GNVQ Intermediate Business

Richard Smith

Lecturer in Business Studies, Stroud College

CAMBRIDGE
UNIVERSITY PRESS

To Mary, Oliver, Aidan and Victoria – to explain how I have
been spending all these evenings!

Published by the Press Syndicate of the University of Cambridge
The Pitt Building, Trumpington Street, Cambridge CB2 1RP
40 West 20th Street, New York, NY 10011–4211, USA
10 Stamford Road, Oakleigh, Melbourne 3166, Australia

© Cambridge University Press 1996

First published 1996

Printed in Great Britain by Scotprint Limited, Musselburgh, Scotland

A catalogue record for this book is available from the British Library

ISBN 0 521 55951 0 paperback

Notice to teachers
It is illegal to reproduce any part of this work in material form (including
photocopying and electronic storage) except under the following
circumstances:
(i)   where you are abiding by a licence granted to your school or institution
       by the Copyright Licensing Agency;
(ii) where no such licence exists, or where you wish to exceed the terms of a
       licence and you have gained the written permission of Cambridge
       University Press;
(iii) where you are allowed to reproduce without permission under the
       provisions of Chapter 3 of the Copyright, Designs and Patents Act 1988.

Contents

	Acknowledgements	v
	Introduction - GNVQ and your portfolio	1
	Grid showing core skills coverage	9
Unit 1	**Business Organisations and Employment**	**10**
	1.1 Explain the purposes and types of business organisations	11
	1.2 Examine business location, environment, markets and products	42
	1.3 Present results of investigation into employment	69
Unit 2	**People in Business Organisations**	**87**
	2.1 Examine and compare structures and working arrangements in organisations	88
	2.2 Investigate employee and employer responsibilities and rights	111
	2.3 Present results of investigation into job roles	129
	2.4 Prepare for employment or self-employment	158
Unit 3	**Consumers and Customers**	**185**
	3.1 Explain the importance of consumers and customers	186
	3.2 Plan, design and produce promotional material	208
	3.3 Providing customer service	239
	3.4 Present proposals for improvements to customer service	260
Unit 4	**Financial and Administrative Support**	**271**
	4.1 Identify and explain financial transactions and documents	272
	4.2 Complete financial documents and explain financial recording	295
	4.3 Produce, evaluate and store business documents	309
	Core Skills	**329**
	Application of Number	330
	Communication	341
	Information Technology	350

Questions   **357**
Business Organisations and Employment   357
People in Business Organisations   364
Consumers and Customers   373
Financial and Administrative Support   383

Answers   **390**

Index   **391**

Acknowledgements

**The author and publishers would like to acknowledge the help
and support of the following organisations in the preparation
and illustration of this book.**

Morgan Motor Co Ltd
Ford UK
British Gas
The Body Shop
Mary Evans Picture Library
Butterworth-Heinemann Ltd (Belbin)
Kelloggs
Coco-Cola GB
Mars UK
Harvard Business Review (Tannenbaum & Schmidt)
Health Education Authority
HMSO
    Figures 21, 29, 30, 31, 53, 54 and 66 are reproduced with
    the permission of the Controller of Her Majesty's
    Stationery Office. © Crown Copyright.
Boots the Chemist
NTC
Tesco Stores

Likewise, the author acknowledges with thanks Clare
Freeman's idea for the individual exercise on pages 183 and
184.

In addition the author would like to thank Henrietta White
and Chris Lee as reliable sources of information on the BTEC
Intermediate study programme, especially regarding core
skills and grading criteria.

He would also like to thank Colin Silk, English teacher at the
County Grammar School for Boys, Lewes, for his painstaking
and illuminating instruction in English grammar all those
years ago.

Introduction

Introduction to the General National Vocational Qualification (GNVQ)

Welcome to GNVQ! Now that you are studying for a GNVQ you will find that doing so will not only gain you a worthwhile qualification, it will also present many opportunities for you to acquire skills and knowledge that are directly relevant to earning a living. You are studying for the Intermediate qualification which represents the second level of a three-part series starting with **Foundation**, followed by **Intermediate** and completed at **Advanced** level. After the Advanced stage has been successfully completed, you may be eligible to study for a Higher National award (HNC or HND) or a Bachelor's degree (BA, BSc or others).

In order to gain the Intermediate Business GNVQ award, you need to demonstrate a level of knowledge and ability in certain subjects which are commonly referred to as **units** or **skills**.

You demonstrate your knowledge and ability mainly by gaining and supplying **evidence** of having performed certain tasks set and assessed by the lecturer, employer, or, in some cases, yourself in agreement with a tutor.

Compiling a portfolio of evidence

You need to collect your own evidence and when it has been checked for accuracy, level and depth of knowledge by your lecturer or teacher, it is kept in a **portfolio**, so that you can provide **proof** of your ability in a given subject.

You need to show that you have produced work which meets all the requirements in each unit before you are awarded a GNVQ. Looking through your portfolio of evidence enables tutors, assessors, verifiers, even prospective employers, to see your achievements.

It is the student, not the lecturer or teacher who is responsible for recording his or her own evidence and proving competence in each subject area. The lecturer or tutor may keep certain records, but the student organises the portfolio to provide the evidence, comments, grades and competencies demonstrated.

You will soon realise the benefits of studying in this way, for the activities you undertake relate directly to business; each one is not only providing proof, but also embracing a piece of knowledge, or a skill well worth acquiring!

Non-written evidence

Your evidence need not always be written down. It may be oral, such as a discussion you take part in or a presentation you give. In this case it is sufficient on the record sheet to describe the event in outline, say how you contributed and finally give a brief indication of the contents. Then, the lecturer (or other assessor) must countersign the record sheet and award grades as appropriate. Grading is discussed later on in this chapter.

Presentations may well be recorded on video for maximum learning benefit, then perhaps stored in the portfolio. Lecturers are strongly recommended not to replay such videos before a large audience of young students. Playback should be in small groups, with only those involved in the presentation present. This will avoid the otherwise inevitable giggles and maximise the learning benefits to the students concerned.

Filing

There is no prescribed format for building a portfolio – you are encouraged to establish your own filing and retrieval system for the evidence you collect.

These are the most common types of portfolio.

- **Lever arch files** – these are useful for holding large amounts of written work securely.
- **Artists' portfolios** – these are particularly suitable for large visual material.
- **Box files** – these hold a combination of flat work such as reports and drawings, or 3-D objects such as video tapes and models.

Figure 1 lists examples of different forms of evidence that you could use. Establishing a successful filing system in your portfolio can also be claimed as a competence. Performance criterion 4.3.5 (page 322) has more details.

Written	Visual	3D	Oral
Written report	Map making	Model	Performance
Diary	Storyboard	Sculpture	Role play
Log	Test paper	Produce	Recorded discussion
Essay	Photograph	Artefact	Recorded conversation
Story	Decoration	Product	Interview
Questionnaire	Graph		Debate
Letter	Printout		Presentation
Notes/draft	Demonstration		Commentary
Newspaper	Picture		Questions and answers
Case study	Poster		
Questions and answers	Diagram		
Display	Film		
	Video		
	Role play		

FIGURE 1 Examples of different forms of evidence

Some words you will need to grasp

Each subject is called a **unit**. The four units covered by this book are called *mandatory units*, because all students must complete them to obtain the intermediate award. Each unit is split into a number of **elements**. Students demonstrate certain levels of knowledge and skill in each element. These are described as **performance criteria** with further guidance from **evidence indicators**.

Look at page iii. You will see that Unit One is called Business Organisations and Employment. It has three elements. The first element *(Explain the purposes and types of business organisations)* has four performance criteria, which develop the purposes and types of business organisation.

> The evidence indicators in the syllabus explain the evidence that is needed in order to demonstrate competence to gain the award.

Whilst the evidence indicators are not the only way to demonstrate competence in a particular element, it has been agreed by the awarding body that they form typical examples, and therefore this book broadly follows them.

At the end of the course, therefore, the amount of evidence in your portfolio should match the requirements of the evidence indicators in each element.

What should a portfolio contain?

Your portfolio of evidence should contain evidence to show that you have met the requirements of:

- all the elements;
- all the performance criteria;
- the range identified in the evidence indicators;
- all the grading criteria.

The illustration given in Figure 2 is an exploded diagram of a typical portfolio.

You should not worry if there are terms here that seem unfamiliar. These will be quickly grasped as the study programme progresses.

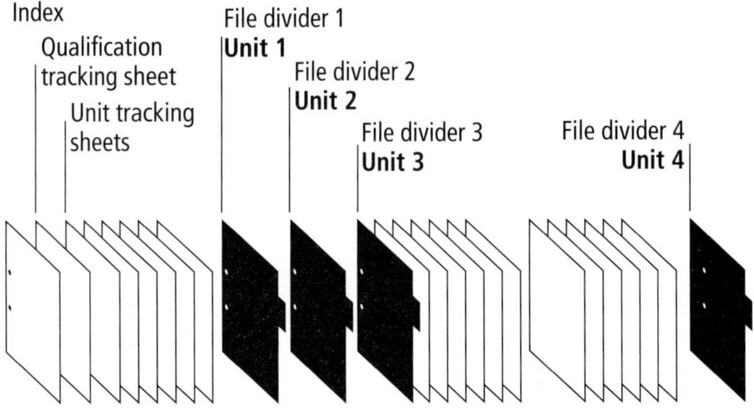

FIGURE 2 Organising a portfolio

Core skills **Core skills** are skills which are essential to a career in any type of business. At Intermediate level, there are three – Application of number, Communication and Information technology. Core skills are demonstrated by students at Intermediate level through the assignments that are undertaken in the four mandatory units. You will find details on the syllabus coverage grid on page 9.

Competence in a core skill is almost always demonstrated through a piece of work that is directly related to a mandatory unit. Only in rare instances will it be necessary to demonstrate competence in a core skill through other work.

You can see that an activity or assignment may demonstrate a number of different skills relevant to both mandatory units and core skills; it may also cover more than one unit and core skill.

Grading

Each piece of work is graded using one of two headings:

1 the **process** necessary to complete the tasks and
2 the **outcome** generated.

This means that even if the result or outcome is not quite right, your thought processes and preparation are still given consideration.

For this reason, the grading of the process is split into four further headings:

- **planning**;
- **information seeking**;
- **information handling**;
- **evaluation**, which follows when the piece of work is complete.

The student evaluates progress, when the piece of work is complete.

The grading of the outcome has just one consideration – the **quality** of the result.

Thus, the final role of a portfolio of evidence is to help determine a student's grade: **pass**, **merit** or **distinction** in each of the ingredients of process and outcome.

Planning

Planning covers a whole host of areas which you should consider.

1 What is the **main purpose** of this activity – **why** am I being asked to do this – what **skill** or **knowledge** can I demonstrate?
   If these questions are kept in mind and answered, the piece of work will be sufficiently long and relevant throughout.
2 Does one task depend upon another?
   Students frequently claim to be unable to make a start on a piece of work, yet there is often one task that is essential

before anything else can be done – perhaps a telephone call or a letter – before any follow-up is possible.

3 Is there a **logical** order to work in, which will cut down the time taken to do the whole task?

4 **How long** will each step take, **realistically?**

5 Can I do it on my own or do I need help from a friend, relative or colleague – perhaps someone else who is better informed than I am and whose involvement will make the task easier?

6 Should I check back with the lecturer or teacher to see if I am doing the right things?

Information seeking

1 What do I need to find out? How easy will this be?
Local libraries, many of which have up-to-date *Yellow Pages* and a useful reference section, are a source of much material.

2 Will my tutor give me any further sources of information?

3 Are some sources better than others? Should I try those first?

Information handling

Is the information up-to-date? Correct? Can I check it somehow?

It may be worthwhile checking with other reference books, or asking an expert.

Evaluation

This takes place after the work is complete, possibly even after the tutor has commented upon it. Student life is one of the very few times when there is an opportunity to reflect on what has been learned from performing certain tasks.

You should consider which tasks were done well, as well as those where mistakes were made or those which might have been done differently, better, or more quickly. The most important thing at this stage is to be **honest**. This will be recognised and rewarded by the tutor.

Some points to consider

1 Is the submission long enough?

2 Is it relevant?

3 Are the facts presented consistently? (Are there any contradictions?)

4 Now that it is complete, what was this piece of work about

and did I realise this at the start?

5 Was there a different way that I could have completed this task – perhaps more quickly?

6 Is there something I can learn from this that will help me in the future?

7 Which parts did I do well?

8 Which parts did I do not so well?

Gaining the Intermediate Award

In order to gain the Intermediate Award, you must:

- demonstrate competence in each element of each of the **four mandatory and two optional units,** as well as the **three core skills.** Evidence for this is built up during the course and stored in the portfolio. The two optional units are the only part of your study programme which are outside the scope of this book;
- pass short (one hour) tests in each of the four mandatory units. Sample questions appear at the back of the book on page 357.

How this book is set out

The book follows the sequence below.

- Introduction
- Syllabus coverage chart
- Mandatory Units
- Core Skills
- Sample Test Questions
- Index

After this introductory chapter, the main part of the book covers the mandatory units. These are:

Unit 1 Business Organisations and Employment (pages 10–86)
- Different types of business, their products, markets and location
- Employment and self-employment

Unit 2 People in Business Organisations (pages 87–184)
- Different roles in business and how these are managed within the organisation

Unit 3 Consumers and Customers (pages 185–270)
- Promoting goods and services
- Providing customer service

Unit 4 Financial and Administrative Support (pages 271–328)
- Financial transactions and documents
- Producing, storing and retrieving business documents

The elements

Each element starts a new section within a unit and this is signalled by a logo. A short introduction to the element comes next followed by the evidence indicators for that element and then the core skills involved. Finally the text will take you through the performance criteria and the activities you should undertake. The structure is as follows.

- New element
- Evidence indicators
- Core skills
- Performance criteria
- Group activities
- Individual activities

Activities

The elements of Units One to Four all contain a number of activities that are designed with the relevant evidence indicators in mind. If these activities are comprehensively undertaken, not only will there be sufficient evidence for you to demonstrate competence in each element, but also in the core skills.

Core skills

The final three sections cover the core skills, which deal with the way people behave and go about their daily commercial lives no matter what their line of business. Figure 3 shows the coverage of core skills in the different elements of this book.

Core skills are as follows.

- Application of number (page 330)
- Communication (page 341)
- Information technology (page 350)

Test questions

Finally, there are test questions with answers; a series of questions on each of the four mandatory units. After that there is the Index.

General advice During the course it is advisable for you to develop contacts with a variety of local businesses – they are an invaluable

Element	1.1	1.2	1.3	2.1	2.2	2.3	2.4	3.1	3.2	3.3	3.4	4.1	4.2	4.3
Core Skills														
Number 2.1							✓	✓	✓		✓		✓	
2.2			✓				✓	✓			✓	✓		
2.3			✓				✓	✓	✓		✓		✓	
Communication 2.1			✓	✓	✓	✓	✓	✓					✓	
2.2	✓	✓		✓	✓	✓	✓	✓	✓	✓	✓		✓	✓
2.3		✓	✓	✓		✓	✓	✓			✓	✓	✓	✓
2.4			✓				✓	✓	✓		✓		✓	✓
IT 2.1				✓	✓	✓	✓	✓	✓	✓		✓	✓	✓
2.2				✓	✓	✓	✓	✓		✓		✓	✓	✓
2.3				✓	✓	✓	✓	✓				✓	✓	✓
2.4				✓	✓	✓	✓	✓				✓	✓	✓

FIGURE 3 Core skills coverage chart

source of information. It is suggested that your school or college establish relationships with some businesses in each of the primary, secondary and tertiary industrial sectors; your tutor or lecturer should arrange this. Direct student contacts of this nature will prove essential when undertaking several of the assignments.

You may well have parents, relatives or friends who work in such organisations – GNVQ students are urged to consult them as much as possible: their encouragement is invaluable and the breadth of experience is likely to be considerable.

Alternatively you may find that a group of students is assigned to one company, or that different groups contact one company at separate times during the year, so that all obtain an insight into and understanding of the various types of industry and business. Talks in school or college by employees of such companies are a valuable complement to student activities.

In all cases, you are encouraged to enjoy the tasks you are set and to make the best use of the experience gained. In this way, you will both retain and benefit from the learning experience that GNVQ undoubtedly provides.

If your group would now like to undertake an exercise to show how GNVQ can provide powerful role plays and learning experiences to develop essential business skills, turn to page 136 and, in groups, try the bridge building exercise. It will also give newcomers an opportunity to get to know each other.

Good luck ... and enjoy the course!

Unit **1** Business Organisations and Employment

The aim of this unit is to encourage students to question what businesses are, and why, where and how they exist. Through investigations into business organisations in the public and private sectors, students should gain a firm knowledge and understanding of business motives and activities, and the way these relate to employment opportunities.

Through their work for this unit, the students should develop skills in: research, analysis, information seeking and presentation. Student are expected to develop a broad understanding of the differences between primary, secondary and tertiary industries and a deeper understanding of the different types of business, their purposes and activities. They also learn about markets, how businesses produce goods and services designed to meet consumers' needs and wants and marketing communications.

From: *Mandatory Units for Intermediate Business*, GNVQ, May 1995

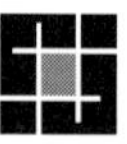 # Element 1.1   Explain the Purposes and Types of Business Organisations

Business exists in many forms and is organised in many ways. However, in all cases it either satisfies people's **needs** – food, clothes and shelter, for example – or their **wants** – holidays, cars and other luxury items.

This element explains **why** business organisations operate. Some exist to make a profit, while others are there to provide basic services and are funded by the state. Charities are also businesses, relying on public donations for their income. Whatever an organisation's purpose, all are businesses.

In the UK some businesses are run by the government: they are defined as being in the **public sector.** Others are run by private people and are said to be in the **private sector,** which includes charities.

Nationalised industries, local government and the Civil Service form the public sector and limited companies, partnerships, sole traders, charities and other categories form the private sector.

Within the private and public sectors there are various **sectors of industry** which define what businesses do: some **manufacture** goods while others provide a **service,** for example. Some make profits, others such as hospitals and the fire brigade, are funded by the government in return for providing essential services.

Sectors of industry

Element 1.1 also examines sectors of industry.

1 The **primary sector** – concerns those businesses which extract materials known as the **natural resources** from the earth. Oil drilling, fishing and farming are examples.
2 The **secondary sector** – concerns manufacturing businesses which convert the output of primary sector business into items which can be put to other uses. Car manufacturing, petrol refining and food processing are examples.

3 The **tertiary sector** – uses the products of the secondary sector to provide a service: car hire companies, tour operators, even schools and colleges.

Current activities and trends in each sector are investigated.

Evidence indicators

- A summary which describes developments in the primary, secondary and tertiary sectors, focusing on present growth or decrease in each sector and typical activities in the sectors.
- Seven examples of different business organisations which have different types of ownership. For each example a summary which explains the purposes and differences between types of business organisation. The seven business organisations should include at least one public sector organisation and small, medium and large private sector organisations.
- A report which focuses on one local or national business organisation, explaining its location, product, purpose, type of ownership and its links with other businesses.

Core skills

In this element, only one core skill is covered:

Communication
Element 2.2. produce written material

Performance criterion

1.1.1 Describe developments in industrial sectors

Business and an economy defined

The headlines in Figure 4 on the next page indicate how important **business** activity is to human social organisation. Everywhere people have **needs**; they need the basic essentials of life – food, drink, clothing and shelter. Others may need an operation in hospital in order to survive.

Once people have the essentials in life, they **want** other goods, such as a new car, a larger house or a foreign holiday.

> All businesses exist to satisfy people's needs and wants by providing goods or services.

FIGURE 4 Newspaper headlines

All business activity takes place in an **economy**. This may be the local economy of your town, county, country, continent or the world. An economy is **any area where there is a defined population and where business is taking place.**

> For an economy to exist, there must be resources: the ingredients needed to produce goods and services. In its simplest form, these resources are land and labour.

Resources
Land
Land is not only the soil, but also the minerals which lie beneath it and the plants and trees that grow upon it. It also includes the oceans and their contents, particularly fish.

Labour
Labour is people working to convert the raw products of land into buildings, machinery and the other goods and services which meet human needs and wants. For this reason, labour includes the **skills** necessary for these various processes.

Resources need to be used thoughtfully: some **natural resources** such as coal, oil and minerals are **non-renewable,** that is once they have been used they are gone for ever. Others, such as fish stocks and forestry can be replaced: they are **renewable** by human effort or by nature.

Industrial sectors

The three main sectors of industry are summarised in Figure 5.

Primary sector

These are industries directly involved with the earth or sea. They are often called **extractive** industries because they take raw materials out of the earth or sea, such as crude oil or mineral ores. Forestry, farming and fishing are examples. **This is the first stage in the manufacturing process.**

Secondary sector

Such industries take the product of primary sector businesses and **convert** it into something else, such as **manufacturing** paper from wood, **canning** and **processing** fish and farm produce, **refining** petrol, **making steel** from iron ore, as well as producing cars from steel.

Tertiary sector

Sometimes referred to as the **service sector**, the tertiary sector takes the products of the primary and secondary sectors and adds value to them. Car hire, hotels, or tourism are examples.

Quaternary sector

It is worth mentioning in passing the existence of this small sector; businesses in the quaternary sector offer indirect **services**, that is they set and maintain standards, or offer advice, usually to other businesses. Unlike firms in the tertiary sector, there is little direct and immediate benefit. Institutes and some government advisory units form this sector.

Sector	Primary	Secondary	Tertiary
Definition	Directly involved with the earth or sea (i.e. *extracts*)	Converts product of primary sector businesses into a usable product (i.e. *manufactures*)	Provides essential and non-essential *services*
Examples	<ul><li>Coal mining</li><li>Mining for metal ores</li><li>Drilling for oil</li><li>Extracting crude oil</li><li>Fishing</li><li>Forestry</li><li>Farming</li></ul>	<ul><li>Steel making</li><li>Car manufacture</li><li>Making jewellery</li><li>Oil refining</li><li>Food processing (e.g. canning and freezing)</li><li>Paper making</li><li>Manufacturing electrical goods</li><li>Generating electricity</li></ul>	<ul><li>Retailing</li><li>Car hire</li><li>Tourism</li><li>Banking</li><li>Airlines</li><li>Hospitals</li><li>Police force</li><li>Armed forces</li></ul>

FIGURE 5 The different sectors of industry

Primary sector industries

Some of the world's natural resources are concentrated in one country. Saudi Arabia has 25 per cent of the world's oil reserves. South Africa has 30 per cent of the world's gold and 34 per cent of the world's chrome reserves.

Although this has brought much wealth to both Saudi Arabia and South Africa, it is not essential for prosperous trading nations to enjoy large quantities of natural resources. The economic success of Japan has occurred despite having very few natural resources of its own. Nearly all of its oil, coal and iron is imported for domestic processing.

America and Australia, on the other hand, have more mineral ores than they need themselves, so they export their surpluses. Some of the states of the former Union of Soviet Socialist Republics (USSR), for example, Khazakstan, Azerbaijan and Turkmenistan have rich deposits of natural gas, oil, coal, metal ores, gold and uranium.

Ownership of natural resources can cause political confrontation in Europe, for example, disputes arise over the rights of one country to fish in another country's sea. Much concern has been expressed over a recent change in European regulations which allows Spanish boats to fish in waters hitherto only used by British vessels. In such instances, the European Union (EU) intervenes to try to resolve the problem.

In the United Kingdom

In the UK major changes have taken place in our primary industries. The size of our coal mining industry has more than halved in the past 20 years. It has recently moved from the public into the private sector (the definitions of these two sectors can be found on pages 20, 22 and 23); the government sold its remaining coal mines to private business enterprises in 1994 and these businesses are seeking to operate them for profit, with varying degrees of success. In addition our steel industry is now based on imported iron ore – less than 5 per cent originates from the UK.

In the last 20 years, the UK has, however, also become a leading European oil producer.

Secondary sector industries

Secondary sector industries are not only those that make goods used in the home or office, such as televisions, computers and cars, it also includes businesses which make machines such as printing presses, lathes and other equipment to enable manufacturers to produce their goods.

Manufacturing industries such as these flourish where labour costs are low or where there is ready availability of people with relevant skills.

In recent years Taiwan, India and Japan have become major suppliers of electrical goods, clothes, vehicles, shipbuilding and other items.

Many such industries based in Europe have shown a decline over the same period due to this increased competition from the East, where labour is generally cheaper and many new factories with the latest machinery have been built.

In the United Kingdom
In the UK, there has been a noticeable decline in manufacturing industries. Although British Steel is one of the most profitable steel producing companies in the world, this growth in profitability has been achieved against a background of massive reduction in output.

The decline of our motor manufacturing is sometimes misrepresented. Although almost all vehicle manufacture that takes place in Britain is now under foreign ownership, the UK economy has successfully attracted more than its share of overseas companies willing to invest in starting a manufacturing plant here.

Ford and General Motors (Vauxhall) from the USA were among the first. In recent years, Peugeot (France), Nissan and Honda (Japan) and BMW (Germany) have followed. In addition, many overseas manufacturers, Volvo and Renault for example, purchase many of their components from UK suppliers.

Tertiary sector industries

Growth among the developed countries such as Europe, North America, Canada and Australia has largely been in the tertiary sector – in service industries.

As well as having a flourishing tourist industry, the UK has long been a leading world supplier of financial services such as insurance and banking.

In the United Kingdom

Napoleon disparagingly described the British as 'a nation of shopkeepers'. UK companies such as Tesco, Marks & Spencer and Sainsbury's support this statement and are respected for their consistent growth and profitability (see Figure 6).

 **Performance criterion**

1.1.2 Explain the purposes of business organisations

All businesses have a purpose, a reason to exist. Many, especially those which are privately owned, are there to generate a profit for their owners.

Others provide an essential service to everybody, no matter what their income or status – hospitals and the fire service, for example.

Charities, such as the Royal National Lifeboat Institute or Doctor Barnardo's exist to help people in trouble, or those with a particular need.

Many businesses have more than one objective. A hotel, for example, exists to generate a profit for its owners. It achieves this by providing a service to its customers: supplying them with a bed for the night and meals, conference facilities or an attractive venue for an exhibition or business meeting.

Achieving business objectives

Now let us consider the achievement of business objectives in a little more detail. Two manufacturers, Morgan Cars and The Ford Motor Company, both make cars; both are in business to generate profits for their owners, but both achieve this goal in quite different ways.

Ford

Ford operates in **mass markets**. The market for mid-size family cars such as the Ford Mondeo is massive, especially when demand is considered on a world-wide scale. Similarly, there is a significant need for a small family 'workhorse' that can carry almost anything its size will allow: the Ford Fiesta is a typical example of a car produced for this market.

Ford sells cars by offering its customers well-designed products, which are readily available almost anywhere in the world. It achieves low prices by selling hundreds of thousands of units of each model – by operating on such a large scale,

Rank	Company name	Country	Core retail activity	Retail sales £m	Year end
1	Metro*	Switz/Ger	Multi-sector	32,219 [1]	31-12-93
2	Tengelmann	Germany	Multi-sector	19,642 [1]	30-06-93
3	Rewe Group	Germany	Grocery	16,271 [2]	31-12-93
4	Carrefour	France	Grocery	13,989 [3]	31-12-93
5	Centres Leclerc	France	Grocery	13,546 [3]	31-12-93
6	Intermarché	France	Grocery	13,337 [2]	31-12-93
7	Edeka Group	Germany	Grocery	11,921 [3]	31-12-93
8	Aldi	Germany	Grocery	11,870 [1]	31-12-92
9	J Sainsbury	UK	Grocery	10,526 [3]	13-03-94
10	Promodès	France	Grocery	10,242 [3]	31-12-93
11	Otto Versand	Germany	Mail order	9,585 [1]	28-02-94
12	Tesco	UK	Grocery	8,600 [3]	27-02-94
13	Ahold	Netherlands	Grocery	8,419 [3]	31-12-93
14	Crai	Italy	Grocery	7,924 [5,1]	31-12-93
15	Auchan	France	Grocery	7,614 [1]	31-12-92
16	Karstadt Group	Germany	Dept stores	7,537 [1]	31-12-93
17	Casino/Rallye	France	Grocery	7,154 [3]	31-12-93
18	Group Delhaize Le Lion	Belgium	Grocery	7,050 [1]	31-12-93
19	Co-operative Societies	UK	Grocery	6,745 [3]	31-12-92
20	Marks & Spencer	UK	Variety	6 418 [3]	31-03-94
21	Quelle Schickedanz	Germany	Mail order	6 098 [2]	31-01-94
22	SHV Holdings	Netherlands	Cash & carry	5,925 [3]	31-12-93
23	GIB Group	Belgium	Multi-sector	5,916 [3,6]	31-01-94
24	Migros	Switzerland	Grocery	5,622 [2]	31-12-93
25	Argyll Group	UK	Grocery	5,608 [3]	03-04-94
26	El Corte Ingles	Spain	Dept stores	5,528 [3]	28-02-93
27	Spar Handel	Germany	Grocery	5,202 [3,5]	31-12-93
28	Cora	France	Multi-sector	5,109 [3]	31-12-93
29	ICA	Sweden	Grocery	4,944 [2,7]	31-12-93
30	Asda Group	UK	Grocery	4,879 [3]	01-05-93
31	Système U	France	Grocery	4,678 [3]	31-12-92
32	Conad	Italy	Grocery	4,626 [1,5]	31-12-93
33	Co-op Italia	Italy	Grocery	4,526 [2]	31-12-93
34	Kingfisher	UK	Multi-sector	4,414 [3]	29-01-94
35	Docks de France	France	Grocery	4,350 [3]	31-12-93
36	Co-op Switzerland	Switzerland	Grocery	4,332 [1]	31-12-93
37	Pinault-Printemps	France	Dept stores	4,217 [2]	30-12-93
38	KF Group	Sweden	Grocery	4,116 [2,6]	31-12-93
39	Lidl & Schwarz	Germany	Grocery	3,770 [2,9]	31-12-92
40	Kesko	Finland	Grocery	3,702 [1]	31-12-93
41	The Boots Company	UK	Multi-sector	3,657 [3,10]	31-03-94
42	Co-op Denmark (FDB)	Denmark	Grocery	3,379 [2]	31-12-93
43	C & A Mode	Germany	Fashion	3,370 [2]	31-12-93
44	Galeries Lafayette	France	Dept stores	3,352 [3]	31-12-93
45	Isosceles	UK	Grocery	2,867 [3]	25-04-93
46	IKEA	Sweden	Furniture	2,825 [1]	31-08-93
47	AVA	Germany	Grocery	2,730 [3]	31-12-92
48	Comptoirs Modernes	France	Grocery	2,664 [3]	31-12-93
49	Kwik Save Group	UK	Grocery	2,651 [3]	28-08-93
50	Vendex International	Netherlands	Multi-sector	2,599 [3]	31-01-94

Notes: * Includes Asko, Kaufhof and Masso. # Exchange rates are averages for the calendar year.
[1] The source for this figure does not specify whether it includes or excludes VAT.
[2] Figure includes VAT. [3] Figure excludes VAT. [4] Estimated figure. [5] Includes sales of all associated retailers. [6] Includes franchise sales. [7] Grocery retailing only.
[8] Excludes foreign operations and UK petrol forecourt sales. [9] Includes cash & carry.
[10] Retail sates comprise Boots The Chemists and the Retail Division.
Source: Management Horizons. For further information please contact Management Horizons' Help Desk on 0181 560 9393

FIGURE 6 Europe's largest retailers

FIGURE 7 The Morgan (above) is a hand-built car, while the Ford Mondeo (right) is mass produced

component prices, new product development and manufacturing costs are kept low. High sales are achieved by heavy promotion using media which are seen by millions of people: the national press, posters and national television, for example. In such a competitive market, **market share** is very important: Ford has in excess of 20 per cent of the UK car market. In other words, more than one in five cars sold in the UK is a Ford.

Morgan

Morgan also manufactures cars. Their product, however is a hand-built sports car sold and well respected throughout the world. It manufactures and sells about 700 cars each year – Ford makes at least one thousand times as many cars in the same period! Clearly, Morgan is not trying to achieve a high market share. However, it is eminently successful in its business as any customer will tell you: there is a waiting list of several years for a new Morgan car!

Business income

> Each business needs an income to allow it to provide its stated product or service.

It was stated earlier that all businesses satisfy other people's needs or wants.

A business may consist of one person, such as a plumber; or it may be a massive corporation employing thousands of people around the world, such as BP. Equally, it may be the police force which exists to protect our society so that the vast majority of people can live their lives freely and securely.

In the case of the plumber or BP, products or services are sold **at a profit**, which the owners of the business keep. With police forces, their income comes from money given to them . Their existence is therefore not for profit, they are there to provide an **essential service**, which they do unhampered by any need to make profits; their income is allocated to them from government funds. This is discussed in more detail on page 22, the public sector.

Charities
The income of a charity, such as the Royal National Life-boat Institution, comes mainly from public donations. Charities exist to provide essential services to certain people or animals – the National Society for the Prevention of Cruelty to Children (NSPCC), the Royal Society for the Protection of Birds (RSPB) the Royal National Institute for the Blind (RNIB) are examples.

Some of these people, such as the blind, elderly or deaf, are entitled to certain state benefits – money or goods provided specifically for them by the government, using funds raised by taxing other people.

Charities support such people with specialist services and supplies which the state does not provide.

Stating business objectives
So that all concerned can understand the purpose of any business, each one will make a statement of its **aims and objectives**. The aims of a business describe what it is trying to achieve – perhaps gain a large market share, offer a high level of service, or raise a large sum of money to help the people it is there to serve.

Private and public sector business

The private sector
Businesses in the private sector are privately owned, possibly by the people who run them such as plumbers, doctors and solicitors mentioned earlier. Others, such as Cadbury Schweppes, are also privately owned – by their shareholders, who are frequently members of the general public.

In recent years, there has been a tendency to move many nationalised industries into the private sector. By doing this, they no longer have the 'safety net' of government funds to support them. Instead, they have to earn profits for their new owners. The government feels that they are run more effectively with **profit as an aim** and **competition to ensure their efficiency.**

There are two features that, with one exception, define businesses in the private sector:

- profit as a motivating force;
- competition to ensure that the customer has choice, that is, that products are up to date and available at reasonable prices.

The exception to this definition – charities and voluntary organisations – will be considered below.

Large, medium or small business?
As we saw on page 17, some businesses in the private sector are very **large** – indeed larger than some nationalised industries – Marks & Spencer, Rover Cars, British Aerospace, Barclays Bank, The Prudential Insurance Company and the Littlewoods Organisation are examples.

Others are **medium sized,** employing from about one hundred people to a few thousand.

Medium-sized businesses tend to specialise in a particular area, or are major suppliers in a small market, such as Renishaw plc, a specialist supplier of industrial probes. Other examples are Boosey and Hawkes plc, a manufacturer of musical instruments and M.Y. Sports and Games Ltd whose major business is making paper coil dart boards. In the next section we will examine more closely the significance of the abbreviations 'plc' and 'Ltd' in their business names.

Small businesses abound everywhere – plumbers, electricians, solicitors, corner shops, local builders, printers and carpenters. Most exist to serve a small community by supplying a product or service for which customers pay, thus generating profits for their owners.

Charities and voluntary organisations
Earlier, mention was made of an exception to the two principles of profit making and competition in the private sector.

The aim of charities and voluntary organisations is generally to raise money to help their cause, such as the Royal National Life-boat Institution and Barnardos.

Why are they not run by the government from public funds, since they provide an essential service? For many years, most people have felt that such businesses are more efficiently and effectively run when the buildings, equipment and people who operate charities are paid with money raised by public donations.

Other organisations in this category are established to support worthwhile causes, but cannot reasonably be run for profit. Cambridge University Press is a charity and some of their publications are academic works intended to further research and knowledge, even though the revenue from their sales is often very small indeed; the benefits to mankind, however, in this case outweigh commercial considerations.

The public sector

The UK is a democracy, which means that the British people themselves choose who is to govern them and their country. At least every five years they make their choice in a general election.

One of the main functions of the government is to manage the UK economy. In other words:

1   to make the most of what the country has to offer: to ensure that the scarce resources of land and labour, as well as the **capital** (the plant, equipment and other productive resources that are made by the combination of land and labour) are used to best effect;
2   to ensure that business can run smoothly and to support it where necessary;
3   to distribute as fairly as possible, the wealth that is created by the nation's resources and business; that is to ensure that the poor, the aged, and people with special needs are properly cared for.

Since the government is elected to provide many essential services, but has no way of generating an income on its own, the funds to do this must come from somewhere. The money is generated by taking a share of the income of the people and businesses which it governs, that is, through levying **taxes.**

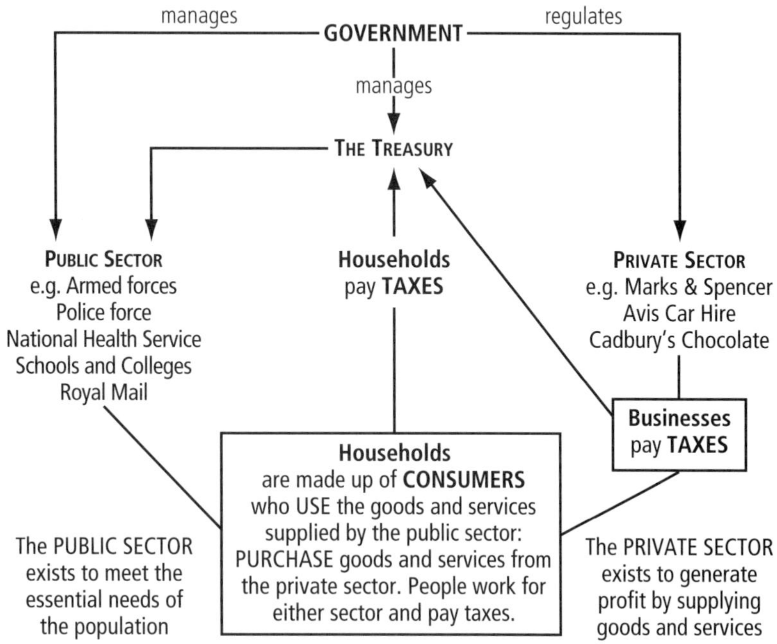

FIGURE 8 The UK economy in outline

Taxes are paid on:

- **profits** from business – (called corporation tax);
- **income** from employees – (income tax);
- **expenditure** by consumers (value added tax – VAT).

The government uses the income generated from taxation in two ways: first, to pay themselves, the people whom the electorate has chosen to serve them; second, to run those businesses that the government manages for the state, known as **state-owned businesses** – the public sector.

Why is the public sector supported by taxes?

Public sector businesses exist to meet the essential needs of the population, such as the fire service, hospitals, schools, street lighting in towns, looking after waterways, building roads. Such services are considered basic to our existence and either difficult or ethically unacceptable to run as profit-making businesses.

> Public sector businesses are not forced to make profits because their revenue comes from taxation.

Imagine what might happen if our armed forces had to make a profit! They might deliberately go out and find an enemy to fight so they could be usefully employed and therefore paid! As it is, our forces are able to spend time training and practising so that they can be called into action for defence and security –or to act as a deterrent to a potential aggressor. However, the idea that essential services should not need to be profit making is quite a new one. Until about 50 years ago, hospitals and doctors' practices were nearly all privately run and had to make a profit to pay the staff. If a patient needed treatment, he or she had to pay. Since many people could not afford high doctors' fees, the less well off had to suffer – they even died – because they could not afford medical attention.

About the time of the Second World War (1939–45) the UK public felt that health care and other such essential services should be available to everyone, regardless of wealth, age, sex or creed, so that such conditions never occurred again. To achieve this, it was decided that the state should run the health service and the costs should be shared by everyone who was working – by paying for it through taxes.

This principle of paying for essential services entirely through taxation runs throughout much of the public sector, which is made up of three parts. Figure 9 illustrates this.

Local Government	Civil Service	Nationalised Industries
• Leisure services • Refuse collection • Hospitals • Local roads • Street lighting • Fire service • Ambulance service	• Ministry of Defence • British Broadcasting Corporation • Ministry of Agriculture and Fisheries • Department of Education and Science • Ministry of Health • Police Force • National Rivers Authority • British Waterways Board • Ministry of Transport • Motorways and major arterial roads	• Royal Mail • Post Office Counters Ltd

FIGURE 9 Businesses in the public sector

To summarise, the three parts of the public sector are:

1   local government;
2   the civil service;
3   nationalised industries.

Performance criterion

Private sector businesses

1.1.3 Explain the differences between types of business ownership

We saw on page 21 that private sector businesses may be large, medium or small. There are also four major types of business **ownership** in the private sector; each is distinguished by the responsibilities of its owner(s).

*   Sole trader
*   Partnership
*   Private limited company
*   Public limited company

Three other types of business deserve special consideration.

*   Multinational companies
*   Franchises
    These form a significant part of private sector business and will be considered on page 30 in this section.
*   Co-operatives
    These are of less significance these days but it is worthwhile to consider their place in commercial history so these, too, will be examined later, on page 32.

Sole trader

Anybody can set up a business and the sole trader is the simplest form. One person sets up a business and simply starts trading, perhaps as a plumber, electrician or solicitor.

The only people he or she needs to tell are potential customers. This is achieved by advertising, or opening a shop or office.

 If a loan, or somewhere to keep the income, is needed, a bank has to be consulted. Later on when trade increases, registration for value added tax may be necessary, and the Inland Revenue will eventually require a tax return. At this time, the sole trader may require the services of an accountant, who, incidentally, may also be a sole trader himself.

Many businesses which are now large started their life in this way, with little or no capital, operating on a very small scale. Richard Branson started his Virgin empire by selling records by mail order. He was about 16 years old and did not even have a telephone! Jack Cohen started Tesco, Alan Sugar started Amstrad; other now large operations were started in similarly modest ways – by sole traders with vision and ambition.

Advantages

This is one of the main advantages of being a sole trader – it is really very easy to start the business. In addition, the owner or proprietor can make all the decisions, which ideally suits those people with a good eye for business. People who have this 'eye' are often known as **entrepreneurs**. They are the 'risk takers' of the business world.

A sole trader can – and frequently does – employ other people, who work for the business but do not own it.

Disadvantages

The disadvantages may be summarised as follows.

1 As the business grows, opportunities for expansion can be limited due to lack of funds. Banks will only usually lend modest amounts of money to a sole trader. The only other potential source of finance is his or her own money, or borrowing from friends, which can lead to disputes when the business either makes large profits or losses.
2 It can be difficult to leave the business behind. When the owner wishes to go on holiday, or have an evening off, there may be no-one in charge to handle telephone enquiries or emergencies (for example a plumber's loyal customer may well call out a competitor if she has a burst pipe and the plumber is on holiday).
3 If there is scope for the business to expand, it may be advisable to recruit other people to invest their money in it. However, it is essential that they share similar enthusiasm, energy and belief in the business's ultimate success and profitability with its owner as they will become **partners** or **shareholders**, as we shall see on pages 27–29.
4 If the business starts to lose money or in extreme cases, goes bankrupt, the sole trader is personally liable for the debts. This means that he or she may be forced to sell personal possessions to pay business debtors. When all but the most basic possessions have been sold, the owner may then be prosecuted and in some cases, sent to prison.

Partnership

Like a sole-trader business, a partnership can be very easy to start: the most important factor at the beginning is that the partners know, trust and respect each other's business judgement.

There is nothing to stop them simply opening their business – by acquiring premises, for example – then starting to trade.

Between two and 20 people may form a partnership. If they have contributed equally and have similarly agreed to share the costs and profits of the business, that may be all that is necessary.

Deed of partnership

However, to start the business on a professional footing especially if there is an unequal distribution of money invested, partners are well advised to draw up a **deed of partnership**. They can do this themselves and it is a document which records the basis of their working relationship, for example:

1   how much each partner has contributed to the business;
2   who is responsible for which duties;
3   how the profits are to be distributed;
4   how new partners would be recruited, if required;
5   how an existing partner may leave the business;
6   what happens if a partner dies;
7   how the partnership may be sold or wound up and how the assets of the partnership (for example equipment and property) are to be divided.

Under the *Partnership Act 1890*, the assets of a partnership would be split equally between the partners if no Deed of Partnership exists.

There are many successful types of partnerships:

1   People of the **same trade or profession**: a group of plumbers, for example may choose to form a partnership; it allows them to share the cost of buying expensive machinery, which individually they may not be able to afford. In addition, their partnership allows them to offer a 24-hour service and they may take turns to be 'on call' during the night and on bank holidays.
2   People of **different trades**: a plumber, bricklayer, joiner

and plasterer may form a partnership to build houses. None of these individuals has the ability to build a house alone, but together they may buy plots of land for just such a purpose, thereby increasing the rewards from their business endeavours.

Another example is where people with different skills join forces. For instance, a solicitor experienced in house purchase may form a partnership with a specialist in contract law, another in business law, another in divorce. In a small town, this may enable their partnership to offer a comprehensive range of legal services to the local population. Alternatively, a group of specialists in business law may form a partnership so that they may share the same offices, equipment, secretarial support and advertising, and all partners may benefit by effectively reducing their individual costs.

A partnership is a suitable form of business when the costs to start are low, if there is little or no need to borrow money and the risks are small. As with a sole trader, partners are also personally liable for any debts that the partnership may incur.

Advantages

The main advantage is that, unlike a sole trader, decisions may be discussed and taken collectively. Although it may take longer to consult each partner, the chances of making a bad decision are reduced, on the principle that 'two heads are better than one.'

Disadvantages

This can, however, be regarded as a disadvantage to a partnership. Shared ownership means shared decision making, which can lead to disputes if there is a clash of opinions, characters or temperaments between two or more strong personalities. This is possibly the most common reason for a partnership failing.

Other advantages and disadvantages that apply to a sole trader equally apply to a partnership, particularly those relating to availability of funds to expand the business.

Private and public limited companies

These are the general characteristics of such businesses.

1 **Shareholders** are the owners of the business.

2   Shares are sold to raise money to start the business.
3   Any two or more people may form a private or public limited company.
4   The owners purchase shares in the business, and once this money has been paid and recorded, **that is the full extent of their liability for any debts that the business may incur.** The shareholders are not responsible for any remaining debts that the business may have.
5   The shareholders elect a board of directors, usually at the annual general meeting, to run the company on their behalf.
6   Some of the profits from the business are distributed at regular intervals – usually once a year – to the shareholders. Such payments are called **dividends.**
7   Directors are **employees** of the business – they may also be shareholders, in which case in addition to their income as employees, they also receive a share of the profits in the form of dividends.

The structure of both private and public limited companies is in principle fairly similar, and is explained in Figure 10.

Many partnerships choose to expand by becoming a private limited company, in order to obtain the benefits of limited liability for all partners. A private limited company can expand by becoming a public limited company (plc) by the issue of shares on the **stock exchange.**

Although plcs enjoy a much larger injection of capital from such shareholders, they may also be taken over (i.e. bought) if somebody is able to acquire more than half of the shares – this is known as a **majority shareholding** in the business.

This could not happen in the case of a private limited company, sole trader or partnership, whose shares are not available on the stock exchange.

> A private limited company is not allowed to sell its shares to the general public.

> A public limited company offers its shares to the general public by selling them on the stock exchange.

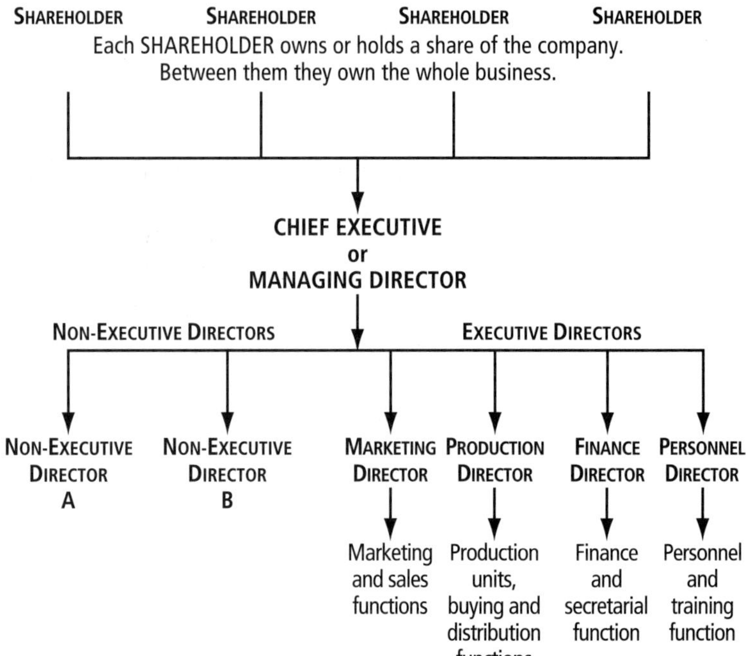

FIGURE 10 Typical structure of private and public limited companies

Probably the best known examples of private limited companies are Addis Ltd (manufacturers of plastic household items and 'Wisdom' toothbrushes) and Littlewoods, the football pools and mail order catalogue operator.

Some special private sector business types
Franchises

A franchise is in most cases a business idea which someone has developed and which the developer (known as the **franchise owner**) allows somebody else to use in return for a fee.

The franchise owner then seeks other people to use its business idea, brand and shop layout. These other people, known as **franchisees**, in some cases, not only purchase their products from the franchise owner, they also pay a percentage of sales value (irrespective whether the business makes a profit or not). This is one of the main business disadvantages of a franchise; however, in return, the franchise owner undertakes not to open a similar business within the same area as his franchisee.

Advantages

These are the main advantages of taking out a franchise.

1 **The risk of failure is reduced** when starting a business.

2 The franchisee has the advantage of having his or her own business, as well as the advantage of **trading under a well known name.** The franchisee is not an employee of the franchise owner and the franchise (i.e. the shop) is financially independent of the franchise owner's business. The franchisee may well be a sole trader.

3 The franchisee **receives help to set up the business**: for example, advice on the best area in which to open the shop, help in obtaining a bank loan and marketing support from the franchise owner, see Figure 11.

In return, the franchise owner is able to expand his business faster by having more money injected into the business from many franchisees. The owner also makes continuous profits from supplying goods to the franchised outlets and of course from the percentage receipts of sales.

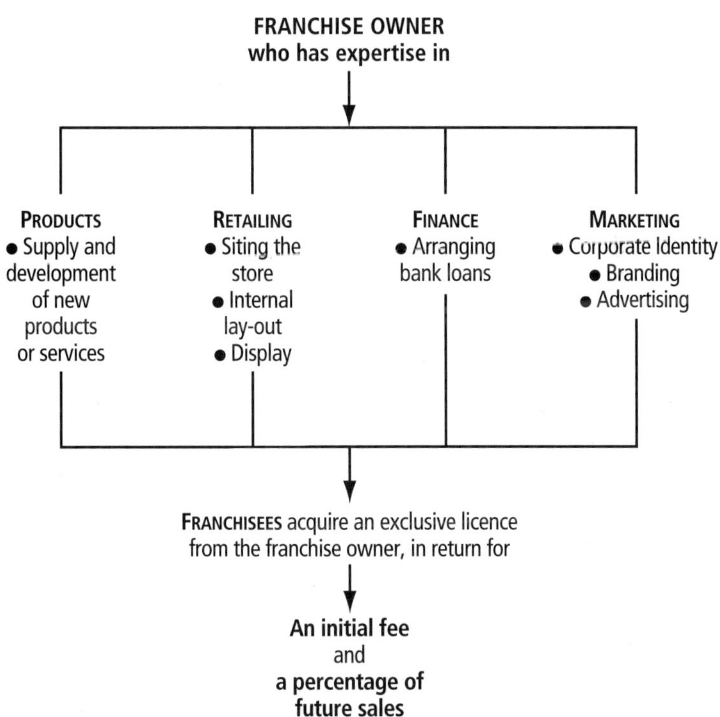

FIGURE 11 The franchise framework

Examples of franchises are MacDonalds (fast food outlets), Swinton Insurance (motor and household insurance and life assurance brokers), Prontaprint (business printing and office services), Fast Frame (picture framing), and Silver Shield (vehicle windscreen replacement).

Multinationals

A multinational business operates in several different countries, although one country houses the head office.

Ford, Coca-Cola and Nike are enormous multinational operations and a major advantage of such businesses is that the costs to develop new products can be recouped (earned back) much more quickly by their ability to trade on a world-wide scale.

The Ford Mondeo, for example, was launched in many different countries at once, thus enabling Ford to gain sales quickly on a world-wide basis. Many of the research costs would have been the same if Ford had only developed the Mondeo for the UK.

Co-operatives

A co-operative is a group of people who choose to form a business together, with all participants sharing the profits of their co-operation. There are many different types, but the most common are retail co-operatives, producer co-operatives and co-operative joint ventures.

Retail co-operatives

These were started in Rochdale in 1844. The 'Rochdale pioneers' as they became known, opened a shop to sell essential food and clothes, with the profits shared among its members according to the amount of money they had spent in the shop over an agreed period. Retail co-operatives (The Co-op) are still run along similar lines, but to become a member a £1 share in the business must be purchased. Most such co-operatives are limited companies.

In their early days, some profits from retail co-operatives were used to improve local conditions for the community by building schools or hospitals.

Producer co-operatives

These are owned by the work force; they share the profits, the work and the decision making. Although this sounds sensible in theory, such a decision-making process can be ponderous and ineffective in practice, which is often the reason for their ultimate failure.

Recent examples of producer co-operatives are the resurgent UK motorcycle manufacturers Triumph and Norton.

Co-operative joint ventures

These are formed when individual businesses combine for a specific purpose. Farmers may purchase machinery which they share and which they could not afford to buy individually. They take it in turns to use and maintain it. Abroad, wine makers from a particular region successfully form such co-operatives to manage the marketing and selling of their wine.

Limited liability

We have seen that sole traders and partners are personally responsible for paying any outstanding debts or resolving problems in their businesses. This is because sole traders and partners are legally part of their business – they cannot keep themselves and their personal wealth separate from their business finances.

This can have advantages – such as claiming against income tax certain household items that are also used for the business. However, it does have disadvantages, particularly if the type of business demands the purchase of a large amount of stock or where a great deal of money is needed to start the business, for instance to acquire a factory, purchase expensive machinery or pay high rent for a shop.

Why have limited liability?

Limited liability is designed to reduce the extent of the owner's responsibility in case of difficulty.

It involves establishing the business as a **separate legal personality** – that is, from a legal point of view the business has a life of its own and an existence separate from its owners. The business, Bloggs **Ltd** (short for private limited company) or Green **plc**, (short for public limited company) can sue and be sued, lend and borrow money, employ people and enter into contracts in its own name rather than that of its owners.

Where there is a high risk, entrepreneurs are well advised to form a limited company. This is achieved by a group of people each contributing a sum of money. If ten people contribute £10,000 each, £100,000 is available to start the company. Each person therefore owns one tenth share of the business. Through limited liability, that is also the extent of any shareholder's liability for debts which the business incurs. In other words, if the operation makes a loss and its creditors (people to whom the business owes money) claim their money, the business is by law obliged to pay only from the value that exists within the business itself. Only in rare instances can the personal wealth of directors or shareholders be called upon.

A business shows that it has the benefits of limited liability by including the word 'Limited' in its business name. As we have seen on page 28, there are two types of business of this nature – public and private limited companies.

Share certificates

The limited business issues certificates to each contributing person to prove the amount contributed. The certificate represents the number of **shares** in the business that person has purchased. Figure 12 shows a share certificate that is issued to each shareholder as proof of the owner's entitlement to a share of the profits – or the extent of his or her liability.

FIGURE 12 A typical share certificate

The law

It is fairly complicated and expensive to form a limited company. Because the owners (or **shareholders**) are no longer personally liable for the business debts, the law is more cautious in allowing it to start trading. It demands certain guarantees about the company's financing and the business aims and objectives. People who have been involved with previous business failures may be excluded from becoming involved with a limited company.

The directors of a limited company are required to file a report every year with Companies' House in London, to give details of profitability. In the case of a private limited company, such reports are available for the public to inspect on request.

Public limited companies must **publish their accounts** every year. This means that they must make details of their trading profits and losses available to the general public.

Public sector businesses

The Civil Service

The Civil Service consists of many departments, most of which are located in Whitehall, London. This is the administrative centre of the country. Figure 13 shows how Civil Service **employees** do not support any political party as part of their jobs, although the Civil Service is run by **ministers** who are politically motivated senior members of the government, such as the Minister of Defence, The Minister of Health and the Home Secretary.

Many of its departments are centrally run, such as the armed forces, responsible to the Ministry of Defence. It is there to ensure that our Army, Navy, Air Force and other services are adequate not only to meet our international commitments (such as the United Nations (UN) and NATO) but also strong enough and located in the right place to defend the UK.

Other Civil Service departments are centrally administered, but run locally, such as health, education, fire and the police services. The central administration is there to ensure that the services operate to a consistent standard everywhere in the country. For example, many schools are run by local authorities, but the Ministry of Education ensures that there are enough schools in each area to serve the needs of that population.

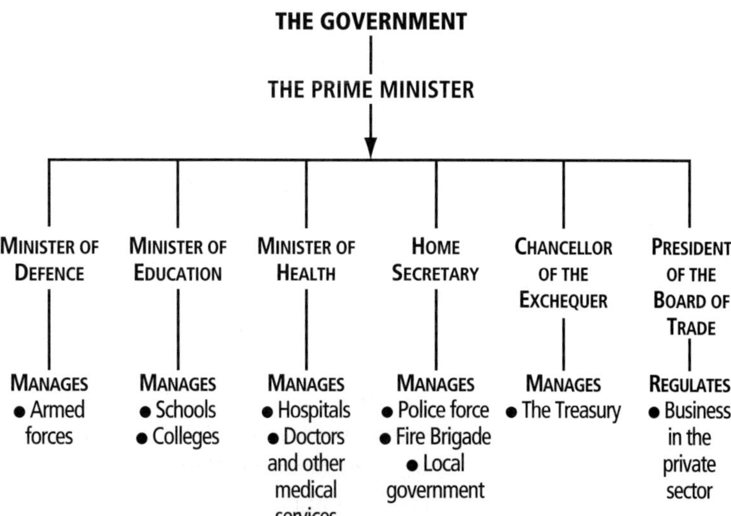

FIGURE 13 Civil Service businesses

Local government

Local government, through the local authority, is tasked with delivering the services listed in Figure 9 referred to on page 24. Not all local authorities are expert at running the diverse range of services they must offer the local community, so some of them – such as leisure centres – are actually run by private companies, but they must conform to standards set by the local authority. It is felt that experts operate them more efficiently and economically thus making better use of taxpayers' money.

Nationalised industries

These are slightly different to the other two types of state-run business.

Historically, there were always businesses that required a lot of money to establish them, such as the Royal Mail. It has had to establish post boxes and sorting offices throughout the country and to employ postmen and other workers to take care of the letters and parcels. It was also necessary to establish standards that would apply throughout the country – whether in far flung areas like the north of Scotland or parts of Cornwall, or in a densely populated conurbation like London.

It was unlikely that such a service could run at a profit, particularly at the start (the Royal Mail was established in 1840), yet it was clearly in the country's interest to make such services available to everybody. It was for this reason that the state established and ran the Royal Mail, and the other nationalised industries mentioned in Figure 9, on page 24.

Use of profit

It was stated earlier that a sole trader and a partnership retains its profits for its own uses. In addition to providing an income for its owners, these profits may be **re-invested** in the business, perhaps to expand and open another shop or branch, or to purchase new equipment.

Public and private limited companies also use their profits to expand the business – buying new machinery and premises, at home or abroad. They may further grow by starting or buying other companies.

Public sector businesses, by contrast, would use any profits to improve the level of service that they offer – perhaps by employing more people, or buying new equipment.

Activities

1   Name these types of businesses in your local area.
    a   Somebody who works by him or herself.
    b   A business run by a group of people of similar skills (e.g. plumbers, electricians, solicitors, doctors).
    c   A business which has the word 'limited' after its name.

2   Where is the nearest fire station? Where is the one after that? How well is your area covered in case of fire?

3   Find out who runs your local leisure centre. Does the council run it themselves or does a private company run it for them?

4   Enquire at three local hotels:
    •   is the hotel part of a national company, or is it run by the hotel owners privately?

Activities

Write a short report using these headings:

1   Primary, secondary and tertiary sectors of industry ...
    a   Give an example of businesses which operate in each sector of industry, that is, one operating in the primary sector, one in the secondary sector, and one in the tertiary sector.
    b   For each, name the industry in which it operates and the country where the head office is situated.
    c   In a few sentences, describe each business and explain why it is in the chosen sector of industry.

2   Businesses in public and private sectors ...
    a   Describe three businesses in the **public sector** in your area. Explain how they are funded and why it is in the public interest that they do not have to make a profit.
    b   Name one large, one medium and one small business in the private sector with which you are familiar. Explain how the profit motive and the need to remain competitive works to the advantage of its customers.
    c   Name a charity and explain how it spends its funds. How would its structure be different if it were to become a business in the public sector?

3   Type of business ownership ...
    Give an example of a:
    •   sole trader;
    •   partnership;

- private limited company;
- public limited company;
- franchise;
- state-owned business.

For each, explain its liabilities, how any profits are distributed and possible sources of finance.

 **Performance criterion**

1.1.4 Explain the operation of one business organisation

Case study

The Body Shop

Anita Roddick and her husband Gordon had an idea for a business. They wanted to manufacture their own soaps, perfumes and cosmetics without testing them on animals and using environmentally friendly materials.

They planned to package their products in simply designed bottles and boxes using re-cycled paper and plastic wherever possible.

They needed money to start the business, so they went to their bank manager. He was not impressed with the idea, because he could not imagine the Roddicks competing successfully with the large companies that dominate the cosmetics industry, such as Max Factor, Christian Dior or Boots.

Anita and Gordon were undeterred; in a casual conversation with a friend they outlined their idea.

He was impressed with their enthusiasm and energy and had a hunch that the idea might just work. He owned a garage that had made enough profits in the past for him to have some money to invest. Instead of lending Anita and Gordon the money they needed (about £5,000), he suggested that they should form a private limited company with the three of them as shareholders. That way, his money would not be re-paid, rather he would receive a share of the profits each year; this arrangement would also limit the extent of their liability for any losses that the business might incur.

The three of them opened their first shop on the south coast in 1976; they created an informal, friendly shopping environment with green as the predominant colour.

Their first products were made at home and customers were even encouraged to return their bottles when they had finished with them. This saved both costs and wastage.

The business grew steadily and profitably.

The Roddicks decided to open another shop. This time, instead of using money from the business, they offered a **franchise** to somebody who had a little money saved. She also had business experience, energy and enthusiasm. Part of the contract which their first franchisee signed, stipulated that all products sold must have been produced by Gordon and Anita.

That business, too, grew steadily and the Roddicks and their garage-owning friend felt that they had a success on their hands far in excess of their wildest dreams.

The business grew and further stores were opened; some were franchised, others were owned by The Body Shop.

They opened their first store abroad, and discovered that their retailing concept was accepted as well overseas as it had been in the UK and both home and export markets grew rapidly.

In order to expand the business without increasing their personal borrowing, the Roddicks offered to sell shares in The Body Shop to the general public. They also continued to expand with more franchised shops and others wholly owned by the company.

Today, there is a Body Shop in all major towns in the UK, and in many overseas' countries. Details of this and the company structure are shown in the two charts (Figure 14 and 15). Anita and Gordon Roddick, and their friendly garage owner, are all multi-millionaires.

They have also established supplier relationships with manufacturers in under-developed nations, thus helping these countries' emerging economies.

Although some of their motives have been questioned in recent times, they continue to support environmentally sensitive charities, and the company continues to flourish.

Worldwide shop list

Europe	Number of Shops Feb 1995	Feb 1994	Year of Opening
Austria	12	9	1986
Belgium	14	11	1978
Cyprus	2	1	1983
Denmark	14	15	1981
Eire	9	10	1981
Finland	20	17	1981
France	26	25	1982
Germany	53	43	1983
Gibraltar	1	1	1988
Greece	37	28	1979
Holland	48	47	1982
Iceland	2	2	1980
Italy	44	38	1984
Luxembourg	2	2	1991
Malta	1	1	1987
Norway	17	14	1985
Portugal	9	8	1986
Spain	54	52	1986
Sweden	41	40	1979
Switzerland	24	21	1983
	430	385	

Asia	Number of Shops Feb 1995	Feb 1994	Year of Opening
Bahrain	2	1	1985
Brunei	2	1	1993
Hong Kong	10	9	1984
Indonesia	5	4	1990
Japan	36	22	1990
Kuwait	2	2	1986
Macau	2	1	1993
Malaysia	14	11	1984
Oman	2	2	1986
Qatar	1	1	1987
Saudi Arabia	18	13	1987
Singapore	9*	9	1983
Taiwan	9	6	1988
Thailand	3	2	1993
UAE	4	4	1983
	119	88	

	Number of Shops Feb 1995	Feb 1994	Year of Opening
UK	243*	239	1976

	Number of Shops Feb 1995	Feb 1994	Year of Opening
USA	235*	170	1988

Americas excluding USA	Number of Shops Feb 1995	Feb 1994	Year of Opening
Antigua	1	1	1987
Bahamas	3	3	1985
Bermuda	2	1	1987
Canada	112	106	1980
Cayman Islands	1	1	1989
Mexico	2	2	1993
	121	114	

Australia and New Zealand	Number of Shops Feb 1995	Feb 1994	Year of Opening
Australia	53	48	1983
New Zealand	9	9	1989
	62	57	

*Our company shops are located as follows: USA 90, UK 43, Singapore 9.

	Number of Shops Feb 1995	Feb 1994
GRAND TOTAL	**1210**	**1053**

Number of countries: **45**   Number of languages we trade in: **23**

FIGURE 14 The Body Shop worldwide shop list

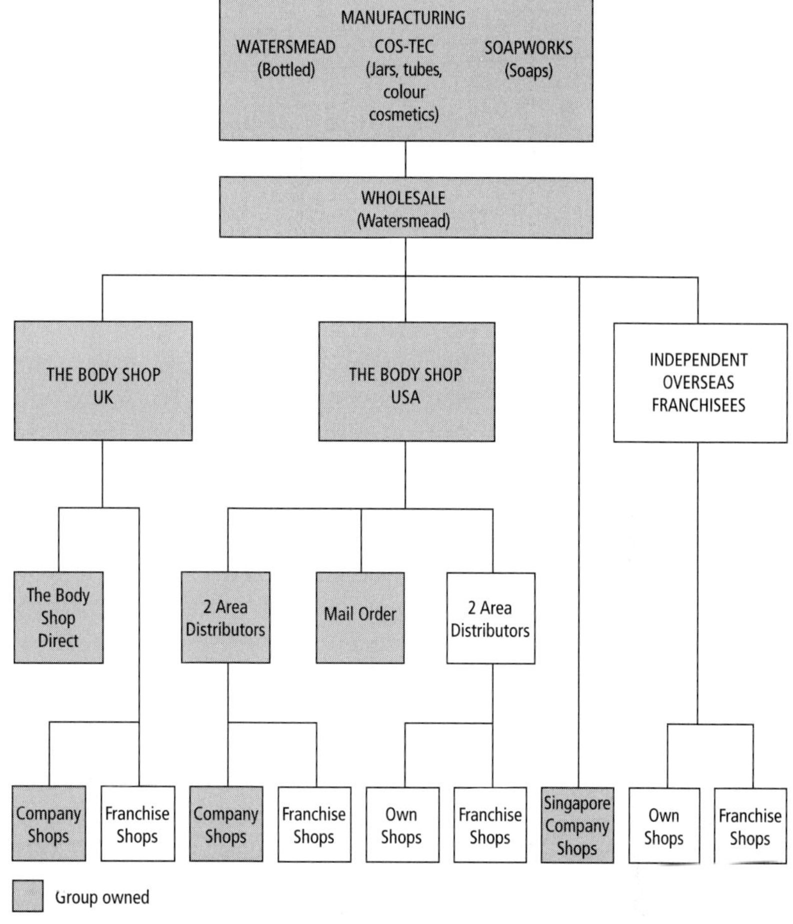

FIGURE 15 The Body Shop operating structure

Activities Write a report on The Body Shop, concentrating on these areas.

a Its purpose, especially the balance between its charitable and campaigning objectives and the need to make a profit for its shareholders.

b The Body Shop has always been a limited company, but the case study describes how it changed its status. Explain why you think it did this, and the benefits of limited liability for the owners of the business.

c Discuss whether The Body Shop is in the primary, secondary or tertiary industrial sector.

d Name other types of business with which The Body Shop employees and franchisees come into contact.

e Describe the stance that The Body Shop takes towards the environment. Evaluate the commercial and other benefits that this brings to the business and the people with whom it comes into contact.

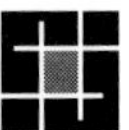 # **Element 1.2** Examine Business Location, Environment, Markets and Products

 Element 1.2 covers the environment in which businesses operate at home and overseas and why businesses are situated where they are – perhaps because they wish to be near their customers or suppliers. For some businesses, such as coal mining or forestry, the location of the business is dictated by the availability of the earth's natural resources – the coal, trees or fish, for example.

Having considered different kinds of businesses in the previous element, let us now examine what they produce – products and services – and for whom: for individual customers, other businesses and the government.

The business environment includes not only the social and physical considerations of geographical location, but also the economic, technological and other aspects that a business must take into account if it is to flourish.

The market has vital implications for a business – who buys, how often, when and where? Answers to all these questions need to be found when deciding where to locate any business.

 **Evidence indicators**

- A map of an area which identifies the location of one business organisation, showing relevant natural resources, the proximity of other businesses, and customers and transport services. The map should be accompanied by a brief explanation of the reason for location of the business.
- A summary which explains the competitive business environment within which businesses operate, with notes referring to legal, environmental and public influences on business organisations.
- A report on one business organisation which describes the market for its goods or services, demand for the goods or services, and explains how marketing communications (e.g. advertising) used by the business has improved its market position.

  • Notes and sketches that support proposals for new or
    developed products.

Core skills In this element two core skills are covered:

Communication
Element 2.2 Produce written material

2.3 Use images

Performance criterion **1.2.1 Explain the reasons for location of business**

Milestones in travel Look at Figure 16 and try to imagine how business functioned before 1730.

From about 1400 to 1700 nothing in the world of business and commerce changed significantly. People worked together in small groups to produce enough shelter, food and clothes for their own needs. Each community was more or less self-sufficient; anything they needed, they made themselves and apart from the development of some skills which were confined to a particular region (such as leather work in Northampton, wool and cloth in the Cotswolds), most business activity required to support the community took place within it.

Date	Milestones
Pre 1730	thousands of small independent communities spread throughout the UK; some international trade (e.g. wool and lace to Belgium); some local specialist skills (e.g. Northampton – leather work; Nottingham – lace). Main transport is by **horse**
1730 onwards	**canals** built – national trade possible
1830 onwards	**railways** built – distribution of products anywhere within the UK in 24 hours broadly possible
1888	Carl Benz launched a **motor tricycle** propelled by **the internal combustion engine**
1913	Henry Ford created the moving production line to cope with high demand for his **car, the Model 'T' Ford**
1935	early commercial **flights**
1957	first UK **motorway** opened

FIGURE 16 United Kingdom: milestones in travel

Although there was some business competition within the communities, it was necessarily restricted – there could only be a limited supply of any particular skill, service or product.

The horse was the main means of transport. Personal travel over any distance was by stagecoach, goods transport predominantly by horse and cart. It took several days to travel from Manchester to London by stagecoach; it was expensive and travellers arrived tired, dirty and possibly robbed of their possessions by highwaymen.

Around 1730, the first canals and inland waterways were built in the UK and on continental Europe; this was a business revolution for canals meant that large quantities of some goods could now be transported around the country. Cloth, coal, iron ore, leather and other non-perishable merchandise could be moved – although slowly, by horse-drawn boat – to the main conurbations, London, Bristol, Birmingham, Leeds, Manchester, Liverpool and the coal mines in Wales.

The development of competition

With the advent of the waterways, **competition** emerged for the first time in any significant degree; coal was produced in several areas in Britain and the cheapest suppliers gained the most business from the emerging factories, especially in the north of England.

One of the first major developments to follow the construction of canals was the movement of the textile trade from the Cotswolds to Yorkshire and Lancashire, where labour was abundant and cheap. The first mechanised textile mills were emerging here and inland waterway transport enabled these businesses to distribute their products widely around the country, including major towns.

The most significant effect of competition was to reduce labour costs – where these were low, work was plentiful; where they were higher, production and trade faded away.

Factories and entrepreneurs

The first factories enabled cloth to be produced in great quantities – far more than was needed in their local communities.

Therefore it was essential to sell their cloth outside Lancashire and Yorkshire and factory owners were continually under pressure to sell the whole of their output to avoid 'stockpiling' and to develop the business.

The owners of factories earned more than their workforce. This was the return for the risk they took in investing large sums of their own money to produce goods in great quantity; risk-taking, or entrepreneurship, earned rewards.

When the railways later established a network which enabled products to be distributed almost anywhere within mainland Britain within 24 hours, other commercial opportunities presented themselves.

A great entrepreneur, W H Smith, hit upon the idea of distributing newspapers which had been printed in London, throughout the whole of the UK. Thus, up-to-date London news was available nearly everywhere. This idea of wide distribution from a central source was taken up by other retailing entrepreneurs such as Lilley & Skinner who opened their first shoe shop in London in 1842. Other retailing pioneers in the UK were John Lewis, who opened his first shop in London in 1864. Mr & Mrs John Sainsbury opened their first grocery shop in Drury Lane, London in 1869.

Once established, such people were encouraged to open more than one store so that they could buy in greater quantity and therefore supply goods more cheaply. Such low costs were partly passed on to their customers in the form of lower prices, but the resulting higher sales meant that the entrepreneurs could still price goods to make higher profits. This enabled them to amass large sums of capital (money) to open more stores in other towns, thus generating even greater profits.

Travel

With the development of the internal combustion engine, a steady growth in the availability of personal transport took place during this century, and people's needs changed: instead of going to their corner shop for groceries car owners could travel further, buy in greater quantities from a large store, and save money.

In this way, the construction of motorways after the Second World War had a revolutionary effect upon the location of the new grocery superstores.

When commercial flight became a reality in the 1930s, organisations could have their head offices in one country, yet travel with ease to subsidiary companies in another country to monitor progress.

The impact of each of these travel developments on business was enormous.

Technology and business

There are other environmental considerations in business, however the impact of technology on business has been immense, especially in the last 15 years.

Look at the photograph of an office in 1926 (Figure 17). In such an office many people would have shared one telephone. Their adding machine would have been an enormous affair with levers and whirring metal – in those days the microprocessor was as much a dream as the computer and fax.

Increased ease of communication and information access has effectively brought towns and business locations around the world closer together. Conference facilities on a telephone now make it possible to have a meeting with Japanese, Thai, German and Nigerian executives without any person leaving the office.

The fax can transmit a page of A4 typescript anywhere in the world in less than a minute.

FIGURE 17 A typical office in the 1920s

Computer technology is now developing so fast that new software is obsolete in the time that it takes to launch the product on the market!

Business location

There are many considerations to debate when a business is choosing its location.

Resources
1 Labour
2 Natural resources
3 Land and premises

Labour
The availability of labour is of prime importance. The supply is affected by:

- availability of relevant skills;
- cost of labour;
- quantity of labour; and
- care for the workforce.

Relevant skills It is vital that the workforce should have the relevant skills that a business requires. It is very much cheaper for the skipper of a trawler, for example, to employ workers who understand fishing. The alternative is to train people in the relevant skills but this is often an expensive and time-consuming business. Unemployed miners from Yorkshire, Wales, Kent and elsewhere, for instance, have much potential which could be an attraction to a firm considering re-locating to any of these areas – but such people would usually need to be paid while they are learning their new skills.

Cost of labour People in the South-east of England are on average paid more than their counterparts in the West, Midlands or North of England and the cost of labour can be a great influence on the overall costs of a business.

Sadly, higher wages or salaries can also have a negative effect on the movement of labour. For example, some people who had lost their jobs in the north-east in the mid 1980s came south knowing of the increased opportunities there. Some were offered jobs, but when they learned the price of houses in the south compared to their cost in the north, they realised they could not afford to sell up and move. They were forced to stop work and return to their native part of the country.

However, it may be cheaper for a company to re-train the miners mentioned earlier than to recruit workers with a rare skill, who, realising their scarcity value, demand higher wages. Plumbers, carpenters, bricklayers and other skilled workers associated with building, frequently adopt this approach when houses are being constructed.

Quantity of labour How many people are available is important. Since a workforce is normally changing constantly – people leave a company, are promoted, retire, fall sick, or simply seek a new environment – it is important for replacements to be readily available. This is one of the main reasons that service businesses stay in London; the advertising industry for example, can more easily replace staff who leave than they can in the provinces where there are inevitably less people with the necessary training and skills to fill any vacancies.

A manufacturer may find the allure of a cheap factory in the country very appealing – until he realises the difficulty of recruiting enough people to work the machines!

Care for the workforce And if this manufacturer decides to import his workforce, he may then face the difficulty of looking after them. They inevitably require medical attention, entertainment, schools for their children, food supplies and such amenities which may be taken for granted in a town, but are not found on an offshore oil rig, on board ship or on an army base.

Natural resources

For obvious reasons, primary sector industries are located at the most convenient place to extract the natural resources. In the case of mines, these are often sited where the ore or coal is closest to the surface. Fishing industries are situated at a port where road, rail or air transport is readily available to distribute the fish to their markets as quickly and cheaply as possible.

Such considerations have far-reaching effects. Electricity generation and steel smelting plants, for example traditionally relied heavily on coal. Thus they are concentrated in an area of ready availability of this natural resource even though they themselves are not primary industries.

As the electricity industry relies less on coal and more on gas for its fuel, so few power stations are built with the availability of gas in mind and the availability of coal becomes of secondary importance.

Land and premises

Government planners strictly control the way in which land may be used. Whether it is for a factory, forest, farm, shop or house, the location of land is at least as important as its price.

The land for a store situated on a prime retail site such as a high street or motorway intersection will be more expensive than that for a back street; this is not surprising as the prime location will attract more passing trade than the secondary one. A factory on an industrial estate will pay even less for its land than one on a back street in a town. Land designated for residential purposes commands a higher price than agricultural land.

Price is not the only consideration, however; the availability of services – water, gas, electricity, drainage and waste disposal – is another feature to take into account. The presence of a nearby stream or river may be a good reason to site a factory which wishes to dispose of a large quantity of non-toxic effluent.

Firms tend to select their location first, then buy the land (once they have obtained **planning permission** from the planning authorities for the use to which they wish to put it).

As business becomes more competitive and developed, it is unsurprising that increasingly large companies have to build new premises for their shop, warehouse or factory in order to meet their precise needs. It is easier and more cost effective for them to do this than it is to move into premises that have previously been used for another purpose.

Incentives Inevitably, there is greater demand in one area for land than in others. Demand for commercial and residential land in London and the south-east, for example, has been greater than in Scotland.

In order to redress this imbalance, and to create new employment opportunities, governments offer **incentives** to businesses which choose to locate their premises in so-called development areas.

Such incentives may take the form of grants to finance some of the building costs, or reduced or no business rates for the first few years, so that the business may establish itself in the new area.

The government calls such places **regional development areas.** South Wales is one, as is the North-West of England.

The government frequently works together with local government to determine the precise amount and type of government assistance, which may include paying to re-train the workforce in an area of high unemployment. In return, the government pays less in unemployment benefit and other subsidies, so there is a financial saving to central government, apart from the undoubted social benefits of having an employed workforce.

The European Union grants finances to encourage industrial growth in poorer member states, such as Greece, Ireland and Portugal.

Proximity of other businesses
One reason for regional differences is that as new industries grow, so they tend to converge on a common area. There are many reasons for this. The most obvious is the availability of natural resources. It was mentioned earlier that the availability of coal in Sheffield and elsewhere in the North of England led not only to the coal mining industry being based here, but also steel refining.

There are advantages in having similar businesses in the same area. One is that specialist suppliers tend to flock to such areas. As motor manufacturers grew and flourished in the Midlands, so their suppliers were based there, too. Engineers, manufacturers of machinery, tyres and other accessories were attracted to that area, since so many of their potential customers – their market – were based there, too.

In France and Germany, wine growing areas attract suppliers of relevant equipment: glass, cork, printed labels. Equally, wine growers in a particular area group themselves together to market their wine as was mentioned on page 33 in the previous element. This has several advantages for them: together they have more power than they do individually. They can buy their components (e.g. bottles, corks, labels) in greater quantity and therefore at lower prices. In addition, they can sometimes achieve greater power over their customers by agreeing to sell their products only in a certain way, sometimes agreeing to hold higher prices, for instance.

Silicon Valley in California and a smaller version west of London near the M4 motorway are examples of modern industries that have clustered together in the same area, although this does not always result in higher retail prices.

This clustering together of industries obviously creates much employment in such areas, which then flourish. However, if the industry suffers a downturn, many people lose their jobs at the same time. For example, when all the motor cycle manufacturers in the Birmingham area lost their market share to more efficient Japanese manufacturers in the 1950s and 1960s, many people in the midlands lost their jobs and prosperity suffered in the area.

Proximity to markets

Some businesses choose their location to be as close to their customers as possible. One obvious example is retailing where the largest companies have created computer models to help them decide where to build new stores. Taking account of the prosperity of an area, location of competitors, and availability of transport, such models demonstrate how far people are likely to travel to make their purchases at the proposed store.

High Streets and shopping precincts generally have a balance of the different types of retailer – newsagents, greengrocers, butchers and chemists exist in even the smallest shopping area. More specialist retailers such as furniture, clothes or musical instruments are more widespread, since people are prepared to travel further to make these more considered – and less frequent – purchases.

Another consideration is the provision of after-sales service, not only in retailing (such as cars and electrical equipment) but also in industrial markets. Suppliers of components and machinery often benefit from being near their customers so that if there is a sudden upsurge in demand or an unexpected problem, they can respond quickly to their customers' needs.

Accessibility to a port, motorway, main line railway station, or airport may be fundamental to a business' success. The proximity of a market town may affect the location of a farm, for example.

The working environment The working environment is a consideration for employers as well as proximity to markets. Research has shown that a workforce performs better when it is comfortable and not distracted. Hence new, custom-built offices command a higher rent than older buildings with less up-to-date facilities.

On the other hand while lack of facilities may command lower rents, workers are often paid higher wages to compensate. An example is an offshore oil rig, where families, shops and other attractions are virtually non-existent, and poor weather and otherwise difficult working conditions prevail.

Performance criterion

1.2.2 Explain influences of the business environment on business organisations

The influence of competition

Everybody possesses a competitive instinct to some degree. In the commercial world, the need to develop, improve and launch new products and to innovate is enhanced by competition from others doing the same thing.

In order to sustain a business, it is necessary to protect that niche which a company has carved out for itself. The major car manufacturers, Mercedes, Ford, Volkswagen and Volvo all have a different approach to the market, yet they are all competing for the same car buyers.

Competition influences greatly the environment in which a business operates. Consider the impact of Virgin and Sainsbury's Classic on the market for Cola drinks. Yet their impact on both Pepsi and Coca-Cola has been tempered by the distribution that these both enjoy in areas where neither Virgin nor Sainsbury is present, for instance, in bar sales and automatic vending machines. In fact, Coca-Cola claimed to have sold more of their drinks in the 12 months after the launch of these major competitors, because the market had grown in size, and the extent of their loss of market share had been less than the market growth.

Another example is the area of domestic electrical products: the life of a CD player as a top of the range product is barely a year, thanks to the continuous innovations of competitors.

Competition and the law

Competition could inevitably tempt some businesses to make untrue or unfair claims about their products.

For this reason, laws exist to give manufacturers and suppliers a framework within which to operate.

In everything they do, they must act with consideration to their customers and community. Harmful ingredients in products are banned, such as some additives in foods, asbestos in any consumer product, and some children's clothing must be fireproof.

Advertising is very strictly regulated, especially where children are concerned. Cigarette advertising on television is banned.

There are strict laws concerning the manufacturer's obligation to replace faulty goods under warranty.

The laws concerning Sunday trading for retailers have been relaxed in recent years.

Laws reflect public and customer pressures. These have an increasing impact on manufacturers. Consider the use of carbon dioxide (laughing gas) as a propellant in aerosols. Although it is still legal to use the cheaper CFC, consumers are prepared to pay a little more for an environmentally-friendly product. Only the most foolhardy manufacturer would fail to heed this strong consumer preference.

Business also has a moral obligation to be concerned about a number of issues – product safety, use and possible abuse, welfare of employees, welfare of customers.

The needs of the local community take a growing importance in commercial life today. When a major operator – manufacturer or retailer – chooses to locate the business in a particular area, planning authorities sometimes make their planning consent subject to certain conditions. For example, permission to build a superstore may be given on the condition that a new children's playing field would be paid for by the retailer for the use of young people in the area.

The environment

The environment is becoming an increasingly important factor for businesses, especially manufacturers.

Some chemical plants emit noxious fumes; other heavy industries not only pollute the atmosphere with emissions, but also with noise. The dangers of nuclear power stations and armaments' factories are all too painful reminders of the consequences of man trying to take the upper hand over nature.

Government planners, however, try to site new factories away from residential areas, with the result that the habitat of flourishing wildlife and sites of natural beauty are often affected.

As consumer awareness of the environment grows, so legislation is made to take account of changing consumer tastes, as well as to protect the public, as innovations in consumer and industrial products appear. We are currently in a transitional phase in environmental law as laws in the individual member countries of the European Union are being brought into line so that common legislation can apply throughout the whole European Union.

Conservation and preservation is a major public concern – recycling materials, replanting forests, replenishing fish stocks and other renewable natural resources, as well as the pollution of air, sea, land, forest and wildlife.

MacDonalds clear rubbish and used packaging away from their restaurants because it improves their image as a community and environmentally aware business; this shows what a powerful influence public concern for the environment exerts, at least over a business's marketing policy.

This public concern over the effect that business and other activities is having on the environment – the earth, sea, air and stratosphere – has affected perceptions of businesses. Here are some examples.

1   There is a growing concern that man is exhausting natural supplies of oil, fish, wood, coal and metal ores too quickly. With fish and forestry, nature does not have enough time to renew natural supplies. In the other examples, non-renewable natural resources are slowly being exhausted due to man's intensive exploitation of them.

2 The conversion process of natural resources into usable products produces pollution that is damaging the environment. Effluent from factories flows into rivers, resulting in poisoned fish; car exhaust fumes and factory chimneys pollute the air. One result of this is an increase in cases of breathing disorders (such as asthma) in industrialised countries.

3 Industrial accidents such as oil spillages from wrecked tankers and polluted gases emitted from nuclear power stations cause death and suffering to people, animals, plants and degradation of the environment in general. The devastation caused by radiation from the damaged nuclear power station at Chernobyl, for example, caused death, disease and disruption extending far beyond Russia's borders.

    Oil tankers run aground, break up and spill their load of crude oil, destroying the marine environment, killing sea-birds and other wildlife dependent on the sea: the *Sea Empress* incident in Milford Haven and other disasters hit the headlines all too frequently.

4 Ingredients used to produce certain products can be harmful to people – for example, lead in petrol and the CFC propellant used in aerosols that was mentioned earlier. Several major steps have been taken to improve this situation and people throughout the world are increasingly conscious of the damage that irresponsible exploitation can cause.

    Practices which are harmful or potentially so are becoming less and less acceptable to consumers, who are even prepared to pay a little more money for an environmentally-friendly product, rather than a potentially harmful one.

5 Even the simple duty of every responsible citizen to dispose of litter and waste thoughtfully is becoming a major issue; penalties are becoming heavier and more widely imposed.

Conservation and environmental protection is likely to assume greater importance as manufacturing techniques develop.

Figure 18 summarises the influences on businesses described in performance criteria 1.2.1 and 1.2.2.

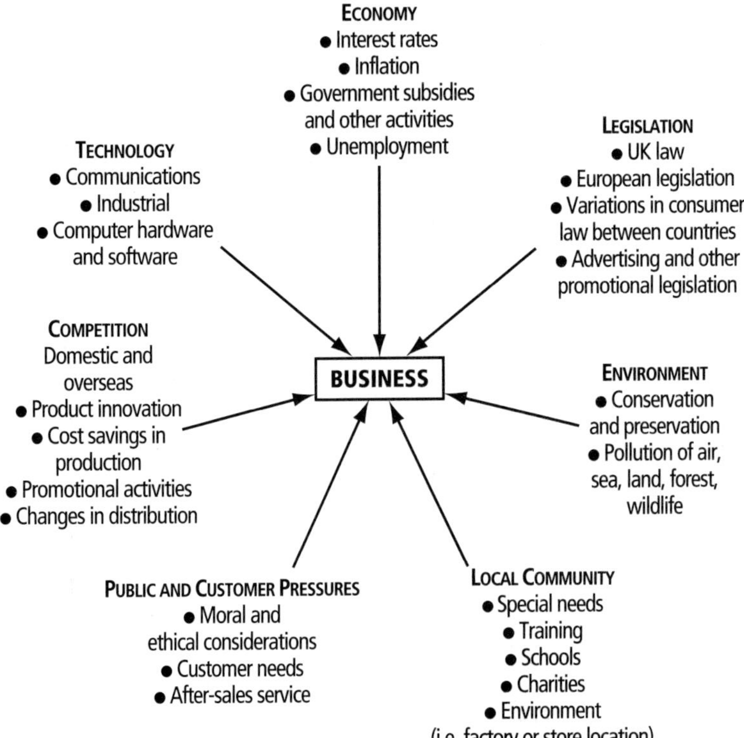

FIGURE 18 Business and the environment in which it operates

Performance criterion

1.2.3 Describe markets for businesses' products based on demand

Markets

Consumer markets

At the beginning of Unit One (page 12), we saw that business satisfies people's needs and wants. People need food to survive, so they buy salt and bread. People therefore create a demand for certain goods and services to meet their needs and wants. It is surprising to note that in 1993, people spent an estimated £20 million on salt in the UK.

From the UK's point of view it may be stated that the **domestic market for salt is £20 million.**

Similarly, people want to travel. Some buy cars, others travel by train, while others hire cars. In 1993, people in the UK spent £35,600 million pounds buying new and used cars, £2,439 million on travel by train and £682 million hiring cars (Source: Marketing Pocket Book).

Expressed another way, it can be said that **the market for new and used cars in the UK is worth £35,600 million.**

> A market is the total demand for identified goods and services within stated boundaries.

The size of a market can be measured in units or value. By measuring it in value its size can be related to other markets. For example, the market for car hire is smaller in value than the market for train travel; about one quarter the size, in fact.

All of the above examples are of goods and services intended for consumers to buy and use themselves. They are called **consumer markets.**

Have another look at Figure 16 on page 43. Prior to 1730, business was parochial; very little trade took place between different regions and even less between nations.

We saw how people's ability to travel improved over the same period in which new industrial processes appeared which enabled greater quantities of goods to be produced, such as cloth in factories.

The development of international trade (export and import) was the inevitable result, to the benefit of all nations. Producing goods on a large scale enabled manufacturers to buy their components in larger and therefore cheaper quantities. Specialisation enabled them to produce greater quantities at reduced costs. Since the cost of distributing such goods had been reduced, those which were surplus to domestic requirements could be sold overseas.

The domestic market

Nowadays, some manufacturers produce goods only for the **domestic market**, either ignoring, or not wishing to take advantage of, the opportunities in overseas markets.

In the Ahr valley just south of Bonn, German wine growers produce a beautiful red wine with a unique light flavour. It is the most northern vineyard in continental Europe and output is restricted by the climate and size of the region; only small quantities of the wines are produced each year. These wines are almost all sold locally. A very small amount is shipped to other regions of Germany; almost none is sold abroad. Yet the farmers make a good living from their domestic market.

The international market

Further south, farmers on the Rhine and the Mosel produce white wines in great quantities. Anybody who has visited or lived in the area will know that much is consumed domestically, but large quantities are also exported. The profits that these overseas sales generate help to fund future investment – new equipment, the development of new production techniques – so that consumers of Rhine and Mosel wines in Germany and overseas benefit as a result.

The **international market** for certain goods is sometimes greater than the domestic market. Volvo, the Swedish car manufacturer, sells more of its cars in the UK than it does in Sweden. Holland, with a population of around 15 million, cannot support enormous businesses such as Philips and Shell without a thriving export market, which far exceeds domestic sales.

Market share

People need to drink in order to survive. Whilst water serves this purpose, some people prefer soft drinks. They do not actually need them, but they like to drink them if they are thirsty.

People spend £6 billion on soft drinks in the UK. This was five per cent more than in the previous year. (Source: *Sunday Times*). A major supplier of this drink is the Coca-Cola corporation, based in America.

In recent times the UK market has become more competitive with the emergence of 'own brand' products from Sainsbury, Tesco and others, as well as Virgin Cola, all of which are generally cheaper than Coca-Cola.

Despite this competition, Coca-Cola claims to have boosted its sales in the UK by 21 per cent in the period July to September 1994, and by ten per cent in the final three months.

It can therefore be stated that **Coca-Cola has a large share of the UK carbonates (fizzy drinks) market.**

It is estimated that people in the UK spent £1,300 million on carbonates in the year ending January 1995. (Source: *Marketing Week*). It is therefore not surprising to learn that the UK supplier of Coca-Cola, Coca-Cola Schweppes Beverages, enjoyed profits of about £140 million in about the same time.

Of course, these figures are changing all the time and are only accurate to a certain degree. But the information is vital to manufacturers, since it enables them to calculate how much **market share** they command. Their competitors obviously have similar information about their own activities.

It is estimated that in the UK about £900 million is spent on recorded music each year (Source: *Sunday Times*). Woolworth claims about two per cent market share; in this case, Woolworth would sell about £18 million worth of tapes and CDs each year.

By comparison, W H Smith has a much larger market share; in addition to its own shops, it also owns Virgin and Our Price record stores and enjoys about 35 per cent of the UK record market. Its turnover in records, from these figures, may be stated to be in the region of £315 million per year.

Some businesses deliberately keep a small market share. This means that in hard times, such as recession and periods of high unemployment, their businesses do not suffer as much as other, larger, suppliers.

 **Performance criterion**

1.2.4 Identify products provided by business organisations

In addition to supplying markets for consumer goods such as music and carbonates, firms themselves make purchases in order to carry on their business. They buy components, packaging, servicing for their machinery, new machines, spare parts and delivery trucks. Offices purchase stationery, photocopiers, and computers.

The industrial market

Businesses which sell mainly to other businesses operate in industrial markets. Such markets are for goods and services not primarily used for direct consumption; rather they help to produce or provide consumer goods or services. They are a means to an end, rather than an end in itself.

Businesses also purchase from the industrial market specialist services, such as advertising from advertising agencies, legal services from solicitors and patent attorneys, information from market research specialists, financial expertise from accountants and auditors.

Governments make purchases of a very specialist nature, such as war planes, armaments, and fire engines. The list of such products is as long as it is diverse.

These are all products of industrial market businesses. Compared with firms operating in consumer markets, such businesses tend to have fewer customers for their products, but in general each customer or "client company" spends a greater sum of money for each purchase.

Goods and services

Products may not only be **goods**; as was seen when the tertiary industrial sector was considered on page 14, the provision of **services** is the source of a growing amount of business – hotels, car hire, holidays and tourism, retailing – all are service industries since the businesses themselves establish their reputation by the quality of the services they provide, rather than by their manufacturing.

Consumables

Consumer goods and services are purchased by the consumers themselves – products that people buy to use immediately and then replace, such as food and drink, batteries for radios, light bulbs, car hire, hotel accommodation and petrol. All are known as **consumable**. For business, stationery and components fall into this category.

Durables

Products with a longer life such as furniture, carpets, houses, cars and clothes are called **durable goods**.

Figure 19 gives examples of consumable and durable goods.

> **Consumer markets** are for goods and services which are provided by businesses for **individuals.**

> **Industrial markets** cover goods and services provided by business for **other businesses and governments.**

EXAMPLES OF CONSUMER MARKETS **for individuals**	EXAMPLES OF INDUSTRIAL MARKETS **for other businesses**	**for governments**
Clothing and footwear	Components	Police services
Trainers	Plastic mouldings	Uniforms
Jeans	Shrink-wrap films	Truncheons
Tracksuits	box bases & lids	Services to convert
Anoraks	Shipper cartons	saloon cars to police
Blouses	Sub-assemblies	cars
Socks	Gearboxes	Handcuffs
Food and Drink	Electrical transformers	Fire services
Instant coffee	Printed circuit boards	Fire engines
Tea	Print	Fire helmets
Fruit juice	Packaging	Extension ladders
Wines	Instruction leaflets	Hose
Cereals	Warranty cards	Protective equipment
Chocolate bars	Stickers	Ambulance services
Toffees	Professional services	Ambulances
Chewing gum	Advertising agency	Stretchers
Fresh fruit	Market research	Medical equipment
Domestic appliances and	Solicitors	Wheelchairs
electronic equipment	Accountants	Armed forces
Camcorders	Trade Mark agents	War planes
Dishwashers	Auditors	Aircraft carriers
Fridge-freezers	Investment consultants	Weapons
Personal stereos	Secretarial services	Ammunitions
Televisions	Cleaning services	Training equipment
Radio cassettes	Goods	Tanks
Household equipment	Office furniture	Local services
Curtains	Stationery	Equipment for
Carpets	Photocopies	children's playgrounds
Light bulbs	Production machinery	Dustcarts
Duvets	Vehicles	Traffic lights
Cutlery	Fork lift trucks	Mowing machines
Leisure	Tractors	Swimming pools
Books and magazines	Panel vans	
Greetings cards	Articulated trucks	
Compact discs		
Bicycles		
Cinema		

FIGURE 19
Consumer and industrial markets

△ Performance criterion

1.2.5 Explain activities undertaken by businesses to improve their market position

Identifying needs

It is said that the most successful salespeople are those who listen more than they speak. By listening, they can find out what their customer needs, then demonstrate how the product on offer meets such needs.

So it is also with successful companies. The business that listens and thereby understands the needs of its customer – individual consumer, other business or government – has a greater chance of success than those which leave it to chance.

Needs and wants are continually changing, due to developing technology, changing tastes and standards of living.

Now that many homes possess a car, there is less need for a corner shop and a milkman to provide food and drink. There is a greater need, however, for large supermarkets so that a family may shop in bulk – perhaps once a week – rather than the 'little and often' shopping pattern that used to be the norm.

Consequently people's requirements in public transport have changed. Bus services no longer need to be so extensive and frequent, since people use their cars. Smaller buses have consequently been designed and now abound on the streets.

Use of the radio has changed beyond recognition since the advent of television. The once large demand for black and white televisions has now dwindled to almost nothing. Use of colour television has changed with the introduction of video recorders and satellite channels.

New developments are taking place constantly and businesses must constantly check that they continue to meet their customers' requirements.

Villiers, BSA, Francis Barnett and Royal Enfield were all successful motorcycle manufacturers prior to 1970. Ekco, Bush, Mullard and Marconi were well known makes of radio in the years before and after the Second World War.

Hardly any of these manufacturers survived because they failed to keep pace with emerging technology and changing customer needs.

In the case of motorcycle manufacturers, competitors introduced dealer servicing, electric starter motors and other improvements to broaden the appeal of motor cycling to meet changing needs and expectations. The UK manufacturers had expanded their businesses in the 1920s and 1930s when customer demands were quite different; if the machine needed attention, the owner did it himself. Since it was predominantly a male preserve, the use of a kick-start showed how macho he was!

After the war, the Japanese were the first to recognise changes in the marketplace and were able to harness new technology to fulfil and foster new requirements.

The same decline was shown in the UK electrical goods industry. When microprocessors and printed circuit boards started to replace valves and transistors, UK manufacturers failed to keep up with technological change and many companies died.

The significance of price

Inevitably, price also plays a part in dictating market position. Innovations are made not only to produce new or modified goods but also to produce goods more easily, more quickly or using less materials. Furthermore, generally speaking, as markets expand, so prices come down. For instance when colour television was introduced in 1967, the price of a set was £200; this was about one third the price of a small car. As more people wanted colour television, so manufacturing techniques improved, components could be produced or purchased in larger quantities, hence more cheaply, and prices came down. As prices came down, so more people were able to afford colour television and prices came down even more, so that even at today's prices, a colour television can be purchased for less than £200; this is probably less than £20 in 1967 prices!

The significance of desirability

It goes without saying that the more attractive and desirable a product, the more people will want to buy it.

A television does not need a remote control, but most people prefer a television to have one. It therefore follows that a television with remote control becomes more desirable to potential consumers than one without.

A car does not need a radio, or electrically controlled mirrors, windows and sunroof, but one with these accessories is more desirable, even if it is more expensive. Some people would like to buy such a car, but cannot afford it, so they settle for a cheaper model with less accessories.

Mechanically there may be no difference; the car will probably last just as long, but will always be less attractive, even more so when improved models with more gadgets are introduced as the original model of car becomes older.

Most manufacturers, therefore include versions of their cars which range from the most simple ('standard' or 'economy') versions to the most complex ('top of the range') models so that a wide range of customer needs are met, and many customers can dream of moving upmarket as their finances improve!

Just as consumers have a wide choice of cars, so the variations open to car manufacturers are also diverse. For example, a manufacturer can choose to add an electric sunroof, or a better quality radio. If both are included the price would be higher than many consumers would want to pay, so the manufacturer must choose which accessory to include.

Marketing research

Most manufacturers recognise that their own opinion may not be what their customers actually want.

In order to discover what customers want, manufacturers conduct marketing research into customer preferences.

Marketing research can take many different forms, depending on the information the manufacturer seeks. but all such exercises involve communicating with customers in some way.

Telephone research, personal interviews and postal questionnaires are all forms of market research. Sometimes it is merely a matter of observing customers or potential customers in a store or other environment to see how they reach their decisions to purchase certain items.

In nearly all cases the results are analysed and used to improve the product or some aspect of it.

It may be the **design** of the product or packaging that is being monitored. Even a basic product like a toilet cleaner can be improved by re-designing the neck of the bottle so that the liquid may be squirted higher up the lavatory bowl to clean the toilet more easily and more effectively! The toilet duck is the result.

Manufacturers do not always produce a product that does a perfect job. The manufacturer of Persil withdrew Persil Power when it was alleged that the manganese or other ingredient in the product had a detrimental effect on the clothes.

Some years ago, Shell withdrew a version of its petrol when it was discovered that the additive that was supposed to improve engine efficiency and cleanliness failed in practice to live up to the public expectations generated by the extensive advertising campaign.

The manufacture of new flavour Coca-Cola ceased when it was found that customers actually preferred the original flavour, despite the fact that research had given the company a much more positive response to the new product.

It can be seen that market research is not an exact science although computer technology has helped to reduce its inaccuracies.

Marrying the aims of production and marketing

There is sometimes internal friction in businesses between production and marketing. Production wants to supply the goods it can produce most easily and quickly, whereas marketing wants them to make what the customer wants, in order to maximise sales! When the production function in a business has a disproportionate input, a product may be launched that the production team likes, but customers do not.

Watney's Red Barrel beer was launched nation-wide in the 1960s amid great furore; the people in production liked it because it was easy to brew and was the same throughout the country so thousands of gallons of the same recipe could be brewed at once. It used fewer hops, and on the face of it seemed a very attractive product. There was one main drawback however; customers did not like it enough! So, despite the advertising campaign, sales of Red Barrel were disappointing and the product was withdrawn.

More positive co-operation between marketing and production can, however, result in product and packaging improvements that mean cost savings. By reducing the labour and material content of a product, a price reduction can be achieved and consequently sales improved. Removing a box lid from a product and shrink- wrapping it can have the two-pronged benefit of reducing the product cost (there is no lid) and increasing its attractiveness at point of sale, that is in the shop, as the contents of the box can now easily be displayed.

Market-led businesses

Figure 20 shows how a market-led business uses its customer orientation to maintain a balance between the various

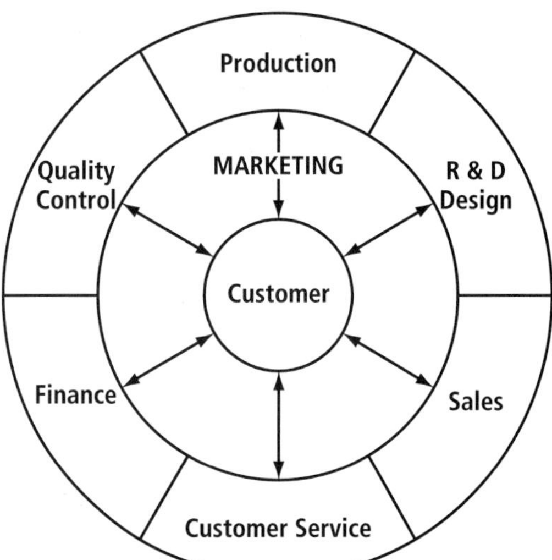

FIGURE 20
Marketing is the key
co-ordinating
function

functions of the business. In such circumstances resources
are harnessed to optimise the running of the business to
meet customer needs – and ultimately, as a successful
business, to generate greater profits for its owners.

Marketing communications

These are the items that a manufacturer provides to support
the product and inform prospective customers about the
product. Advertising can be as lavish as an extensive
television advertising campaign costing millions of pounds,
in the case of a mass-market product, to a modest
advertisement for the plumber in a local paper.

Other outlets for advertising are posters, press, commercial
radio, the cinema and more unusual forms such as air
balloons, carrier bags and T-shirts.

Personal contact

For industrial markets, much of marketing communication is
by personal contact – at exhibitions and through visits by the
sales force. It is most important that customer confidence
and contact is maintained in industrial markets, for the
customer needs to be reassured that if there is any problem
the supplier will be there to sort out difficulties!

Sales literature

There are times when it is desirable to compare one product
with another to determine the most suitable. This is
particularly true of **consumer durable** purchases that last a
long time, such as washing machines, curtains, carpets, cars

and video recorders. Some people wish to compare the performance and features of one model with another and **sales literature** in the form of leaflets and brochures is a useful source of reassurance and information for prospective customers. These can also be read and considered away from the point of sale.

After-sales service

Another aspect of marketing is the level and availability of **after-sales service.** When purchasing a car, it is helpful to know that the dealer is in the nearest town, and that it will not be necessary to take the car miles across the countryside for repair or inspection!

It can be a drawback with some imported goods or goods purchased from a large warehouse to know that after-sales service could be difficult should the product not function as intended.

Small local shops, suppliers and tradesmen enjoy a considerable advantage in these conditions, where some customers are prepared to pay a higher purchase price in order to have the security of the helpful local supplier being available if necessary.

Performance criterion

1.2.6 Propose products which would meet market demand

Activities

1 Sketch or describe two new products or services which you have devised. Explain the needs and wants which they are designed to meet. They may well be refined versions of existing products.

   Notes and sketches should be used in support of your proposals.

2 Select a large business in which you are interested; a manufacturer of food, drink, cars, hi-fi, for example.

   Draw a map of the area where it is are located. Show the relevant natural resources (for example, water, raw materials, food or wood). Show also where the suppliers of the business are located; if supplies are imported show its proximity to a harbour or airport and explain the relevance.

Show how transport services distribute the product to the consumer.

Your map should be accompanied by a brief explanation of the reason for location of the business.

3 From the text in this chapter and your own notes, explain the competitive environment within which businesses operate, with specific reference to legal, environmental and public influences on business organisations.

4 Choose a business and write a report describing the market for its goods or services, including how the product is made available to potential consumers. Identify the main competitors.

Describe the nature of the demand for goods or services; who purchases a good or a service, when and why – the benefits that consumers derive from doing so for example.

Explain how a business uses marketing communications such as advertising to improve its market position.

Element 1.3 Present Results of Investigation into Employment

Element 1.3 focuses on **employment** in its broadest context. Narrower concentration on aspects such as employment legislation, administrative procedures and specific personnel matters is covered in Unit 2 **People in Business Organisations**.

This element considers how some people work for themselves, yet others work for other people; the conditions in which they work, how people are paid and how their taxes and other deductions are made at source by the employer. Some business skills and training are also covered. Finally, we look at the impact of new technology on peoples' jobs, where they work and the environment in which they do it.

Before looking in detail into this element, students may like to refresh their memories about data presentation. This is covered in Core Skills 2, on pages 346–349).

Evidence indicators

- Seven examples, with descriptions, of different types of employment, including full-time, part-time, permanent, temporary, skilled, unskilled and self employment.
- A summary which analyses employment information about two EU regions (one should be the UK), including a graph or chart showing percentages of people in employment with a breakdown by gender, age and sector. The summary should explain differences in the number of people employed and describe the growth or decline of one manufacturing or service sector in those regions.
- A short report which describes and compares the working conditions of two individuals working for different organisations. The report should compare the individuals in terms of: hours of work, career opportunities, training opportunities and use of new technology.
- A record of a presentation, supported by visual aids, showing percentages of people employed and employment opportunities across at least two EU regions, or a record of a presentation, supported by visual aids, comparing working conditions of two individuals.

Core skills

Although the activities in this element can link with all three core skills in varying degrees, these elements are the main focus:

Application of number
Element 2.2 Tackle problems

2.3 Interpret and present data

Communication
Element 2.1 Take part in discussions

2.3 Use images

2.4 Read and respond to written materials

Performance criterion

1.3.1 Describe and give examples of types of employment

People earn their living in many different ways. Some have their own business and work for themselves, others work for somebody else.

> An **employer** is the person who offers work in return for payment and the **employee** is the person who performs the job. The employer pays the employee a wage or salary.

Types of employment

There are various types of employment:

Self-employed
A person with his or her own business, perhaps a sole trader or partnership, is known as **self-employed**. The self-employed person has no legal right to a salary or wage; he or she retains the profits that the business makes or, in the case of a partnership, the owners take their share of the profits. It will be seen that large variations in income are possible for self-employed people: in a good year profits can be large, in a bad year profits may be non-existent.

As the business grows, the owner can employ other people who are not self-employed; they are **employees** of the business.

Examples of self-employed people are plumbers, electricians, accountants and solicitors who work on their own or in partnership with others.

Employed

Anyone who works for a living and is not self-employed, is an employee of a business. Such a person does not own the business, he or she works for it. If that person works for longer than 16 hours per week, it is considered **full-time** employment; if less, it is classed as **part-time** employment. Part-time work often takes place in the evenings, at weekends, or to help at busy times of the week.

Permanent employment

Permanent employment can be for full-time or part-time employees and reflects a longer term, continuing commitment on the part of both employer and employee.

With this comes greater job security, and includes extras such as holiday and sickness pay, the opportunity to join the company pension scheme, maternity (and, increasingly, paternity) leave as well as enhanced prospects for promotion.

Temporary employment

Such employment exists to help an employer over a short-term situation – perhaps an exceptionally busy period, or to fill in while the permanent employee is off sick, on maternity leave or on holiday.

It frequently takes the form of a short-term contract, which can be for full-time or part-time employment.

Temporary employment tends to exist in seasonal businesses; in shops during the peak-purchase time leading up to Christmas, at seaside resorts during the traditional holiday periods of July and August. In the service sector, hotels and restaurants, in manufacturing, building and printing typically offer similar temporary employment.

Skilled and unskilled employment

One of the effects of technology is the reduction in the range of menial tasks that are undertaken in business. E-mail, for instance, is reducing the amount of staff required in the post room, as well as administrative and other tasks.

Unskilled workers are those with few skills other than the basic ones of literacy and the ability to undertake simple manual, menial and labouring tasks; on building sites, in parks and gardens, usually quite low paid, repetitive manual work exists in decreasing amounts.

Skilled workers are those with qualifications from a recognised training: bricklayers, carpenters, plumbers with qualifications are skilled. In the professions, surgeons, doctors, architects, accountants, solicitors and others have all undertaken specialist training for their professions.

In order to carry out skilled work, the employee has spent time and effort training to develop academic or craft skills. These have a value to employers. This enhanced value is reflected in the higher wages or salary that such people earn.

Performance criterion

1.3.2 Collect, analyse and explain information about employment in different regions

The pie-chart in Figure 21 shows the number of people in employment in the UK in June 1994.

Male and female employment figures

The largest number is the 9.6 million males in full-time employment. The female counterpart is 5.7 million, the second largest total.

The total workforce is shown to be 24.6 million people, 13.2 million males and 11.4 million females.

The Institute for Employment Research reports that women will become increasingly involved in employment. Details are illustrated in the bar chart in Figure 22. The number of women in employment is expected to increase four times faster than the number of men. By the year 2000, women are expected to make up 45 per cent of the workforce, compared with 39 per cent in 1974.

Small firms and self-employed people

Overall, employment is predicted to grow by the year 2001. Part of this growth will be made up from the increasing numbers of self-employed people.

Researchers believe that the reduction in the size of the employed workforce caused by the recession in the early 1990s will be more than compensated by people setting up their own

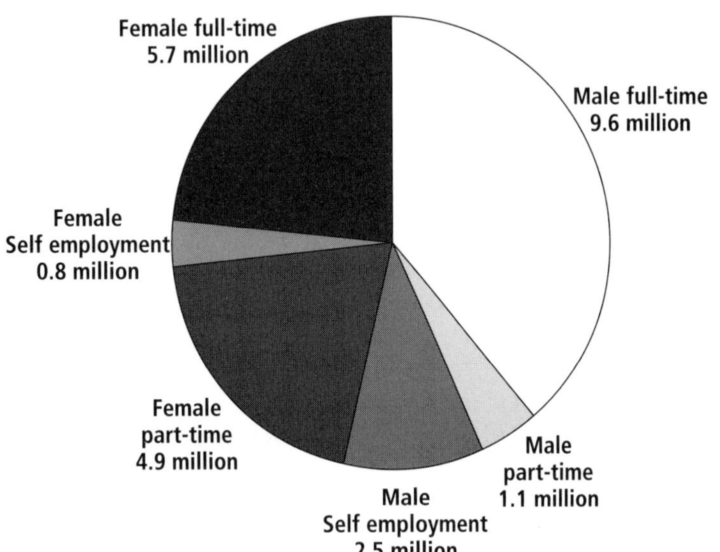

FIGURE 21 The employment of the UK workforce – June 1994

Note: Excludes H.M. Forces and government programmes

Source: **Census of Employment –** Employment Gazette

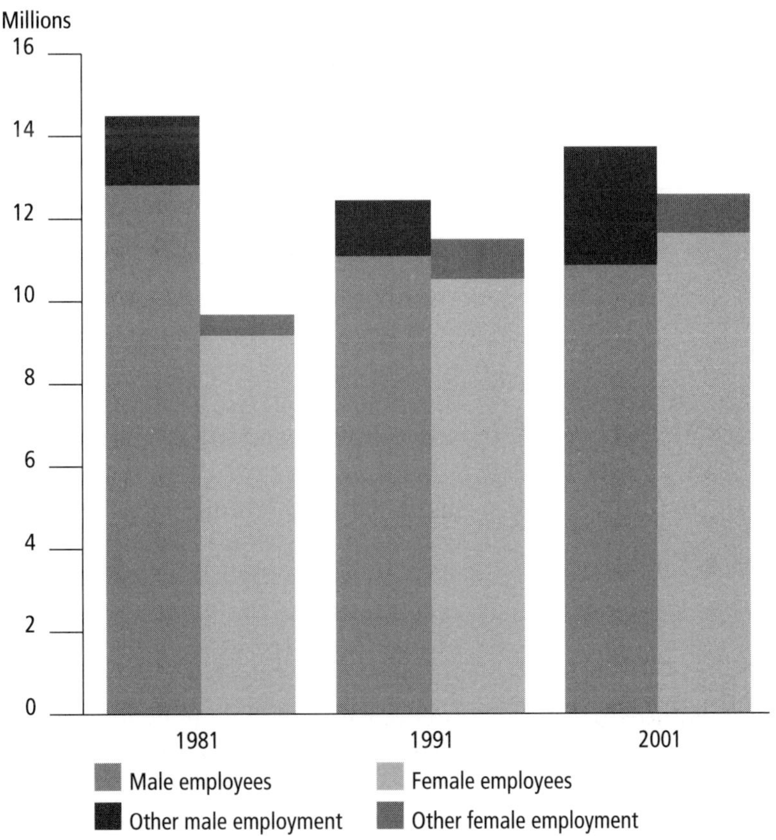

FIGURE 22 The increasing involvement of UK women in employment 1981–2001

Source: **Review of the Economy and Employment: Occupational Assessment, 1994**
© Institute for Employment Research, University of Warwick

businesses. As these grow into small firms, their self-employed owners may then start to take on employees of their own.

Some of the self-employed may well be the same people who lost their jobs as employees in the 1990s.

The report suggests a rise in part-time and self-employment, with the numbers of people in full-time employment remaining static, and women's employment continuing to grow faster.

Employment across different industries

The exploded pie chart in Figure 23 shows the different industries in which people in the UK are employed.

During the 1980s, growth was virtually dominated by the numbers employed in the service sector, which rose by over 2.3 million.

The overall growth in employment was only 1.4 million due to the decline in employment in primary and secondary industries.

The bar chart in Figure 24 shows how these trends are predicted to develop in the immediate future. It will be seen that employment in the whole economy is projected to grow by six per cent by 2001.

The disproportionate growth in the service sector, particularly in business and miscellaneous services, is countered by the continuing decline in primary and secondary industries, with the exception of construction, which includes building houses, roads and industrial premises.

'Utilities' covers those people employed in the gas, electricity, water and waste disposal industries. Such employment is classified as being in the primary industrial sector as the vast majority of the raw material is extracted from the earth; for example, electricity is greatly dependent on gas and coal supplies for its existence.

Most of the growth is predicted to occur in the period 1997 to 2001. The report continues:

> Because of its close relationship to the level of demand in the economy, **construction** employment is expected to

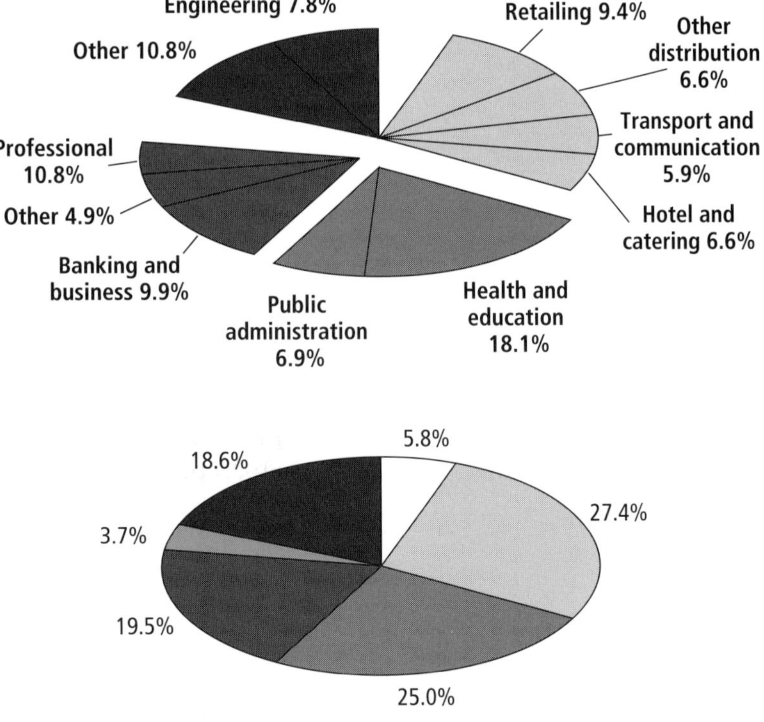

FIGURE 23 Where the jobs are – employees by industry 1993

Source: **Review of the Economy and Employment: Occupational Assessment, 1994**
© Institute for Employment Research, University of Warwick

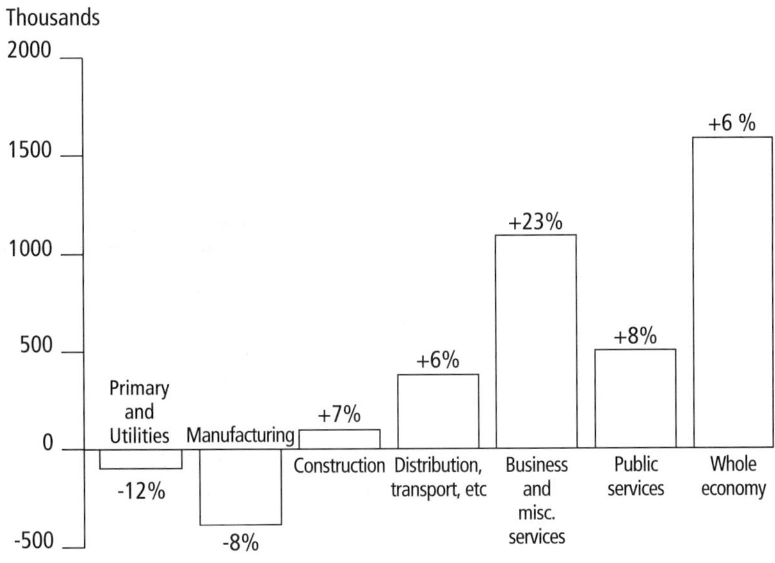

FIGURE 24 Overall employment change in the UK 1993–2001

Source: **Review of the Economy and Employment: Occupational Assessment, 1994**
© Institute for Employment Research, University of Warwick

increase almost three times as fast between 1997 and 2001 as in the 1993 to 1997 period.

As technological change and pressure to reduce labour costs continue, **manufacturing** employment is projected to fall by 1.3 per cent per annum in the second part of the period compared to 0.9 per cent in the first part.

Over the decade as a whole, manufacturing is expected to lose not much less than 385,000 jobs from its total; primary and utility industries will also continue to decline up to 2001.

Employment in the public sector

This last statement reflects the move of the gas, electricity and water businesses into the private sector, as the government sold utilities shares to the public in the 1980s and 1990s.

The **public sector** covers those people employed by the state. We saw in Element 1.1 that this means county councils, local government, the civil service and nationalised industries.

Figure 25 shows 1993 employment at 5.9 million people. Note that this chart shows total employment in the public services, including employees in private sector businesses which *supply* the public sector; for example, some leisure and refuse collection services are provided to councils by private firms.

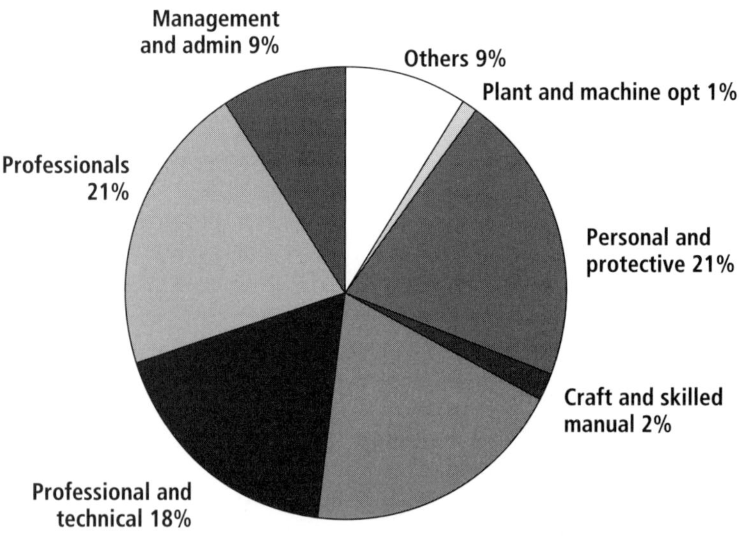

FIGURE 25
Breakdown by
occupation in the UK
1993

Source: **Review of the Economy and Employment: Occupational Assessment, 1994**
© Institute for Employment Research, University of Warwick

European employment

Thus far, statistics concerning national UK employment have been considered. However, such information may also be considered on a local level, and, internationally, on a Europe-wide and even broader world-wide basis.

The map of Europe in Figure 26 shows unemployment across the Member Countries of the EU in April 1993. It demonstrates how unemployment varies by region, and by country.

Activities

1 Name the areas (north, east, south, west or central) in the countries where unemployment is over 22 per cent.

2 Ireland receives regional development finance from the EU. From studying the map, why do you think this is so?

FIGURE 26 Total European unemployment rates, April 1993

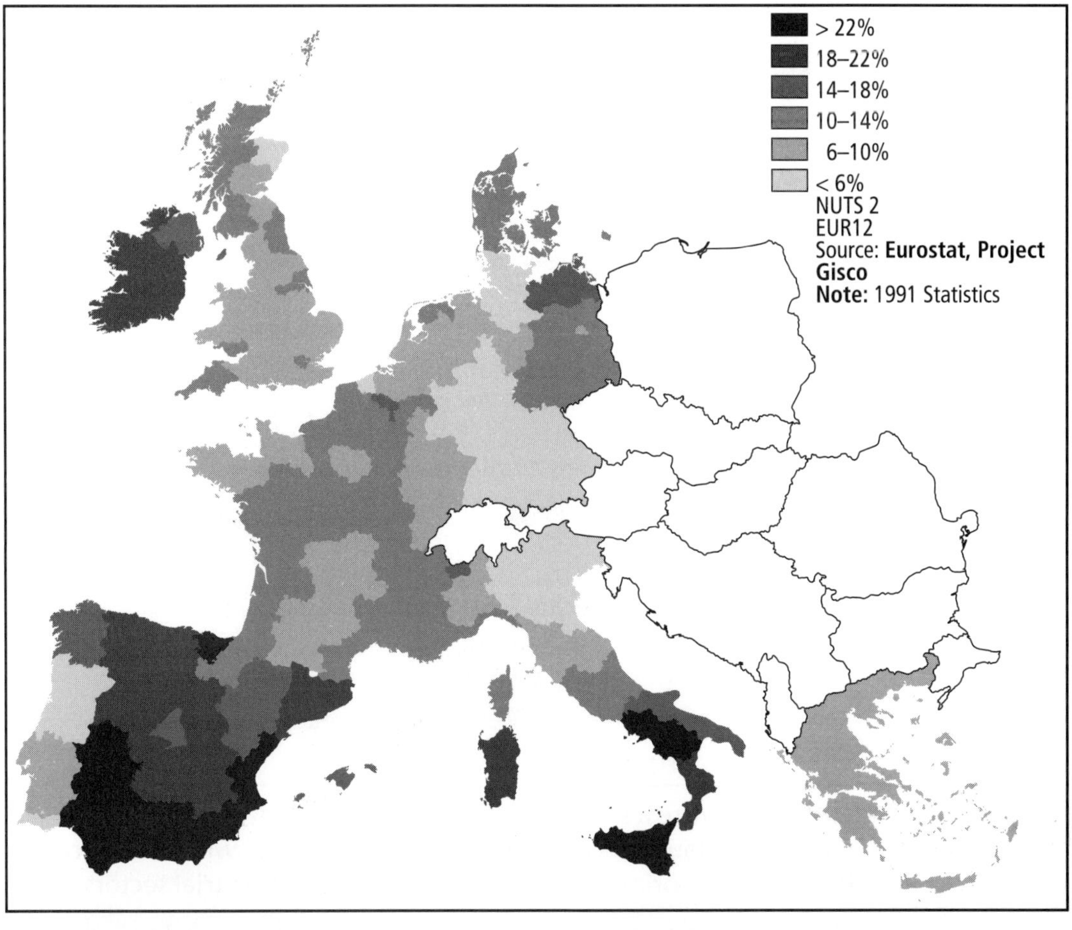

Activities

1   Name the country where there are many areas with unemployment at between 10 to 14 per cent. Discuss with your lecturer or teacher why you think this might be so.

2   Germany and Northern Italy show unemployment below 6 per cent. Discuss the type of employment predominating in these areas in terms of agricultural or industrial – primary, secondary or tertiary sectors.

Case study

Employment in Gloucestershire

Figure 27 shows how the industrial employment structure for Gloucestershire compares with the UK overall.

Gloucestershire has fared slightly better in the period than the national average in certain sectors, due to these facts:

* the stability of jobs at one of the county's largest employers, Nuclear Electric, compared to national losses in mining and other energy supply industries.
* Large companies supplying defence-related products have given some job security to an otherwise declining sector.
* Gloucestershire has a lower than average number of people employed in construction.
* The Bank of England, Laurentian Life and Eagle Star all moved into Gloucestershire during the 1980s; before then, the financial services sector employed less than the national average.

Figure 29 shows male and female activity rates within the county compared to the UK overall.

* Easy access to employment and a wide range of opportunities means that there is higher than average female participation in the employment market in three urban centres.
* Lower rates of female participation in three rural areas are caused by lack of transport infrastructure and limited range of employment opportunities.

Activities

1   Write a short report comparing employment activity in Gloucestershire with the UK as a whole, with reference to the primary, secondary and tertiary industrial sectors.

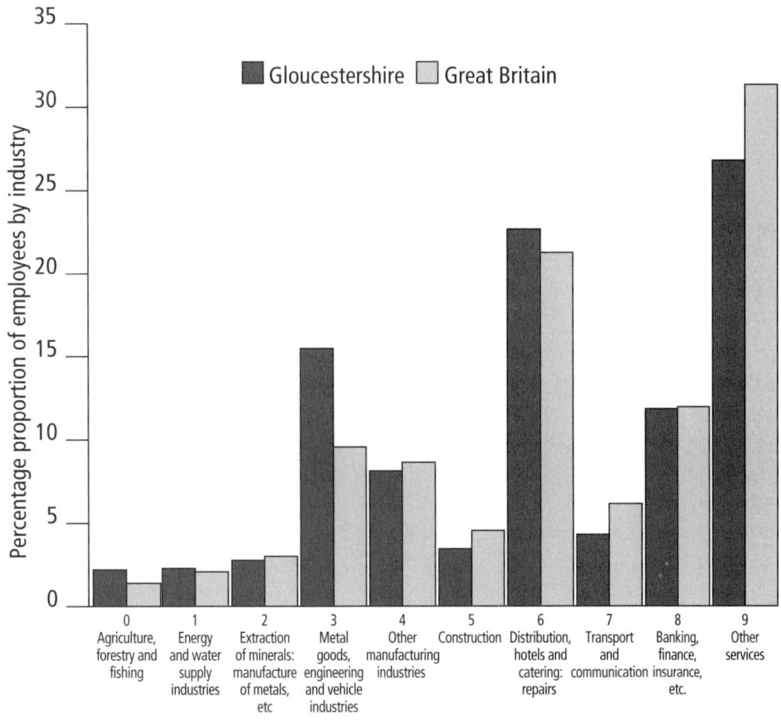

FIGURE 27
Industrial
employment
structure for
Gloucestershire and
the UK

Source: **Review of the Economy and Employment: Occupational Assessment, 1994**
© Institute for Employment Research, University of Warwick

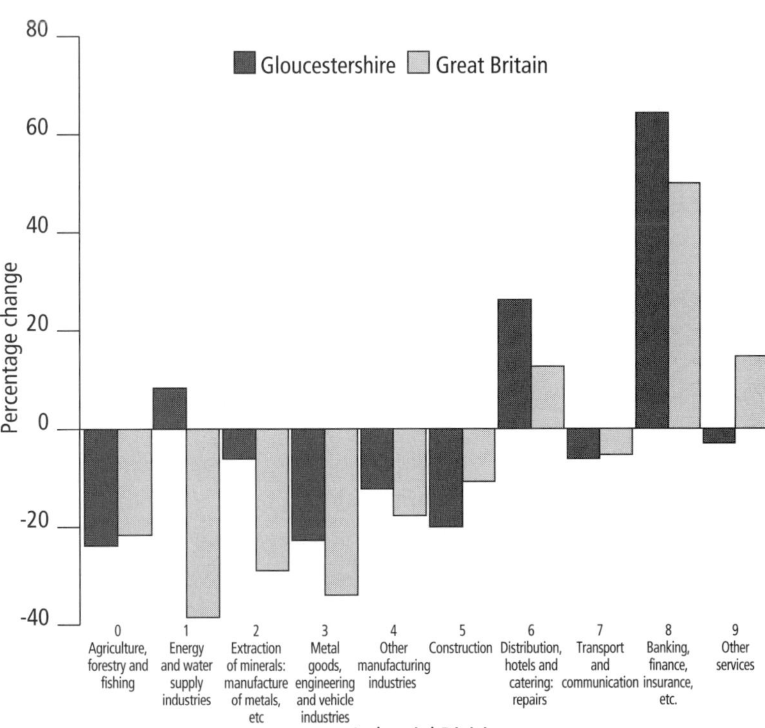

FIGURE 28 Change in
employment
1981–1991 for
Gloucestershire and
the UK

Source: **Review of the Economy and Employment: Occupational Assessment, 1994**
© Institute for Employment Research, University of Warwick

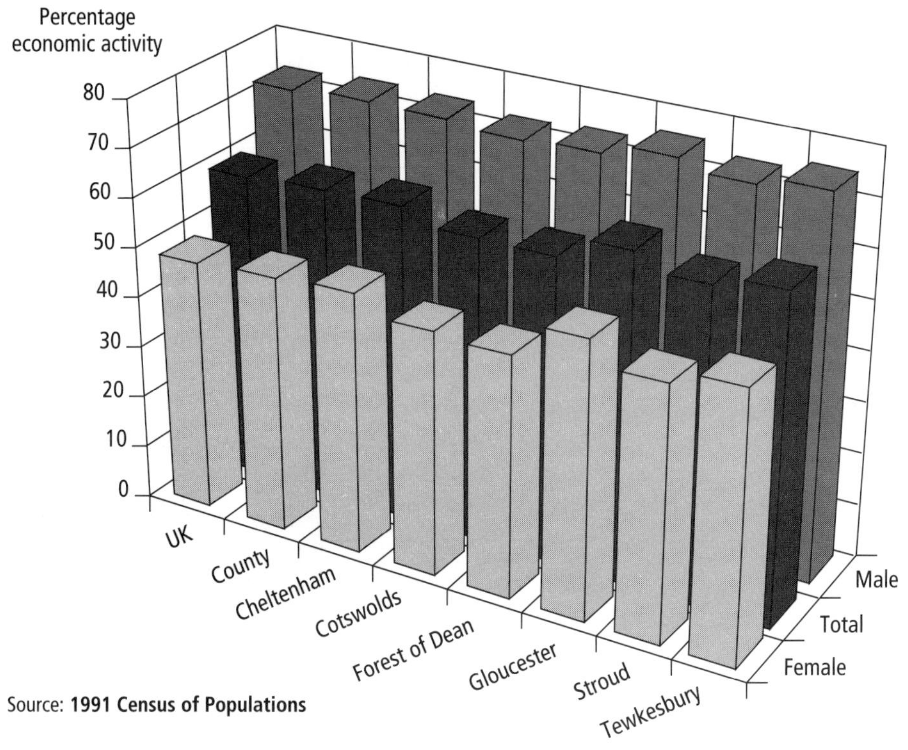

Source: **1991 Census of Populations**

FIGURE 29 Economic activity rates in Gloucestershire

2 Name the three places in Gloucestershire where
   a there are fewer females employed than the national average, and
   b there are more females employed than the national average.

   What are the causes given for these deviations from the national average?

3 Present the data given for the whole of the UK in the form of a pie chart.

Regions	June 1993 (000s)	June 1994 (000s)	% Change
South West	**1,685**	**1,693**	**0.5**
Wales	958	960	0.2
East Anglia	786	788	0.3
Northern	1,078	1,084	0.6
West Midlands	1,973	1,948	−1.3
East Midlands	1,498	1,504	0.4
Scotland	1,984	1,962	−1.1
Yorks and Humb.	1,832	1,821	−0.6
South East	6,906	6,871	−0.5
North West	2,311	2,270	−1.8
Great Britain	**21,011**	**20,902**	**−0.5**

FIGURE 30 Employment by UK region June 1993–June 1994

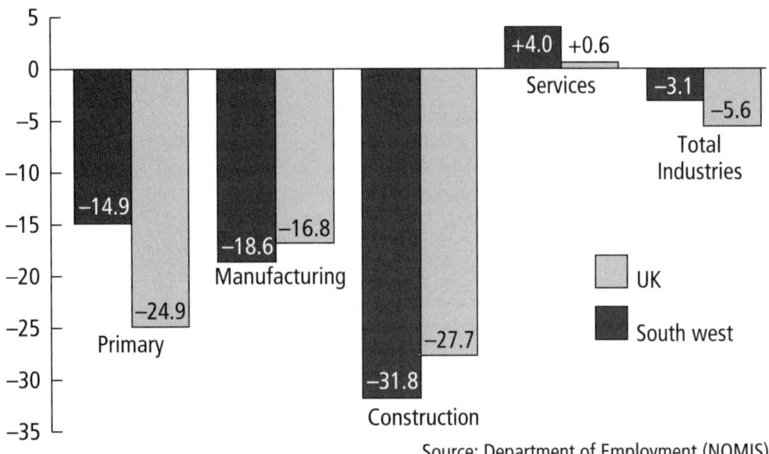

FIGURE 31 Change in employment in the UK and the south-west, June 1989–June 1994

4 Figures 30 and 31 form part of a report on regional and national trends in employment. It covers the year June 1993 to June 1994 and the change during the five years June 1989 to June 1984. Using your college or school library as reference, discover and state some of the reasons for the regional variations in these figures.

5 Summarise the employment information contained on the map of Europe above, (see Figure 26, page 77) with respect to one other region in Europe.

FIGURE 32

	EUR 12	B	DK	D	GR	E	F	IRL	I	L	NL	P	UK
Economic Indicators:													
1992 Gross domestic product (GDP)													
At current prices (bn ECU)	5,421*	169	110	1,499	60	444	1,020	39	945	8	248	74.0*	806
Per inhabitant (1,000 ECU)	15.7*	16.8	21.3	18.7	5.9	11.4	17.8	10.9	16.6*	21.0	16.4	7.8	14.0
1991 Gross value-added by sector (%):													
agriculture, forestry, fishing	2.7	2.1	4.2	1.4	16.3	4.2	3.5	8.1	3.8	1.7	4.6	7.3	1.5
industry	33.5	33.1	28.5	42.0	27.4	36.2	32.6	35.8	37.2	39.8	34.4	46.5	36.2
services	63.7	68.9	71.7	64.1	56.3	59.6	68.6	56.1	67.4	63.7	68.1	62.9	66.3
1991 Private consumption/inhabitant													
(ECU): total[1]	9,035	9,936	10,546	9,494	4,058	7,134	10,415	5,453	10,063	11,503	9,159	2,162	8,751
Breakdown by purpose (%):													
food, drink and tobacco	21.7	18.5	21.2	16.2	37.0	20.9	19.0	36.4	20.2	18.6	15.4	37.1	21.9
clothing and footwear	8.0	8.0	5.4	7.3	8.7	8.8	6.2	7.2	9.9	5.9	7.0	10.3	5.9
gross rent, fuel and power	17.8	16.7	27.7	18.2	12.5	12.6	20.0	10.3	15.4	19.8	18.4	5.0	18.6
housing, etc.	8.0	10.9	6.3	8.4	8.0	6.5	7.6	8.0	9.5	10.8	7.2	8.6	6.4
medical care and health	8.0	11.4	2.3	14.4	3.5	4.1	9.7	4.0	6.7	7.3	12.7	4.5	1.6
transport, etc.	14.6	13.4	16.0	16.6	14.9	15.2	15.9	13.4	12.1	19.1	12.7	15.4	17.2
recreation, education, etc.	8.3	6.6	10.2	9.0	5.7	6.6	7.5	11.1	9.1	4.2	10.5	5.7	9.9
miscellaneous	13.6	15.6	10.8	9.9	9.7	25.3	14.1	9.5	17.1	14.3	16.1	13.4	18.5
87-92 Annual growth of GDP at													
market prices (constant prices) (%)	2.9*	2.8	1.1	4.7*	1.8*	3.7*	2.4	5.3	2.4	3.9	2.7*	3.5*	1.6*

Source (Figures 32, 33 and 34): **Facts Through Figures.**
Office for Official Publications of the European Communities, 2 Rue Mercier, L-2985 LUXEMBURG

	EUR 12	B	DK	D	GR	E	F	IRL	I	L	NL	P	UK
Employment: 1													
1991 Activity rate (%)	55.4	49.3	67.8	57.4	48.3	48.2	55.4	53.2	50.7	51.9	57.7	60.5	62.7
(labour force as a percentage of population aged 15 and over):													
men (%)	68.6	61.4	74.3 7	71.0	64.7	65.3	64.7	70.6	66.7	68.8	71.0	72.6	73.8
women (%)	43.2	38.0	61.7	44.9	33.1	32.6	46.9	36.0	36.0	35.9	44.8	49.9	52.3
1991 Total civilian employment per sector of activity (%):													
agriculture, forestry, fishing	6.3	2.7	5.7	3.5	22.2	10.9	6.0	14.0	8.5	3.5	4.3	17.4	2.3
industry	32.8	30.5	27.4	40.1	25.7	33.0	30.0	28.9	32.2	29.0	25.4	34.0	30.9
services	60.6	66.8	66.3	56.4	52.1	56.1	63.7	56.8	59.3	67.6	69.6	48.5	65.9
1991 Total civilian employment by professional status (%):													
employers, self-employed	15.6	14.9	9.0	9.2	35.2	20.3	12.6	21.5	24.3	9.2	9.8	26.4	13.0
family workers	2.6	2.3	1.8	1.8	11.7	5.0	2.7	2.0	4.1	1.5	1.7	3.9	:
employees	81.6	82.7	89.2	89.0	53.1	74.4	84.8	76.5	71.6	89.2	88.5	69.7	86.0
1991 Part-time employees (x 1,000):	15,736	409	566	3,989	54	392	2,302	78	791	11	1,816	123	5,207
% of working men	3.7	2.2	10.9	2.2	1.7	1.1	3.2	3.7	2.5	1.5	15.5	1.6	5.3
% of working women	29.4	30.5	38.4	34.0	4.9	10.6	23.6	17.2	9.7	18.2	58.5	6.5	43.3
1993 Unemployment rate (Eurostat estimates, yearly averages) (%):													
total [2]	10 5	9.4	10.4	5.6	7.2	21.5	10.8	18.4	11.1	2.6	8.8	5.0	10.5
men [2]	9.3	6.5	9.5	5.2	4.8	17.9	9.1	17.4	7.7	2.0	6.9	4.3	12.2
women [2]	12.3	13.7	11.3	6.1	12.8	28.2	13.0	20.1	16.9	3.6	11.7	6.0	8.1
aged under 25 [2]	20.3	19.6	11.4	4.9	24.6	37.5	23.1	27.9	30.6	5.7	15.0	10.3	16.9

FIGURE 33

a Using the three tables for reference (Figures 32, 33 and 34) and your nearest reference library for information, draw a chart to show employment activity in one region with a breakdown by gender, age and sector (e.g. primary, secondary, tertiary industries).

b Using the information in this element as a guide, explain the differences in your chosen region in terms of the number of people employed and describe the growth or decline of one manufacturing or service sector in the region.

FIGURE 34

	EUR 12	B	DK	D	GR	E	F	IRL	I	L	NL	P	UK
Education: 1													
1991/92 Number of pupils and students (full-time and part-time excl pre-primary) (×1000)	66,677*	2,039	933	13,338	1,861	8,741	11,586	877	9,539	51	3,537*	1,974	12,205
1991/92 girls per 100 boys at:													
secondary level	99	107	97	91	92	103	101	99	94	109	91	130	108
higher level	95*	93	111	71	103	105	114	85	100	:	84*	153	95*
1991/92 Pupils and students among all people													
between 5 and 24 (%)	72*	80	72	71	65	74	72	68	64	55	87*	63	76*
Employment: 2													
(Data from labour force surveys in springtime)													
1991 Civilian working population (×1000)	146,763	3,998	2,899	30,488	3,935	15,014	24,347	1,347	23,947	165	6,928	5,038	28,658
1991 Total civilian employment (×1000):	134,245	3,719	2,635	29,238	3,632	12,622	22,115	1,134	21,520	162	6,420	4,839	26,207
% men	60.3	61.6	53.9	59.4	66.3	67.7	56.9	66.2	65.2	64.6	61.6	57.0	56.3
% women	39.7	38.4	46.1	40.6	33.7	32.3	43.1	33.8	34.8	35.4	38.4	43.0	43.7
% aged under25	15.3	11.3	18.4	15.4	11.4	16.1	11.3	20.3	13.9	16.0	18.9	17.7	18.5

▲ **Performance criterion**	### 1.3.3 Compare working conditions for employees in different organisations

Employers are becoming more and more aware of the relevance of peripheral aspects of employment, for example:

Travel to work

A long or difficult journey to work often results in an employee arriving tired and hardly in a fit state to work hard. For this reason companies increasingly offer their own transport, especially buses, to reduce the stress of travel to work for their employees.

Some employers also pay for this, because in relatively low-paid jobs the cost of travel to work is a significant factor in deciding whether it is worth working at all.

This type of employee benefit support can be very cost effective for the employer – a small additional cost increases employee output quite considerably.

Physical conditions

Research has proved that people perform best in a supportive environment.

Equipment needed is to hand and well maintained Any specialist equipment should be easily accessible. It is clearly time-wasting if it is kept in a remote cupboard so that people have to rummage beneath a pile of other odds and ends to find it. It is even worse if it is then incapable of doing the job for which it is intended, due to ill repair or poor maintenance.

It has been established that if people are responsible for their own equipment in a business, that equipment is more likely to remain in a usable condition.

Equipment used is up to date, to maximise efficiency It is frustrating, inefficient, and time-wasting if employees are forced to use out-dated equipment, due to lack of investment by the employer.

However, if the firm is struggling for its existence, and employees are working together to save the business, people will understand the short-term need to contain costs by not investing in new equipment. If such lack of investment persists, however, the long term effect tends to be demoralising.

Care is taken to protect employees from potentially dangerous equipment Clearly both employees and employers require protection from dangerous equipment, particularly in production. Laws cover many eventualities but it is also in everybody's interest to treat such equipment with respect and keep it away from high-traffic areas on the factory floor.

Both employer and employees have a legal duty to act responsibly with dangerous equipment.

Working conditions appropriate to the job Clearly there is wide variation in appropriate working conditions depending on the particular job. It is unrealistic to expect anyone who works outside, such as a window cleaner, bricklayer or veterinary surgeon, always to have warm conditions with plenty of space. However, research has shown that the more supportive the surroundings, the better the output.

Health and safety regulations and other legislation makes certain stipulations which will be covered in the next section on page 118.

There is sufficient space for immediate needs and storage A vital part of good working conditions is having sufficient space to work effectively; this means being able to have easy access to the tools of the job, and space for visitors, if necessary. Too much space can be as much a hindrance as too little. More space requires more heating and more opportunities to misplace things.

Mental conditions
In addition to the physical conditions discussed above, there are other considerations to take into account when human beings, not machines, are at work.

Regular breaks Depending on the nature of the task, people complete jobs to a higher standard, and, surprisingly, quicker, when they have regular breaks. This applies both to mentally and physically demanding work.

Opportunities are given for training and personal development People work best if their contribution to the business is recognised, and their skills encouraged and developed. It engenders a feeling of belonging and recognition in an environment where strong performance is applauded.

Entitlement to regular holidays Just as regular breaks encourage enhanced performance, so holidays play a part, too. A complete break after a period of sustained effort is useful to 're-charge the batteries' in preparation for a return to work. Without such a rest, performance suffers as stress, tiredness and, in extreme cases, exhaustion, follows. This can affect the physical and mental well-being of the person concerned, as well as the morale of colleagues.

In addition, people's morale is sustained with psychological reassurances such as the following.

1 They are satisfactorily paid in relation to their value to the business, in comparison with wages paid by competitors, and overall labour market price. This may include bonus payments, such as completion of a project on time, or commission for achieving a sales target.
2 The workforce enjoys job security in return for loyalty.
3 Sustained high performance will be recognised by promotion and enhanced career prospects within the business.
4 Adequate provision is made for employee welfare in case of retirement (i.e. pension schemes), sickness, and prolonged absence such as maternity.

Human beings become tired after sustained effort, so performance suffers if working hours are too long. New technology has reduced many of the mundane tasks in business – addition, typing, stamping the post are just a few examples.

The bad news is that people also need regular breaks from using new equipment, especially where exposure to VDU screens and other equipment is concerned.

| **Performance criterion** | **1.3.4 Present results of investigation into employment, or comparison of working conditions** |

| **Activity** | Split into groups of four or five people. |

Identify eight or ten different occupations, possibly involving people who are well known to the group, so that each group member can conduct two interviews, with employees in two different businesses.

The two occupations should be contrasting in terms of:

a Factory work, manufacturers or service providers;
    indoors, outdoors;
    frequent travel and office-based;
    age;
    temporary, permanent; self-employed.
b Types of employment, such as self-employed, employees who are full time, part-time, permanent and temporary.

Prepare questions, to identify if and how employers (and the self-employed) take account of the physical and mental conditions mentioned above.

Make one of the questions a list of the conditions to be considered in a working environment and ask your interviewee to rank them in order of importance.

As a group, analyse your findings with respect to the age range of the people you interviewed, the jobs they were doing and the type of employment (self-employed, employees who are part-time, full-time, permanent and temporary).

Individually, choose seven of the people your group interviewed, including the two which you interviewed yourself. Write a report of your findings with respect to these seven people.

Describe and compare the working conditions of the two individuals you interviewed, covering these areas.

- Hours of work
- Career opportunities
- Training opportunities
- Use of new technology

Unit **2** People in Business Organisations

The aim of this unit is to look at organisational structures, how these structures affect the way in which people work and how productivity, competition, quality assurance and technology cause change to working arrangements. Students should investigate why people work, how they work, particular team working, including the benefits of team membership and the rights and responsibilities which come with employment. They should begin to assess the skills required to seek employment or self-employment, develop organisational and planning skills as well as presentation skills. Students are expected to understand the general significance of employment law, focusing specifically on equal opportunities and health and safety regulations.

From: *Mandatory Units for Intermediate Business*, GNVQ, May 1995

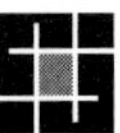

Element 2.1 Examine and Compare Structures and Working Arrangements in Organisations

About this element

The last element started to consider working arrangements in different organisations. This element develops this by considering different organisational structures and the different functions. It also looks at some of the aspects of change management.

Evidence indicators

- Two organisational charts illustrating the difference between two working structures. One chart should illustrate a hierarchical structure and the other a flatter, or matrix, type.
- Notes describing the work in each department of an organisation, including an explanation of the ways in which the work of one department links with the work of another (interdependence).
- A short report comparing working arrangements in two organisations, with particular reference to team working. This should include an explanation of why team working is introduced and how team working operates within one business organisation.
- A summary which explains how at least one of the following – productivity, quality assurance, competition or technology – has caused change in one business organisation.

Core skills

This element gives students the opportunity to demonstrate these core skills:

Communication
Element   2.1 Take part in discussions

             2.2 Produce written material

             2.3 Use images

Information technology
Element   2.1 Prepare information

2.2 Process information

2.3 Present information

2.4 Evaluate the use of information technology

Performance criterion

2.1.1 Describe organisational structures

There are three indispensable characteristics that any entrepreneur seeking to launch and sustain a successful business must display:

1   a **will to win**;
2   a **vision** for success and
3   the **stamina** to see the whole task through.

Such characteristics are not always conducive to an amicable working atmosphere, for in all businesses there are good and bad times and a successful entrepreneur must be ready to tough out the hardest of trading circumstances.

The path to success inevitably involves expanding the business. As it builds, more staff will be required; at first one or two employees, later, additional people form whole departments.

> The skills that are required to found and build the business are not the same as those required to employ and motivate staff.

The founding of a business

Imagine two friends start a printing business. One looks after the printing side, the other handles sales and marketing. Both partners work harder than they have ever worked before, letting nothing stand in the way of the growth of their business.

Success allows the business to expand; four staff are employed, one to help with the printing, one for distribution, one for sales and one for marketing. They are directly responsible to the two owners.

They, too, feel closely involved with the business and play a large part in its continuing success. A small, flat structure is developing, which is illustrated in Figure 35.

Figure 35 is a simple **organisation chart** of the business. It looks like a family tree and shows how the two partners are the most senior members of the business, and how four other people report to the two owners.

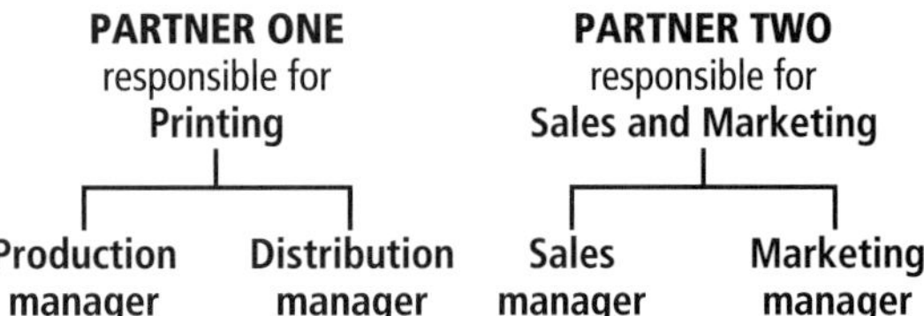

FIGURE 35 A flat company structure

The business continues to flourish; more employees are recruited. They also report to the partners; these two people maintain their demanding work rate and keep a watchful eye on everybody's activities within the business.

The structure would then look like Figure 36 below:

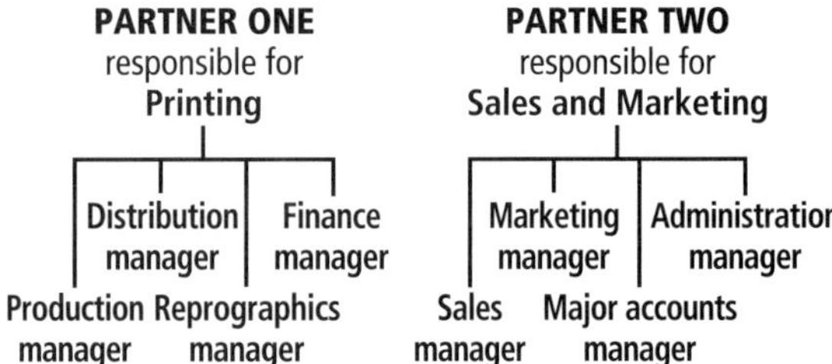

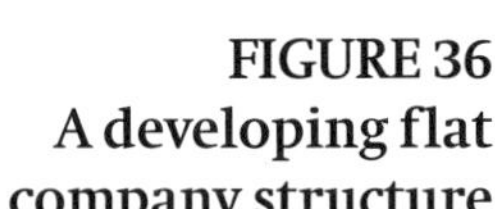
FIGURE 36 A developing flat company structure

The business expands

One day another printer decides to sell his business; the two partners buy it, not only to acquire more equipment but at the same time to gain access to their competitors' customers.

In order to raise the finance for the purchase of their former competitor's business, they issue shares to business associates and form a private limited company.

At this point, the business must change; no longer can the erstwhile partners run the business by keeping a watchful eye on everything that happens – it is now too big for that. They will probably have to spend days in the premises of their new business and quite possibly it will be necessary to travel to visit the customers they have acquired.

It is not only the business that has to change – the way that the business is run, **the management style**, must also change.

Until now, the two founders had adopted an **autocratic** approach to the business – they knew exactly what each employee was doing. They had a vision of the direction the company was taking and how it was going to get there.

They could explain to their employees what was required of them, give instructions as necessary, and make sure their orders were obeyed. Business exists in a very tough world and, especially at the beginning, a streak of ruthlessness is frequently necessary to enable the business to flourish. Swift corrective action is essential to correct any mistakes or omissions of slack employees.

Specialists

When the business expands, greater opportunities present themselves to the owners. They can employ specialists to allow the business to continue to flourish. An expert paper buyer, for example, may be able to save a large amount of money by buying different papers. If these pass through the printing presses faster, the business can run more efficiently, and savings of an amount greater than the paper buyer's salary would justify his or her employment. Other new employees, who may be specialists in a particular type of production or export sales, for example, could be employed on the same basis.

The reason that such specialists are employed is that they have an expertise that the owners do not have. They know their specialist field and neither need nor want to be constantly supervised; they work much better on their own using their professional skills and judgement. All that they require of their superiors is an understanding of the company's objectives – the direction in which it is now heading.

These more senior employees may also have an input into the business objectives, such as warning of difficult trading times, shortages, or areas of opportunity in their specialist areas.

Democratic decision making

A more **democratic** managerial approach is now required to allow the specialist employees to do their job properly. Democratic means 'of the people'; a democratic business allows employees greater involvement in the direction the business takes and in its day to day running.

Decision making is now passed down to subordinates – senior, middle and junior managers. So decisions are made lower down the organisation. There are many advantages to this, one of which is that decisions are made by those who experience the good and bad effects of their decisions on a day-to-day basis.

This also allows their superior, for instance the managing director, to concentrate on looking further afield for new business opportunities, perhaps acquisitions, new customers, new products, new markets (at home or abroad) or relocation.

Hierarchical company structure

This more democratic approach to running the business is illustrated in the hierarchical company structure in Figure 37.

By this time the business is working on three sites, and the three unit managers (A, B, and C) are charged with the day to day running of each.

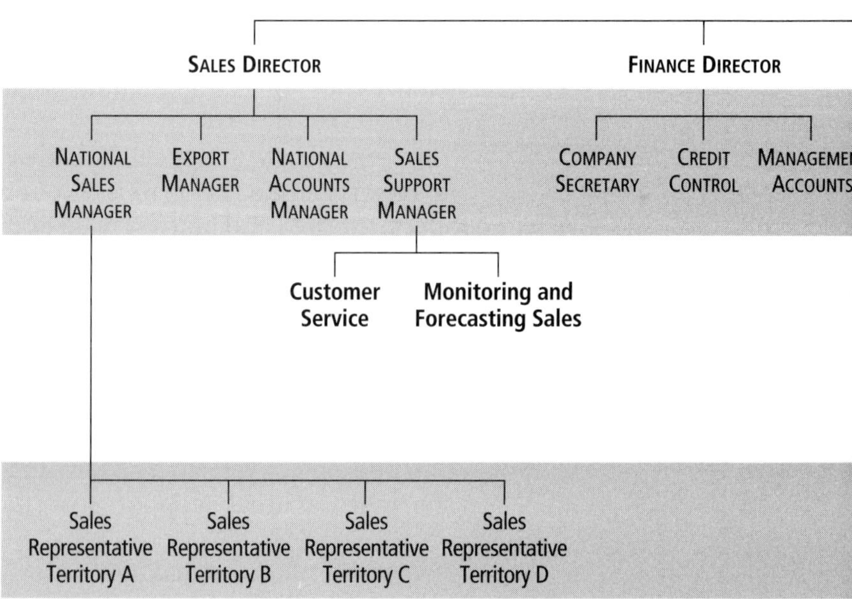

FIGURE 37
A hierarchical company structure

One founder has become the managing director, the other has assumed the role of sales director.

It can be seen that it is totally impractical for an autocratic management style to remain effective in this new structure. Successful businesses change their management styles as they grow, to reflect the changes that have happened both inside and outside the business.

There is a clear **chain of command** which extends from the directors, through their senior, middle and junior managers and supervisors, to the front line staff. In brief, directors set the direction that the business is to take, managers manage the business in the given direction, and supervisors supervise the workforce to ensure the business performs according to agreed objectives.

A TYPICAL MANUFACTURING ORGANISATION

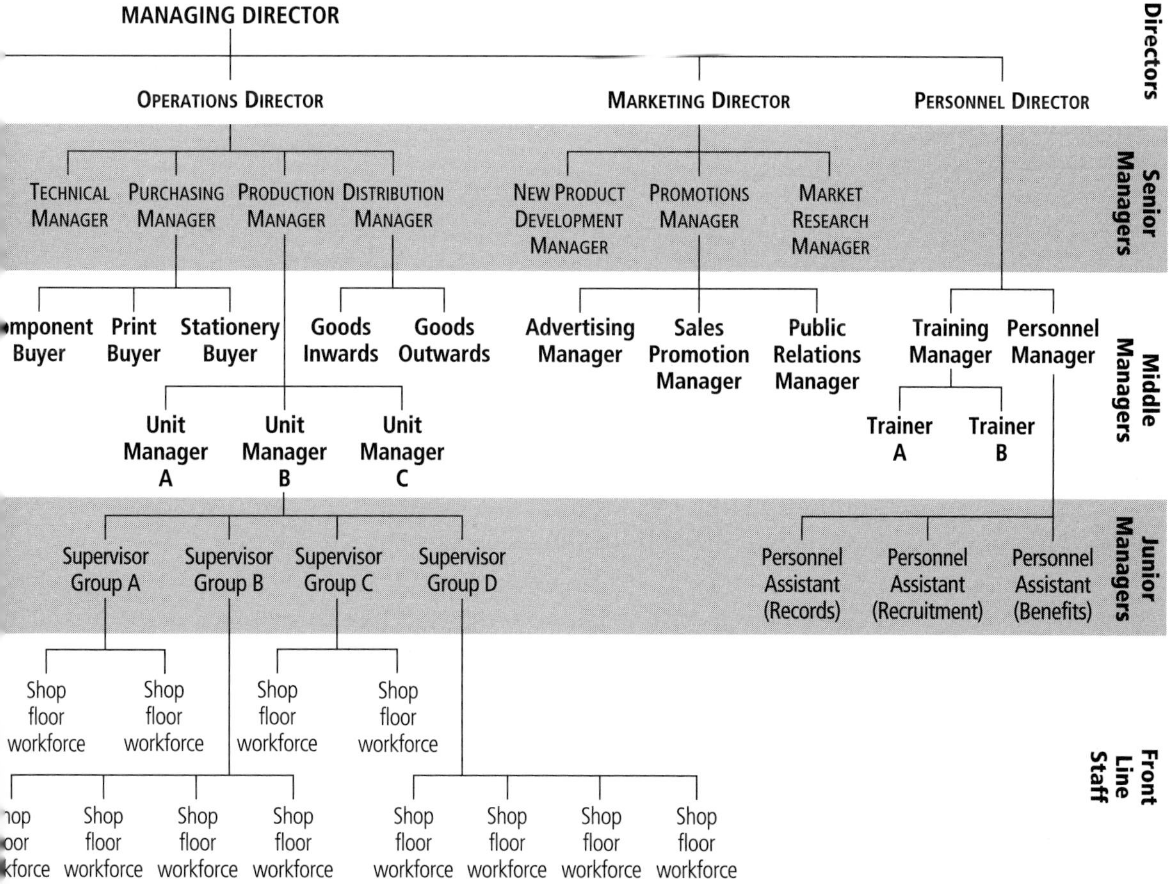

Matrix company structure

A **matrix** structure groups people by **function** rather than by department. This means that in a company which has more than one business stream, people in any one function would operate in all business streams.

The diagram in Figure 38 shows an example of a company operating in three areas – manufacturing, retailing and mail order. It can be seen that employees working in accounts, marketing, personnel, IT and administration service all three business streams. People tend to work together in project teams, within a particular business stream.

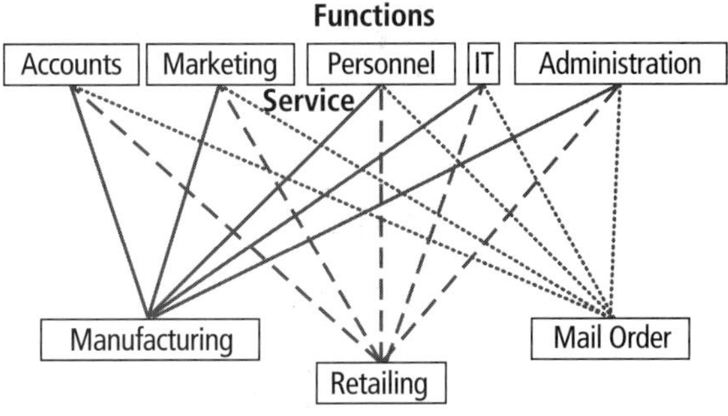

FIGURE 38 A matrix company structure

The major advantage of such a structure is that it avoids duplication of function throughout the business. In other words, there is only one accounts department, not one for each of the three business streams.

The major disadvantage is that people can avoid taking responsibility for any one operation, since their involvement encompasses the whole business and a project team can function like a bad committee – that is, they could avoid responsibilities by hiding behind corporate decisions.

| ▲ **Performance criterion** | **2.1.2 Produce organisational charts showing departments** |

Grouping employees

There are many ways of grouping employees logically within an organisation. The grouping can be done as follows.

Grouping by function
This reflects the contribution of each department to the overall running of the business. Typical departments in a manufacturing company are as follows.

- Personnel
- Production
- Sales
- Marketing communications
- Finance and administration

If each such function within a manufacturing business had a director responsible for it, the organisation chart could look like Figure 39.

FIGURE 39 A typical manufacturing company identified by departmental function

Grouping by process
Each operation is run like a separate business. In a printing operation, such departments could be board printing, paper printing and mailshot printing.

Grouping by location
Ford of Germany is a separate company from Ford, UK; there is duplication of function here because the sales department has to be run differently in Germany than in the UK. The production function may also be operating differently; perhaps the Escort is made in the UK, the Mondeo in Germany.

Grouping by product or product group
Homebase is run as a separate business from Sainsbury supermarkets within J Sainsbury plc. This is because Homebase sells totally different products (DIY, electrical and garden products) from those in the supermarkets.

Grouping by customer type

The wholesale newspaper sales business within W H Smith deals with newsagents who buy their papers and magazines in bulk. The retail business deals with the general public and most stores are located in high pedestrian traffic areas. W H Smith wholesale outlets are located near major roads, motorways and railway stations because early delivery to the newsagents is an essential part of the business.

Performance criterion

2.1.3 Describe the work and explain the interdependence of departments within business organisations

Let us examine the main departments shown in Figure 39.

Personnel

The personnel function takes care of all aspects of the labour resource of the business. Personnel departments are now frequently called human resources departments. It embraces the following activities.

Recruitment and selection

This is the complete process from identifying a vacancy and where it fits in the organisation, to describing the tasks involved and the type of person required to do them. It then includes advertising, receiving applications and interviewing, drawing up a shortlist of candidates, final selection, making the job offer, confirming it in writing and welcoming the new recruit to the company with an induction programme.

Training

Training is available in many different forms, dependent upon employees' needs. It may be to develop technical skills such as those required of a mechanic or fitter. It could be function specific, such as financial, accounting, or marketing skills.

Alternatively, management skills can be practised and learned on a management development programme, especially prior to an employee's promotion.

Training programmes can be run at the place of work or in another location – by the company's own trainers or external ones. Typical training programmes are as follows.

- Time management
- Managing meetings

- Presentation skills
- Customer Care
- Leadership skills
- Negotiating Skills
- Supervisory skills
- Team building

Staff administration

This covers such areas as paying wages, recording holiday entitlement, communicating arrangements for statutory bank holidays, as well as maintaining personnel, sickness and other absence records.

Other personnel matters covered by this area include:

- hours of working;
- pensions;
- discipline;
- termination of employment through giving notice; retirement; redundancy or dismissal;
- social activities, for instance, sports and social club;
- trades union liaison.

Staff welfare

This aspect includes health and safety matters, as well as the provision of rest rooms, medical attention and insurance matters such as provision for the rest of the family should the employee be injured or even killed at work. Some companies provide hairdressing and dental services at the place of work. In the armed forces, shops, schools, hospitals and accommodation are provided for troops stationed abroad.

Other staff welfare issues include maternity and paternity leave, granting of compassionate leave and staff benefits.

Production   In a manufacturing company, production embraces not only all aspects of the **manufacturing** process, it also includes the operations surrounding it such as **purchasing** components and machines, and **warehousing** goods inwards and the **distribution** of finished goods to customers.

In a service organisation, the operation's function concerns that part of the business connected with delivering the service, that is, in retailing, the actual running of the stores; in a car hire business, the acquisition of the vehicles and looking after the premises.

Production monitors factory performance to minimise

wastage through production control, future production schedules through production planning and quality control to ensure product consistency.

The technical department
The technical department works closely with marketing to develop new products for the company, especially those that are manufactured in house, rather by outside suppliers.

Purchasing
The **purchasing** function plays a vital role in any organisation. Their principal job is to source components – print, packaging, plastics, metals, or other components required by production.

The expertise of purchasing lies in obtaining reliable suppliers who can produce components of the correct specification, deliver consistently on time, in the quantities required and at a competitive price.

For this reason, purchasing frequently requires people with expert knowledge and skill in a particular area such as print, plastics or engineering.

Transport and distribution
Transport and distribution covers the vehicles that the business runs – company cars, trucks, delivery wagons and vehicles used in the factory. Distribution covers the essential task of delivering the finished goods from the warehouse to the customers. This may use the company's own fleet of vehicles or a carrier, such as TNT or Captain Cargo. This decision depends on how many parcels are distributed daily, and their nature – for example, extremely delicate or frozen goods need special handling which may best be covered by the company's own fleet of vehicles. A small business with packages of standard size and weight is probably better served by outside carriers which have hundreds of vehicles covering the country on a daily basis. They frequently offer different levels of service: delivery next morning (i.e. overnight), next day, within two days, or within one or two weeks. The rate structure, naturally, varies according to the service chosen.

Sales The sales department is responsible for selling the company's products to its customers.

The size of the sales force depends on the number and size of the company's customers. If the company has many customers, each perhaps placing small orders with the company, the company will need a large sales force to look after them. Confectionery, greetings cards and grocery producers are examples.

On the other hand, some businesses only require a small number of sales people. Examples are producers of machinery, packaging, exhibition materials, furniture and goods such as stationery which is widely sold through the wholesale trade.

An essential part of the success of most sales forces is the sales plan, which breaks down into targets for each sales person.

The performance of the sales force is constantly monitored against the budget, that is the forecast sales are constantly compared to actual sales to check whether the sales revenue will be more or less than that forecast for the year; appropriate remedial action can then be taken, such as cutting internal budgets, redundancies or recruitment throughout the business.

Customer services

Customer services typically falls within the sales function, although this can vary depending upon the focus of the organisation. The role is to answer customer queries which can vary from complaints of faulty product or service, to detailed technical questions about the product's manufacture. In all cases, prompt, polite conduct reaps rich rewards in terms of customer satisfaction and future loyalty, since it is usually only customers who are genuinely interested in the organisation who contact this section.

Marketing Marketing is a function that permeates through every consumer-led business. In a profit-making organisation, marketing is the process of identifying what the consumer requires, then fulfilling that need or want profitably.

This starts with research into the products that the company can supply with respect to customer requirements. Once such needs and wants have been identified it is the responsibility of marketing to ensure that products or services are developed and designed to fit them.

Research and development

Research and development (R & D) within a market-led business falls within the marketing function. The role is to identify fully what customers expect and require, then to devise product to fill these identified gaps profitably. This is considered in more detail in Unit Three.

The role of R & D starts with market research. It goes on to develop prototype products (or services), followed by further research. The department then liaises with production to ensure that the business can deliver the goods or services in the way in which the customers require them. Packaging for a new product is devised elsewhere within the marketing team.

Marketing communications

Marketing communications are inside and outside the company. Internally, liaison with production is essential to ensure that products are devised and costed with mass production in mind. Co-operation with the sales function is important to ensure that products meet customer needs in as many aspects as possible. Externally, working directly with consumers is a vital task, often done through market research. Outside suppliers such as advertising and sales promotion agencies are essential to the final realisation and launch of long-prepared marketing plans.

Marketing plans

Successful marketing plans detail how the company will find out what consumers want, the price they are prepared to pay, where and how they can obtain the products, and how they will learn of its existence, for example through advertising and promotion.

This is known as the **marketing mix** and should be the basis of all marketing – indeed all company – activities.

Promotion of products

Promotion of the company and its products is the responsibility of the marketing function and this includes advertising the company's products on television, posters or in the press, including trade magazines.

Public relations controls such areas as editorial coverage in the media, and promotional competitions. Maintaining the overall image that the business wishes to convey to the media is the responsibility of the public relations function.

Administration

Administration covers several different areas.

Legal
Patents, trade mark registration, copyright. This can require specialist legal skills and in many businesses these are handled by the company secretary.

Basic supplies
Basic needs such as company stationery, note paper, envelopes, and so on. In the case of stationery, central acquisition allows the stationery buyer to obtain preferential prices by buying in greater quantities for the whole business than would be possible by individuals purchasing only for one function.

Support functions
Reception, switchboard, internal and external mail and, less frequently nowadays, centralised secretarial duties. These are frequently the first point of contact that customers have with a business and it is essential that they are handled sensitively.

Maintenance and security
Maintenance and security of the buildings; maintenance of common equipment such as photocopiers.

Computer services
Computer (IT) services frequently fall within the administration area. The employees' role is to commission and maintain the company's main frame computer and other data recording and communication systems.

IT services also supply individual PCs to company personnel, as well as telecommunications including fax machines.

Such operations need to be handled centrally to ensure a consistent level of service and uniformity throughout the company.

Accounting

The role of the finance or accounts department is crucial to the success of the whole operation. It starts by ensuring there are enough funds to run the day to day business.

Budget control
Incoming payments are monitored so that accounts people can regulate the amount of goods that customers are receiving before having to pay for them.

Outgoing payments are also monitored, so that the amount of internal spending is known, that is how much each department is spending. This is known as **budget control.**

The finance department is also involved in longer term planning such as moving site – purchasing the ground, building and moving staff.

Working as a team

'Business is people' and the ability to work with other people is nowhere more important than at work. Teamwork is paramount and some companies spend thousands of pounds training their people to work as a team.

A good hockey team consists of different people with different skills. Its goalkeeper defends them when necessary and knows the right place to be to minimise the opposition's chances of scoring a goal. Good forwards know how to put themselves into scoring positions, to take maximum advantage of limited goal-scoring opportunities. Different skills are required to succeed in the different positions.

So it is in business. People depend upon each other for support and co-operation.

Marketing is responsible for identifying opportunities for new products. A working prototype may be designed, working in co-operation with the **technical function**, which is part of production. The technical function would be ill-advised to design and suggest a product without consultation with the **production** people to make sure that the suggested product can be manufactured – it is important to consider ease of bulk production at the design stage.

Co-operation through computers

Increasingly, new product development takes place using computer-aided design (CAD), which allows marketing, computer and technical personnel to work closely together, especially at the concept stage, to work on prototypes for testing.

The use of computerisation in product development not only encourages closer teamwork, it also accelerates the whole process by avoiding the need to make many hand-built models. Virtual reality computer modelling speeds up the process dramatically, and cuts long-term development costs.

Production people are also involved at this time, and computer-aided manufacture (CAM) optimises the use of materials, labour and space in the production process.

Input from customers

Similarly, it is important that sales are involved at an early stage of design. They may wish to involve their customers with the product and give them an opportunity to express their thoughts (good and bad) about the proposal. Often a customer who is consulted at the design stage will feel more inclined to stock the product when it is produced.

Recruitment of new team members

It is possible that if a new product is to be launched, production may have to recruit new personnel – perhaps with specialised skills to use certain new machine, perhaps simply because the output of the factory will increase and more people are needed.

Thus the personnel function will need to be involved in the recruitment process, and work closely with production to ensure that people with appropriate skills are selected.

Unskilled workers are less expensive to employ, but more limited in their capabilities. They may improve with training, a further expense, but one which may give the new recruits a greater loyalty to their new employer.

Co-operating over product costs

In order for the new product to be made, costings will need to take place to determine the following.

The 'once only' costs of:

- developing the new product, packaging and advertising;
- purchasing new machinery for bulk production;
- training for the workforce and
- recruiting new workers.

Ongoing costs once the product is launched, comprising:

- component materials – packaging;
- distribution costs.

These need to be compared with the price and profit margins that the product can achieve in the market place to assess how long it will take to re-coup the 'once only' costs, and to judge the likelihood of sustained profitable sales in the long term.

The establishment and checking of such costs show how important it is that somebody from finance with the relevant skills is involved before much investment and commitment is made in a possibly unprofitable product.

 **Performance criterion**

2.1.4 Identify and explain differences in working arrangements

Team work

It should be clear by now that the ability to work as a team member is a fundamental pre-requisite of most employees. This means that a good employee should have the ability to:

1 take, understand and carry out commands;
2 make suggestions and take part in constructive discussions concerning company business;
3 on occasion, lead a team working on a project.

Note, however, that even a company director has to take orders from his or her managing director as well as leading his or her own team or department. The ability therefore, to take and carry out orders is as important as the ability to give them.

In general, a hierarchical structure (see Figure 37, pages 92–93) is more conducive to harmonious teamwork, since there are fewer departments and a greater variety of junior, middle and senior managers.

This creates opportunities for people of similar levels to work together and to allow specialised tasks to be allocated to appropriately qualified team members.

All businesses are dynamic, meaning that they must change to meet market needs as they evolve. The decline of the UK motor car and cycle manufacture in the 1950s and 1960s is sufficient evidence of what happens when businesses fail to take account of changed market conditions.

As conditions change, so the need for different working arrangements evolves.

Centralised systems

A centralised system in an organisation means that business employees throughout the country are controlled by head office, typically based in London, but as communications improve throughout the UK, head offices are increasingly re-located to a part of the country where land, buildings and housing are cheaper.

The main advantage of centralisation is consistency and conformity throughout the business. The main disadvantage is the 'ivory tower syndrome' – personnel in head office become remote from the daily business operations and produce systems and make decisions which are impracticable or inefficient. Furthermore, local market opportunities can be completely ignored because head office is located far away.

De-centralised systems

A de-centralised structure devolves decision making to the operational area. Such a UK structure tends to have a small head office, between five to ten **regions,** which are split into five to ten **areas.** Where day-to-day contact with customers is concerned this is almost always more effective than a centralised system, for it allows for flexibility to make decisions according to the needs of the moment.

The main disadvantage is inconsistency; for example one region may be more casual in its approach to customer service than another.

Attendance at work

Depending on the type of business, a shift system of working may operate. This involves starting at perhaps 6.00 a.m., working until 2.00 p.m., when the day shift starts. At 10.00 p.m. the night shift may take over – in a 24-hour day, each shift has worked eight hours.

Such arrangements exist in manufacturing, where it is expensive to shut down plant. Shift systems also operate in the retail trade, where long opening hours and Sunday trading necessitate shift-working to allow people adequate rest.

Flexi-hours

Flexi-hours are sometimes worked in offices where it is not necessary for everybody to be present together. Somebody may start at 6.00 a.m., if he or she chooses, then finish at 1.00 p.m. Provided that person works a pre-agreed number of hours in a day, week or month, the employer is happy for the employee to have added freedom of time off to suit individual requirements.

Contracts

Working contracts increasingly reflect the need for additional flexibility. A **fixed-term contract** may guarantee work for three years, after which time the employee is free to take employment elsewhere. Similarly, the employer has no obligation to pay redundancy, pension, sickness benefit and holiday pay when the contract is finished.

If, however, the employer wishes to terminate it early, there is a liability to pay the employee for the rest of the duration – if, three months into a two-year contract, the project changes and the employee is no longer required, the employer is liable to pay the employee a further 1.75 years of the contract.

Many contracts are **permanent** – this means that the person is employed until an agreed period of notice is given by one party to the other.

Workbases

Increasingly, employers seek greater flexibility in the location and availability of employees.

Many employees are needed in their office, factory or store. The difference between such conditions can be considerable. Offices often have air-conditioning, comfortable seating, plants and other luxuries, whereas the office in a factory may be no more than a screen with some old chairs, a desk, a lot of dirt and a fair amount of noise!

Many people work outdoors, from home, or on the move. As technology improves, such flexibility has the attraction of being where the activity is most critical, such as with a customer, or visiting a supplier.

Telephone and fax facilities are available for use in cars, thus improving communications enormously, and the need to visit an office base is now frequently reduced to attendance at meetings and for information briefing.

Performance criterion

1.2.5 Explain and give examples of reasons for change in working arrangements in one business organisation

Organisations can undergo changes for a wide range of reasons.

> Most changes are **market driven**. This means that an **external change** has triggered the need for **internal response.**

Three reasons for changes within an organisation are illustrated in Figure 40.

Developments in technology

Developments in technology resound throughout business. In the example, a technological innovation such as the use of robots for mass production on an assembly line means that the business must acquire a new factory to meet the exacting demands of robotic equipment – constant temperature, clean atmosphere, for example – which may not be possible in the current premises.

FIGURE 40 Some reasons for changes to organisational structures

A new site is purchased. This creates new positions in the company because, as the diagram shows, the business is

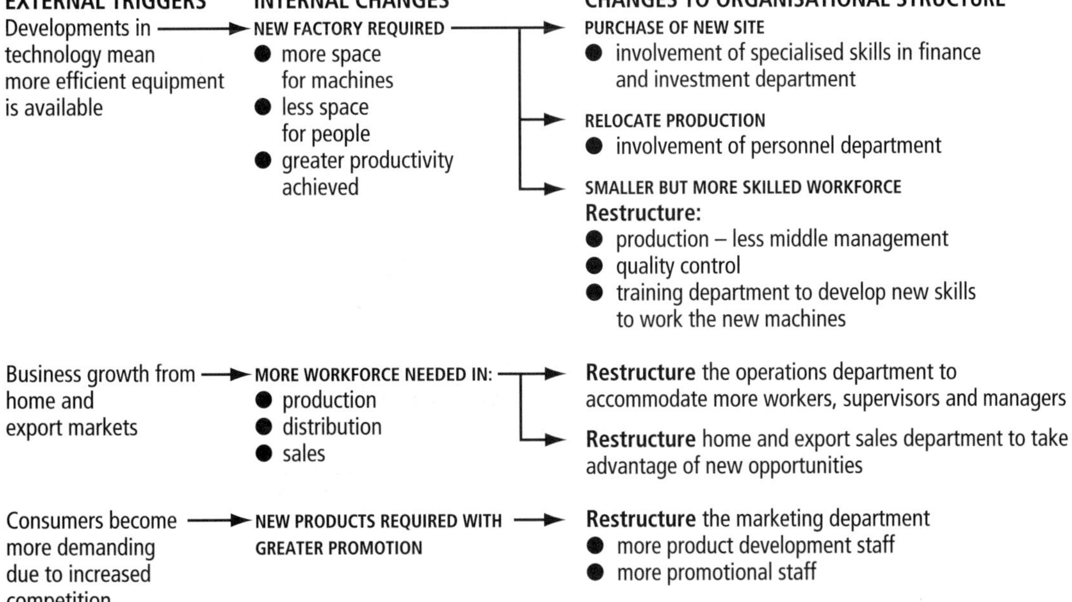

investing in new buildings, machinery, people and training. The business structure changes to incorporate the new positions as well as the redundancies resulting from tasks and skills no longer required. The net result is an increase in **productivity** and, since machines tend to bring increased consistency and reliability, a similar increase in **quality assurance**.

Business growth

Business growth from home and export markets opens up new opportunities in production, distribution and sales. It could mean starting new subsidiary companies in overseas markets, bringing in the need for extensive restructuring at all levels within the business.

**FIGURE 41
Restructuring the
organisation of a
business**

Our example in Figure 40 shows how the organisation would change to accommodate new production techniques, more people involved in distribution (especially on the export side where documentation is different and usually more complex) and more representatives in home and export sales.

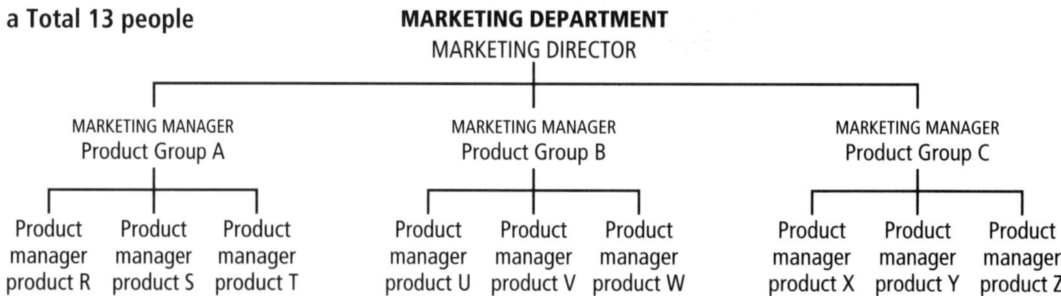

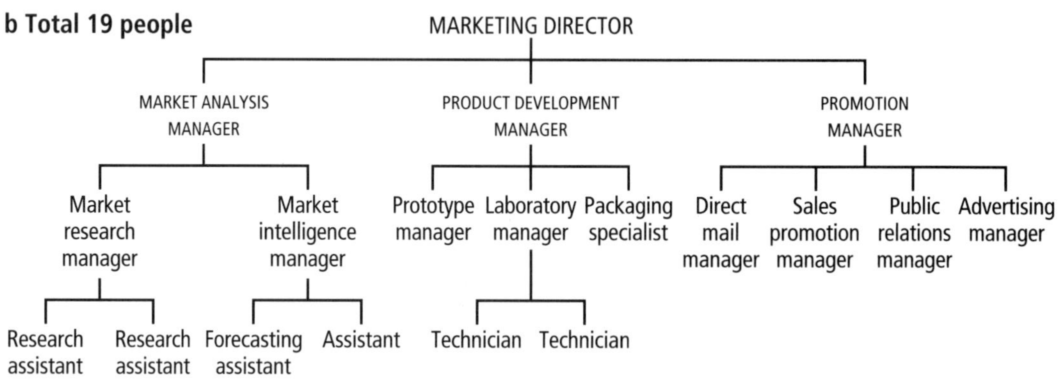

Demanding consumers

Consumers become more demanding for many reasons: perhaps they become more aware of alternative products or **competition** is increasing.

Our example in Figure 41a and b above shows how a marketing department could be restructured to accommodate the changed market conditions. The new structure (b) is no longer arranged by product, with managers for each as in the old structure (a). If many new products are to be launched there is a need for a product development manager, and the new department should be organised by function. Market analysis must keep abreast of the latest changes in consumer demands, competitors activities and the performance in the marketplace of the company's product range. The promotion manager looks after the increased activities in developing consumer awareness of the company's new products.

Thus the marketing department grows from 13 to 19 people.

Activities

1   In pairs, choose two businesses to which you have access. They should preferably be in the same area of operations, for instance printers, engineering works, supermarkets, but with contrasting organisational structures.
    a Obtain an organisation chart of both businesses.
    b Examine the structures and compare them.

    Identify similarities in terms of structure and function; indicate whether they are flat, matrix or hierarchical structures.

    Describe the work that each department or function undertakes, with reference to the descriptions contained in the text. Explain how one department links to the work of others and is dependent on their services to function on a daily basis.

2   Draw a new structure for the company, using a different approach (i.e. if the present structure is flat, re-draw it as hierarchical). Departmental functions should be shown.

3   Choose three people's functions in either organisation. Describe the tasks that they are required to do in their jobs.

Particular reference should be made to the way in which they function as part of a team. Describe the overall objective of the team, and the input that the three people have into it.

4 Summarise how **productivity, quality assurance, competition** or **technology** has caused change in one of the businesses examined.

NB Students are encouraged to use IT for written work, charts, figures and diagrams in order to claim the common skill competencies required to gain the GNVQ award.

Element 2.2 Investigate Employee and Employer Responsibilities and Rights

The previous element having presented the overview of structures and departments, Element 2.2 will now consider the more specific role of the individual within an organisation.

This includes the employment relationship and its considerations, which are examined in some detail, as is the interaction with other individuals within the organisation.

Evidence indicators

- A report which explains the benefits which one business organisation has gained from employee and employer co-operation. The report should include examples of disagreements between the employer and one or more employees, and explain how they are resolved. The report should show that the student understands how the trades unions and courts may be involved in resolving disagreements.

  One section of the report should explain at least two examples of employers' and employees' rights and responsibilities, showing that the student understands how both employers and employees are affected by legislation, in particular equal opportunities legislation.

Core skills

Although this element does not address a particular core skill, it is strongly recommended that students should use the report writing opportunity to practise and, if desired, claim competence in these core skills:

Information technology
Element   2.2 Prepare information

2.1 Process information

2.3 Present information

2.4 Evaluate the use of information technology

Communication
Element 2.1 Take part in discussions

2.2 Produce written material

Performance criterion

2.2.1 Explain the benefits of employer and employee co-operation

Consider the effects of a rail strike. The employees go on strike, and lose one day's pay. The employees lose money. The railways are shut down for a day. They lose revenue: money. The customers lose because they either have to stay at home or choose another means of travel.

In short, everybody loses, employees, employer and customers.

The benefits of co-operation

When employer and employees co-operate, the opposite happens. Each helps the other, attitudes change, any omissions are spotted and corrected, the business flourishes.

When this happens, profits become greater and so there is more money to pay the employees.

Co-operation means employer and employees working together for the benefit of the business. Frequently, it is a matter of changing the attitudes of both employer and employee to make it happen.

The recent success of the Rover car group represents an enormous change in the relationship that previously existed between employer and employee, when strikes, sabotage by the workforce, work to rule and other obstacles were placed in the way of success because the employees felt they should have been treated better.

Improved commitment by employees to the employer's business is gained in a number of ways:

- through open discussions regarding finances, including pay;
- by the establishment of trust between both parties;
- by giving people greater involvement in decisions;
- by providing training programmes for all employees.

The result is improved efficiency, since everybody is pulling in the same direction.

Difficulties with co-operation

If only life were so easy! Sadly, external events sometimes work against co-operation. For example, when business takes a downturn or new equipment is introduced the net result is often a reduction in the size of the workforce.

A tense atmosphere develops as employees find out who is to remain with the company and who is to be made redundant.

Sometimes, employees try to dissuade their employer from purchasing new machinery that will cost them their jobs; such a short-sighted approach may mean that a foreign competitor who has the machinery wins business at the expense of the manufacturer who chose not to buy the new equipment.

Employee consultation

It has been proven by research that most employees work best when they are able to contribute their own ideas to the business. The old adage that 'two heads are better than one' is testimony to the positive effect that can result when people are consulted about situations, changes or decisions that affect relevant parts of the business.

This process is sometimes formalised by the employer establishing advisory or consultative panels to meet regularly to discuss matters.

In this way, greater use is made of employees' experience and specialist skills. In addition, potential disputes can be avoided.

'Quality circles' are a very successful example of employee participation. Employees from different parts of the business form a team to address a particular issue relating to an aspect of the quality of the product or service. The concept originated in Japan and has been implemented in the UK, notably in the production of Jaguar cars, where reliability and rust problems existed in the late 1970s. By setting up quality circles and other consultative bodies, these problems were very successfully overcome, the business flourished and the contribution of all employees was very much valued.

It can be seen that transferring some decision making to the employees resulted not only in improved company performance, but also employee motivation.

Regular and open communication with employees is known to enhance the relationship of employer and employee, as well as the effectiveness and efficiency of the business. Employee briefing sessions, where senior representatives from the business inform the workforce of recent developments in the business, are one example of how employee communications take place in practice.

In continental Europe, employees are frequently represented at board meetings and at director level.

Performance criterion

2.2.2 Describe ways to resolve disagreements

There are always many different solutions to disagreements; most involve discussion, negotiation and , most importantly, **communication** between the parties concerned.

As a dispute develops, other parties may become involved. In ascending order of seriousness, these are as follows.

- Trades union negotiation
- Legal representation
- Industrial tribunals
- European Court of Justice

Trades union negotiation

As their title suggests, trades unions are groups of workers who join together to protect themselves against exploitation by unscrupulous employers. They exist on the basis of 'united we stand, divided we fall' and date back to the days when state benefits were virtually non-existent and, in the event of unemployment or industrial accident, many families were sent to the workhouse.

The groups tend to form themselves by **industry** (such as the National Union of Mineworkers), by **sector** (such as UNISON, the union for all workers in the public sector – nurses, education assistants and council workers) or **trade,** such as The Musicians' Union.

Any employee may join a trades union and their purpose is to look after the interests of its members, in matters such as:

- wage negotiations;
- employee discipline or dismissal;
- appeals against decisions made by the employer and
- the establishment of working hours and conditions.

Legal representation Both employer and employees can call on the services of a solicitor for advice, or to write a letter pointing out the alleged wrong doing.

Alternatively, there are some legal bodies with a specific remit for cases of dispute between employer and employee.

ACAS

The Advisory, Conciliation and Arbitration Services (known in Northern Ireland as the Labour Relations Agency) exists to become involved when an employer has a dispute with employees to which neither can find a solution agreeable to both parties. It publishes codes of practice for employers and employees to follow.

Although these are not legally binding, either party may run into difficulty if in the event of a subsequent dispute, it is found that the codes have not been followed. A court is likely to rule against the offending party.

In this case, ACAS is called in as an arbitrator, or 'referee'. If both parties agree to abide by the decision reached, the matter is not taken to court, thus saving high costs and further loss of working time.

Industrial tribunals

If negotiations break down – firstly, between employer and employee and secondly between trades union and employer with or without ACAS involvement, then the case goes before an industrial tribunal. There is a panel with a chairperson which hears both sides of the case before reaching a decision.

Typical industrial tribunal involvements are in disputes over pay, unfair dismissal of an employee, and claims regarding equal opportunities, sex discrimination and race relations.

In the event of the employer being found acting wrongfully,

compensation, sometimes amounting to thousands of pounds, may be payable to the wronged party.

European Court of Justice
In the event of dissatisfaction with the verdict, it is possible to appeal to a higher court against a decision. The highest such court in Europe is the European Court of Justice, based in the Hague, Holland. It consists of 13 judges, who are called upon to make:

- **regulations**, to be immediately obeyed by all EU member countries;
- **directives**, to be obeyed but which may be introduced at a later date more convenient to each member state;
- **decisions**, to be obeyed in a particular case, but not necessarily with implications for all member states.

 **Performance criterion**

2.2.3 Explain employer rights and responsibilities

When people go to work for someone else, a relationship is established between the employer and the employee.

> Employment is a two way agreement: the employee agrees to do a certain amount of work, and in return the employer agrees to pay a certain amount of money.

This forms the basis of the employment contract, to which other considerations are added, such as breaks, holidays and working conditions.

Contract of employment

Within the first 13 weeks of starting a new job, the employer has a legal obligation to present to the employee a written confirmation of the terms of employment. This is called the **contract of employment**, which must contain:

- the names of employer and employee;
- job title;
- the duties that the employee is expected to perform;
- date employment began;
- hours of work;
- holiday pay;
- sick pay;

- pension scheme;
- the length of notice to be given by both employer and employee in the event of termination of employment;
- grievance procedure – if the employer or employee is unhappy about the treatment of certain issues relating to the employment, there are set paths to follow, and the grievance procedure describes them;
- disciplinary procedure – the way the business handles any breach of conduct, rules or safety procedure.

In addition, it addresses a number of areas, which are considered below.

Employer rights

In addition to the terms and conditions of an employment contract, there are some legal obligations that must be respected by both employer and employee.

Employers generally seek to ensure an orderly working environment for all employees. An important part of this involves employees working according to the terms of their contracts.

Employers are usually disposed to understand when employees first show tendencies troublesome to business such as lateness, regular absence, or lack of effort. In such instances, the employer may seek to cajole the employee concerned by gentle hints that such behaviour is falling short of the requirements of the business.

If such transgression of the employment contract continues, however, disciplinary action may result. The employer formally advises the employee verbally of the misdemeanour and of future actions that may be taken or penalties imposed if improvement does not result.

The employee is required to observe the terms of the contract. The employer is entitled to take the remedial action described above, if the employee fails to do so.

In general, the employee is required to perform as follows.

1 He or she should observe a **duty of care** to the employer, other employees and people when on the employer's premises. In general, this means that the employee must act in a reasonable and responsible manner.

2 Reasonable and legal instructions from a supervisor or manager should be observed.

3 Work should be carried out conscientiously and in good faith. This includes respecting confidential information relating to the business; profits, profit margins or trade secrets.

4 He or she must be entirely trustworthy and honest in all matters especially where finance is concerned.

> **The employer owes a duty of care to the employee.**

This means that the employer must act in good faith, paying wages promptly, providing work, re-imbursing expenses, providing a reference when required, providing safe working conditions and practices.There needs to be trust between employer and employee and if this is broken, many problems result, which sometimes result in court action being taken by either party.

Equal opportunities

The employer has an obligation not to discriminate against people because of certain features or characteristics. This means an employer is obliged to select people because of their suitability for a task, and to avoid bias in the selection procedure especially as regards the following.

- **Sex**
  Women tend to select women for a particular job, men tend to select men; others stereotype men irrationally for certain jobs such as driving, and women for others, such as secretarial or nursing tasks. This is illegal and employers have a responsibility to discount this in their selection and other working practices, giving everybody equal opportunities for all positions and tasks within the organisation.
- **Race**
  It is similarly illegal to select against people because of their origin – place of birth, skin colour, race or religion.
- Physical disability.
- Homosexual or other sexual orientation.
- Age, both young and old.

Health and safety at work

Health and safety at work is a paramount responsibility of the employer with strict legal implications. *The Health and Safety at*

Work Act 1974 places obligations on both employer and employee.

Employer's responsibilities

The employer must:

1   provide a safe working environment;
2   provide adequate welfare facilities, including medical attention when necessary;
3   record and investigate accidents thoroughly, implementing improvements that may be learned from such occurrences;
4   keep exits and entrances safe;
5   keep systems and equipment in safe working order;
6   ensure that components and packaging components are safe and that storage procedures take care of employees;
7   ensure that toxic or dangerous substances necessarily used in manufacture and employment are stored safely;
8   provide appropriate training and supervision on health and safety matters in the workplace.

Remuneration

In addition to the legal requirements relating to remuneration, the employer must arrange for the employee to receive remuneration either in cash, by cheque or credit transfer to his or her bank account. Furthermore, the employer must deduct at source PAYE (short for 'pay as you earn'), income tax and National Insurance contributions which must be remitted to the Inland Revenue on the employee's behalf.

National Insurance is the employee's contribution towards health care, pensions and other benefits for all citizens which the state provides.

Employee welfare

Responsible employers take employee welfare seriously. It concerns the effect of their work on employees' private lives. Undue stress at work, for example, causes anger, illness including nervous breakdowns, and the break up of families. A sensitive employer will monitor workloads and performance to avoid such occurrences.

At best, the employer will enrich the lives of employees and their families. This can happen in several ways:

Sports and social club   A sports and social club is sometimes formed by the business. Like a staff association, this is established to promote a feeling of belonging within the organisation. It focuses on events that are not related to the business. Sports teams are often formed to play in leagues and tournaments.

At Christmas and other festive occasions, dances and other social events are organised and often subsidised by the employer.

Subsidised canteen A subsidised canteen is one way of ensuring that employees eat properly when they are at work. It also has the side effect of ensuring that employees are able to perform satisfactorily during the afternoon for it is well known that lunch-time drinking reduces employee effectiveness afterwards.

Health checks Health – medical and dental – checks are a thoughtful way in which the employer can show concern for the welfare of employees. These can take place either on site or on the premises of a nearby doctor or dentist.

Some employers engage a hairdresser to visit their premises! Not only does this demonstrate the employer's concern for employee welfare, it avoids employees taking extended lunch breaks to allow this necessary task to take place!

Crèche or nursery facilities Crèche or nursery facilities reassure parents that their young children are close at hand and well cared for. Such a service may be entirely or partially funded by the employer. In some cases it is merely a service supplied by the employer, but entirely paid for by the employees. It is still worthwhile for the convenience and peace of mind of employees.

Compassionate leave Compassionate leave is usually allowed when a death or serious illness befalls a close relative of an employee. This amounts to one or two days paid leave to attend hospital or make arrangements and attend a funeral.

Paternity leave Paternity leave is increasingly granted to a new father. This enables him to visit the mother and child as well as to prepare the home for the needs of the new addition to the family.

Season ticket loans Season ticket and other loans by the employer relieve the employee of some of the financial stress related to travel to work. This is particularly the case where employees live some distance away from their work (usually to live in the country) and work in a large town or city.

Company visits Company visits or excursions are a pleasant way of rewarding employees for achievement or abnormally sustained effort.

Staff discounts Staff discounts and access to seconds (i.e. slightly imperfect but still acceptable goods) enable the employer, at little cost, to give employees access to goods that may not be available elsewhere and to which they are privy because of their employment.

Employee benefits Employee benefits such as purchase of private health insurance for all family members are another way of the employer showing concern for the welfare of employees and their families.

Disciplinary procedure

It is the responsibility of the employer to instigate and implement an effective disciplinary procedure.

This is not only a legal requirement, it also ensures that employees work in a safe, supportive environment, secure in the knowledge that insubordination and anti-social behaviour is not tolerated.

The disciplinary procedure normally begins with informal warnings. If these are not respected, a **verbal warning** is usually given by a supervisor, immediate superior or somebody from personnel. The employee is asked to sign a confirmation that such a verbal warning has taken place.

If there is no improvement, a **written warning** may result. This will state that if there is a recurrence of the transgression within a stated time, the employee may be dismissed.

Dismissal, the last resort, means that the employer terminates the working relationship with the employee under the terms of the contract.

For very serious matters such as theft, dismissal may be instant, with no necessity to go through the stages of verbal and written warnings.

In any case, proof or written confession is essential if the law is to be observed and fair dismissal results.

Performance criterion

2.2.4 Explain employee rights and responsibilities to their employers

Employee rights

Remuneration

This includes:

- pay and method of calculating pay (e.g. so much per hour or per unit of work if payment is by piece work);
- frequency of pay (e.g. weekly or monthly).

Remuneration is the amount of money that a person receives in return for doing a certain job. It may take the form of **wages**, which are paid in cash or by cheque weekly, **salary**, which is paid monthly by cheque or credit transfer through the bank. Incentive schemes such as **bonuses** for production workers who complete certain tasks within an agreed time scale, or **commission** for sales personnel for achieving sales targets, are also part of the remuneration package.

Some businesses allow their employees to participate in **profit sharing schemes**. In such cases, at the end of each year, they would receive an additional payment which would vary dependent upon the amount of profit that the company has made.

Sometimes the profit sharing may take the form of share ownership in the business. If profit hits a certain level, employees are either given or able to purchase a quantity of the company's shares at a preferential price.

Safe working conditions

The employee is entitled to expect to work in safe surroundings.

Because many businesses demand the use of special equipment which can have hazardous side effects, the *Health and Safety at Work Act 1974* is the latest in a number of laws designed to protect employees from dangerous working conditions.

This includes the necessity:

1   to fit guards to sharp blades, lathes and similar machinery;
2   to ensure that toxic or corrosive chemicals are stored away from danger;
3   to protect employees when working in potentially dangerous circumstances such as on gantries;
4   to protect employees from air pollution or exposure to dangerous inhalation.

This law is covered in greater detail later on page 127. It embraces such areas as the provision of fire exits, extinguishers and sprinklers. It covers the provision of medical help in case of emergency and training in first aid and fire evacuation procedure.

Health and safety inspectors are employed by the government. They are empowered to ensure that employee safety procedures are correctly implemented in businesses and can close businesses that do not conform to exacting requirements.

Staff associations

Staff associations are formed by either the employer or employees of a business. Their function is to promote a sense of belonging within the organisation by encouraging employees to enjoy themselves as a group engaged in an activity entirely divorced from work. Thus, such organisations arrange theatre visits, parties, open days and other events for employees and their families.

Sometimes a staff association may have its own premises in the business, even a bar which is open at strictly controlled times. One employee usually takes the role of secretary and a committee is formed from employees to arrange a timetable of events for the coming months.

Compliance with terms of contract

It has been stated that the employee agrees to work for the employer and in return the employer agrees to remunerate the employee.

Health and safety

The Industrial Revolution of the 18th century brought about significant changes to people's working lives. Previously they had lived and worked in small communities, using little mechanical equipment and life at work had differed little from their home lives.

With the advent of factories, canals and mines, all this changed. Workers were now vulnerable to dangerous machinery and surroundings, resulting in a succession of industrial accidents and deaths, which more often than not left the bereaved families homeless and penniless.

After a number of unsuccessful attempts at reform, legislation was passed which not only stipulated the rights and responsibilities of employer and employee with regard to safety, it also established teams of inspectors whose sole job was to travel around the country to ensure that this legislation was observed by all parties.

Employee
responsibilities

Capability and qualifications

The employee must be capable and qualified to perform the tasks of the job.

Capability includes the physical strength, mental and physical ability and skill to perform the required tasks.

Qualifications are formal recognition that the person possesses the requisite skills to undertake particular tasks. For example, a plumber may possess City and Guilds qualifications.

At interview, the prospective employee must be honest about declaring capabilities and qualifications to perform certain tasks. If the employer asks about specialist knowledge, the employee must discuss previous experience, capability and qualifications. If dishonest claims are made, the employer is entitled to dismiss the employee instantly.

Conduct

Part of the employee's duty of care relates to conduct at the place of work. This embraces the personal behaviour of the employee, particularly with the employer and other employees. Good business conduct includes the following areas.

1 **Competence** to undertake the tasks required by the employer.
2 **Complying with instructions** from the supervisor or manager.
3 **Morality,** including sexual and ethical behaviour at work. The employee must tolerate and respect other people's race, colour, religion and sex, and in addition behave in a

manner which promotes safe working practices.

4 **Safety** – the employee must not behave in an unsafe or reckless fashion where he or she and colleagues are concerned. Employees have a responsibility not to endanger the health of others. In recent times, this has been extended to passive smoking, where successful court cases have resulted in employers paying out large sums of money to ex-employees who have suffered the effects of inhaling other employees' smoke at work. This has led to many employers banning smoking at work.

5 **Punctuality** – that is, arriving on or before the required time, and leaving on or after the agreed finish. Frequent absence from work is liable to disciplinary action by the employer.

Criminal activity

The employee has a responsibility to the employer regarding disclosure of conviction for certain criminal offences. Theft from the employer, or wider public issues such as a delivery driver convicted of drinking and driving will nearly always result in dismissal.

> The employee owes a duty of care to the employer and to other employees.

This means that the employee must behave responsibly during the employment and work loyally, conscientiously and honestly. The employee has an obligation to work to the highest reasonable standards.

This includes acting in good faith towards the employer, accounting for cash and money handled on behalf of the business, respecting trade secrets, and obeying reasonable orders by the employer.

Legislation The main legislation that concerns employment is a rag bag of laws that date from different times and which affect different employment areas. This is not wholly surprising. As industry has evolved, so has the need to protect its workforce in the various types of workplace.

Of course, in every workplace the fundamental principal applies, that employees should be able to work in safe conditions without adverse affect to their health. However, the implementation of this principle varies widely over different jobs; basic farm work as we know it is well over one thousand years old, welding is an early 20th century innovation, and North Sea oil rigs with their specialist workforce date from the 1970s.

The passing of legislation affecting any job arises from the identification of a need. Once a need has been identified and legislation to cover it has been created there still remains the fundamental need to enforce the law. Without enforcement legislation is powerless. Governments, however, have an interest in enforcing their own legislation for to do so maintains their credibility. It is in this way that legislation has evolved over hundreds of years.

The principal laws, with their implications, are given below.

The Factories' Act 1961
This Act concentrates on the use of industrial machinery and other provisions, essentially for factory workers, providing for:

- adequate toilet and washing facilities, heating and ventilation;
- unobstructed floors, stairs and passageways, with non-slip surfaces on all floors;
- adequate protection to potentially dangerous machinery and equipment;
- fire doors which must be kept unlocked and unobstructed, and adequate fire escapes which must be well signed and maintained.

This Act is strengthened by the *Provision and Use of Work Equipment Regulations 1992*; the *Manual Handling Operations Regulations 1992* and the *Personal Protective Equipment at Work Regulations 1992*.

These stipulate that equipment must conform to EC directives on safety, training, servicing, the provision of guards and the wearing of protective clothing.

The Offices, Shops and Railway Premises Act 1963
This Act is the major legislation governing workers in shops and offices stipulating that:

- the temperature must not fall below 16°C;

- there must be adequate lighting and fresh air supply;
- sufficient toilet and washing facilities for the number of employees must be provided, as well as soap, clean towels and hot and cold running water;
- at least 12 square metres of working space per employee must be available.

The Health and Safety at Work Act 1974

This Act protects employees from having to work in hazardous conditions. It not only places obligations on the employer to provide a safe working environment with remedial measures (such as first aid and medical attention where appropriate) and training on specialised safety equipment. It also places obligations on the employees following such training to use the equipment properly and with regard for other employees and other people in the factory such as visitors.

It furthermore splits the country into areas, each with a health and safety inspectorate to implement the Act and close any businesses which persistently contravene it.

The *Management of Health and Safety at Work Regulations 1992* and the *Health and Safety (Display Screen Equipment) Regulations 1992* make further provision for the protection and monitoring of the health of employees who are exposed to hazardous conditions in the workplace.

In the case of employees frequently using display screens, the employer must provide regular eye tests, sufficient breaks away from the screen, adequate lighting and ergonomically designed furniture.

The Equal Pay Act 1970 and The Race Relations Act 1970

These Acts stipulate that men and women should be treated equally in every way, including pay, conditions and opportunities for promotion. This applies to people of all races, colours, nationalities or ethnic origins.

The Disabled Persons (Employment) Act 1958

This Act obliges firms employing 20 or more people to employ at least three people who are registered as disabled. Whilst there are exceptions due to the nature of the work, some jobs such as switchboard operators dictate priority for disabled people (in this case the blind).

The Rehabilitation of Offenders Act 1974

This Act concerns the necessity to disclose to an employer previous criminal convictions by potential employees. Some convictions are regarded as 'spent' after some time has elapsed (the precise amount depends on the gravity of the offence) and there is no need to disclose them. Others must be disclosed; if not, dismissal can result.

The Employment Protection (Consolidation) Acts 1975 and 1978

These Acts cover the obligation of an employer to provide to the employee a contract of employment within 13 weeks of starting with the company.

The Employment Acts 1980–1990 and the Trade Union Act 1988

These Acts identify the extent to which trades unions and their members may strike and take other industrial action in the event of industrial disputes.

The Trade Union Reform and Employment Right Acts 1992

This Act stipulates that a female employee is entitled to take maternity leave with a guarantee that her position will be held until her return to the company after a maximum 14 weeks.

Activities

1 Investigate a local business – for example, a shop, a factory, or a hotel – which has gained from employer and employee co-operation.

   Write a report which includes examples of disagreements between the employer and one or more employees.

   Explain how they were resolved.

   Describe the further legal action that would have resulted if the disagreement had not been resolved in this way.

2 Give two examples of employers' and employees' rights and responsibilities, quoting the relevant legislation, particularly that relating to equal opportunities.

Element 2.3 Present Results of Investigation into Job Roles

Having started to explore the interface between employer and employee and the relationship of individuals in organisations, this element looks at the different roles undertaken by different people in organisations.

Evidence indicators

- A summary describing three job roles at different levels within one organisation. The summary should describe the day-to-day activities and tasks of those job roles, and explain the extent to which team membership enhances individuals' ability to perform their job roles.
- A record of a presentation describing one job role and the activities and tasks undertaken by a person carrying out that role. The presentation should either describe how an individual, or an individual operating within a team, deals with:
  - a one routine problem-solving task (e.g. how to keep sufficient stocks to meet needs);
  - b one non-routine task (e.g. dealing with an emergency, which should be illustrated with posters or signs giving instructions for an emergency such as the evacuation of a building in the event of a fire).

Core skills

This element gives students the opportunity to demonstrate these core skills:

Communication
Element 2.1 Take part in discussions

2.2 Produce written material

2.3 Use images

Information technology
Element 2.1 Prepare information

2.2 Process information

2.3 Present information

2.4 Evaluate the use of information technology

 **Performance criterion**

2.3.1 Identify and describe individual's job roles at different levels within organisations.
Look again at the organisation chart (Figure 37) on pages 92 and 93. The right hand side shows the rank order of positions within the organisation.

In all medium to large organisations there are **levels of seniority**; a hierarchy or 'pecking order'. This reflects the level of responsibility and authority which employees have within the organisation.

In this example, the **managing director** is the most senior employee. This job is to manage the direction that the company takes.

Next in line are the **directors**. They set the direction for day-to-day operations of the business.

Senior managers manage major functions of the business. **Middle managers** look after large sections of these (e.g. advertising, print buying), while **junior managers** are responsible for a specific area (personnel assistant, supervisor over a group of front line staff). The **front line staff** and the **workforce** are responsible for performing particular tasks.

Job roles

Managing director
This is frequently the most senior position in the business. The managing director is in overall charge of the company, overseeing all its functions. The position should be occupied by somebody with many abilities.

1 The managing director should have much experience in a senior managerial role (i.e. managing people and resources).
2 The person should possess a good understanding of the business concerned, even if appointed from another business.
3 The person should possess the ability to communicate with people at all levels.
4 The person should demonstrate achievement and success in previous positions.
5 The person should be a good decision maker.

The managing director is involved in developing the business strategy and plan. In a democratic business, the directors are also involved in setting the direction that the business will take.

As has been said, in an autocratic organisation, the managing director writes the strategy and makes the decisions (see Figure 42).

The managing director has two important types of function; **internally**, to oversee the successful running of the business and **externally,** to be aware of opportunities that may arise – perhaps the opportunity to acquire, another business, perhaps a competitor, perhaps a supplier or customer.

In all events, a watchful eye must be kept on developments in the external business environment for such opportunities as they arise.

Directors

One benefit of a democratic approach is that the directors, too, are involved in setting the strategy and writing the business plan. Thus, continuity is achieved because their next task is to write plans for their own function, for instance in marketing, sales, operations, personnel and finance. A democratic organisation will involve the senior and middle managers in this activity as well, in order to gain their commitment to the short, medium and long term tasks.

Directors report to the managing director and are appointed because they have special expertise and skill in their chosen area, perhaps personnel management or marketing.

In any event they are people with seniority, usually paid a considerable amount of money, and although they report to the managing director, their opinion is also respected and considered by their superior.

As Figure 37 on pages 92–93 shows, **executive directors** (for instance, the sales director) are responsible for the successful operation of their particular function. They attend board meetings and are expected to report on activities that have taken place on their side of the business.

Non-executive directors also attend board meetings, but are appointed not in order for them to manage or direct a function within the business, but because of the expertise and experience that they bring to the company. They advise and add to the debate on matters of strategy and management, but take no part in day-to-day operations. Their role is to attend board meetings and advise on other matters as the need arises.

Managers

Figure 37 on pages 92–93 shows managers at various levels within the organisation – junior, middle and senior. Managers are people who have gained skills and knowledge through experience and training, then shown potential or ability to manage or oversee that function when it is performed by other people.

The manager's function is to ensure that the area of responsibility delegated to him or her is run as efficiently as possible with available resources.

Resources are not only the people reporting to the manager, but also the equipment that they use, the area they occupy and the money allocated to them.

A manager takes care of the day to day running and decision making of a defined function, be it sales promotion, a production unit, or personnel, the precise area of responsibility depending on the nature of the job. Some managers may also involve other people in the decision-making process – subordinates and colleagues – depending on the personality of the person concerned, the preferred managerial style (see the Tannenbaum and Schmidt management style continuum given in Figure 42 below) and the company culture.

FIGURE 42
Tannenbaum and Schmidt management style continuum

TELLS	SELLS	CONSULTS	SHARES	DELEGATES
Manager makes decision, **announces** it to subordinates	Manager makes decision, **explains** it to subordinates	Manager makes suggestions, subordinates make suggestions	Manager **defines** limits, lets group make decision	Manager allows subordinates to function within defined limits

Supervisors

Supervisors are people who have demonstrated commitment, ability and skill in a particular area and have been promoted to their first managerial position. It gives them responsibility for a small group of people – perhaps workers all involved in the same area of production, or assistants in a sales office.

It is here that early management skills are developed; the ability to command respect without appearing authoritarian, the skill to engender a sense of discipline, the ability to get a job done, withstand pressure and develop new ideas.

It is said that any person, supervisor, manager, director or managing director can only be an effective direct manager of up to seven people. Above this number it is not practicable to oversee fully the roles that they are supposed to be playing.

Operators

Operators, operatives, front-line staff or workforce are those people on whom the business depends for ultimate success – they are the people who actually do the work – in the factory, on the switchboard, as a salesperson travelling from customer to customer or as an executive in purchasing, personnel, warehousing or finance.

An operator has responsibility to carry out the tasks allocated, or in management terms **delegated**, to the position.

It is from the operators that future supervisors and managers are found.

There are also people who are quite content to be efficient operators and have no desire to progress further within an organisation.

Dependent upon the actual job, the position of the operator is the most junior within an organisation, but a skilled operator often commands the respect of his superiors and colleagues.

Team Members

As may be seen from Figure 10 in Element 1.1, (page 30), rarely do individuals work alone in an organisation.

Increasing emphasis is placed on sharing tasks and delegating them to the person most skilled in handling them. The logic is based on the old saying that 'many hands make light work'.

Activity

Think of a team sport. Consider the different roles – or positions – that people play in them. Identify the various skills needed to make that team successful.

In business, a team is a group of people working together to achieve a common objective, just like a team taking part in a sport. The team captain is the leader; the business equivalent is the supervisor or manager.

Performance criterion

2.3.2 Explain the benefits of team membership in performing job roles

Training for team work

Team work clearly has many advantages to an organisation. Many large companies like to recruit their staff early in their careers (prior to about age 27), so that training can take place in the style and culture of the business. Thus the approach to problem solving, decision making and management skills can be moulded in the required way, and the executive will not only have a long career with the company, he or she has not been deflected from the company way of thinking by many outside influences.

Meredith Belbin, a well-respected Professor of Business Studies, has identified eight individual team roles which make an ideal team.

His eight team roles are listed below.

1 **Company worker:** the workhorse or 'implementer' who turns ideas into action.
2 **Chairperson:** not necessarily the team leader, but a co-ordinator who gets on well with people.
3 **Shaper:** a self-elected task leader who is dynamic and finds ways around obstacles.
4 **Plant:** creative, imaginative ideas person.
5 **Resource investigator:** a 'fixer', exploring opportunities and getting other people to do things.
6 **Monitor evaluator:** a strategist and analyst.
7 **Team worker:** a social, accommodating person who promotes harmony within the team (the opposite to the 'shaper').
8 **Completer/finisher:** a person who likes attention to detail, to setting and keeping to deadlines.

Activities

1   Copy and complete the questionnaire in Figure 44, on pages 138–141 and follow the instructions to identify your natural primary and secondary roles in a team. Please note: in order to gain the most out of this exercise it is essential to be honest! There are no right or wrong answers. Take as long as you need, but do not think for a long time over any one question.

Compare your results with others in the group.

2   Consider people whom you know. Which parts do you think they would fulfil in a successful team?

3   Split into groups of eight people. Six are required to complete the exercise, and two to observe.

Complete the bridge-building exercise on pages 136–137.
Instructions for the two observers:
Take a sheet of paper and list the eight different roles that Belbin identified in all successful teams.
While the six people are undertaking the bridge building exercise, the two observers should identify, with examples, which group members took the different Belbin roles.
Examples should mention specific tasks and the way they were carried out.
When the task is complete, all eight people should discuss the experience and what has been observed.
Identify the tasks which were undertaken by individuals and those which were undertaken by the team working together.

Individual work

Individual work is required when a separate task needs to be done, figures need calculation or plans need formulation and cool, calm reflection is required. Some tasks require specialist skills, such as accountancy, writing promotional literature and some product design. In a company only one person may possess such skills. Alternatively a consultant or specialist outside the company may be consulted and that person devises proposals for group consideration within the company.

Activity   Bridge Building Exercise

Briefing
You will be allocated to a group by your tutor. In this group, you have 30 minutes to make plans for the construction of a bridge, which must be built quickly. Use as little paper as possible and use as few bridge supports as you can.

Your group will be given 10 sheets of paper only to plan and practise with. When you come to build the bridge, you can use as much paper as you need, but remember the costs! The group making the biggest profit wins.

After you have built your bridge, you will be asked by your tutor to identify the different Common Skills used in completing the task.

The task
As a group, you are required to build a bridge over the 'river' which your tutor will mark on the floor of the room. The bridge must be:

- made out of the materials provided and nothing else;
- capable of standing by itself for two minutes without any extra support; **at least 30 cm above the river** at its central point.

N.B. The river is one metre wide

You may build supports for your bridge, but see the section on costs!

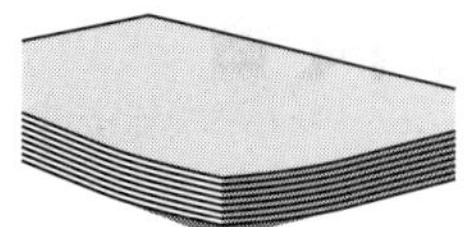

Materials
You may use only the material provided for the construction of your bridge. These are:

- paper clips
- A4 size paper

Payment
Your group is under contract to be paid £10,000 for the bridge, as long as you follow the rules. Out of this, you have to pay the following costs:

- £100 for every sheet of paper used in the bridge;
- £2,000 for every support which stands in the river;

- £100 for every 10 seconds (or part of 10 seconds) that it takes your group to build the bridge

Planning

Building the bridge is a group exercise and you will need to plan carefully the following:

- how to build your bridge;
- how much you will lose in costs;
- who in your group will do what.

If you choose, you can make a written plan before constructing the bridge.

FIGURE 43 Types of bridges

A self-perception inventory for team members

Directions

For each section distribute a total of ten points among the sentences which you think best describe your behaviour. These points may be distributed among several sentences: in extreme cases they might be spread among all sentences or ten points may be given to a single sentence. Enter the points in the Table after section VII.

I What I believe I can contribute to a team:

	Statement	Points
a	I think I can quickly see and take advantage of new opportunities	
b	I can work well with a wide range of people	
c	Producing ideas is one of my natural assets	
d	My ability rests in being able to draw people out whenever I detect that I have something of value to contribute to group objectives	
e	My capacity to follow through has much to do with my personal effectiveness	
f	I am ready to face temporary unpopularity if it leads to worthwhile results in the end	
g	I can usually sense what is realistic and likely to work	
h	I can offer a reasoned case for alternative courses of action without introducing bias or prejudice	

II If I have a possible shortcoming in teamwork, it could be that:

	Statement	Points
a	I am not at ease unless meetings are well structured and controlled and generally well conducted	
b	I am inclined to be too generous towards others who have a valid viewpoint that has not been given a proper airing	
c	I have a tendency to talk too much once the group gets on to new ideas	
d	My objective outlook makes it difficult for me to join in readily and enthusiastically with colleagues	
e	I am sometimes seen as forceful and authoritarian if there is a need to get something done	
f	I find it difficult to lead from the front, perhaps because I am over-responsive to group atmosphere	
g	I am apt to get too caught up in ideas that occur to me and so lose track of what is happening	
h	My colleagues tend to see me as worrying unnecessarily over detail and the possibility that things may go wrong	

III When involved in a project with other people:

	Statement	Points
a	I have an aptitude for influencing people without pressurising them	
b	My general vigilance prevents careless mistakes and omissions being made	
c	I am ready to press for action to make sure that the meeting does not waste time or lose sight of the main objective	
d	I can be counted on to contribute something original	
e	I am always ready to back a good suggestion in the common interest	
f	I am keen to look for the latest in new ideas and developments	
g	I believe my capacity for judgement can help to bring about the right decisions	
h	I can be relied upon to see that all essential work is organised	

IV My characteristic approach to group work is that:

	Statement	Points
a	I have a quiet interest in getting to know colleagues better	
b	I am not reluctant to challenge the views of others or to hold a minority view myself	
c	I can usually find a line of argument to refute unsound propositions	
d	I think I have a talent for making things work once a plan has to be put into operation	
e	I have a tendency to avoid the obvious and to come out with the unexpected	
f	I bring a touch of perfectionism to any job I undertake	
g	I am ready to make use of contacts outside the group itself	
h	While I am interested in all views, I have no hesitation in making up my mind once a decision has to be made	

V I gain satisfaction in a job because:

	Statement	Points
a	I enjoy analysing situations and weighing up all the possible choices	
b	I am interested in finding practical solutions to problems	
c	I like to feel I am fostering good working relationships	
d	I can have a strong influence on decisions	
e	I can meet people who may have something new to offer	
f	I can get people to agree on a necessary course of action	
g	I feel in my element where I can give a task my full attention	
h	I like to find a field that stretches my imagination	

VI If I am suddenly given a difficult task with limited time and unfamiliar people:

	Statement	Points
a	I would feel like retiring to a corner to devise a way out of the impasse before developing a line	
b	I would be ready to work with the person who showed the most positive approach, however difficult he or she might be	
c	I would find some way of reducing the size of the task by establishing what different individuals might contribute	
d	My natural sense of urgency would help ensure that we did not fall behind schedule	
e	I believe I would keep my cool and maintain my capacity to think straight	
f	I would retain a steadiness of purpose in spite of the pressure	
g	I would be prepared to take a positive lead if I felt the group was making no progress	
h	I would open up discussions with a view to stimulating new thoughts and getting something moving	

FIGURE 44 A self-perception inventory (pages 138–141)

VII With reference to the problems to which I am subject in working in groups:

	Statement	Points
a	I am apt to show my impatience with those who are obstructing progress	
b	Others may criticise me for being too analytical and insufficiently intuitive	
c	My desire to ensure that work is properly done can hold up proceedings	
d	I tend to get bored rather easily and rely on one or two stimulating members to spark me off	
e	I find it difficult to get started unless the goals are clear	
f	I am sometimes poor at explaining and clarifying complex points that occur to me	
g	I am conscious of demanding from others the things that I cannot do myself	
h	I hesitate to get my points across when I run up against real opposition	

Self perception inventory analysis sheet

Section		CW		CH		SH		PL		RI		ME		TW		CF
I	g		d		f		c		a		h		b		e	
II	a		b		e		g		c		d		f		h	
III	h		a		c		d		f		g		e		b	
IV	d		h		b		e		g		c		a		f	
V	b		f		d		h		e		a		c		g	
VI	f		c		g		a		h		e		b		d	
VII	e		g		a		f		d		b		h		c	
Total																

CW COMPANY WORKER   CH CHAIRPERSON   SH SHAPER   PL PLANT
RI RESOURCE INVESTIGATOR   ME MONITOR EVALUATOR   TW TEAM WORKER   CF FINISHER

The highest score on team-role will indicate how best the respondent can make his or her mark in a management or project team. The next highest scores can denote back up team-roles towards which the individual should shift if for some reason there is less group need for a primary team-role.

The two lowest scores in team-role imply possible areas of weakness. But rather than attempting to reform in this area the manager may be better advised to seek a colleague with complementary strengths.

Company worker
This person is disciplined, conscientious and aware of external responsibilities such as the need to keep other people informed about what the team is doing. He or she respects established conditions in the organisation and one weakness of the role is a degree of rigidity. On the positive side, this person is very practical, trusting and tolerant of other people. The Company worker's strengths lie in putting other people's ideas and plans into operation and carrying out plans which the team has agreed in a systematic and efficient way.

Chairperson
As you might expect, this denotes the ability to lead the team towards its objectives through effective use of team members. The Chairperson is able to recognise individual strengths and weaknesses in other members of the team and ensure that the best use is made of every person's potential. This role has many positive aspects, he or she is likely to prefer a participative, consultative style of leadership, carrying all the rest of the team with them. In case where the team needs to act under pressure and at high speed, the Shaper can take over.

Shaper
Shapers are people who have strong need for achievement and success. They are highly competitive with an active desire to win, they put life into a team and can drive though change at the expense of popularity. On the negative side, Shapers are often seen as pushy and aggressive and insensitive to the feelings of others.

The Chairperson and Shaper roles are complementary; the former pulls a team together while the latter challenges the status quo and goads other team members into action.

Plant
The Plant is the creative member of the team, full of new ideas and ways of doing things and particularly concerned with finding innovative solutions to major issues. They generally have higher than average intelligence. Often, however, they are weak in communicating their ideas to others and can appear to be on a different wave-length, they are also very sensitive to criticism or praise. If a team contains too many people who are strong in this role, they can conflict with each other over ideas.

The name derives from Belbin's experiments in which he 'planted' individuals who scored highly on creativity in psychometric tests into the companies he was studying (Belbin, 1981).

Resource Investigator
When studying managers who might be classified as 'Plants', Belbin identified another, complementary role - the Resource Investigator. More outgoing and communicative than the Plant, this person gets around, finds out what is going on, meets people and asks relevant questions. This person is often described as 'never being in the office and, if he or she is, always on the telephone'. Resource Investigators are good communicators and negotiators, always ready to explore new opportunities and make new contacts. They are also good at thinking on their feet and getting information. However, they can quickly lose enthusiasm if the task is not stimulating enough for them.

Monitor/Evaluator
Although both Plants and Resource Investigators are valued by teams for their ideas and enthusiasm respectively, both can get carried away if there is no Monitor/Evaluator present. This person is serious-minded and judicious, valued for an ability to make shrewd judgements and able to debate with a Plant over the latter's ideas. To other team members, the Monitor/Evaluator can appear as rather dry, boring and over-critical, but this role is essential in a team where the decision-making process is complicated and it is difficult to reach consensus; the Monitor/Evaluator can be relied upon to reach the optimum decision.

Teamworker
Teamworkers are diplomatic and perceptive with a strong interest in people. They are good at building on other people's suggestions, improving communications between different members of the team and generally fostering team spirit. They are particularly effective at averting interpersonal conflict and dealing with difficult team members. The Teamworker will let the Plants in the team have their say even if their ideas may appear impractical to others; he or she can draw out the slower but essential Monitor/Evaluator. A team composed of Teamworkers might sound ideal, but they lack the attributes of some of the other roles and members of such a team would spend all their time supporting one another!

Completer/Finisher
So far we have identified team members who represent the aims of the organisation, who can lead the team during stable times and in periods of crisis, people who will have ideas, people who communicate well, people who can reach decisions and people who encourage co-operation; the Completer/Finisher is the final ingredient. He or she is the person who has the ability to carry anything through to its conclusion with complete thoroughness. A team may have many brilliant ideas and even reach decisions, but if the agreed action is not carried out, it will fail in its objectives. This person checks on every detail and ensures nothing is overlooked. Completer/Finishers have high standards for themselves and others and may often be intolerant of people who do not share these standards.

Specialist
This is the person with professional expertise in an area valued and needed by the team in order to achieve its objectives. A team may need more than one Specialist at different times in its evolution. For example, a team involved in a building project would need an architect at the design stage and perhaps someone with expertise in the different properties of particular building materials: they might also need expert help on costing, on computer trunking and so on.

Of course, these team roles are stereotypes and individuals are usually strong in one or two aspects and weak in others. The same person can, therefore, perform more than one role in a team; you do not have to have teams of nine people to fulfil all the roles. The important point is that teams which are well-balanced in terms of the roles team members play will be more effective than teams which are unbalanced and where one or more essential team roles is missing.

FIGURE 44 continued

 **Performance criterion**

2.3.3 Identify activities performed by individuals at different levels within organisations

Achieving business tasks

In all business there is a variety of general tasks to undertake.

- **Decision making**
- **Problem solving**
- **Setting and achieving targets**

The abilities and skills required to perform these general tasks may be summarised as follows.

- Creativity
- Communication
- Analysis
- Planning
- Control
- Maintenance

Creativity

People who are able to use their creativity generate new ideas for application in many areas of business, not only for new products and advertising, although these roles are of course vital. Creativity includes finding more efficient ways to produce goods. By being creatively innovative, Henry Ford solved the problem of keeping up with demand for his product (the Model T Ford) by setting up the first moving production line in 1913. At the same time he saved money, thereby making the business more profitable.

So creativity goes right through any successful business. Sadly, devising new ways of performing business tasks can mean people losing their jobs and skills becoming outdated. Computer aided design (CAD) has resulted in technology taking over the jobs of many model makers and designers.

Communication

Communication is vital throughout the company, if people are fully to understand their mission and role within the business.

This will be examined more fully in Element 4.3, page 309.

A disgruntled employee once described his work situation as 'like growing mushrooms – you are kept permanently in the dark, except that now and again someone opens the door and throws a load of muck over you in the hope that you develop into something worthwhile.'

Effective communication is essential to maintain the commitment of employees if the 'mushroom' syndrome is to be avoided!

Communication may be verbal or in writing; formal or informal, as will be seen on page 341.

Analysis

Analysis covers the monitoring of the actions of other people and activities. People include competitors, customers, suppliers as well as those working within the business. Activities embrace sales, customer preferences, technological innovations, new products launched by competitors, the money available within the business, how much is owed to the business by other people, and how much the business owes.

This area also embraces market research which will be considered later on in more detail. (See page 153.)

Planning

Planning is essential if the business is to run smoothly. Change is such an ever-present force within business that planning is essential to bring stability and direction. The diagram in Figure 45 shows how the planning process starts by developing a strategy. This identifies and considers market opportunities that the business plans to exploit. A strategy is devised to answer the question 'where is the company going?', in the short, medium and long term. The strategy may include plans to develop new products for the existing market or to develop new market opportunities at home and overseas; these developments may involve the existing product range in the short term but in the long term it may envisage new ones.

The mission statement

The mission statement encapsulates the strategy in a simple sentence. The mission statement of Next, the high street clothes retailer is:

> To be the natural choice national fashion retailer in the UK for fashion-aware men and women who expect style and distinction from their clothing (Source: *Next Annual Report*).

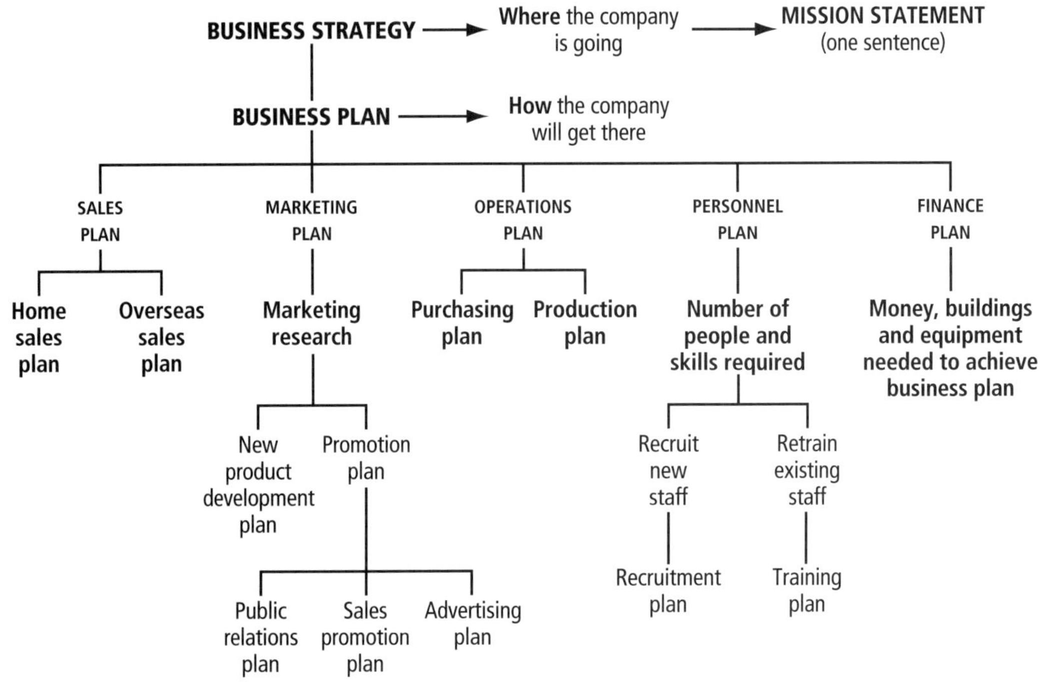

FIGURE 45
A business planning model for a manufacturing company

The business plan

Out of such strategic statements the business plan is developed. This is essentially practical and details how the company is going to reach the destination described in the business strategy document.

In a democratically run business, as many people as necessary are involved in developing the business plan, which can be a very exciting phase of business development. They not only feel involved in the business, they can also comment on the likelihood of achieving the targets and goals identified and the best way of achieving them making best use of available resources.

If innovation is to be introduced into the business, it is essential that all involved understand why and where it fits into the plans of all the functions in the operation – in this example, sales, marketing, operations, personnel and finance.

Planning takes into account the direction in which the business is going, the industry in which it is operating, the skills that the workforce will require, the amount of money necessary to make the required investments and the resources (buildings, land, vehicles, machinery) that will be needed. Other aspects are identified in the diagram in Figure 45.

Control

Control is essential to achieve goals within the agreed time. For example, creative people love being creative – this brings tremendous benefits to a business. There is a time, however, when somebody has to blow the whistle to say 'enough is enough. Now let us put these new ideas to good use within the business'. Otherwise, the creative team simply keep coming up with new ideas which never get used.

For this reason, forecasts, budgets and targets are made so that results can be monitored and evaluated against them. This means that if sales exceed forecast, budgets can be increased and the benefits may immediately be felt within the business. If no target or forecast is available, nobody knows how well the company is doing until the end of the year, by which time the implementation and availability of additional financial benefits are long delayed.

Control involves discipline and effective management of available resources.

Maintenance

Maintenance concerns not only the machinery and equipment, it also concerns the values that the business holds. For example, there is no doubt that Mercedes could make a lot of money by introducing a cheap family car to compete with the Ford Fiesta, Vauxhall Corsa and Rover Metro. They choose not to. Why? Because the Mercedes name is associated with a level of quality, size, engineering and price that is incompatible with building such a car.

No doubt, creative and new product development teams within the company have suggested such ideas, even perhaps made prototypes.

The directors and managers within the business have argued against such a development because of the values within the business, which reflect the values that their customers perceive from outside the business – in other words, the value of the Mercedes brand.

Decision making

Decision making requires abilities and skills frequently referred to above. The decision maker needs to make correct choices about:

- **whom to involve** in the decision (communication skills);
- **when to make** the decision? (have we got enough information and if not, when will it be available?);
- **how and when to communicate** the decision to others?

Of course, much depends on the **implications** of the decision being taken.

In hierarchical, democratic businesses, decisions are made at the lowest possible level, so that the people who take the decisions have to live with their consequences. It is proven that decisions are more effective when taken by people who are better informed about the day-to-day implications that their decision may have.

In autocratic organisations, decisions are taken by the senior managers. Junior staff thus feel excluded from the business and tend to develop an attitude of 'oh well, if that's what they want, they can have it' – lack of motivation frequently results. In these circumstances, the best staff tend to leave, obtaining new positions in companies where their decision making skills are developed, encouraged and respected.

Problem solving This embraces decision making, but is just one ingredient of many in the problem-solving process, which may be summarised as follows:

- **recognising** that there is a problem;
- **defining** the problem;
- **finding out information** relating to the problem;
- **discussing** the information;
- **devising alternative solutions** to the problem;
- **discussing** them with the appropriate people;
- **evaluating** the alternative solutions;
- **choosing** the most appropriate one;
- **communicating** the decision;
- **implementing** the decision;
- **monitoring** the implications and **following up** the results of the decision.

It will be seen that discussion and communication are frequent terms used in connection with problem solving. The implication of this is – listen to as much informed advice and comment as possible before taking any decision. In addition, when all the people concerned are consulted they feel part of the problem-solving process and more involved in the decision.

This may include not only employees, but also outside agencies (advertising, market research) or consultants for areas such as finance and production.

Setting and achieving targets

Targets can be set in all areas of the business:

- home sales;
- export sales;
- production levels;
- output per person;
- cost reductions in an area of particularly heavy spending;
- improvement in response times to customer enquiries and others.

Setting a target establishes a set of 'stepping stones' or benchmarks against which performances may be judged. The targets may be monthly sales during the year, as the example below shows.

Sales target – Territory X   All values in £,000

		JAN	FEB	MAR	APR	MAY	JUN	JUL	AUG	SEP	OCT	NOV	DEC
1995	Actual	345	132	168	478	490	265	354	467	576	689	467	280
1996	Target	395	150	185	490	525	280	375	485	595	725	485	300
	Actual	375	138	175	480								

Total 1995 actual   £4,711
Total 1996 target   £4,990. This represents a 5.9 per cent increase over 1995 actual

In this example, although the salesperson for territory X is achieving sales figures in 1996 above those for 1995, they fall short of target by £52,000. Some investigation is necessary to discover why. Perhaps a competitor has launched a superior product, or the customers are overstocked from the previous year – perhaps the sales person is not performing satisfactorily – the reasons can be many and varied. However, a target gives the opportunity to monitor and reflect on performance.

The practice of setting targets has benefits in all areas of the business.

1   To give people something to aim at.
2   To establish a benchmark against which remedial action can be taken if performance falls short of target level. Such action could involve increasing the level of promotion, reducing costs to maintain profitability, or increasing the size of the sales force.
3   It gives the business the opportunity to compare current performance with that of previous years.
4   To present an opportunity for a considerate manager to reward hardworking staff with a well-deserved treat. Achieving targets is often a cause for celebration, particularly in difficult trading times.

Performance criterion

2.3.4 Identify tasks in job roles

Let us consider the tasks that certain individuals have to undertake in business, and the type of people who consequently are likely to possess the skills and ability to perform them.

Human resourcing

In business, there are four resources required:

1   money or capital;
2   land and buildings;
3   machinery and components;
4   **labour** – the human resource.

It is this last, and most important resource, labour or human resource, that is the responsibility of Personnel. The function of this department entails many tasks which may be summarised as devising and operating systems that take account of employees' needs and those of the organisation.

The tasks involved in personnel may be summarised as follows:

1   to **recruit** staff for the organisation;
2   to **establish appraisal systems** so that supervisors and managers can review employee performance regularly;
3   to **maintain employee records** confidentially;
4   to **devise and run training programmes** to meet company objectives;
5   to **terminate employees' service** – through giving notice by either party, retirement, redundancy or dismissal;

6 to **operate employee benefits** such as private health insurance, company car policy, discounted products and services;

7 to **devise and implement a disciplinary system;**

8 to **administer the company pension scheme;**

9 to **devise and implement health and safety policy** for employees;

10 to **run the sports and social club;**

11 to **liaise as necessary with outside bodies** such as trades unions and arbitration bodies in case of dispute with employees.

It embraces creating advertisements for vacancies, interviewing, making and confirming in writing job offers to new recruits, introducing them to the organisation, transferring pension funds, and other matters that relate to employee needs.

The sort of people who work in personnel are by nature caring and considerate but with an analytical, dispassionate facet which allows them to distinguish between genuine employee needs and abuse of the system.

Producing goods or services

This involves making the product that keeps the company in business; many of the same attributes apply both to manufacturers and to service deliverers.

Manufacturing is the process which converts raw materials, components and sub-assemblies into finished product by adding labour and technology.

It embraces packaging and packing the products into shipper cartons, for onward despatch to the finished goods warehouse or direct to the customer.

The tasks involved are set out below:

1 **to set up machinery** accurately to work raw materials and components consistently to product specifications;

2 **to ensure that sufficient component stock and materials** are situated in the factory to keep up with production requirements;

3 **to assemble raw materials and components** into sub-assembled and finished product;

4 **to package finished product, place and seal in shipper cartons.** A shipper carton is the outer packaging – frequently a large box made of corrugated cardboard – in which multiples of the finished product are sent to retailers. Finally, manufacturing has to arrange

5 **to transport the finished product** either to the warehouse or onto a vehicle for delivery to the customer and

6 **to ensure efficient production** by effective supervision and management of production teams.

The personal qualities required in production are:

1 to be scrupulous about observing **health and safety** requirements;

2 to pay **attention to detail** in setting up equipment safely and effectively;

3 to show **leadership, supervision and management skills** and

4 to demonstrate **a practical approach to problem solving** – machine adjustment, machine breakdown, and the problems arising from human frailties (e.g. managing the illness and holiday leave of others and industrial disputes).

With service deliverers (such as a hotel or car hire company), much liaison is needed with outside suppliers (car manufacturers or brewers, for example), and it is necessary to **maintain a consistent external corporate image.**

Both of these requirements for producing services apply equally to manufacturers.

Accounts Since the main purpose of most businesses is to make profits, it follows that the function of accounts is pivotal to the organisation's success.

The role is to:

1 **monitor the requirement for funds** to run the different functions effectively within the business;

2 **to ensure that customers pay their invoices** on time;

3 **to check new customers** for their creditworthiness;

4 **to implement procedures for customers who do not pay** their invoices;

5 **to obtain the best return for invested capital** that is not immediately required to run the business;

6 **to negotiate with the bank agreed borrowing facilities** at competitive rates of interest.

The type of people involved have necessarily a good head for figures, and an analytical approach to business. It is no help to the business if an accountant is swept up in the emotion of an advertising campaign, or the development of a new product, spending large sums when the real financial need is to reduce company spending.

Administration

Senior level

Administration takes place at many levels within a business. At the most senior level the tasks are:

1 **to negotiate contracts** and agreements for the business;
2 **to register and protect patents, trademarks and copyrights** that the business has originated.

Patents

Patents are documents which register the origination of a device or gadget that does a job in a different way than before.

Trademarks

Trademarks identify the business and its products in the marketplace. 'Coca-Cola', 'McDonalds' and 'Reebok' are trademarks which are immediately recognised by consumers and goods which carry these names represent a certain level of value in the marketplace.

Copyrights

Copyrights exist in packaging designs and promotional copy as well as in music, art and literature. Copyrights exist to protect intellectual property from unlawful copying.

Junior level

At a more junior level the administrative tasks are as follows.

1 Maintaining, and inputting information into, the company's **computer system** which handles much of the record keeping and communication within a business, especially where the company operates on more than one site (an initially expensive system repays the high outlay by reducing the need for large numbers of expensive clerical assistants).
2 The **secretarial function,** which can fall within administration if IT is not so well developed within a

business. In this case, the responsibility for company stationery and paperwork comes within this function.

The type of person required in administration should be ruthlessly efficient, to avoid waste of scarce resources.

Cool, analytical negotiating and record-keeping skills are required at all levels in administration.

Selling

Figure 46 shows how it is that customers of the business are unlikely to be the ultimate consumers of the product. Thus customers may be wholesalers, national retailers, mail order or in the case of drinks manufacturers, off sales, on sales, or any other customer who purchases product or services to resell to the ultimate consumer. In this case it is necessary for the sales function to develop a discount structure that makes the price of products attractive to a customer who wishes to make a profit by selling them on.

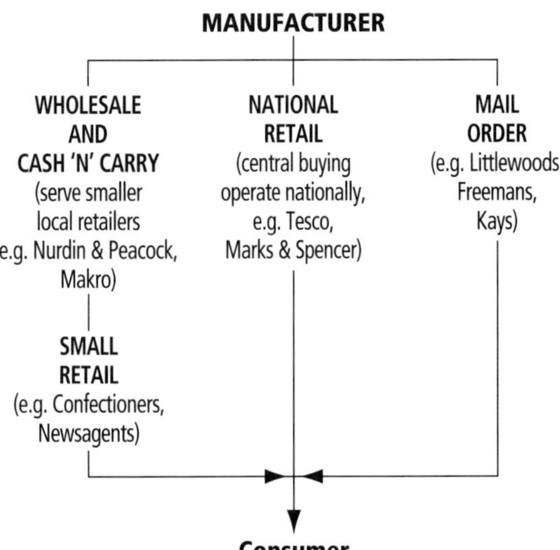

FIGURE 46 Distribution pattern for a typical manufacturer of consumer goods

The tasks involved in this essential sales function are:

1 **to identify and interest potential customers** in the company's products;
2 **to sell products and services to customers** – discount structures are often related to the quantity or value of products ordered by a customer;
3 **to introduce new and re-packaged products successfully to customers** of the business;

4 **to introduce sales promotions** and other promotional material at point of sale;
5 **to set targets for each territory** covered by the sales team, to monitor progress during the year and to take appropriate remedial action where necessary. This is a sales manager's job.

It is often thought necessary to be a good and confident talker to be successful in sales. This is quite wrong.

Successful sales people are invariably good **communicators**, but this is not the same thing at all.

The most successful sales people are those who listen well, then are able to match customer need with the product on offer. In other words, the successful sales person listens to what the customer requires, then demonstrates how selected products can match those needs.

A considerate, caring attitude is necessary to be sensitive to customer needs; however, a competitive streak is extremely desirable if the competition are consistently to be beaten and appropriate selling space to be won for the salesperson's own products.

A strong character and a degree of self reliance is essential, as it can be very tough when working alone in a sales territory and business is hard to find yet targets are relentlessly high.

Marketing Marketing is at the hub of any successful business. The marketing philosophy for commercial businesses, as indicated earlier, is to identify and satisfy consumer needs profitably.

The tasks involved are as follows.

1 **Analysis and research**
   a to identify consumer needs;
   b to monitor competitors' activities, predominantly in the areas of new product development and promotion;
   c to consider the profitability of a proposed product.
2 **New product development** which involves marketing working in conjunction with technical staff and production, while taking the responsibility of ensuring that new products meet market needs. Trade customers and end consumers must both be considered.

3 **Product re-juvenation.** This involves devising new packaging for existing products and re-formulating existing products to meet changed market needs, such as competitor innovation.
4 **Setting prices** so that the products compete effectively in the marketplace, yet generate sufficient profit for the business so that development and promotion costs are recouped in an acceptable time (often two or three years), and sufficient funds are generated for future investment in the business, for instance, in new machinery.
5 The **devising of promotion**, for instance:
   a advertising on television, posters, radio, in the press and other media;
   b sales promotions such as in-store or on-pack competitions, and the design of store mobiles and other display material;
   c public relations, including press releases, photographs, consumer competitions and giving television, radio and press interviews as required.
6 The **agreement of distribution channels** together with sales, to decide which customers should be offered the products, at what prices/discounts. Marketing is also responsible for the provision of after-sales service, including customer service and the implementation of guarantees.

The type of person involved in marketing has an all-round interest in and understanding of the major facets of business from finance (especially profit and loss) to the practical aspects of working with production, personnel and sales. Finally, the person needs to possess a commercial flair for successful design and promotion of products.

Distribution It was stated above that distribution is the responsibility of marketing. The distribution function of a business is responsible for the physical shipping of the products, the delivery of boxes of goods to the customer.

Credit control (a part of finance) then follows up to make sure that the customer pays for the goods received.

The tasks involved in distributing are:

1 to take care of products in the finished goods warehouse;
2 to know the value of goods in that warehouse at any time (stock-taking takes place at about six-month intervals);

3   to arrange with carriers or distribution companies for the despatch and transportation of finished product to the company's customers within agreed time scales;
4   to negotiate rates with parcel carriers and haulage companies. These may be based on mileage or price per packet;
5   to handle trade enquiries from company customers and, occasionally, prospective customers;
6   to obtain a signature on delivery notes (See Element 4.1, page 285), which is then returned to the distribution manager. This is usually the signal for the invoice to be sent, so it is fundamentally important to complete deliveries correctly.

The type of person who succeeds in distribution is an effective administrator with an eye for detail. Much of the company's money can be wasted through the shipping of incomplete orders, incomplete paperwork, damaged goods or poor timing.

Successful distribution is based on an ability to administer correctly the handling of many different packages going in different directions. Much of the information required is computerised, but manual intervention is also required on occasions.

Providing customer service

Many people maintain that everybody within an organisation is responsible for providing customer service.

A separate function within an organisation, however, is normally tasked with:

1   answering potential and actual customer enquiries in person, by telephone or letter;
2   responding to customer complaints through the same media;
3   responding to trade enquiries from existing customers, such as retailers;
4   responding to enquiries from potential trade customers.

Cleaning

This is an essential role for not only does it help the company conform to the requirements of the *Health and Safety at Work Act 1974,* it helps to make the whole work environment more comfortable for employees, customers and visitors alike.

The cleaning function involves:

1 sweeping floors and hoovering carpets to maintain clean floors;
2 washing down and removing dust from walls;
3 maintaining toilets to a clean standard of hygiene;
4 maintaining adequate stocks of cleaning materials and reporting faulty cleaning equipment.

Security Security personnel are required to make regular tours around the premises to watch for break-ins and other breaches of security.

Other tasks are:

1 to ensure that people entering the site are bona fide visitors;
2 to keep a record of such visitors' names, business addresses and whom they are visiting during their visit;
3 to set and monitor the effective functioning of any mechanised alarm systems;
4 to observe and check employees for any breaches of security.

Performance criterion 2.3.5 **Present results of investigation into job roles**

Activity Split into groups of three or four. Make a presentation to the whole class, describing three different job roles at different levels within the business which you have chosen to visit.

Use audio-visual and visual support where possible, including handouts and posters, possibly promotional material from your selected business.

Describe the activities that the three people perform in their jobs during a typical week. Your presentation should be supported by brief written descriptions of day-to-day activities undertaken by the three selected members of staff.

You should include details of which tasks are undertaken alone and which in teams. Find out and report how the people themselves think about individual work and working in teams.

(You should note that different people prefer different methods of working.)

The presentation should describe either how an individual, or an individual operating within a team, deals with:

a one routine problem-solving task, (e.g. how to keep sufficient stocks to meet needs) and

b one non-routine task, (e.g. dealing with an emergency) which should be illustrated with posters/signs giving instructions for an emergency such as the evacuation of a building in the event of a fire.

Your presentation should last about 30 minutes and be supported by a brief written summary for inspection by your lecturer or teacher.

Element 2.4 — Prepare for Employment or Self-employment

At some stage as they emerge into adulthood, and for a very long time thereafter, most people need to earn money to sustain themselves and dependants with food, clothing and shelter. In addition, many people are able to save the balance or spend some of it on leisure activities. In short, they have to earn a living and must either become an employee, or run their own business.

Becoming an employee is a relatively straightforward procedure of application, interview, offer and acceptance.

There are two ways for people to have their own businesses. They can **start their own**, by identifying a gap in the market, then finding a profitable way to fill it. Or, they can **buy or take over an existing business** or franchise. The skills needed to **start** a business are not the same as those required to **sustain** it.

In any event, a career is a marathon, not a sprint. A lot of hard work is required, plus the personal characteristics that will be examined later in this element.

What personal characteristics are desirable or essential to start and then run a business? What skills are involved? What does it take to be a successful employee?

Evidence indicators

- A record of interviews with people in three different types of employment, including the names of interviewees, how they came to be in their current employment, and a summary of the skills which those types of employment require.
- A summary which describes three local, national and international employment or self-employment opportunities. The summary could include job advertisements, media articles and careers information, and should include supporting information collected from relevant sources.

- A chart showing the skills needed for employment and self-employment, matched with the student's analysis of their own achievements and how they could improve and develop each skill.
- A record of a discussion of the student's strengths and weaknesses in relation to skills for employment or self-employment, stating when the discussion took place, who was involved and summarising the content of the discussion.

Core skills

This element can give students the opportunity to demonstrate all 11 elements of the three core skills. This is an integral part of the programme to identify individual strengths and weaknesses. For this reason it is recommended that 'calculating costs for a business plan' from Core skills – Application of Number, pages 337–340 be introduced into this element.

If it is found that the demonstration of some skills in this context becomes a hindrance to understanding and successfully completing the mandatory unit activities in this element then simply omit whichever core skill activity is involved (e.g. Information Technology). There are many other opportunities to demonstrate core skills in other elements.

Application of number
Element   2.1 Collect and record data

2.2 Tackle problems

2.3 Interpret and present data

Communication
Element   2.1 Take part in discussions

2.2 Produce written material

2.3 Use images

2.4 Read and respond to written materials

Information technology
Element   2.1 Prepare information

2.2 Process information

2.3 Present information

2.4 Evaluate the use of information technology

 **Performance criterion**

2.4.1 Identify types of employment and self-employment

Types of employment

There are many different ways of earning a living. Paid employment comes in different shapes and forms.

The public sector
Working in the public sector means working for a local authority, the Civil Service or a nationalised industry – perhaps the police force, a hospital, the armed forces, the Inland Revenue collecting income tax or working in a county council.

It used to be said that working in the **public sector** offered greater **job security** than employment in the **private sector.**

Whilst this may still be broadly true, even in the public sector redundancy and job loss is becoming an increasingly common occurrence. However, in return for the relatively more secure employment in the public sector, people are generally paid less, with fewer benefits such as company cars and private health insurance, than is the case in the private sector.

The private sector
As was seen earlier, this embraces just about everything else, from a large public limited company such as Cadbury plc to a small, local builder.

Voluntary work
This type of work exists in both public and private sectors and involves any kind of unpaid activity – from serving meals to the elderly, sorting out patients' files in the local hospital, to auditing the financial accounts of the local branch of the RSPCA.

Self-employment

Starting and running a business can take several different forms, as we saw in Element 1.1.

The family business

'Brown & Daughter – Butcher' – this is a family business proclaims the shop sign proudly and many people will recognise such a business that is handed down from parents to children. Relatives of Sir John Moores, the founder of Littlewoods football pools to mail order company, are today still actively running this exceptionally successful family business started in the early years of this century.

The Cadbury and Sainsbury families still hold senior positions in these well-known confectionery and grocery businesses. Most family businesses are, however, more modest and the successful transfer of a family business from parents to children is an effective way to pass wealth from one generation to another, as well as providing employment and real career opportunity.

The Yorkshire adage should be noted in this context: 'clogs to clogs in three generations'.

The first generation is founded by the starving person with no money (and only wooden clogs to wear) who starts a business, works extremely hard and makes it thrive, providing a comfortable livelihood for the family. The next generation takes over, but the younger ones are not so hungry, do not work as hard as the founder; the business starts to falter, although still generating a fair living for the family.

The grandchildren continue to live off the money in the declining business and, because they have no concept of the hard work involved in avoiding failure, when the once flourishing business transfers to them, it is a shadow of its previous success. It continues to suffer under their mismanagement, ultimately falls apart and the third generation is left in the same penniless state as the grandparents were when they started.

Government enterprise scheme

Recognising the difficulties facing somebody starting their own business, the government does give some small assistance.

The Government Enterprise Scheme was introduced so that the initiative of budding entrepreneurs was not discouraged by lack of opportunity to claim life-maintaining unemployment benefits.

The scheme provides participants with an allowance of about £40 per week and it is payable for the first 12 months of trading.

The effect that it has on businesses is to give £2,000 income for the first year, which can have a significant effect on early profitability, considering the start-up costs and inevitably lower level of trading in the early stages.

In addition, schedule 'D' income tax is not payable until the first trading year is complete, so demand for payments is eased further. The idea is to give a new business the best possible opportunity to establish itself. Taxes are therefore paid when the business grows and the returns are higher.

Partnership and franchise

The advantages and disadvantages of a partnership and franchise were considered in detail in Element 1.1 on pages 28 and 30–31. Both reduce the element of risk in starting a business, but neither guarantees success.

A sound piece of advice to those considering self-employment was given by Jack Cohen, who built the Tesco business from very humble beginnings. On his tie-pin was engraved the initials YCDBSOYA – you cannot do business sitting on your backside – it is *essential* to put in a lot of hard work.

Performance criterion

2.4.2 Identify opportunities for employment or self-employment

Market and catchment areas

At all stages from conception, it is necessary to recognise where the market is located, and how large it is. This was considered in Element 1.2, page 51.

Some businesses, such as a newsagent, have a relatively small **catchment area**. In other words, their customers do not come from far away. However, since many people are customers for confectionery, **tobacco** products and **newspapers**, (often abbreviated to **ctn** in marketing publications) there is enough trade to sustain the business from such a relatively small area.

More specialised businesses usually operate over a larger area. The customers for a shop selling fishing tackle may travel several miles for service, especially if the service is reliable.

Some operations, such as theatres, are regional and tend to be situated in large towns and cities throughout the country.

It will be seen that other businesses such as Debenhams, Argos and Vauxhall operate nationally and internationally, but have many outlets for their products.

Great Ormond Street Hospital in London offers medical services for children that do not exist anywhere else in the UK. Children with certain illnesses therefore have to travel to London for treatment, so that the hospital's catchment area is the whole of the country and sometimes abroad.

Advertising agencies and record companies operate internationally, but only have perhaps one or two offices in any one country because of the nature and demands of the business.

Activity

In groups of three or four, identify examples of businesses that are:

a local to your area;
b local to your region (perhaps located in the nearest large town or city);
c operating nationally so that some people have to travel many miles if they require that product or service;
d operating on a European scale;
e operating internationally.

Performance criterion

2.4.3 Select information from relevant sources which applies to identified employment opportunities

Sources of information for the employee

Employment opportunities are advertised in various places.

Job centres
Job centres are a good starting point. They have details of employment vacancies; in addition, they are staffed by people trained to support job hunters and to keep informed of local opportunities.

Careers offices
Referral to careers offices, which tend to exist in larger towns and cities, can be made through a job centre. On file they

have details of professional and executive positions, as well as a database of employers in the region.

Employment agencies

Employment agencies are usually privately run and are hired by the recruiting company to shortlist suitable candidates for a specific vacancy that exists within their organisation. The recruiting company interviews the shortlisted candidates and pays the agency when the position is successfully filled.

The media

Newspapers, specialist magazines, television, teletext and radio all carry advertisements for career opportunities. From a vacancy for a car park attendant which may be advertised in the local paper, to a chief executive for an oil company in Saudi Arabia, which may well be advertised in the quality Sunday newspapers, such media carry an abundance of general and specialist opportunities.

Sources of information for the self-employed

The vast majority of the input and thought for the self-employed has to come from the person or people concerned, if the business is to succeed.

However, advice and information is usually worth listening to and its value considered to the fledgling business.

It should be borne in mind that any employee of an organisation is somebody who, for whatever reason, has chosen not to start his or her own business, so inevitably any advice that they may give will be limited to the extent of their training and outlook.

The most valuable use of such sources of information is the information – the facts, rather than the opinions – that such people can offer.

The Federation of Small Businesses

The Federation of Small Businesses is based in London and has 50,000 members. Through its publication *First Voice,* press releases and personal contact, it seeks to ensure that the opinions, problems and needs of owners of small businesses are heard and understood in government, the Civil Service and other relevant arenas.

Chambers of Commerce

These are local organisations, set up as a forum for local business people to meet and address issues that affect them.

In this way, a chamber of commerce allows local traders to work together, for example with the local police against shoplifters and other criminals.

Another example of their co-operation is in negotiations with the local councils over parking regulations and restrictions in a town.

Banks

Despite their efforts to woo small businesses, banks themselves are businesses and exist to make profits for their shareholders. It should be borne in mind that they will look after themselves first.

1 First, and probably most importantly, they are a source of money. It should be borne in mind that bank charges can be a very expensive drain on profits and should be avoided if possible.
   It is not without coincidence that the most successful trading nations in recent times, Japan and Germany, have a strong commercial tendency to borrow very little money from banks. Thus the relationship that exists between companies and their banks is more equally balanced.
2 The business banker should be a source of confidence and trust. If, for example, a business starts to trade with a new customer, perhaps abroad, the bank can be very helpful in ensuring that this new customer pays invoices at the correct times. In this respect, it is advisable to involve the bank at the start of the business relationship with the new customer.
3 They offer the opportunity to invest capital saved from previous year's profits, or capital set aside to pay tax demands from both Customs and Excise and the Inland Revenue.
4 They deal in foreign currencies, and can therefore arrange to supply appropriate currency for overseas visits and convert payments from customers abroad into local currency.
5 They offer some peripheral financial services of mixed quality, such as insurance policies and small business advice. It is always advisable to check these services against others for quality and value for money.

Training and enterprise councils (TECs)

These are regional organisations which were set up in the late 1980s, to identify the need and arrange for the supply of training services for businesses in their region.

There are around 60 TECs in the UK, often delineated by county. The reason for this is that training needs tend to differ between areas and it was felt that regional units were the best way to handle such a situation.

TECs were established by the government, run as a joint venture between businesses and education providers.

Details are in the telephone directory and under Training and Enterprise Council in the training section of *Yellow Pages*.

Government departments

For businesses, the most relevant departments relate to the Board of Trade. These are The Department of Trade and Industry (DTI) and the Employment Department (ED).

The Department of Trade and Industry (DTI)

The DTI offers most help, for it has access to much world-wide trade information.

This includes a directory of businesses broken down by trade sector by country. If, for example, a UK business operating in the music industry seeks potential German piano dealers, the DTI has such information, which it holds on computer and, for a small fee, will generate a customised list.

Another database which the DTI holds is a directory of consultants operating in the UK, with details of their area of specialisation. In this instance, it is up to the business to agree the fee structure direct with the consultant concerned.

Frequently, the advice given in these circumstances is well considered and relevant.

The DTI is a good starting point for information. If it does not itself have access to the required information, it may well advise on a suitable alternative source.

The DTI is located regionally, with a base in most major towns and cities throughout the UK.

The Employment Department (ED)

The ED keeps a register of people who are unemployed, but seeking work, with details of their professional or trade skills.

In addition, ED job centres display vacancies locally, and for small business owners it is therefore a useful source of casual, unskilled and some skilled labour. The ED has offices in most medium and large towns and cities throughout the UK.

Voluntary Service Overseas (VSO)

This organisation recruits young people from the developed world and uses their labour to help third world countries.

Projects can vary enormously depending on the needs of the country concerned; from engineering projects to farming, to assisting in a school.

It is highly recommended for students who wish to take a year out between finishing full-time study and starting full-time employment, espccially if they are not certain which career path to pursue.

The benefit is two-fold; for the country concerned they have access to western labour and expertise, while the students are tested personally and professionally and learn much about their own abilities and character. VSO service also gives a 'breathing space' between study and work, and the opportunity to identify one's own values in life.

Citizens Advice Bureau (CAB)

One of these is situated in most UK towns and cities; it is a source of information on a range of subjects from legal matters, entitlement to centrally offered services and funds, to local tourist information.

If there is any doubt about where to go for information on anything, this should be the first port of call. Details are in the telephone directory.

Performance criterion

2.4.4 Analyse skills for employment or self-employment

There are many skills involved in running a business and, surprisingly, they are common to many businesses.

Some of these relate to **core skills**, which will be examined on page 329 onwards. Other skills may be summarised as follows.

- Organisational
- Decision making
- Problem solving
- Setting and achieving targets
- Working with others
- Working alone
- Communication
- Application of number
- Information technology
- Occupational skills particular to the type of business

Organisational skills

It is essential to prioritise time and other resources when starting or running a business so that maximum gain is achieved from the considerable effort that is involved, even if the business involves employment of or partnership with other people.

Organisational skills require clear thinking – identifying what needs to be done and making sure that the task is completed.

The resources of money, time, materials and labour can only be used once and effective organisation skills will focus on the priorities.

Organisation is required **at the start:** having first found a room, office or building in which to work it is necessary to organise the **essential** things in order to get started. This may involve arranging for a telephone to be installed, decoration, or opening a business bank account.

It may be as simple as ensuring that customers are visited at the right place, at the right time and in the appropriate manner – it still requires organisation.

In order to ensure the continued success of the business, organisational skills are required to make sure all employees are working at the right things and pulling in the same direction. If a stock room is required, organisation can save a lot of time when empty shelves need replenishing. A simple and effective system for re-ordering goods will save time and avoid embarrassing lapses which could lose future trade.

If the premises need attention, this should take place where possible outside business hours, or at least when it disturbs the business as little as possible; this requires careful organisation.

Belbin's "Completer/Finishers" (see page 141), tend to be organised themselves, and make good organisers of others as well.

Decision making

There is an art to decision making. The first decisions are not always the best, since not all facts may be to hand. Emotion, too, can play a part and a dispassionate decision is often more considered and the consequences more beneficial.

Some decisions are obviously more important than others.

It is crucial that extra time and attention is given to the more important decisions. It is equally important to persuade other people to agree and work with the results of those decisions. So employee or partner involvement at the appropriate time is also essential.

Decisions may be classified into three categories:

1 **emergency** decisions, which require clear, speedy and accurate thought;
2 **routine** decisions, where usually nothing has changed and approval is all that is required;
3 **debatable** decisions, which can be borderline decisions, or ones which affect other people. In this instance it is advisable to involve those concerned. They should be made with mature thought and approached logically.

There are five main steps involved in reaching such a decision.

1 **Fact finding**: what information is required and when.
2 **Asking other people**: people like to be involved in decisions that affect them. They also frequently make useful suggestions. Consultation pays dividends.

3 **Deciding**: identifying the options and evaluating each. At the right time, deciding which is the best. Then sticking to it!

4 **Communicating**: telling the people concerned – all together if possible. Of course, the result of confidential decisions should be given in private, such as salary increases, or positions becoming redundant. Important decisions should be confirmed in writing. The importance of sticking to a decision once made is that it may be necessary to sell the decision to those affected. This should be easier to do, if they have been involved at an earlier stage.

5 **Following it up**: this may be a matter of observing people's reactions over time, or review and discussion with those concerned.

Problem solving

Problem solving, like decision making, can be classified into three categories:

1 **logistical problems**, involving a person having to be in two or three places at the same time;

2 **resource problems**, where the best use has to be made of money, equipment, and people;

3 **unforeseen circumstances**, when something goes wrong.

Such situations need to be addressed quickly in order to avoid later, more serious, consequences.

A problem frequently has two solutions, one **long term** and one **short term**. The short-term solution is the 'quick fix' which saves the situation in question. The long-term one avoids the same situation occurring again in the future.

The steps in the problem solving process are as follows.

1 **Analysis**: to identify and isolate the real causes of the problem. This is an information gathering process and should take place objectively. When other people are involved, the discussion should be unemotional and dispassionate. Any suspicion or recrimination should be avoided.

2 **Identifying alternative courses of action – short- and long-term solutions**: each alternative should be considered for the consequences.

3 **Choosing two solutions – one for the short-term and one**

for the long-term. The short-term solution usually considers the circumstances, such as the implications, the consequences (what will happen if we do nothing?) and the timing. The long-term solution should consider the resources available.

4 **Putting both short- and long-term solutions into effect.** The short-term solution should be implemented immediately to limit the damage. If the long-term solution is more complex (as is often the case), an acceptable timescale should be agreed, then put into practice and its progress monitored.

In both cases, the people concerned should be informed when each solution is complete.

The benefit of such a systematic approach is that each problem should only occur once.

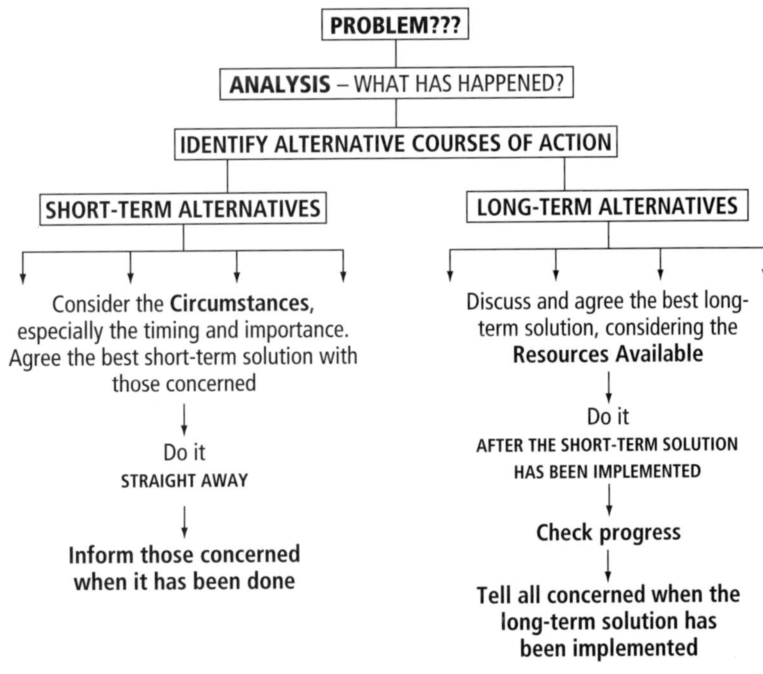

FIGURE 47 The problem solving process

Activity

Think of a problem associated with your school or college. It may be connected with the canteen, library, availability of computers, accommodation or facilities for students.

In groups, use the step by step guide described above to identify and analyse the problem. Devise alternative short- and long-term solutions.

Discuss them with your teacher or lecturer.

Choose the best short- and long-term solutions, then work out a plan to overcome the problem.

Put it into practice.

Review its success over an agreed timescale.

Setting and achieving targets

Even if there is only one person involved in the business, a plan is essential if the business is to succeed. It may be a vague sketch in the owner's mind, but some sort of plan of action is essential.

If more than one person is involved in the business, or if the owner is asking the bank (or other source of funding) for financial support, that body will almost certainly want to reassure itself that the business is well thought through and on a firm footing.

Targets are fundamental in the planning process.

A target is what the business is aiming to achieve. Targets are usually expressed in the short, medium and long term, which varies dependent upon the size and type of business.

In the record business, three weeks represent the short term, one year the long term.

In the aircraft industry, the long term may be more than ten years.

Meeting targets

A target may state the intended:

1 sales (by product units and revenue);
2 output (in product units and cost);
3 profit (by value – revenue less costs);
4 goal.

The goal may be an agreed timescale to achieve something, perhaps a factory relocation or training employees in first aid and fire prevention.

Targets should be **specific**, **quantified** and **achievable**, otherwise they act as a de-motivator for the employees struggling to achieve them.

They should state what is to be achieved, by when, the resources available for use, and who is responsible for achieving them.

For example, 'in co-operation with the local fire service, the personnel manager will ensure that all employees are trained by 31 March in the fire-evacuation procedures of the factory.'

This is a target for the personnel manager – it is **specific,** in that the subject is the fire-evacuation procedure of the factory. It is **quantified** – all employees are concerned. It is **achievable,** especially if the personnel manager concerned has been involved in setting the target.

Progress should be monitored during the period concerned, so that corrective action may be taken if necessary.

In the case of targets for the whole business, they are usually reviewed together at progress and planning meetings of directors or senior managers.

Even if targets are being met exactly, they should be analysed. The business may have changed and despite the sales revenue being on target, the source and type of business may have changed, requiring new initiatives, perhaps to develop new sources, or to re-kindle existing business which has gone off the boil.

Regular review is a good idea even for a sole trader working alone. It may be a job for a Sunday afternoon, looking at the records and analysing actual sales for the year to date (i.e. from 1 January to the present) compared to the target.

Exceeding targets

If targets are exceeded, reasons should be sought. If it is because business that was originally anticipated to come later in the year has been brought forward, then it may be possible to have a holiday at that time.

Alternatively, if the business is additional, and if it is business that is likely to recur, more staff may be required.

Missing targets

If targets are not being achieved, reasons should also be sought. Corrective action needs to be taken, such as more advertising, or reducing temporary or permanent costs dependent on the reasons for the shortfall.

Only by setting and monitoring targets can the owner know if the business is performing as planned, and that targets are being achieved. When this happens, it is frequently a cause for celebration!

Working with others

'Business is people, knowledge is power'. The importance of the first half of that expression cannot be overstressed and it explains why the subject of working with others occurs frequently throughout this book and the study programme.

Self-employed

As a self-employed person, the need to work and co-operate with others is present but the relationships are often different from those experienced as an employee.

The following are the main people with whom the self-employed person comes into contact.

Customers

With a small business, the relationship with customers can be more personal. Since a sole trader or small business may well deliver goods at very short notice to unusual sites at strange times, opportunities exist to become better acquainted with customers who appreciate the personal, high level of service, and the additional effort required to provide it.

Suppliers

Whatever the business, a new company needs suppliers for all kinds of support – stationery, printers, component suppliers, wholesalers, many of whom are also running small businesses themselves. Because of this strong common bond, a kindred feeling exists between them, and they tend to work closely together.

Neighbours

If the business is situated on an industrial estate or in a parade of shops or if it is based in the owner's home a sense of instinctive mutual understanding may well develop in a similar way to the relationship with suppliers.

Competitors

There are times when even competitors must work under the same roof, for example at trade fairs and exhibitions, or perhaps a chance meeting while visiting the same customer.

They sometimes work together to protect or further the industry which they share.

For example, rival banks sit on credit-rating panels and share information about people who have a track record of defaulting on debts.

Other competitors co-operate at trade meetings, such as 'The Fence Club' where toy manufacturers, wholesalers and large retailers meet regularly for dinner, entertainment and discussion of issues affecting them all.

The Society of Motor Traders and Manufacturers (SMMT) is a similar organisation for the car industry.

Relationships with competitors are sometimes good, sometimes bad and sometimes strained due to the tension which can exist. However, there are also many instances where competitors in business are close friends outside.

It should be borne in mind that competitors are professional people, running a business and facing the good and bad times that most people in business face at some stage. They always deserve respect and civility.

Employees

The relationship with employees is necessarily different from that with others, and aspects such as motivation, employee involvement and other aspects of personnel management have been covered in the previous three elements.

It was once said that an advantage of self-employment is a better opportunity to choose who to work with.

It follows that business owners tend to work with people with whom they get on well, which fosters the feeling of co-operation, especially when trading is difficult.

The importance of being able to work with other people professionally cannot be overstated.

Working alone

On the other hand, the successful entrepreneur who shows self reliance and independence also has a larger than normal capacity for working alone.

Working alone successfully requires self discipline, high motivation and an ability both to define goals and then take steps to achieve them.

Some tasks require the newly self-employed person to work alone.

1 Working out the financial side of the business. An accountant will advise how to set the figures out but many hours will be spent both at the outset and in daily business, in documenting income and expenses. This requires patience, attention to detail and concentrated effort if the finances are to be efficiently calculated with no wastage.
2 Writing brochures and promotional material. This, too, sometimes requires hours to be spent working out the most appropriate words, phrases and ways to describe the services on offer.
3 Travelling to visit customers and suppliers. This is the same task as that carried out by a sales employee, but there are no expense accounts to pay for cars and petrol! The approach and responsibilities require a single mindedness that will be reflected in many hours working alone.

For this reason, it is worthwhile having a permanent base for the business, even if it is shelves and a desk in the corner of the dining room of the owner's home! It is at least somewhere to be alone to concentrate on the business. As the business grows, it can move to its own office and greater things.

Communication

The ability to communicate follows from working with others. This is so important that a core skill has been devoted to it (see page 341).

Technological innovation has made so many improvements to speed, quality and cost of communication that many different means are now available:

1 in writing – reports, memos, letters, faxes and electronic mail (E-mail);

2   over the telephone – individually and through conferencing facilities;
3   visually – by satellite link;
4   through personal visits, meetings, conferences and presentations.

Before deciding which method of communication to use, it is advisable to consider the importance of the communication, how much time it will take (e.g. travel time, report writing time) and the best time of the day to do it. When other priorities are considered the method of communication may be determined by circumstances.

Application of number

This, too, is a core skill and the subject of a separate section, a testimony to its importance in business in general, and to the self-employed person in particular.

Simple arithmetic, percentages, averages and the ability to monitor performance against forecast are essential skills for any business person in order to monitor cash flow and profitability.

Information technology

This is such a fundamental part of business these days that is almost essential for everybody to have some form of IT resource to call on. This may be achieved by using the local secretarial agency – even sending and receiving faxes in this way to keep overhead costs as low as possible.

The problem with IT and the self-employed is the cost of keeping the hardware and software up to date.

It should therefore be established precisely what is needed of IT for the business; if it is a plumber, the requirement may be met in total by using the secretarial agency. If it is a professional office, desk-top publishing may be updated at sensible intervals so that documents look attractive and up-to-date.

Clearly an artwork studio needs considerable investment in IT and this must be budgeted into the costing structure from the outset and as the business develops.

Occupational skills

These are the professional skills required and the main reason for establishing the business. It is not enough to be qualified in a trade or profession, the skilled worker needs to keep up to date with developments in the trade or profession concerned. Refresher courses may need to take place from time to time; these are often arranged to take place at weekends or evenings, to minimise time spent absent from the business during normal work hours.

Business requires certain skills that are common to both employment and self-employment, since providing goods or services for other people and handling money in some way permeates paid and unpaid employment, whether in people's own businesses or when working for somebody else.

This is why the course contains the three core skills considered in the final three sections of this book.

Setting up business in self-employment

Self-employment has good and bad aspects.

The best part about self-employment is the opportunity to choose and develop a business idea, with no manager or supervisor to watch over every move.

The bad part is that the business world is unforgiving, and while the rewards may potentially be high, the wind can blow very cold when business is slack, the bills still come in, and the bank manager asks awkward questions.

Business is a jungle – competitive, tough, with danger lurking around dark corners. It is challenging, but can be immensely enjoyable and rewarding.

There are two sets of skills and personal characteristics required to become self-employed. The first set relate to **setting up** the business, when life can become almost a day to day affair. The second set start when the business is established and these skills are involved in **sustaining** it, keeping going against sometimes fierce competition, difficult trading conditions and changing technology.

Many new businesses fail, for many different reasons:

- perhaps insufficient planning took place before the business was set up;

- too much money was spent before the real financial needs of the business had been identified;
- the gap in the market was not as large as originally thought;
- competition both big and small drove out the new entrant.

Before starting out, there are some fundamental questions to ask.

1 Is there a genuine market need for the product or service in mind?
2 Is anyone else supplying it?
3 What is **unique** about the business idea?
4 If there are no competitors, why not? There may be very sound reasons why nobody else is offering that product or service; perhaps the potential is small, perhaps there are hidden snags.
5 If there are competitors, who are they? Why should the proposed new business attract customers away from the existing businesses? Are they so big that they might retaliate (by offering low prices, or poaching customers, for example) and kill the new business before it really starts?
6 How much will it cost to start?
7 How much will it cost to sustain the business?
8 Is the money available or can it be borrowed?
9 Is the market opportunity attractive enough to warrant taking the risk? Can the risk be reduced, by working in partnership with somebody or by starting on a smaller scale?
10 Is the owner prepared to work night and day to make the business work?

All these questions need to be answered before any worthwhile business can start.

Starting up
Possibly, just possibly, there is a market opportunity and the risk is worth taking. What is needed to start?

As little as possible. Many start off in a garage, a shared desk in an office, or half a shop – anywhere to keep the overhead costs low.

The only essential is customers or potential customers. All successful businesses start off with boundless enthusiasm, optimism and capacity for hard work.

If the business is retailing, the importance of choosing the right site cannot be overstated (see page 49).

Against such a background, it is essential to identify objectives and opportunities for self-employment.

It is often advisable to set the business up simply, with the minimal administration to reduce costs. It was stated earlier that a sole trader is the simplest form. Dependent on the nature of the business, a sole trader simply needs to start trading!

If more than one person is involved, the business becomes a partnership and it is essential to agree between the partners where the responsibilities lie for each partner and how costs and profits will be shared (see pages 27–28 for more details).

A start-up checklist

A person considering employment or self-employment should consider all the items on the following checklist carefully.

- What skills do I have to offer?
- How much are people prepared to pay for them?
- What does the market need?
- Is the market:
  local,
  regional,
  national or
  international?
- Who else is supplying that market?
- What is unique about what I have offer? In other words, why should people come to me rather than somebody else?
- Has anybody tried it before? Are there lessons to be learnt from that past experience?

Businesses come in all shapes and sizes. Many middle managers who were made redundant during the recession of the early 1990s set up consultancies as a result of answering such questions. Many had wide experience in different areas, such as marketing, sales, account handling (selling), accountancy, production control or purchasing, and such skills could be transferred to other disciplines.

Most consultants are sole traders, or, where a group of colleagues have set up a consultancy together, partnerships.

Sustaining a self-employed business

Not everybody needs or wants to work to be paid.

If somebody has taken early retirement, inherited or made a fortune, there may be no need for more income and a person may therefore choose to work for a voluntary organisation, purely for the satisfaction of helping people in need.

For most, however, they have no choice, since the costs of living need to be met by generating an income. Business is competitive, unrelenting, and sometimes creates unimaginable pressures. Whilst, as stated earlier, self-employment can be immensely enjoyable and rewarding, it is certainly not a soft option for the faint-hearted.

It demands certain attitudes and character.

Self-reliance

Independence of character and thought is essential. Owners of businesses will inevitably be faced with difficult problems and decisions. It is essential that the person has self-reliance to cope with them. This means the ability to assess the information available and make a considered judgement.

Circumstances will also arise where the business owner will have to play the part of an escapologist to get out of a seemingly insoluble situation!

Sometimes there is somebody with whom to discuss such situations, especially if the business is a partnership. At other times there is nobody and still the decision has to be made or the situation faced.

Self reliance is essential.

Determination

Determination to succeed is also essential.

Determination can only originate from two sources, the natural inborn characteristic and firm belief in the potential success of the business. If either is missing, the business will fail in almost all circumstances.

Such determination is essential because of all the obstacles to success and the fact that they recur throughout the life of the business, although as the business grows and strengthens it becomes relatively easier to overcome them.

Resilience

Resilience is the ability to bounce back after misfortune, or the ability to continue under every circumstance including illness. Being self-employed, especially in the early days, is unlike being in employment because there is nobody to fill in during absence; in other words, 'the buck stops here' and the sole trader, partners or owners of the business must take full responsibility for what happens – good and bad.

Resilience is vital.

Patience

Patience is not always needed to found and run a successful business.

Some businesses succeed from the start and self-reliance, determination, resilience and hard work are all that is needed.

However, few businesses trade successfully from the outset, and rarely according to plan. Even when a person buys a business as a going concern, there may well be a period of transition where customers are watching to see how the new owner continues to run the business – shop, office or agency. As the business trades, the owner is learning a lot about it and him or herself. Meanwhile, constant adjustments are necessary to take account of changes in customer needs.

The perception to recognise such changes and the ability to respond to them is essential: patience greatly increases the chances of ultimate success.

Performance criterion

2.4.5 Discuss own strengths and weaknesses in relation to skills for employment or self-employment

It will be seen from the above that the features of self-employment fall into three main areas: ability, interests, and opportunity.

1 **Ability** relates to the skills covered in an earlier section (see pages 168–178).
2 **Interests** are covered under attitudes on page 181.
3 **Opportunities** were covered in part in the opening paragraphs of this element, on page 158. The entrepreneur must be highly self-motivated and alert to market opportunities. How is this done?

There is no easy answer, otherwise everybody would be self-employed.

Activities

Consider the area where you live. What shops **and other businesses** (e.g. solicitors, builders, furniture makers, advertising agency) are there? What businesses are **not** there? This is what the instinctive marketing person describes as 'gap analysis', identifying gaps in the marketplace. Each is a hole, and one of two things can happen to anyone trying to fill it. The person will either fall in or enlarge it into a fully fledged business. The outcome rests on the three above considerations, ability, interests and opportunities, together with mature consideration of the market.

Photocopy the two lists of businesses so that all group members have a copy.

Now consider the opportunities identified. Which one, if any, appeals to you most?

Activities

You will need five blank sheets of paper.

1 On the first, write a description of your personality as if written by someone who knows you well. Use three headings:

- Abilities and skills
- Personality
- Interests

2 On the second, list the six things in life that have given you the greatest satisfaction in achieving. This should relate to commercial life if possible.

3 Underneath, write the six things in life that have caused you the greatest dissatisfaction – even embarrassment. These experiences too, should relate to commercial life as much as possible. Discuss them in groups of three; listen to each person's list and comment positively on the discussion with regard to the person concerned.

4 Consider your attitude to the list of opportunities prepared earlier. Which of these appeal to you, if any? On the third sheet, list these areas of opportunity.

5 On the fourth sheet of paper, consider what you have written above and write a brief summary headed:

   'My attitude to and suitability for employment or self-employment'.

6 Finally, consider the type of organisation in which you wish to work.

   - Large, medium or small
   - Service or manufacturing
   - Public or private sector
   - Your own business or somebody else's

When you have completed all of the activities discuss your findings with your lecturer, your personal tutor, and, if appropriate, your parents, friends and potential business partner.

Unit ③ Consumers and Customers

Introduction to the unit

The aim of this unit is to build on the knowledge and understanding gained in Unit One, Element 1.2, about business markets, competition and demand, and to develop an understanding of the significance of the individual needs and wants of consumers and customers. The student should be aware that promotional activities and customer service contribute to the marketing activities of a business.

Through this unit the students are expected to build on their personal experience as a consumer and customer to understand the effects consumers and customers have on business; the differences between consumers and customers and the vital role played by each in a modern market economy, and the way in which demand stimulates jobs to provide products and services that people and other businesses want. Students should also understand the principle of customer service underpinning the success of business organisations.

As part of their work for this unit, students should gain some practical experience of providing customer service in business organisations. This may be achieved through work experience, work shadowing, part-time employment, or through customer-focused activities based at school or college (e.g. front-of-house for a play, office services provided by the school or college, or an enterprise project). The experience should be as realistic as possible, but if necessary can be role play in a simulated situation. Students should not only practise serving customers but also examine existing customer services (e.g. local bus or train services) and suggest improvements. This work can often be undertaken with the support of the organisation whose services are under review.

Students undertaking an enterprise project could use their work as evidence towards some of the requirements of this unit.

From: *Mandatory Units for Intermediate Business*, GNVQ, May 1995

Element 3.1 Explain the Importance of Consumers and Customers

About this element

Consumers and customers have been mentioned often so far; their importance to business can hardly be exaggerated. Element 3.1 seeks to explain this, the relevance of positive customer relations and how the development of the supplier – customer relationship makes for successful market-led businesses.

Grouping customers with similar characteristics for market research and other information, is also considered, so that businesses operating in mass markets ensure their products consistently meet with consumer approval.

Evidence indicators

- A summary which describes the way in which consumers can create demand, cause changes in demand and stimulate supply for one type of good and one service.
- A summary of three changes in buying habits over the past two to three years which describes the consumers' characteristics and suggests why their buying habits may have changed.
- Three product descriptions supported by computer or manually generated graphics that illustrate past trends in demand for these products. For each product description an explanation of the factors influencing change in demand and suggestions about how consumer demand is likely to change over the next two to three years.
- Notes which explain why customers are an important source of income, repeat business and information, with examples taken from business contexts.

Core skills

This element gives students the opportunity to demonstrate these core skills:

Application of number
Element   2.1 Collect and record data

2.2 Tackle problems

2.3 Interpret and present data

Communication
Element 2.1 Take part in discussions

2.2 Produce written material

2.3 Use images

2.4 Read and respond to written materials

Information technology
Element 2.1 Prepare information

2.2 Process information

2.3 Present information

2.4 Evaluate the use of information technology

Performance criterion

3.1.1 Describe the effect of consumers on sales of goods and services

Consumers are essential in an economy: not only do they supply the labour, they also generate wealth by their demand for goods and services.

Types of consumer

There are three kinds of consumers, as Figure 48 shows:

- Individuals
- Businesses
- Governments

Individuals

Individuals work for businesses, which produce goods and services. Businesses sell these products, receiving money in exchange. With some of this money, they pay their workforce. The workforce then change roles and become consumers, using most of their earnings to pay for the goods and services they require.

Individuals buy what in marketing terms are known as **consumer goods.** Consumer goods fall into two categories.

Consumer durables are are the capital purchases made by most households – a house, a car, television and furniture. There are two major categories of consumer durables:

1 **brown goods**, so called because their cabinets used to be made of wood, such as televisions, radios and hi-fi equipment;
2 **white goods**, such as refrigerators, ovens and washing machines which are traditionally in white cases.

The second category is **fast moving consumer goods** (usually abbreviated to FMCG), which are the consumable items we buy frequently such as food and washing materials.

The services that consumers purchase also fall into two categories:

1 **essential services**, most of which are provided by the state, such as education, medical and emergency services;
2 **non-essential services** such as banking, travel agents, hotel services and car hire.

Businesses

Businesses are themselves also consumers. They use industrial goods, which fall into two categories:

1 **capital goods**, which are the major purchases that companies make, such as machinery, lorries, fork lift trucks, computers, telephone systems, specialist design

FIGURE 48 An economy has different types of consumers

GOVERNMENT
uses
- Weapons, ammunition, war vehicles for land, sea and air
- Uniforms
- Medical equipment – capital and consumable
- Educational equipment – capital and consumable
- Emergency equipment – capital and consumable
- Snow clearing
- Waste disposal equipment
- Public toilets

BUSINESSES
use
Industrial goods
- Capital goods – trucks, machinery, computers
- Consumable goods – components, stationery

INDIVIDUALS
use
Consumer goods
- Capital goods – consumer durables
- Consumable goods – fast moving consumer goods

equipment (in financial terms, these have a life longer than one year) and

2 **consumables**; these are the goods that a business buys on a day to day basis, such as paper, headed notepaper, printed paper and brochures, components to manufacture goods and replacement parts for machines.

Governments

Governments also purchase capital and consumable goods, some of which are of a very specialist nature, as Figure 48 shows.

Consumer demand

All three types of consumers listed above **create demand** in an economy. If, collectively, they do not create demand, the only way in which an economy can grow is to sell its goods and services into another economy – that is, export. Although this is theoretically possible, in practice the output of most businesses is sold into their own (domestic) economies or markets.

Thus it may be shown that demand is essential in an economy, and that consumers are the source of that demand. At the beginning of this book (on page 12), it was observed that consumers have needs and wants – and that it is **essential** to fulfil **needs, desirable** to fulfil **wants.**

In an economy, demand exists naturally from consumers; if human beings are deprived of salt, we suffer. So there is a demand for salt. If human beings are deprived of sleep, we also suffer. However, we do not need a bed on which to sleep, but it is much more conducive to sleep if we have one. So there is a demand for beds.

But let us consider this a little closer. Doctors observe that too much consumption of salt is bad for the heart. As a result, consumers demand a different kind of salt, with different ingredients that are less harmful to the heart.

So, the nature of the demand for salt changes.

Similarly, if houses are built with fewer rooms, demand will increase for beds which fold up into the wall. If demand for caravans increases, demand for bunk beds to fit them will similarly increase.

In short, demand is not constant for any type of goods. As circumstances change, so demand changes.

> The needs and wants of individuals are continually changing; this changes the demand for goods.

For different reasons, the needs and wants of governments and businesses also change.

Governments change to meet the ever-changing economic and political climate. The huge improvement of international relations with Russia has meant that in some countries there is no longer such a large requirement for armed forces, so the demand has changed for weapons and armaments.

In industry, the recession has stimulated demand for cheaper foods. Food-processing plants have had to amend their products (perhaps by cheapening the packaging and including goods of a slightly lower grade) to meet the changed demand.

The world economy exists on the concept of individuals, firms and governments demanding goods, paying for them with money in whatever currency.

Performance criterion

3.1.2 Identify and explain the buying habits of consumers with different characteristics

Central to the marketing concept is finding out consumers wants and needs, then designing products and services to meet them.

Successful businesses seek to identify their consumers closely in order to find out more precisely their wants and needs. Who are their consumers? Why do they choose a certain product in preference to another? Is it the product, the packaging, where they bought it, the price, the television commercial – all or some of these?

For example, most people need to travel; perhaps to work, school or to go out for the evening. There are many different ways to make a typical five mile journey to work: on foot or bicycle, by bus, train, moped, motorcycle or car.

People need to travel. The main determinants of the way they travel are cost, speed, comfort and personal preference.

Choosing a bicycle

Some people will cycle, simply because they enjoy cycling. If they cycle five miles to work, that is ten miles per day, 50 miles per week, 2,500 miles per year, it is logical that they are prepared to pay more for their bicycle than somebody who only uses it at weekends to travel short distances.

Furthermore, such a person may wish to purchase a cycle cape and leggings, so that the bicycle may be used throughout the year.

In other words, that person will probably buy a different bicycle and different cape and leggings than the casual week-end cyclist.

So, suppliers of cycling equipment will need to cater for the preferences of both types of cyclist – their customers.

Activity

Now let us consider the same situation from the point of view of car purchasers.

Potential customers for new and used cars have many different needs. Some live alone, are high earners, who seek to impress their friends with a high-performance sports car.

Others are in the same bracket but are uninterested in driving quickly.

Other people may have lower incomes, a young family and need plenty of space to transport the family and their belongings.

Companies provide some of their employees with a car. A junior manager has a less prestigious car than a senior director, whatever the personal needs might be of the person concerned. A nature of the company car makes a statement about the company to any other company or customers that the employee may visit.

In groups of three or four, identify the needs of 16 different types of car driver.

Identify the cars available for such people – new and used. Discuss your findings with the rest of the class.

Case study

Cadbury's 'Marvel'

Cadbury's was among the first suppliers in the UK of a milk substitute product. Before 'Marvel' was launched, the only alternative to the genuine article was condensed or evaporated milk, which, when kept in its tin, could be kept for years. In tea or coffee, however, it tasted dreadful.

'Marvel' was, as its name implied, a genuinely novel product which could not only be stored for a long time, but, by simply adding water, could be made up to a very acceptable milk substitute in tea, coffee – even on a breakfast cereal.

It was therefore a success from the moment of launch.

It inevitably attracted the interest of competitors, who took their time to develop products which were packaged in a more acceptable way for many consumers – in sachets (such as 'Coffee Mate') or in plastic bottles (such as St Ivel '5 Pints') – than the tins in which 'Marvel' was packaged. Slowly, the competitors eroded the massive market share that 'Marvel' had won for itself.

The marketing people at Cadbury's did not panic. They researched the market and discovered that 'Marvel' possessed a feature that gave it a competitive edge in a key part of the market-milk made from 'Marvel' contained less fat than any competitor's version, even less fat than milk itself!

Cadbury's recognised that the market had changed since the launch of 'Marvel' and devised new promotional and advertising material that emphasised its low calorific value. They even included a picture of a measuring tape around the circular tin.

The product was unchanged, the packaging was still the same-sized tins. It was the **promotion** that was different. This time, instead of 'Marvel' being promoted as a milk substitute – something you used when you had run out of milk - it was promoted as having less calories than milk with the result that to some people it was in fact better than milk! Sales increased once again.

The people to whom the new promotion appealed were predominantly people concerned with diet and healthy family eating – often the very people who did most of the shopping for the whole family!

There was no reduction in price, no change in the product, only a small change to the design of the packaging.

Because Cadbury's had taken the trouble to find out key information about their customers, they maintained their market share, profit margins and the product.

This illustrates the advantage of finding out as much as possible about the customers for a product – their needs, wants, age, sex, where they expect to buy certain products, how often they visit such outlets, how much they expect to pay, and the use to which they put the products.

It also demonstrated that a major competitor 'Coffee Mate', appealed to business people who preferred to offer neat sachets of milk substitute to guests in their offices and boardrooms, rather than offering them a tin or plastic bottle with a spoon stuck in it!

Activity Who do you think would find (a) sachets and (b) plastic bottles of milk substitute powder more acceptable than a tin?

To help you here are six factors which play a key part in determining the type of product that different people will choose to suit their needs:

- age
- sex
- size of family and their role within it
- stage of life that they have reached
- social and educational circumstances
- rural or urban neighbourhood and type of housing.

Performance criterion

3.1.3 Identify trends in consumer demand

> The one thing that is certain is change.

Changes in one area, such as new inventions in technology, bring about changes in the way people live and the goods and services they want.

In recent years there have been many changes to the way in which people live their lives. These have been brought about by different developments in many areas. Some examples are given below.

1 **People have fewer children** than earlier this century. If the family is smaller it means that more can be spent on each child. Toy manufacturers have therefore developed more expensive toys and a wider choice is available. There is wider availability of activity holidays and pursuits for children and young people of different ages.
2 **Wider car ownership** has caused a decline in demand for public transport. There is greater choice in individual travel, although this is increasingly limited by the ability of public authorities to keep up with increased use of the roads, and the consequent need for more, wider roads and motorways.
3 **Improvements in telecommunications** have allowed for wider ownership of telephones, which are more widely used, with more overseas phone calls (such calls have become relatively cheaper due to advances in technology). In business, this has led to general availability of faxes and international computer communications.
4 **Other advances in technology** have resulted in a wider availability of a greater range of domestic gadgetry: more labour-saving devices, such as dishwashers, washing machines, and vacuum cleaners. Less time is now spent maintaining the everyday running of a house than in previous generations, when a whole day might have been taken up with clothes washing, for example.
5 **More leisure time** due to earlier retirement and, for some people, a shorter working week, together with **higher disposable income**, has meant a growth in leisure pursuits such as golf, squash, leisure centre activities, and foreign holidays.
6 For many middle and senior managers, **an increase in**

stress levels at work – hence the need to relax more often at evenings and weekends.

7 **Greater integration with Europe** both physically (the Channel Tunnel) and economically has resulted in more travel to continental Europe. This has changed our attitude to food which is now more influenced by Italian, French, German and other countries' cuisine than it was earlier in the century.

Furthermore, there is greater business co-operation in Europe – in retailing, financial services, manufacturing. The German mail-order giant Bertelsmann bought the Yorkshire-based company Grattan; BMW bought Rover.

8 **Change in demographic structure** has increased the pressure on individuals to provide for their own old age pensions and other aspects of their welfare rather than rely on state provision.

9 **The growth in Sunday trading** has meant that shopping for groceries and DIY has become something of a leisure pursuit (look for the ice-cream vans outside the stores on a Sunday!).

10 **Growing concern for the environment** has meant that products and packaging are more environmentally sensitive, with greater use of recycled packaging, the steady increase in the sole use of unleaded petrol, and the introduction of CFC-free propellant in aerosols.

11 **Increased concern for safety** has, for instance, increased sales of cycle helmets, and made the use of seat belts compulsory in cars, while the desirability of air bags and side-impact protection in cars is constantly stressed in promotions. Cars have consequently become more expensive.

Concern for personal safety, together with an intensive promotional campaign by the Department of Transport, has caused a dramatic reduction in the numbers of people driving with excess alcohol in their blood. This reflects social change: the importance of abstaining from alcohol when driving is now far more widely accepted than it was perhaps 20 years ago. As a result, there is now a much greater demand for, and acceptance of, non-alcoholic drinks at social gatherings.

In the home, smoke alarms and fire extinguishers are more prevalent; awareness of health and safety issues in offices and factories, hotels and public places has brought about changes in equipment and the way offices are built.

12 **Concern for personal health matters** has led to a decline in smoking, lower consumption of red meat and greater

Women take over as breadwinners

by Lesley Thomas

RECORD numbers of women are taking over as the main breadwinner in their families, leaving some men depressed at the reversal of roles and others delighted at the chance to pursue alternative interests.

New research reveals that the number of women earning more than their partners has trebled in the past decade, increasing from only one in 15 in the early 1980s to one in five today.

The rise is attributed by experts to the growing success of women in securing senior jobs in the professions and the decline of the traditional male manual job It follows big improvements in the educational achievement of girls: they are now outperforming boys at almost every level, are more likely to get jobs after university and are shown by surveys to be more ambitious.

Susan Harkness, a researcher at the London School of Economics (LSE) and an author of the study, said the emergence of the female breadwinner was common in all social classes. "Not only are more professional women earning more than their partners but also the demand for male manual workers has fallen, forcing more women out to work to sustain the family income," she said.

The rising number of "kept men" has resulted in a shift in traditional family roles. Men are increasingly prepared to put their partners' careers first.

Typical is Susan Singleton, 33, a solicitor with her own practice who earns about £90,000 a year. Her husband, Martin, 39, a preparatory school teacher, brings home less than half her salary. "We always prioritised my career over his

because we always thought I would earn more than him," she said.

The couple, from Harrow in northwest London, have three children aged six, eight and 10. "If either of us was ever going to give up work we always thought it would be him," said Susan. "We were earning the same when we were first married, but within a year my salary escalated beyond his."

Martin, who teaches music and mathematics, said: "There isn't any specific demarcation of tasks, but I do most of the housework. How could I be disappointed that Susan works and earns more than me? I probably spend most of it anyway.

"I've never described myself as a new man, but I'm newer than a lot of people. I see a lot more of my children than most fathers do. A lot of people think our arrangement is a bit strange, but we're more than happy and out children are extremely well adjusted."

For others, however, the rise of the woman breadwinner is not a welcome change, Surveys suggest as many as two-thirds of women believe men are threatened by women who earn more than them, leading to tensions within relationships. Last week the Samaritans revealed that, for the first time, more men were phoning the organisation than women.

Denise Knowles, of Relate, the marriage guidance group, said there were still many men who found it difficult. "it's not always the money that they are bothered about, it's the fact that their girlfriend or wife is capable of earning as much if not more than them. It's to do with image. Their role as breadwinner is being chipped way and they have to adapt."

The biggest pressures have come in areas where men once relied on jobs in heavy industry but have now been forced into unemployment or part-time work. In some mining communities, one former pitman in five has suffered stress or a marriage break-up, according to an investigation by Derbyshire County Council.

For Jimmy Lees, 41, a former miner from Ollerton in Nottinghamshire, who has been unable to find work for 10 years, and his wife, Kate, it has meant a sea change in attitudes. The couple, who have two teenage children, now rely on her income of £120 a week as catering assistant to support the family. "In mining villages you used to expect the man to bring in the money," said Kate. "But I have to work because I'm the only one who can get a job."

Jimmy, who worked at the Bevercotes colliery, is unhappy playing the homemaker. "I do a lot of the housework, but not the ironing. It's been terrible for the kids and frustrating for me. It's just impossible to get work. I was in a job club for about five years and I was applying for 12 jobs a day. I only had two replies."

The LSE research, based on representative samples of British households, confirms the trend: over the past decade the proportion of working wives has risen from 55% to 71%, while the number of working husbands has fallen, albeit marginally, to 90%.

Sociologists believe men should be philosophical about the change. Anna Coots, social policy director at the Institute for Public Policy Research, said: "If women's success at work means that fathers spend more time with their families, it can be no bad thing."

FIGURE 49 Extract from 'The Sunday Times' 21 May, 1995

resistance to the idea of food additives due to awareness of their possible side effects.

13 **More awareness of and greater freedom to discuss sexual issues**, together with the spread of sexually transmitted diseases, has brought about wider availability of contraception. This had led to far-reaching changes in our social and family expectations of both sexes.

14 **More women work and have a career;** this has caused a change in child-bearing patterns, and in some cases brought higher disposable incomes to families in which both partners work. This situation fosters the further advances in domestic technology mentioned in number 4: there is a greater demand for sophisticated labour-saving devices for the home. There has also been a social change in the traditional role of women as childbearers; as women concentrate on their careers, some men now stay at home to care for the children. Figure 49 discusses this significant development. It may be noted that these changes have also caused major changes in legislation, such as the ability to trade legally on a Sunday and legal requirements for health and safety provisions in the workplace.

Performance criterion | **3.1.4 Produce graphics to illustrate the trends**

Activities | Figure 50 gives some statistics to illustrate the changes in demand mentioned above. Figures 51–53 give further information.

a From the information given in Figures 50–53, choose three major changes in buying habits in recent years which illustrate changed consumer characteristics.

b Write a short report to explain which of the facts in the list 1 to 14 on pages 194–197 are the main causes for these changes.

c Describe three products that have changed in recent years.

d From the information given on pages 198–201 and using IT, draw at least one each of: (a) a graph, (b) a pie chart and (c) a bar chart to clarify the figures and illustrate a change in demand.

e Describe how IT has improved the graphic representation of the above information. Which software did you use? Make a log of any errors, faults and difficulties that occurred while this task was being undertaken. Discuss them with your lecturer or teacher.

f From the evidence, and from your own research, how do you think consumer demand is likely to change for these products over the next two to three years?

	Measurement month in 1993	1989 %	1990 %	1991 %	1992 %	1993 %
Washing machine	Dec	88	89	89	90	91
Clothes dryer	Dec	44	44	43	42	41
Dishwasher	Dec	11	13	14	15	16
Gas cooker, freestanding[1]	Dec	43	43	42	41	41
Electric cooker, freestanding	Dec	37	36	37	36	36
Microwave oven	Dec	48	52	55	60	63
Refrigerator, incl. fridge/freezers	Dec	99	99	99	99	99
Separate freezer	Dec	37	38	37	38	37
Fridge freezer	Dec	49	50	52	54	55
Vacuum cleaner	Jun	98	98	97	97	97
Central heating system[1]	Mar	78	80	82	84	84
Electric space heating	Mar	51	47	43	40	40
Gas space heating[1]	Mar	44	43	41	42	42
Oil/paraffin heater	Mar	5	3	3	2	2
Water heating	Mar	99	99	99	99	99
Shower fitment	Mar	43	46	46	53	53
Colour and/or monochrome television	Dec	98	98	98	97	98
Colour television	Dec	94	94	96	97	97
Television sets, two or more	Dec	52	55	55	52	52
Video recorder	Jun	58	62	69	70	71
Kitchen gadgets						
Coffee maker		33	31	32	32	31
Deep fat fryer		34	33	35	36	35
Electric toaster		55	56	58	58	59
Food mixer		46	43	42	43	41
Sandwich maker		39	39	39	41	40
Slow cooker		21	21	21	22	21
Loft insulation	Dec	73	75	75	73	71
Cavity wall insulation	Dec	14	15	16	17	16
Double glazed windows	Dec	42	45	48	52	55
Power lawnmower, rotary		42	42	45	47	46
Power lawnmower, cylinder		20	19	18	18	17
Hand lawnmower		13	12	11	11	11
Electric hedge trimmer		15	15	16	17	18
Electric drill		54	54	55	58	58
Car, one only		44	44	45	45	–
Car, two or more		22	23	23	23	–
Car, one or more		66	67	68	68	–
Telephone		87	90	89	89	93

FIGURE 50 Changes in demand for consumer durables in the UK 1989–1993

[1] 81.0% of households had a gas meter in the first quarter of 1994.

Sources: GfK Marketing Services Ltd © except kitchen gadgets & garden tools: Target Group Index (April–March), © BMRB. Cars: Department of Transport.
Telephone: BT, ITC. The 1993 figure includes cable TV telephone lines.
Reproduced in **Marketing Pocket Book**, 1995

Kiiograms per head per annum[1] except where otherwise stated

	1980	1985	1990	1991	1992	1993
Dairy Products[2]						
Liquid wholemilk	121.22	95.74	62.62	56.22	49.86	45.21
Low fat milk	–	12.78	36.84	40.41	50.16	53.46
School & welfare milk	1.55	2.36	1.33	1.11	1.77	2.88
Condensed milk & other liquid						
milk derivatives	4.51	2.51	2.58	3.03	3.18	3.04
Dried & instant milk	4.58	4.21	3.46	3.25	3.18	3.04
Yoghurt	2.44	3.84	4.94	5.69	6.28	6.01
Cream	0.89	0.66	0.74	0.81	0.96	0.92
Butter	5.97	4.18	2.37	2.28	2.12	2.08
Cheese	5.73	5.78	5.88	6.06	5.91	5.68
Soft	0.45	0.53	0.62	0.69	0.67	0.65
Hard	4.94	4.85	4.82	4.88	4.71	4.53
Processed	0.34	0.39	0.44	0.48	0.52	0.50
Total	**146.88**	**132.06**	**120.75**	**118.85**	**123.42**	**122.32**
Eggs number	191.75	163.67	114.22	117.13	108.16	99.73
Meat & Meat Products						
Fresh meat	41.89	35.41	32.46	32.19	30.55	30.69
Beef	11.97	9.59	7.70	7.88	7.32	6.89
Lamb & mutton	6.65	4.82	4.30	4.44	3.67	3.43
Pork	6.08	5.08	4.36	4.23	3.73	4.17
Bacon & ham	6.18	5.44	4.45	4.43	4.01	4.00
Poultry	9.49	9.31	10.91	10.51	11.24	11.62
Offal	1.52	1.17	0.74	0.69	0.59	0.57
Sausages	4.79	4.39	3.55	3.95	3.20	3.14
Cooked & canned meat[3]	5.46	6.01	5.66	5.52	6.03	5.73
Frozen convenience meat	2.17	3.10	3.13	3.33	3.70	3.84
Other meat & meat products	3.93	4.00	5.36	5.72	5.91	6.41
Total	**58.25**	**52.90**	**50.16**	**50.72**	**49.38**	**49.81**
Fish & Fish Products						
Fresh fish incl. shellfish	2.17	2.06	1.94	2.03	1.82	1.92
Frozen fresh fish	0.81	0.91	0.98	0.93	0.85	0.87
Canned & bottled fish	0.94	1.04	1.50	1.56	1.66	1.56
Processed fish	1.70	1.46	1.29	1.09	1.36	1.43
Fish products	1.46	1.76	1.76	1.61	1.68	1.75
Total	**7.08**	**7.22**	**7.47**	**7.21**	**7.37**	**7.52**
Oils & Fats[4]						
Margarine	5.64	5.54	4.70	4.63	4.11	3.64
Lard & compound cooking fat	2.67	2.12	1.18	0.91	0.84	0.81
Reduced & low fat spreads	–	0.70	2.33	2.44	2.66	2.55
Other fats incl. vegetable oils	1.56	2.31	2.67	2.66	3.01	2.89
Total	**9.87**	**10.67**	**10.88**	**10.63**	**10.61**	**9.88**
Sugar & Preserves						
Sugar	16.47	12.39	8.87	8.67	8.13	7.86
Preserves	2.42	2.17	1.97	2.11	1.86	1.75
Honey syrup & treacle	0.60	0.58	0.53	0.54	0.49	0.46
Total	**19.49**	**15.15**	**11.37**	**11.32**	**10.47**	**10.06**
Potatoes & Potato Products						
Fresh potatoes	60.38	60.37	51.71	49.85	46.77	45.50
Canned potatoes	0.18	0.25	0.32	0.33	0.42	0.39
Instant potatoes	0.13	0.10	0.07	0.08	0.10	0.10
Chips excl. frozen	1.46	0.94	1.01	0.78	1.23	1.29
Frozen potato products						
incl. frozen chips	1.74	3.26	3.79	4.25	4.80	4.93
Crisps & other non-frozen						
potato products	0.99	1.50	1.81	1.89	2.18	2.30
Total	**64.89**	**66.42**	**58.71**	**57.17**	**55.49**	**54.52**

FIGURE 51
Household food and
drink consumption
in the UK 1980–1993
(continued on page
200)

	1980	1985	1990	1991	1992	1993
Other Vegetables & Vegetable Products						
Fresh vegetables	41.66	37.57	38.19	37.45	37.74	37.32
Green vegetables	18.31	14.43	14.39	13.47	13.04	12.51
Root vegetables	8.64	8.29	8.24	8.43	8.75	8.85
Other fresh vegetables	14.70	14.86	15.55	15.55	15.95	15.96
Frozen vegetables	5 04	5 54	5.83	6.11	5.52	5.65
Canned vegetables	13.09	14.20	12.47	12.63	12.62	11.73
Vegetable juice	0.21	0.28	0.30	0.33	0.41	0.44
Other vegetable products	0 50	0 75	1.46	1.61	1.87	1.97
Total	**60.51**	**58.34**	**58.25**	**58.13**	**58.16**	**57.11**
Fruit & Fruit Products						
Fresh fruit	30.68	27.31	31.36	31.74	32.22	32.10
Citrus fruits	7.76	6.01	6.89	6.89	6.77	6.31
Apples	11.57	10.22	1 0.42	9.87	9.70	9.32
Bananas	4.54	4.15	6.46	6.71	7.48	7.86
Other fresh fruit	6.81	6.94	7.59	8.27	8.27	8.61
Canned fruit	4.11	3.03	2.69	2.73	2.68	2.48
Fruit juice	4 55	7.69	10.47	13.00	11.56	12.27
Other fruit products	1.40	1.25	1.11	1.23	1.15	1.17
Total	40.74	**39.29**	**45.63**	**48.70**	**47.61**	**48.03**
Nuts & Pulses						
Nuts & nut products	0.63	0.64	0.79	0.77	0.83	0.84
Dried pulses	0.48	0.45	0.35	0.33	035	037
Total	**1.11**	**1.09**	**1.14**	**1.11**	**1.18**	**1.21**
Cereals & Cereal Products						
Flour	8.36	5.97	4.70	4.19	4.18	4.28
Bread	45.86	43.59	36.78	35.11	36.73	36.79
White bread	32.23	28.56	21.71	20.21	22.32	22.39
Brown & wholemeal	8.20	10.80	10.70	10.77	10.53	10.33
Other bread	5.43	4.23	4.37	4.12	3.88	4.07
Cakes, buns & pastries	5 50	5.62	6.05	6.73	6.84	6.98
Biscuits	7.61	7.43	7.45	7.38	7.42	7.14
Breakfast cereals	5.16	5.96	6.58	6.96	6.87	6.70
Other cereal products	9.17	8.71	10.07	11.27	11.47	11.54
Total	**81.66**	**77.28**	**71.63**	**71.64**	**73.51**	**73.43**
Beverages						
Tea	3.02	2.57	2.23	2.19	2.01	1.90
Coffee, incl. coffee essences	0.98	1.00	0.92	0.98	0.93	0.93
Instant	0.79	0.79	0.70	0.77	0.71	0.70
Bean & ground	0.16	0.20	0.21	0.20	0.21	0.23
Cocoa & drinking chocolate	0.18	0.22	0.24	0.21	0.18	0.15
Branded food drinks	0.24	0.20	0.23	0.31	0.34	0.36
Total	**4.42**	**3.99**	**3.62**	**3.68**	**3.46**	**3.34**
Mineral Water[2]	–	0.64	2.90	3.63	5.08	7.97
Alcoholic Drink[2,5]						
Beer	147.20	134.50	135.70	130.90	126.80	123.70
Cider & perry	5.07	6.94	7.89	7.94	9.40	9.59
Wine	10.20	13.52	15.79	15.73	16.44	17.31
Spirits, (LPA)	2.24	2.13	2.11	1.99	1.84	1.88

Notes: [1] Domestic consumption.

[2] Litres (or equivalent) per head per annum, except * foods.

[3] Includes 'Cooked & canned bacon & ham' and 'Cooked, uncanned chicken'.

[4] 'Butter' is included in 'Dairy Products'.

[5] UK data, based on population aged 15 years and over, on and off trade consumption.

Sources: NTC Research, HM Customs & Excise, NFS, SPCS.
Reproduced in **Marketing Pocket Book**, 1995

**FIGURE 51
(continued)**

(a) Volume consumption 1983 1993*

Beer	1983	1993*	Shares by type	1981 %	1993* %
m hectolitres	62.08	56.84	Bitter	44	39.3
Index	100	92	Mild	9	5.5
			Lager	32	46.3
			LPE	7	3.5
			Stout	6	5.4

Cider, perry	1983	1993*
m hectolitres	3.26	4.49
Index	100	138

Wine of fresh grape	1983	1993*	Shares by type	1982 %	1993* %
'000 hectolitres	4,810	6,962	British	10	12
Index	100	145	Imported heavy	22	4
			Imported light	68	84
			Sparkling	4	4
			Still	64	80

Wines, British	1983	1993*
'000 hectolitres	549	962
Index	100	175

Spirits	1983	1993*	Shares by type	1981/82 %	1993 %
'000 HL pure alcohol	916	868	Whisky	51	41
Index	100	95	Gin	13	12
			Vodka	13	16
			Rum	8	9
			Cognac	4	4
			Other brandy	3	5
			Others	8	13

* Year ending October.

(b) Volume shares by type of licence, 1993

	on-licence	off-licence
Beer, total	82	18
packaged	24	76
Fortified (= heavy) wines	11	89
Spirits, bottled	29	71

Source for (a) and (b): The Drinks Market Profile (the annual Off-Licence News/Stats MR review of the industry's structure and performance), published April 1994. Reproduced in **Marketing Pocket Book**, 1995

FIGURE 52 Consumption of alcoholic drinks in the UK 1983–1993

Cigarette smoking by sex in persons aged 18 and over in the UK

		1982 %	1990 %	1992 %
Men	Current cigarette smokers			
	Light (under 20 per day)	20	17	17
	Heavy (20 or more per day)	18	14	12
	Total current cigarette smokers	38	31	29
	Ex-regular cigarette smokers	30	32	32
	Never or only occasionally smoked cigarettes	32	37	38
Women	Current cigarette smokers			
	Light (under 20 per day)	22	20	19
	Heavy (20 or more per day)	11	9	9
	Total current cigarette smokers	33	29	28
	Ex-regular cigarette smokers	16	19	21
	Never or only occasionally smoked cigarettes	51	52	52

Average weekly consumption per smoker by sex — Number

	1982	1990	1992
Men	121	118	112
Women	98	97	97

FIGURE 53 Changes in smoking habits 1982–1992

Source: **Family Expenditure Survey**, 1993

Item	1971	1981	1986	1990
white sliced loaf	9 min	8 min	6 min	5 min
1 lb rump steak	56 min	60 min	46 min	40 min
500 g butter	19 min	20 min	16 min	13 min
pint of milk	5 min	4 min	4 min	3 min
12 eggs	22 min	17 min	15 min	12 min
100 g coffee	22 min	20 min	21 min	14 min
pint of beer	14 min	13 min	13 min	11 min
20 cigarettes	22 min	20 min	21 min	17 min
car road tax	40 h 31 min	27 h 11 min	25 h 39 min	17 h 55 min
colour TV licence	19 h 27 min	13 h 12 min	14 h 37 min	12 h 32 min
1 litre of petrol	8 min	8 min	6 min	5 min

FIGURE 54 Changes in the working time required to purchase every day items in the UK, 1971–1990

Source: **Family Expenditure Survey**, 1993

Performance criterion

3.1.5 Explain causes of change in consumer demand for consumer goods and services

Some of the causes of change in consumer demand were considered above. These are mainly concerned with external changes that have developed as technology and other changes have taken place.

Here are some of the major influences which cause **temporary changes** in consumer demand:

Money to spend

It was noted earlier that people are in general better off now than in previous years. Look at Figure 54, an excerpt from the Family Expenditure Survey, to see how the work time needed to pay for everyday items has changed over four sample years from 1971.

In 1971, on average, a person had to work for 40 hours and 31 minutes in order to pay the car road tax (road fund licence). This represents more than an average week's work for many people. By 1990, the amount of time had more than halved to 17 hours and 55 minutes – just over two day's work. It may be seen that the real cost of a road fund licence has consistently reduced since 1971.

This trend is equally true, if less dramatic, with other products. It now takes an average of only three minutes to earn enough money to buy a pint of milk – in 1971 the average person had to work for five minutes; real incomes have increased, and we are now able to buy more in real terms than was possible just over 20 years ago with the average wage.

Confidence to spend

Confidence plays a great part in an economy. Sometimes, even though people and businesses have sufficient money to make purchases, they choose not to. If a person is afraid of losing his or her job, then the likelihood that he or she will spend a lot of money on new items – especially luxury items – diminishes.

Similarly, if companies are uncertain whether sales will maintain their current level, they are less likely to buy new equipment and machinery. In short, they lack confidence.

Confidence enables consumers and businesses to continue their business or lifestyle secure in the knowledge that their income or revenue will continue at a comparable level for the foreseeable future.

In the early 1990s, when recession and unemployment prevailed, confidence was low. Despite the fact that people had money for purchases, lack of consumer confidence meant that they chose to save it. Spending was greatly reduced, causing many retailers to go out of business.

Cost of living

The cost of living is the amount of money required to provide the basic necessities and expectations of living; it includes the cost of housing, clothes, food, motoring, most needs and some wants.

It is measured by finding out the prices of the same items all over the country at regular intervals and using these figures to calculate an average person's expenditure on basics on one given date. This is known as the **Retail Price Index**.

We have seen in Figure 54 opposite how the cost of living has fallen in real terms since 1971.

Clearly, the cost of living for individual families depends on their circumstances; for example, whether they have a high mortgage and other borrowings. If they have a large house the council tax, gas and electricity charges are likely to be higher than average.

A change to rates of income tax will affect different people according to their income.

All these factors, however, influence the cost of living.

Changing needs, changing wants

Needs and wants change for two reasons:

1 **People get older.** Hearing aids and zimmer frames are generally of greater interest to senior citizens than to teenagers.
Teenagers and young people tend to buy goods such as CDs and fashionable clothes. As people take on the responsibilities of a family, however, purchases tend to extend to include products which are an investment in the future, such as life assurance, pension contributions and furniture. Tastes in clothes and entertainment often change.
2 As the world around us changes, so **opportunities change** and awareness grows of different lifestyles that exist in different countries.

In the 1920s, foreign holidays were more or less limited to France, and that then only for the very rich. In the 1960s, however, the concept of the package holiday made Spain affordable for a far greater number of people.

Nowadays, holidays in America, Australia and other non-European countries are chosen by many people.

As prices decrease, products containing relatively sophisticated technology become quite commonplace – telephone answering machines, camcorders and home computers are examples.

When people become aware of the existence of such items, their list of wants changes, since humans are by nature acquisitive.

Peoples' needs change also. When public transport services had greater coverage of rural areas, people who lived in the country could travel by bus to neighbouring towns.

Nowadays, such public transport services have diminished and for people who live in the country a car is a necessity. Where people once needed a bus, they now need a car instead because expectations of convenience in transport have changed.

 **Performance criterion**

3.1.6 Explain and give examples of the importance of customers to business organisations

> Sir John Egan, a major British industrialist who is currently Chairman of British Airports Authority plc, once said;
>
> 'Business is about making money from satisfied customers. Without satisfied customers, there can be no future for any commercial organisation.'
>
> This is probably the most important sentence in the book.

Dissatisfied customers

Without customers, it is impossible to have a business. Dissatisfied customers tell their friends about their dissatisfaction. Dissatisfied customers reduce morale in the business concerned.

Dissatisfied customers mean that the business must constantly find new customers for its goods or services. They are then 'stitched up' or 'ripped off' in some way, before they go away, having been relieved of as much money as possible. They tell their friends, relatives, television watchdogs, the press, of their experience, so that people soon keep away from that business.

In the short term, the business may trade very profitably. In the long term such a strategy is disastrous, since finding new customers is very expensive – it requires constant promotion, advertising and aggressive selling.

There are enough badly-run double-glazing, timeshare and refitted kitchen businesses who bear witness to this fact of business life; such a commercial approach is very short term, since it is a very expensive exercise to keep finding new customers.

Satisfied customers

By contrast, the recommendation of existing satisfied customers may not be so thrilling, but it is a very cost effective way to build a business. Existing customers recommend good suppliers to their colleagues, friends and relatives.

This establishment of trust, goodwill and confidence between supplier and customer means that satisfied customers return at a later date to make further purchases. The success of the major supermarket chains and other large brands – retailers and manufacturers – provides ample evidence of the truth of this statement.

The failure of businesses which have ignored this essential business practice – for instance the decay of the UK motor cycle and car industries in the 1960s – is a sad reminder of its importance. The product was not what the public wanted; after-sales service was lacking and the 'take it or leave it' attitude meant that many potential customers chose to leave it when the more attractive, market-led Japanese and European products became available.

We have already observed how customers are not solely individuals; they may also be companies or governments. Whatever the business, the same applies. Satisfied customers – individuals, other businesses or governments – are absolutely essential to business success.

Activities   Split into groups of maximum four, minimum three students.

1   You are asked to find out the buying habits of one of these:

    a   the purchasers of an economy range of foods in a large supermarket chain near where you live;
    b   users of fast-food outlets such as MacDonalds;
    c   purchasers of CDs and cassettes in general;
    d   purchasers of CDs and cassettes of a particular act or artist;
    e   holidays in Florida or Australia.

(Note to lecturers: ensure that as many topics are covered as possible, so that the results may be compared and contrasted.)

Devise a market research project to determine how attitudes have changed in the past 12 months, compared to five years ago.

Present your findings to all the students. It should include your analysis of why you think sales patterns have changed in the past five years.

Your presentation should be supported by computer or manually generated graphics to illustrate buying habits and trends.

In a report:

a explain what led you to collect the data in the way you chose;
b explain the method you chose to collect the data (i.e. whether you chose telephone questioning, leaflet questionnaire or personal interview) and why;
c explain how you decided to record the data.

Include in your portfolio the rough mathematical calculations that led you to draw your charts in the way you did.

All students should now collect their individual presentations together, to provide each with a comprehensive record of changing purchasing habits, consumer attitudes and the importance of satisfied customers to business success.

2 Look again at Figure 54 on page 202.

Draw a bar chart to illustrate how long it took to earn all the items which could be earned in less than one hour in 1990.

Now do the same for 1971, superimposing the results on the same diagram, to highlight the differences.

Using the diagrams, identify the main differences between the two years in terms of time taken to earn the different items.

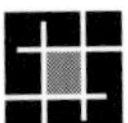

Element 3.2 Plan, Design and Produce Promotional Material

In the last element, mention was made of businesses promoting their products in certain ways.

This element examines the different ways in which manufacturers and service providers make their customers aware of the products they have to offer.

Evidence indicators

- Examples of three types of promotion to include sponsorship and an advertisement. The examples should describe the product being promoted, the content of the promotion and the constraints on the content in terms of the *Consumer Protection Act* and Advertising Standards Authority.
- A plan which explains the purpose of the selected promotional materials and estimates the time, people, materials, equipment and costs to produce those materials.
- Promotional materials for one product which either advertise the product, outline a sponsorship scheme or detail a competition to promote goods or services (services could be an event). The promotional material could include: poster, leaflet, video and audio-tape, and the student could produce computer-generated material.
- Summary notes evaluating the success of the promotional materials in terms of achieving the stated purpose and the response of the targeted audience.

Core skills

This element gives students the opportunity to demonstrate these core skills:

Application of number
Element   2.1 Collect and record data

          2.3 Interpret and present data

Communication
Element   2.2 Produce written material

2.4 Read and respond to written materials

Information technology
Element   2.1 Prepare information

 **Performance criterion**

3.2.1 Identify and give examples of types of promotions used in marketing goods and services

Promotional material is all around. Its purpose is to **inform** potential customers of one or more of the following aspects of a business's activities.

1   The **benefits** of using a particular product or service; perhaps a new or existing one, or a changed version of a known item.
2   A change in **price**: this may be permanent or temporary.
3   The **availability** of a product or service: where and how it may be acquired.
4   The scope of a large corporation, or the benefits associated with a particular brand or group of brands.

Any of these promotions can be achieved in many different ways. If, for example, somebody has a bicycle to sell, the person may write out the details on a post card, and place it in the nearest newsagent's window. Alternatively, a small advertisement may be placed in the local paper.

Both of these are examples of promotions. Somebody wants to sell something, and informs potential buyers of the benefits of purchasing it.

The person doing the selling chooses the place most likely to be seen by people who may be interested in buying, having considered the price of alternative outlets for the information.

Types of promotions

Point-of-sale
Promotions that take place at point-of-sale are those that advertise the product *at the place where it can be purchased.*

Manufacturers of cosmetics and feminine fragrances are amongst the most frequent users of this method, since the final decision which perfume or nail varnish (for example) to purchase is not made until the customer is actually in the store and standing at the display.

Furthermore, at this point the customer has the opportunity to try out the product, then make the purchase knowing for certain that it is the right one for the particular occasion.

A new product launch, especially where a television and press campaign is involved, is frequently supported by quite lavish point of sale display materials so that the new product can stand out in the store.

This is essential since the newcomer has to establish itself beside strong competition – existing products are already favourites, tried and trusted by their customers.

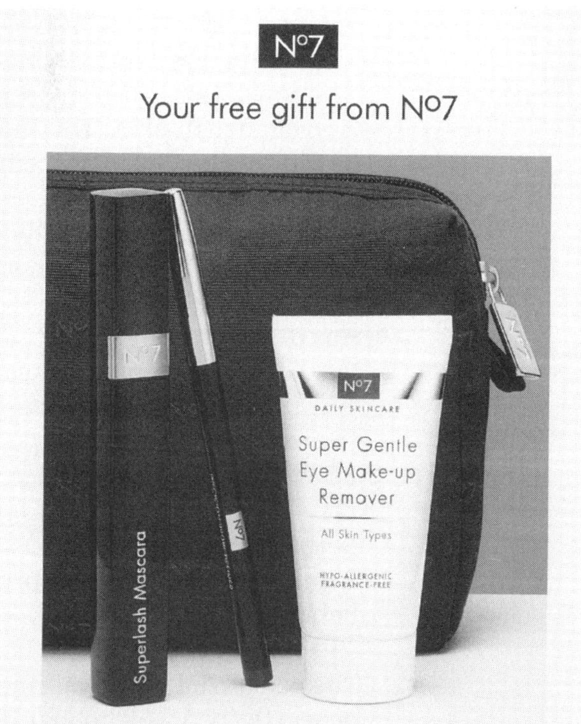

FIGURE 55 A point of sale advertisement for cosmetics

Advertisements

Advertisements can be made in many different ways and use many different outlets, varying from internationally distributed magazines to the local paper. These outlets are called collectively media (the plural of medium).

The advertisement may be associated with a brand name, a colour (such as the Cadbury's milk chocolate mauve or the Coca-Cola red, both of which are instantly associated with their products by many purchasers), an activity (such as a new

FIGURE 56 Coca-Cola advertisements have a consistent approach that purchasers immediately associate with the product

Coca-Cola, Coke and the contour bottle are registered trade marks of the Coca-Cola Company

board game or the reduced effort required when using a new floor cleaner, for example), sound, music, static or moving pictures.

The choice of medium depends on the nature of the message that is to be conveyed and to whom the advertiser wishes to convey it.

Simplicity is the key to successful advertising, so that the message is received and understood by as many people as possible in the market for whom it is intended.

There are many different media available for advertising. Each has different features, hence specific advantages and disadvantages. Each therefore, is particularly suitable for different occasions.

Posters
Although many are static, there are also many types of moving-poster sites. These are on buses, taxis, supermarket trolleys; even hoardings can rotate to carry more than one advertisement.

Posters cover virtually the whole country and exist in all kinds of forms: milk bottles, hot-air balloons and even T-shirts can act like a poster to convey a message! Posters always use large, bold print to fit the space available – small print with a lot of copy would be largely ignored by the target audience.

By contrast, large, bold print is noticed.

Most outdoor poster sites in the country are managed by three or four companies.

Radio

Radio reaches an increasing number of the population, but tends to concentrate its activities on the larger cities and towns. In addition to the regional ILR (independent local radio) stations, there are also national commercial radio stations such as Classic FM and Virgin Radio, as well as community radio stations for minority interest groups.

Radio advertisements clearly have to rely on spoken words, music and sounds to make their message memorable. The advantage of radio is that many people listen all day as an accompaniment to their work.

The main disadvantage of radio advertisements is that they generally need to be heard several times by their target audience before much impact is made.

Newspapers

There are many different types of newspapers and this medium is almost universal in its appeal.

Newspapers may be national (such as *The Daily Express*), regional (such as *The Birmingham Post*) or local (such as *The Hampstead & Highgate Herald*). They may be distributed free of charge, or paid for. They may appear daily – every morning or evening, weekly, or occasionally (such as a special edition). Furthermore, they may be small (tabloid) or large (broadsheet). Parts may be in full colour, others partly (e.g. spot colour), others in monochrome.

The advertising is possibly even more diverse and covers a very wide range of needs.

Newspaper advertising may cost as little as four or five pounds for a classified advertisement (so called because they are classified under their different headings, such as advertisements by builders and other trades people, items for sale, holiday lettings and so on). Alternatively, a national manufacturer or retailer may take a full page in colour in 'The Daily Telegraph' for around £45,000.

Magazines

These fall into two categories, consumer and trade.

Consumer magazines cover virtually everything from trout fishing to economics, personal finance to knitting. One of the greatest assets they offer to advertisers is precise targeting of their markets.

Trade magazines exist for almost all trades and professions: farming, toy manufacturing and retailing, the motor trade, accountancy and electronics, for example.

Trade magazine advertising can be an effective means of one-way communication with a company's customers.

They are excellent for speaking to specific audiences, such as grocers or printers. They are likely to be interested in the information and so considerable detail can be incorporated in advertisements.

A very cost-effective way of advertising in trade magazines is to have four pages printed and stitched into the middle of the magazine. This avoids paying their page costs – the advertiser supplies the four pages – as only the relatively low additional production costs are charged and the insert can be made to look very much like part of the magazine's editorial.

Television

Until quite recently, television could almost guarantee a huge audience every evening. Although greater use of video recorders, satellite and cable broadcasting has diluted its effect somewhat in recent years, it is still a very powerful medium in terms of audience reach.

The ITV and Channel Four stations cover virtually the whole country and both are watched by millions of people every day.

Features of television are moving images, colour and sound, with very wide audience reach.

Television can be geographically selective (such as the HTV region) and selective by time – for example, children can be targeted while they watch earlier in the evening, adults later at night.

Since it is expensive (Kellogg's spent over £59 million on television advertising in 1993 (source: Marketing Pocket Book, 1995), television is only appropriate for mass-market products, but for them it is ideally suited.

Sponsorship

Sponsorship can take a wide variety of forms. Perhaps the best known is the sponsoring of television programmes, such as Inspector Morse or the weather forecast; and sports events, like the Littlewoods FA Cup or a motor racing team such as that sponsored by Benetton.

Sponsorship also embraces charities: a company may donate a sum of money to a charitable event, which is acknowledged perhaps by giving the company's products some advertising space in the programme for that event. The charities involved can be of national importance and thus offer opportunities for national promotions. Local issues can also be an effective vehicle for smaller business promotions: a local supplier might sponsor a fun-run or other charitable event in return for some publicity or simply to foster the image of the business as one with a positive interest in local affairs.

Sponsorship tends to be most effective when a known brand or product is involved because space on which to advertise is often very restricted. In this case the brand name is used boldly and repetitively; certainly there is scant opportunity for taking in product details on a fun-run!

Some examples of current sponsorship are:

- football Premier League, sponsored by Carling Lager;
- television national weather, sponsored by PowerGen;
- television local weather, sponsored by Legal & General Insurance.

The benefits of sponsorship are various. The sponsor is often mentioned in the media – in newspaper articles, BBC and other television reporting concerning the event – in circumstances where advertising is not the primary concern and people see the company's, or product's, name associated with something they find interesting or meretricious. Some sponsorship gives the sponsoring company an opportunity for corporate hospitality: the ability to entertain important customers in style for a memorable occasion such as the Littlewoods Cup Final, or the Benson & Hedges Trophy.

This also applies to the sponsoring of an artistic event, like an opera, the Young Musician of the Year Award (sponsored by National Power), a concert or theatrical production.

A company may sponsor a sports or television personality. Whilst this has the positive effect of association with an idol of the target market, it can also have a negative side should the artist fall out of favour with the public. Pepsi-Cola withdrew the company's involvement with Michael Jackson when stories of alleged child abuse began circulating.

Competitions

Competitions can be a very effective form of promotion. They are an especially effective means of promoting a new product launch, where the features of a product can be itemised and the consumer has to rank them in order of importance; this makes entrants closely consider each feature and the benefit it gives the consumer.

Competitions are also relatively cheap to run and bring additional appeal to the medium in which they appear: more people may buy a newspaper which is carrying an interesting advertiser's competition.

Competitions must have some element of skill in them, otherwise they become a form of gambling. Thus many competitions include a so-called tie-breaker, requiring entrants to complete a sentence pertaining to the product or manufacturer.

Performance criterion

3.2.2 Describe constraints on the content of promotional materials

In general, companies wish their business and products to be perceived in a positive light and will avoid association with any controversy or apparently unfair advertising.

There is also some legislation to protect the public (and competitors) from false claims, unfair or unethical practices in advertising or publicity.

It is declared not to be in the public interest to promote certain products in certain media: tobacco companies are not allowed to promote cigarettes using television, for example. So, tobacco companies take greater advantage of those opportunities left to them in order to promote their products to the mass market, poster and magazine advertising as well as sponsorship, for example.

Legal constraints

The Trades Description Act

The main purpose of this Act is to protect consumers from traders who deliberately give a false description of their goods or services, or price.

It is enforced by trading standards officers (see below).

The Sale of Goods Act

Descriptions of goods or services must be accurate and the goods themselves must be 'of merchantable quality', that is fit for sale, unless the existence of the defects are clearly displayed; for example 'shop soiled' goods offered in sales.

The Consumer Protection Act

This Act allows a consumer to claim for damages on behalf of anyone who suffers a personal injury or damage to property resulting from a defective product.

The onus is on the consumer to supply proof that the product or service was defective.

Once this is proven, however, the Act particularly protects consumers from faulty imported goods; previously, the consumer could be forced to sue an overseas' supplier in a foreign language, with little hope of compensation. Under this Act, the onus is on the retailer who is liable to the consumer. The retailer may subsequently sue the overseas supplier if appropriate.

In addition to legislation, there are also a number of standards set by tradition, the companies themselves, and administrative organisations, that are maintained by a number of government bodies.

The Trading Standards Office

The Trading Standards Office is part of the local authority and is staffed by officers who are there to investigate consumer and trade claims of malpractice in local businesses. If a complaint is made, the officer investigates and involves police or the legal profession as appropriate.

The trading standards officer is empowered to prosecute in cases of malpractice.

However, the office only becomes involved when requested, and does not act on its own initiative.

The Advertising Standards' Authority

Often abbreviated to the ASA, this body states that 'all advertisements should be 'legal, decent, honest and truthful'.

By keeping a keen eye on their competitors' activities, most advertisers regulate their own behaviour.

There are however, several areas of controversy, such as the content and approach of advertisements aimed at children, or promoting tobacco and alcohol products, feminine hygiene products and contraceptives. The ASA mediates between the advertiser and the public in such areas; it also controls the use of product endorsement by famous people (for example in the advertising break between a chat show personality's actual programme) and will prevent one company directly comparing its product with a named competitor, who is shown as inferior.

The ASA also assists the public should they wish to complain about an advertisement. It will investigate the complaint and make a judgement on it. If it finds that the complainant is justified, the offending advertiser may be asked to change the advertisement, or even to withdraw it altogether.

Other regulatory bodies exist to check an advertisement at draft stage (to avoid unnecessary expense for the advertiser) and approve an advertisement at most of its significant stages of preparation. The ITC is one such body.

Performance criterion

3.2.3 Plan to produce promotional materials to promote particular goods or services

Promotions need to be meticulously planned for many reasons.

1 It is vital to ensure that the production department have had a chance to manufacture sufficient stocks of the product in question, so that when it is promoted maximum advantage is taken of further orders from the retail trade.
2 Similarly, the sales people need sufficient time to visit all relevant customers to inform them about the promotion.
3 Sufficient resources must be allocated to the promotion so that it has the best possible opportunity to succeed.

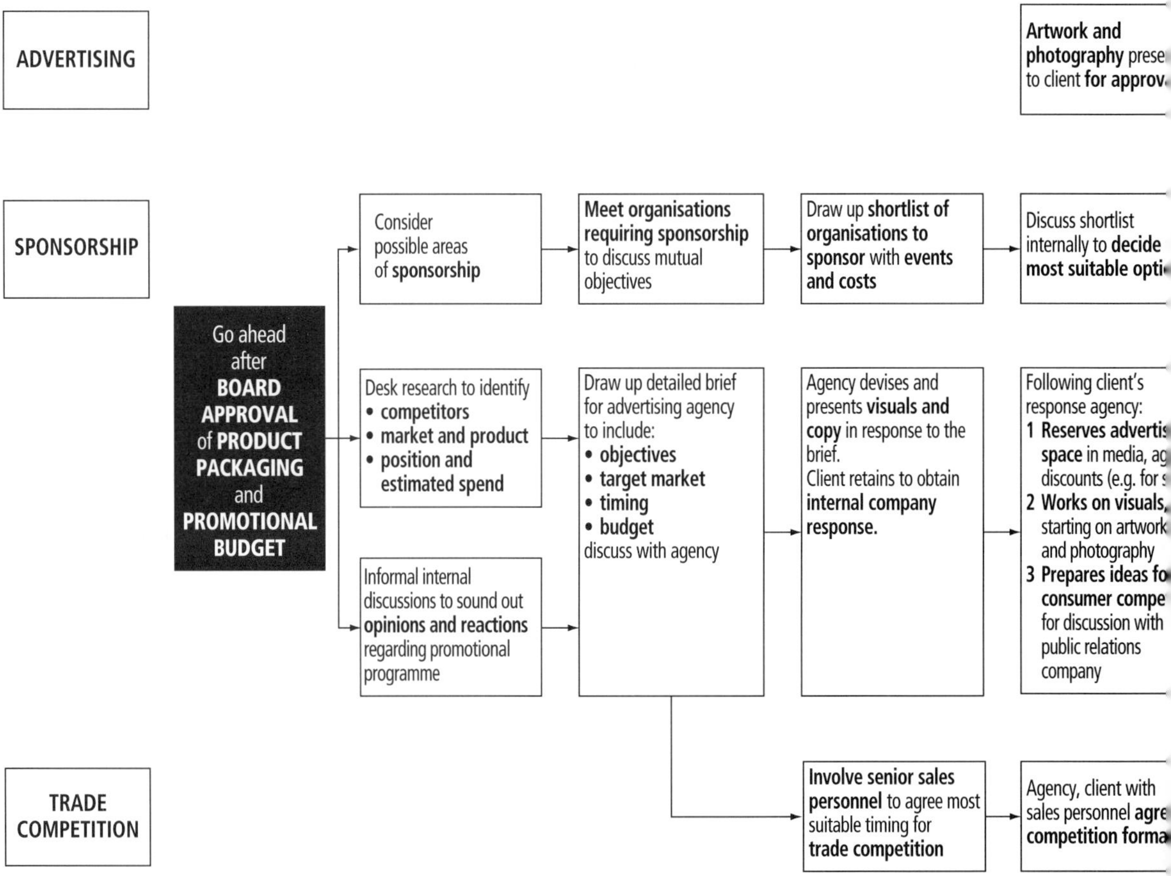

FIGURE 57 The development stages of a promotional plan

In other words, it is essential to **plan the promotion.** Figure 57 shows the stages in a promotional plan.

Planning involves allocating the correct amount of **time, the** proper materials, the right people with the appropriate skills, adequate equipment, and sufficient money – the correct budget.

An advertisement, a sponsorship arrangement and a competition are examples of promotion.

Advertising involves using the most resources, and for this reason each step is detailed in the following pages.

Advertising

Timing

Timing is vital. Commercials that promote products at Christmas are shown to the toy retail trade at toy fairs in the previous January, and to the national retailers (such as 'Toys 'Я' Us and W H Smith, Woolworth and Boots) at previews in the previous November. In order to do this, work will have started on the commercial around August, 16 months before the Christmas in question! However, the commercial can only be started when the product is fairly well developed.

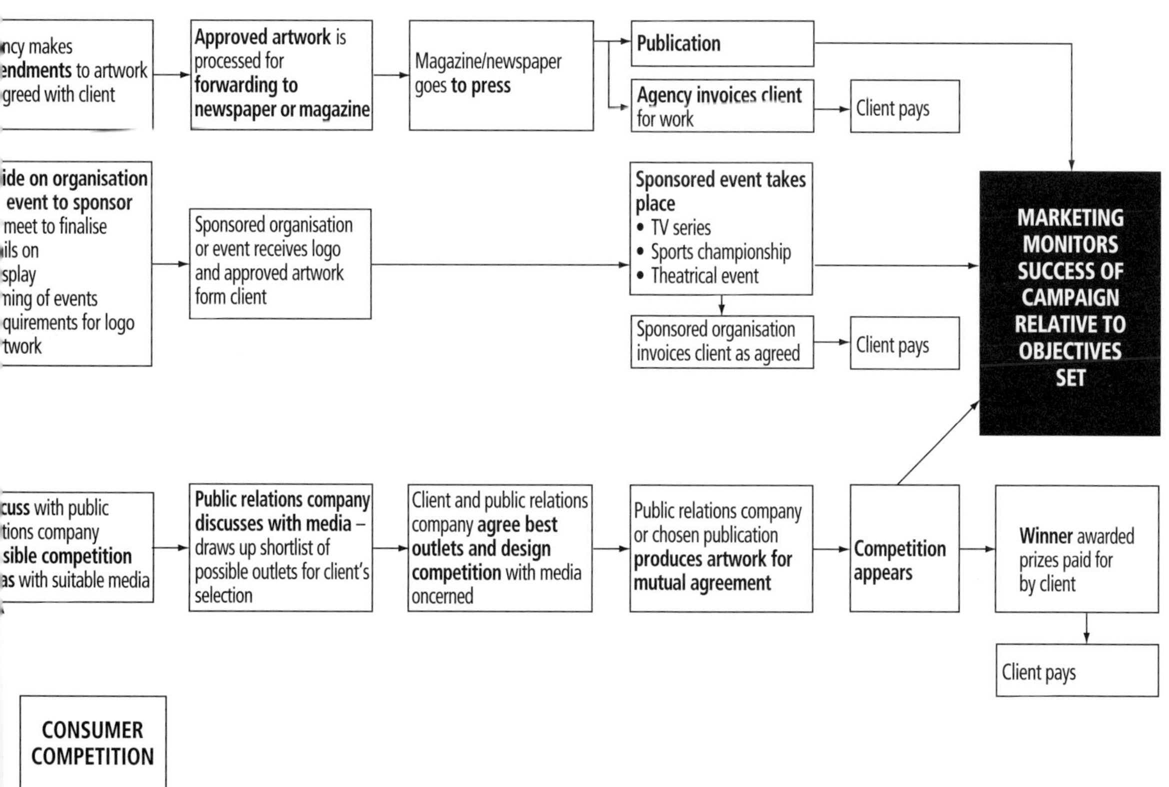

(Surprisingly, it does not necessarily need to be entirely finished, just good enough for the manufacturer to feel reassured that it is justified in spending its promotional resource on it).

The new Christmas products that appear on a television commercial in October, were therefore probably developed a full 20 months ago!

The complete timescale for an advertisement or a promotion may be summarised as follows.

1 Planning

The planning stage is when the shortlist is drawn up of products that could be selected for promotion, together with the objectives for the promotion of each product.

Once the objectives are established, a methodology can be devised to achieve them – whether television supported by press and posters, or commercial radio, for example. In the case of an industrial product, it may involve recruiting a new sales force, or booking and building a stand at an exhibition.

It is likely that outside suppliers would be used to devise and supply each promotion. In the case of press, radio, television or poster advertising, an advertising agency would probably devise and produce the advertisement, as well as reserving the media space and agreeing with the owner (the newspaper or television company) how much the space, slot or spot will cost.

At this stage, an outline budget can be considered.

A timetable can now be drawn up to identify when each stage of the promotion must be complete. This can be very complex as the launch schedule in Figure 58 illustrates. This launch was for a new range of clarinets for a musical instrument manufacturer and did not include national advertising. Nonetheless, it took over a year to implement and involved many different operations.

One of the benefits of such a planned approach is that not only can the manager concerned maintain an overview, it also allows for the early identification of any delay and allow time to develop contingency plans.

MUFFET RELAUNCH

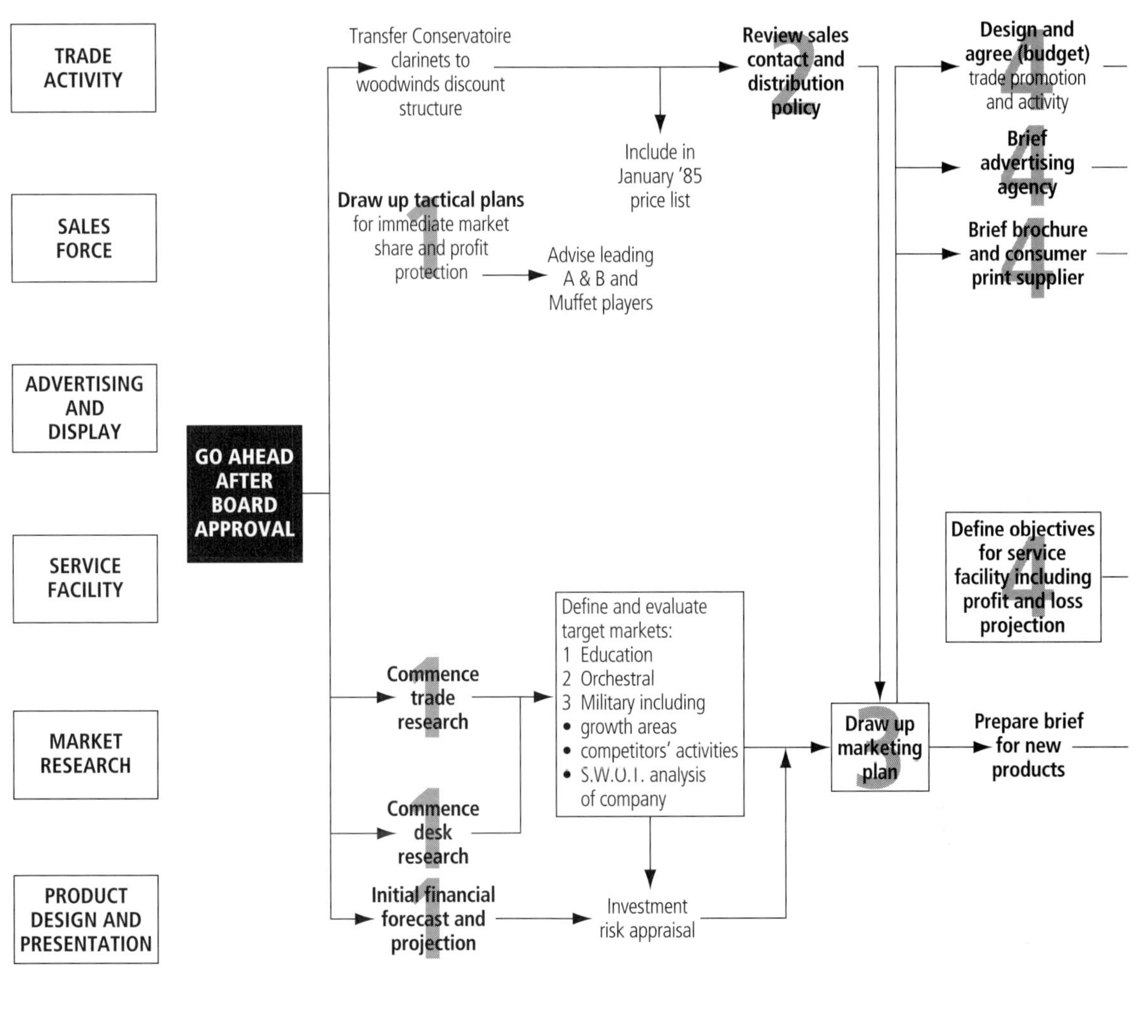

FIGURE 58 The launch of a new range of clarinets (continued on page 222)

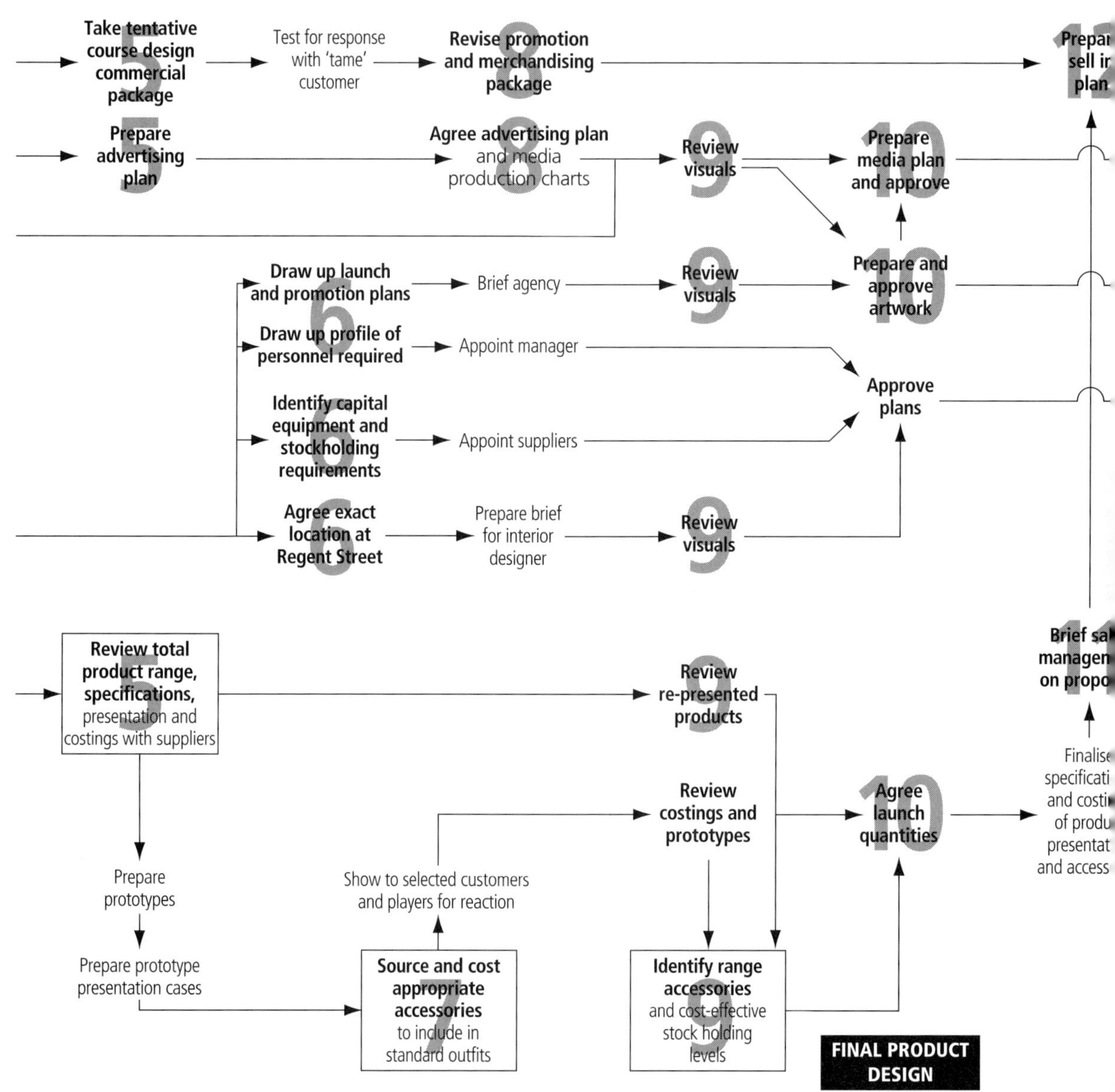

FIGURE 58 The launch of a new range of clarinets (continued from page 221)

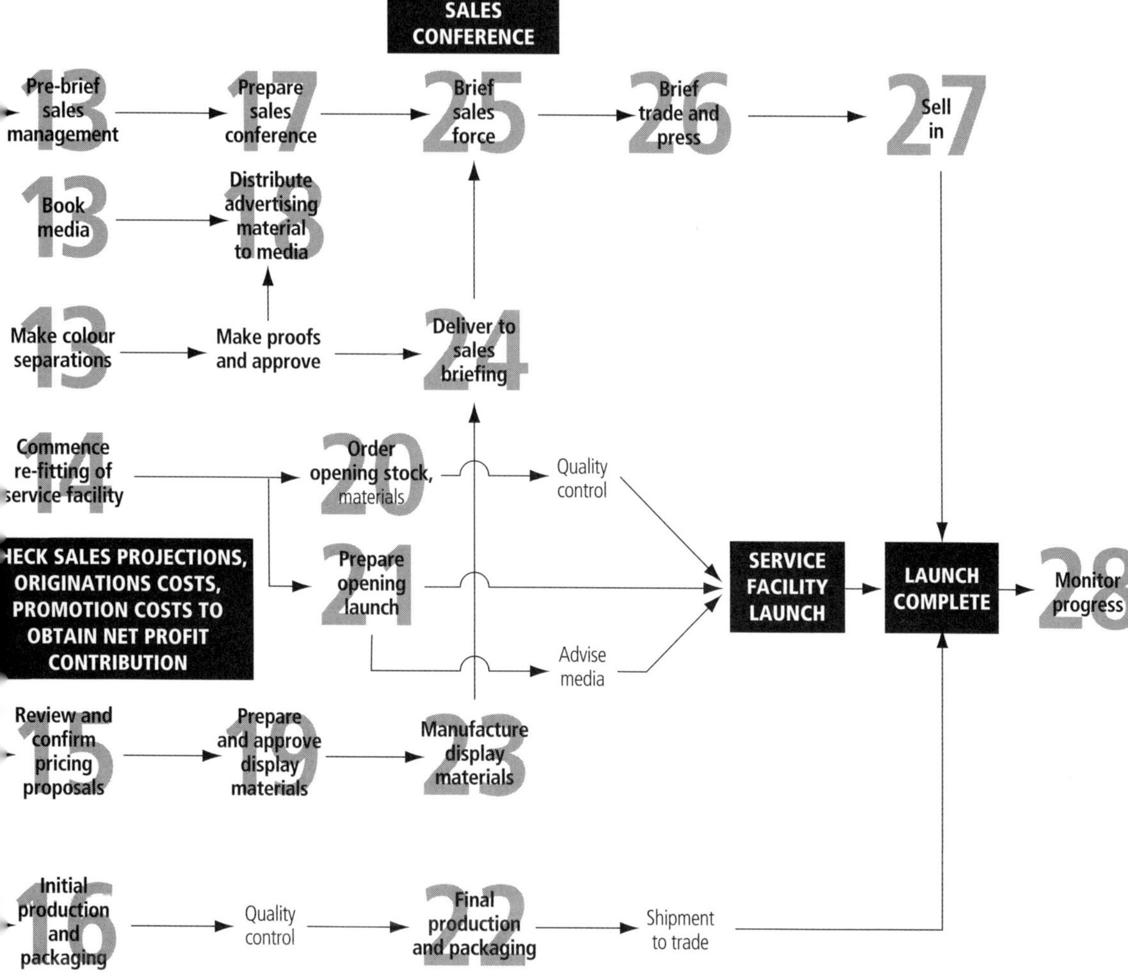
SALES CONFERENCE
Pre-brief sales management
13
Prepare sales conference
17
Brief sales force
25
Brief trade and press
26
Sell in
27
Book media
13
Distribute advertising material to media
18
Make colour separations
13
Make proofs and approve
Deliver to sales briefing
24
Commence re-fitting of service facility
14
Order opening stock, materials
20
Quality control
CHECK SALES PROJECTIONS, ORIGINATIONS COSTS, PROMOTION COSTS TO OBTAIN NET PROFIT CONTRIBUTION
Prepare opening launch
21
SERVICE FACILITY LAUNCH
LAUNCH COMPLETE
Monitor progress
28
Advise media
Review and confirm pricing proposals
15
Prepare and approve display materials
19
Manufacture display materials
23
Initial production and packaging
16
Quality control
Final production and packaging
22
Shipment to trade
MANUFACTURE STARTS

2 Production

Having decided which products to promote, the objectives for each promotion, the approximate methodology and the budget, now is the time to realise those plans.

Production is the practical process of taking the promotion objectives and coming up with advertisements which realise them. The first thing to do is to establish a theme for the whole promotion. At this point, photographers, artists, copywriters and other creative people, possibly from an advertising agency, will become involved.

Photographers take colour and monochrome prints or transparencies, using both the outdoors and the inside of a studio. Extremely specialised skills are required to photograph, for example, a plate of chicken curry for a food manufacturer. It can easily take a whole day, and the resulting picture must look as if the food has just been freshly prepared, perhaps with steam rising from it! Very different skills are needed when a similarly painstaking approach is necessary and young children are involved. Their attention span is a matter of minutes and they need constant attention to keep their clothes clean and their interest alive!

Artists also specialise in certain areas: drawing products interestingly and designing brand logos. Radio and television commercials usually involve actors, who bring a different set of skills to bear on the task of appearing ecstatically happy over a new brand of washing up liquid, for example.

Such professionals make it all look so easy, when the reality is quite the reverse and their expertise is therefore expensive. A television commercial involving parachutists and helicopters in addition, for example, can easily run into hundreds of thousands of pounds to make.

Radio commercials are generally much cheaper to produce, but even jingles can be expensive, requiring musicians, singers and studio time to record and re-mix.

After the filming has taken place, television and radio commercials need to be edited, that is produced in their final form. When they are approved by the client (the person or company who commissioned the agency to make the commercial in the first place), copies are then sent to the broadcasters.

So, the advertising agency takes the theme and turns it into an advertisement. One of the benefits of having an overall theme is that all the posters, press, television and radio advertisements will have a common approach – using the same words, slogans, personality, and visual or aural motif.

The media-buying department will reserve the space required for advertisements in newspapers and ensure that printers allocate production capacity on the printing presses for any promotional literature, while the creative people get down to producing the advertisement itself.

When all the promotion has been decided on and realised – the campaign can start!

3 After the launch

Once the campaign has been launched, the lion's share of the work has been completed.

The job now is similar to that of a pilot once an aircraft has taken off; monitoring and making adjustments where necessary.

Monitoring

As far as a manufacturer or service provider are concerned, there are three key points to monitor.

1 The effectiveness of the campaign

If an advertising campaign involves television advertising for a particular product, there may well be an almost immediate upswing in sales, especially if the promotional campaign is to launch a new product or service.

It is important to monitor that the advertisements are appearing as agreed; on the correct poster sites and at the right time in the correct newspapers or magazines. The quality of reproduction (the clarity of printing and colour) also needs monitoring; in case of shortcomings, redress in the form of free repeat advertising is normally offered, so it is well worthwhile – as well as sound management practice – to undertake this monitoring task.

Any discussion with the media will normally take place through the company's advertising agency which is responsible for devising the creative ideas for the advertisement, carrying out the artwork, supplying it to the correct media when requested, and booking the media space.

2 Sales increase

The second area to monitor is sales activity. There is little point in advertising anything unless it brings a measurable result, and this is frequently increased sales.

An effective marketing executive will therefore check with the sales department for increased sales throughout a campaign, as well as taking note of any customer reaction to a campaign.

Checking may well include which customers have bought the goods or services initially, then who is ordering again as the campaign progresses – it may be argued that repeat business is the most profitable business of all. If this happens, the source of the repeat business can be monitored – perhaps a particular sector such as supermarkets are buying, but not garage forecourts (for example). If this is the case it is worth finding out the reasons. It may be something that can be put right, thus making the campaign even more successful.

3 Despatch and distribution

When a major promotional campaign is running, it is vital that priority is given throughout the business to those promoted items. When re-orders start to come in, it is vital that they are despatched to the customer without delay.

Effective distribution managers know this, but may be distracted by other day-to-day events, hence they may need reminding of the promotion and its importance to the whole company.

It can be seen that people involved with marketing need to be effective communicators, to ensure that the right people are involved at the right time, to devise the best campaign for a well-researched product.

When the campaign is over, a reflective meeting is almost invariably worthwhile; to find out what went well, what can be improved for the future and anything else to be learnt from the campaign. This meeting should take place between the advertising agency, sales and despatch, either as teams or, more likely, with three individual representatives.

Sponsorship

With sponsorship, the monitoring process is likely to continue over a longer period. The benefit of PowerGen sponsoring the television weather forecast, or the sponsorship of the Football League by Endsleigh Insurance is likely to raise consumer awareness of the product in the longer term. It may be necessary not only to monitor overall sales, but also to commission some market research to ascertain increased consumer awareness of the brand.

It may not be necessary to involve an advertising agency at all in sponsorship. The agreement may have been reached within the two organisations concerned (the sponsor and the beneficiary of the sponsorship). It may only be necessary to provide the beneficiary with some studio-produced artwork of the logo.

If an event is sponsored, such as the All England Tennis Championships, a Covent Garden opera or an art exhibition, there may be some **corporate hospitality** involved: the sponsor invites major customers to attend the event as guests of the company. Frequently they will be entertained to a meal beforehand, drinks during the interval, and have certain preferential treatment, like very good seats, which makes the whole event memorable and enjoyable for all concerned.

Where sports and the arts are concerned, large sums of money are donated each year through sponsorship, which enables the participants in particular and their vocation in general – musicians, artists, sportspeople – to benefit.

Competitions

Competitions can be run with or without involving an advertising agency. It is difficult to isolate the effectiveness of the competition itself. It could be argued that a competition is most effective when combined with other forms of promotion, such as press, television or poster advertising.

The deadlines to supply the relevant media with artwork and other materials for the competition must be identified and adhered to, so that the competition schedule coincides with any associated advertising campaign.

During the monitoring process, it is essential to identify a winner and ensure that the prizes are distributed at a fitting time and place and presented by the correct people.

It is worth mentioning that competitions can be run on three levels.

1 Consumer competitions

In this kind of competition customers are invited to enter – typical of these are newspaper competitions and those on the back of cereal packets.

2 Trade competitions

These can be competitions run for the retailer, wholesaler or other intermediary who has sold the most product, noted the greatest increase in sales or whatever the originating company chooses as the objective of the promotion.

3 Internal competitions

These are useful to motivate the company's sales force in a particular direction. It is inevitably harder to sell an untried and unfamiliar product and the natural inclination is to concentrate on the proven, known, and tested products. To counteract this, companies sometimes run competitions offering the sales force an opportunity to win something if sales targets for new products are met.

The cost of promotions

Effective promotions are almost always expensive. However, if the stakes are high, so are the rewards.

Figure 59 gives examples of advertising costs in printed media.

Publication	Circulation	Cost per monochrome page
National papers:		
The Sun	4,071,000	£28,000
The Daily Mail	1,794,000	£22,680
The Daily Telegraph	1,008,000	£35,500
News of the World	4,774,000	£29,750
The Sunday Express	1,563,000	£29,864
The Sunday Times	1,221,000	£47,000
Magazines:		
Radio Times	1,438,000	£13,300
Hello	404,000	£6,370
Just Seventeen	259,000	£4,900
Smash Hits	326,449	£7,780
Trade press:		
Architects Journal	15,122	£1,485
Retail Newsagent	16,240	£1,004
Sports Trader	2,404	£775

Source: BRAD, 1995

FIGURE 59
Advertising rates in printed publications

It should be noted that the costs given in Figure 59 are purely for space in the publications; origination (artwork and photography, for example) costs extra.

It should also be noted that the cost per thousand readers varies considerably. This is because as the interests catered for by magazines become more specific, it follows that their readers are more likely to purchase from advertisers.

For example, if you are a manufacturer of building materials and you wish to advise architects of your new products, *The Architect's Journal* may be a good choice for your advertising, even though it is only read by an average of 15,122 people. The chances are high that they will be interested in learning of your product – in percentage terms, the returns may be much higher than that achieved from the 4 million plus readers of The Sun – and there is an enormous difference in cost.

It is generally recognised that the most authoritative source of information on charges for space and airtime is a publication known as BRAD, short for British Rate and Data. It contains details of charges for terrestrial and satellite television stations, posters, independent radio, national, local, regional and trade press.

Normally, the purchasing of such space is handled by the advertising agency, most of which have a buying department specialising in this area. There is often a large difference between the 'rate card' (i.e. published) rate and the fee that is actually paid. This depends on specified space (e.g. the back page), how far forward the booking is being made and how many times the advertisement is due to appear.

Performance criterion	### 3.2.4 Explain the purpose of the planned promotional materials

Promotions are costly in terms of human and financial resources. It is essential to obtain the maximum benefit from them.

The best promotions are simple, and keep to the point. It is the message that is important, not the media or the advertisement itself.

There are many different reasons why major suppliers decide to promote their company, group of brands, logo, corporation, products or services. Four will be considered here.

Communicating a message to an audience

If a company is launching a new product or service, sales will be small unless potential customers are tempted to try it! Thus, not only must they learn about it, they must know where to go to try then buy it.

The unique selling proposition

It was demonstrated above how expensive it is to promote products through mass media such as national newspapers and television, so it is vital to **identify the objectives** of the promotion.

In order to do this, the question has to be asked: what is **different** about the product? What will make customers forsake their existing brand in order to try the one being promoted? The answer should help define the objective of the promotion and is sometimes known as the **unique selling proposition**, or **usp**.

Baked Beans Anybody can make baked beans: they are simply a vegetable cooked in tomato sauce, then canned. Only Heinz can make Heinz Baked Beans. Through their consistent promotion of a fundamentally good product, Heinz has won for itself a large share of a huge market. The company launched its baked beans in the UK in 1905 since when the recipe has remained unchanged; a perfect example of a simple product, packaged effectively, well promoted through different media.

Chocolate 'Maltesers' were launched in 1928; the unusual combination of honeycomb and chocolate was an innovative use of two familiar 'sweet treats'. The next step was to package them both attractively and robustly, so that they could travel to different retailers all over the country.

The final step was to promote them – they were not advertised as 'bits of honeycomb dipped in chocolate'!

One of the features of honeycomb is that the air that forms the bubbles makes the product light – and also cheaper to make, since less material is used! There are also less calories present because the honeycomb contains air.

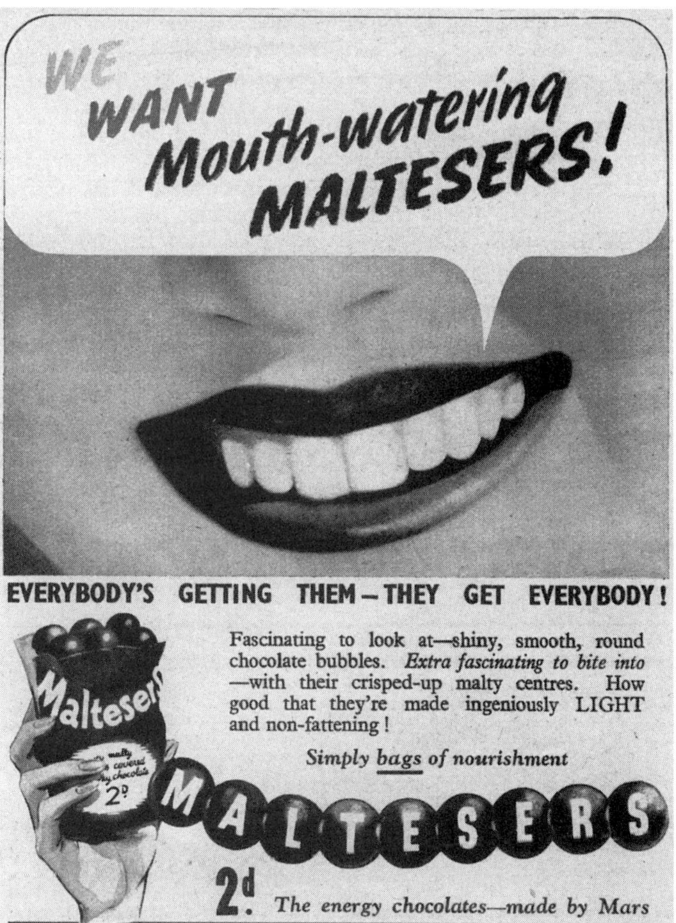

FIGURE 60 An advertisement in 1939 for 'Maltesers'

The unique selling proposition for 'Maltesers', today therefore, is that people can eat them without putting on as much weight as they would if they were to eat a competitive product. The usp for 'Maltesers' has developed further to be 'The lighter way to enjoy chocolate.' This captures both the physical and emotional pleasure of eating the product. It has proved such an effective focus for promotion that 'Maltesers' are still available over 60 years later.

One difficulty with chocolate is that it melts, especially in your hand.

In 1940, Forrest Mars launched a new chocolate-based product which was clean to eat and did not melt in your hand. 'M & Ms' were launched in the UK in 1988 as 'the sweet which melts in your mouth, not in your hand'.

This characterisation of a product is known as **positioning**, that is gaining a (unique) position for a product to enjoy in the marketplace. For example, there are many different types of washing-up liquid. It is generally accepted that these detergents wash up, that is remove grease from the dishes. Unfortunately, they also remove the natural oils from the hands of the person washing up!

Fairy Liquid is positioned as the most concentrated washing-up liquid, the most effective remover of grease from dirty dishes, and the most caring on the hands washing up. This is the usp of the product. As a result of its successful occupation of this position in the marketplace the manufacturer can charge a higher price than competitors.

Activity   List five well-known products. Identify their unique selling proposition.

Collect examples of their advertisements to demonstrate how the usp is reflected in the promotion.

Creating sales   ### Indirect sales
Sales may be created directly or indirectly. The **indirect** approach was largely dealt with in the previous element (page 209 onwards): an advertisement tells potential customers about the product, but frequently omits where it may be purchased. In many instances this is because most people know where to go to buy washing-up liquid or confectionery.

Nonetheless, such promotional messages are designed to create sales.

Direct sales
Direct sales stimulation names specific suppliers of the product being promoted. When a commercial or advertisement for the latest version of the Ford Fiesta (for example) extols the many benefits of ownership, it will also name the local Ford dealers where the vehicle may be purchased or leased. The same commercial or advertisement may be used all over the country but the dealers' names are different for each area.

Similarly, advertisements in the press and on television promote, for example, a compilation CD that can only be purchased by ringing the 0800 number specified in the advertisement and quoting a credit card number.

A coupon offering money off the purchase of a product is a promotion to create sales. When the coupon is included as part of the packaging of the product itself, that is offering money off the next purchase, the objective of the promotion is to generate **customer loyalty**; in other words the intention is to encourage consumers to acquire the habit of regularly purchasing a particular product.

The Tesco Clubcard is a variation on this idea. In return for giving Tesco the customer's name and address, an ongoing discount is allowed against purchases in a Tesco store and money-saving vouchers from their suppliers are given; all in the cause of generating sales.

FIGURE 61 Part of a brochure, promoting Tesco's Clubcard

FIGURE 62 A still from Kellogg's Corn Flakes' 'Have you forgotten how good they taste?' campaign

'Kellogg's Corn Flakes; have you forgotten how good they taste?' is a slogan designed to create **sales from a definite source**. It is designed to appeal to **lapsed users** – those people who used to eat the cereal, then stopped for some reason.

The theory is that Kellogg's Corn Flakes are so well known that it is only necessary to bring their name from the back to the front of potential consumers' minds and sales will increase.

Influencing customers' perception

The third example of a reason for wanting to use promotion is the need to influence the way in which the customer considers the product. This is nowhere near as subversive as it may sound!

Let us consider Kellogg's Corn Flakes once again. Another of their advertisements states that they taste good at any time of the day. Yet the vast majority of cornflakes are eaten at breakfast time.

Kellogg's advertisement is designed to alter that perception; it is exhorting us to consider eating them as a snack during the day, or as a supper last thing at night! The intended consequence is that instead of just eating one bowl per day at breakfast, we eat another when we come home, and perhaps another last thing at night. This only happens in the rarest cases, but the intention is to change consumers' perception, or **re-position the product** in consumers' minds so that it is considered as an all-day snack rather than solely a breakfast cereal.

Providing information

Side-impact protection systems, airbags, even seat belts, advanced braking systems are just some of the product benefits that are communicated in commercials for cars.

Although the information may well be biased in favour of the manufacturer concerned, one of the objectives of the commercial is to provide information to potential purchasers and customers.

FIGURE 63 Advertisements for BT's services in print and on television have a consistent theme

Most people know what a telephone is and does. BT advertisements inform potential and existing users of the new products that BT is introducing. At the same time, of

course, it stimulates telephone usage, but services like 'call interrupt', the BT charge card and other new developments do need to be communicated to existing users.

Some promotions are designed to convey information beneficial to public safety – self-protection against the AIDS virus, the benefits of fitting a smoke alarm in the home, the dangers of fire on bonfire night, the dangers of drinking and driving are all promotions designed purely to inform, rather than sell a product, although obviously the information is presented in such a way as to influence behaviour.

FIGURE 64 An advertisement by the Health Education Authority giving information about contraception

Performance criteria

3.2.5 Design and produce promotional materials and use them to promote goods or services

3.2.6 Evaluate how successful the promotional materials were in achieving the stated purpose

Activities

By looking through back copies of newspapers and magazines, identify the following three types of promotion:

a consumer competition;
b an advertisement;
c sponsorship.

Cut out the examples and stick them on a blank page in your portfolio.

Collect examples of how products competing against the ones you have chosen are promoted. In each case, describe:

a the product that is being promoted;
b the content of the promotion;
c the benefits offered compared to those of its competitors;
d any constraints on the promotion in terms of the **Consumer Protection Act**, and the Advertising Standards' Authority.
e for each of your chosen three products, write a critique of the promotional material, evaluating:
- likes;
- dislikes;
- suggestions for improvements.

State how successful you think each item of promotional material is in achieving the stated purpose, in terms of:

a effectiveness in communicating to its audience;
b effectiveness in creating sales;
c influence on customers' perceptions;
d effectiveness in providing information.

Activities

Divide into groups of three people. You work in the creative department of White, Starchy, Benson & Bowles, a leading London advertising agency. Your client Bradbury's has just developed a new chocolate-coated biscuit-based bar. It is intended to compete in the snack market, where the major competitive products are 'Kit-Kat' and 'Twix'.

The retail price is higher than your competitors, since you have identified a gap in the market for a high-quality product which serves not only as a snack but also as a reward for a job well done. In this way it also competes with 'Crunchie'.

Your product has thicker chocolate than 'Kit-Kat' and 'Twix', and has an airy cream-based filling similar to a walnut whip, hence the premium price.

a Invent a brand name for your product, to reflect its positioning and its value.
b Design and produce a logo for it.
c Design a cardboard dispenser, to be printed in colour. It should contain 48 units of the product and be capable of being displayed on the shelves of newsagents, college canteens, cafés and other outlets where such merchandise is on sale.
d Design a competition for the consumer press, to stress the different facets (i.e. positioning) of the product.
e Design an advertisement which could appear in the national press to promote your product.
f Draw a chart similar to the model on pages 218–219, to illustrate the amount of time you would require to complete your suggested programme. You should allow sufficient time for your client (Bradbury's) to approve your suggested artwork, and for the magazines or newspapers to print the advertisements.
g When all groups have performed these tasks, place the promotional material together and compare the results. Individually, list your:
  - likes;
  - dislikes;
  - suggestions.
Compare them with the individual work undertaken in stages a–e above. How effectively do you think each:
  - communicates its message to the audience;
  - stimulates sales;
  - provides information about the product;
  - influences customers' perceptions of the product?

# Element 3.3   Providing Customer Service

It is one thing to write about market-led organisations – another to be part of one. The first step towards becoming an effective part of such an organisation is to understand the needs of customers in a variety of situations. This element seeks to identify and address some of these areas.

Evidence indicators

- A summary which identifies a business organisation's customers, describes its customer services, gives examples of one oral and one written business communication within that organisation, and describes its procedures for dealing with customer complaints.
- A brief summary which identifies the four Acts of Parliament which protect customers.
- A record of a demonstration by the student of oral communications with customer(s) which includes greeting the customer, establishing the customer's needs attempting to meet the customer's needs and finishing the communication. The demonstration should include customers who: wish to make a purchase, require information, a refund, to exchange goods, make a complaint, have a special need.

If there is no opportunity to demonstrate service to a customer with a special need a description should be substituted.

If the opportunity to work with actual customers is not available, it is acceptable to use customer simulation.

Core skills

This element gives students the opportunity to demonstrate these core skills:

Communication
Element   2.2 Produce written material

Information technology
Element   2.1 Prepare information

2.2 Process information

Performance criterion   3.3.1 **Identify an organisation's customers and its customer needs**

Activity   In pairs, discuss why it is important to an organisation to identify its customers. Consider why an organisation might try to group customers in some way and what those groups might be.

Who is the actual customer?   It is not always so easy to identify an organisation's customers.

Customers are frequently the people who buy the product or service, but this is not always the case. At Christmas, children work on their parents for a particular present; the parents actually buy it.

So, perhaps it is the people who **use** the product? There again, parents pay for breakfast cereals, but often it is the children who make the buying decision and eat the product. Doctors prescribe medicines; the patients buy and use them.

Perhaps the **people who make the decision to purchase** a particular product or service. However, they are not always the users. Music teachers often tell their students which music book to buy. The student then tells his or her parents, who go out and buy the book.

So identifying an organisation's customers is not always as simple as it seems.

Let us start with a simple customer identification and worry about the more complicated ones later.

I want to buy a bar of chocolate. I have a **need** for a snack. I go into a newsagent's and am faced with a huge selection. I pick one; perhaps the one that was nearest so that I do not have to bend down and drop all my other shopping. Perhaps I choose the bar in the middle because I am not tall enough to reach the one I really want at the top of the pile.

Perhaps I consider the options before entering the shop – turkish delight, bar of milk chocolate, nougat-covered chocolate, chocolate-covered biscuit, and so on. Having recognised that I actually wanted the turkish delight, that was the one I actually chose. I pick it up, take it to the till and pay for it.

I am a customer of the confectionery company that manufactures the turkish delight.

When I make that purchase, I am also a customer of the newsagent.

While I am in the newsagent's shop I also buy *The Daily Mirror*. That is of direct interest to the newsagent, who orders it for me every day. The only interest that this may be to the chocolate manufacturer is that if a high enough percentage of its customers read *The Daily Mirror*, it may be useful for advertising its products.

Why is customer identification important?

We saw in Element 3.1 how important it is for an organisation to know who its customers are. The reasons are summarised below.

1   To enable the organisation to provide its customers with with products that they actually **need**;
2   to offer **additions** to the product that the customer considers useful and relevant;
3   to develop the business by launching **new products** that will also appeal to these customers;
4   to provide **after-sales** services of a level and type that the customer expects and wants;
5   to promote the organisation's products using **media** that customers actually read or with which they otherwise come into contact;
6   to communicate with customers (through advertisements, press releases, competitions and other ways) using the language and terms that they use themselves;
7   to anticipate changes in their purchasing needs or buying habits;
8   to avoid offering customers products, services or benefits that they do not want or need and
9   by doing all the above, to remain competitive in their chosen market.

How does a business find out who its customers are?

In two words, marketing research. The purpose of such research is frequently to confirm the astute marketing person's belief or hunch that such a product might appeal to this group of people.

The prime-target market

In the last element (on page 213) we saw how certain magazines appeal to certain people.

In Gloucestershire, where I live, many people enjoy riding horses and things equestrian. In Stroud there is a shop which specialises in supplying and repairing saddles, bridles and most of the leather articles connected with riding horses.

It follows that this business may well choose to advertise in *Horse and Hound* magazine.

The readers of this magazine who live in the Stroud area, are the **prime-target market** of that business. In other words, these are the people with whom the owner of the business is most interested in communicating, to spread the word about the goods and services he offers. In other words, if this business wants to communicate with its customers, *Horse and Hound* would be one possible advertising outlet.

The secondary-target market

Another possibility is the *Stroud News and Journal*, our local paper. Although this paper is read by a lot of people who have no interest in horses the advertisement may not be wasted on them. I am not interested in riding horses. However I have a leather briefcase; it broke and I needed to get it repaired. By chance, somebody told me about this particular shop in Stroud, which was the only one able to repair my briefcase. Despite my lack of interest in riding, but because of my possession of a leather briefcase in need of repair, I am part of the **secondary-target market** for this business – local people who need somewhere to take their leather goods for repair, but have no interest in horses.

So, perhaps the *Stroud News and Journal* is an effective outlet for the business after all, and the wastage is smaller than imagined.

It clearly benefits a business to know who its customers are – both prime and secondary target markets.

Affinity groups

Identifying customers by an interest that they share is known as placing them into **affinity groups**. Such people are easy to reach – anglers, cyclists, classic sports-car enthusiasts, and the like. This is clearly very effective for manufacturers of fishing rods or organisers of motoring events, but less interesting to chocolate-bar or washing-powder manufacturers, whose markets are much broader.

Social grading

For businesses operating in these **mass markets,** there are many other ways to identify and classify their customers. Figure 65 is an example of one of the simplest. It categorises people by social grade.

FIGURE 65 NRS social grade definitions

Social Grade	Social Status	Occupation
A	Upper middle class	Higher managerial, administrative or professional.
B	Middle class	Intermediate managerial, administrative or professional.
C1	Lower middle class	Supervisory or clerical, and junior managerial administrative or professional.
C2	Skilled working class	Skilled manual workers.
D	Working class	Semi and unskilled manual workers.
E	Those at lowest level of subsistence	State pensioners or widows (no other earner) casual or lowest-grade workers.

These are the standard social grade classifications using definitions agreed between Research Services Ltd., and NRS.
Source: National Readership Survey as quoted in **Marketing Pocket Book**, 1995

In its time this grading was innovative because it recognised that people have different tastes and this was a way to isolate and group together people with similar preferences.

Its main weakness is that it is *too* simple; there are many people of D group who share the same interests, hobbies and purchasing power as people in group A.

There are also people in group A who have dissimilar tastes from other people in group A. For example, group A includes bishops, surgeons and stockbrokers. This group obviously covers a wide range of backgrounds, interests, incomes, family types and sizes.

The NRS social grade definitions are used less and less these days but they serve to illustrate a simple way of grouping customers together.

ACORN profiles

Another example of mass market identification is the ACORN profile (Figure 66). ACORN stands for 'a classification of residential neighbourhoods' and is based on postcodes. It is suitable for most market research, and particularly for direct mail promotions. It is much more detailed and accurate than the NRS classifications, and much more reliable.

Customer needs

Identifying the needs of customers brings fundamental benefits to a business.

Customers wishing to make a purchase

Different people have different needs. In a retail environment **parents of young children** need, among other facilities:

- wide aisles for the shopping trolley and buggy;
- changing facilities;
- the availability of nappies and OTC children's medicines (OTC is short for over the counter – a common marketing term in the pharmaceutical world).

On the other hand, **less able-bodied people** may need:

- ramps to allow access for wheel chairs;
- specially adapted shopping trolleys;
- the availability of help to pack the purchases and take them to the customer's vehicle.

The availability of children's medicines, however, may not be relevant to their needs at all.

The current emphasis major supermarket chains place on providing customer service is a reflection of the fact that they have researched their markets and discovered the needs of customers wishing to make a purchase.

Manufacturers also need to consider the needs of customers wishing to make a purchase; for example, they need to produce items which are easy to carry individually and yet equally easy to carry as part of a mixed bag of shopping. This puts all kinds of demands on the designers of packaging.

Customers needing to obtain information

The customer need to obtain information is vital at all parts of the distribution chain. The manufacturer needs to be able

CACI's ACORN classification profiles in a trading area or on a database into 6 Categories, 17 Groups and 54 Types (plus unclassified), so that marketers can understand more about their likely consumer characteristics. The table below shows the ACC profile of CACI's 1995 population projections for Great Britain.

ACORN Categories	ACORN Groups	ACORN Types		Number
A THRIVING	**1 Wealthy Achievers, Suburban Areas**	1.1	Wealthy suburbs, large detached houses	1,442,502
		1.2	Villages with wealthy commuters	1,797,707
		1.3	Mature affluent home owning areas	1,528,768
		1.4	Affluent suburbs, older families	2,097,330
		1.5	Mature, well-off suburbs	1,691,487
	2 Affluent Greys, Rural Communities	2.6	Agricultural villages, home based workers	913,933
		2.7	Holiday retreats, older people, home based workers	397,028
	3 Prosperous Pensioners, Retirement Areas	3.8	Home owning areas, well-off older residents	798,595
		3.9	Private flats, elderly people	538,478
B EXPANDING	**4 Affluent Executives, Family Areas**	4.10	Affluent working families with mortgages	1,209,200
		4.11	Affluent working couples with mortgages, new homes	727,725
		4.12	Transient workforces, living in their place of work	199,689
	5 Well-Off Workers, Family Areas	5.13	Home owning family areas	1,473,807
		5.14	Home owning family areas, older children	1,708,143
		5.15	Families with mortgages, younger children	1,265,830
C RISING	**6 Affluent Urbanites, Town & City Areas**	6.16	Well-off town & city areas	615,061
		6.17	Flats & mortgages, singles & young working couples	425,844
		6.18	Furnished flats & bedsits, younger single people	253,342
	7 Prosperous Professionals, Metropolitan Areas	7.19	Apartments, young professional singles & couples	644,936
		7.20	Gentrified multi-ethnic	545,485
	8 Better-Off Executives, Inner City Areas	8.21	Prosperous enclaves, highly qualified executives	419,968
		8.22	Academic centres, students & young professionals	374,489
		8.23	Affluent city centre areas, tenements & flats	252,981
		8.24	Partially gentrified, multi-ethnic areas	399,302
		8.25	Converted flats & bedsits, single people	498,993
D SETTLING	**9 Comfortable Middle Agers, Mature Home Owning Areas**	9.26	Mature established home owning areas	1,874,129
		9.27	Rural areas, mixed occupations	1,962,700
		9.28	Established home owning areas	2,275,878
		9.29	Home owning areas, council tenants, retired people	1,504,114
	10 Skilled Workers, Home Owning Areas	10.30	Established home owning areas, skilled workers	2,568,946
		10.31	Home owners in older properties, younger workers	1,737,110
		10.32	Home owning areas with skilled workers	1,768,020
E ASPIRING	**11 New Home Owners, Mature Communities**	11.33	Council areas, some home owners	2,160,798
		11.34	Mature home owning areas, skilled workers	1,753,391
		11.35	Low rise estates, older workers, new home owners	1,608,442
	12 White Collar Workers Better-Off Multi Ethnic Areas	12.36	Home owning multi-ethnic areas, young families	633,900
		12.37	Multi-occupied town centres, mixed occupations	1,037,306
		12.38	Multi-ethnic areas, white collar workers	602,606
F STRIVING	**13 Older People, Less Prosperous Areas**	13.29	Home owners, small council flats, single pensioners	1,083,493
		13.40	Council areas, older people, health problems	969,253
	14 Council Estate Residents, Better-Off Homes	14.41	Better-off council areas, new home owners	1,368,305
		14.42	Council areas, young families, some new home owners	1,711,087
		14.43	Council areas,, young families, many lone parents	894,221
		14.44	Multi-occupied terraces, multi-ethnic areas	483,733
		14.45	Low rise council housing, less well-off families	1,002,866
		14.46	Council areas, residents with health problems	1,097,833
	15 Council Estate Residents, High Unemployment	15.47	Estates with high unemployment	631,135
		15.48	Council flats, elderly people, health problems	382,915
		15.49	Council flats, very high unemployment, singles	495,479
	16 Council Estate Residents, Greatest Hardship	16.50	Council areas, high unemployment, lone parents	1,055,713
		16.51	Council flats, greatest hardship, many lone parents	516,253
	17 People in Multi-Ethnic, Low Income Areas	17.52	Multi-ethnic, large families, overcrowding	358,707
		17.53	Multi-ethnic, severe unemployment, lone parents	553,009
		17.54	Multi-ethnic, high unemployment, overcrowding	297,252
	Unclassified			**280,967**
	TOTAL			**56,351,706**

FIGURE 66 CACI Acorn profile of the United Kingdom

to inform potential customers where the product may be purchased, the level of warranty, where after-sales service may be obtained, price, and where accessories are available for example.

Another need is for customers who want to know how to obtain a refund – either because the goods proved faulty, or because the product was purchased as part of a promotion promising a refund on part of the price. They need to know how to go about this: whether to return to the store where the goods were purchased, or to apply to the manufacturer.

Customers may need to know how to exchange the goods they have purchased. Clothes for example, may be the wrong size, colour or fitting. Alternatively, the customer may have decided that the goods were simply unsuitable for the purpose for which they were intended.

Sometimes, the customer may need to know how to make a complaint. In most cases contacting the retailer or manufacturer brings a satisfactory response. In rare instances it may be necessary for a customer to see the trading standards officer, or even a lawyer, who can advise on the legal aspects of customer protection and where the customer stands from this point of view. More details of this procedure are on pages 216 and 217.

Customers with special needs include those with visual and aural impairment as well as the less able-bodied. They also include children who need special protection, the elderly and people who need regular medication (such as diabetics).

Ethical standards require consideration: people of certain religions need to worship regularly; they also observe certain feasts. On these days they may not be available to work and a caring employer will respect these needs, yet still ensure sufficient staff are available to meet customer needs.

 **Performance criterion**

3.3.2 Identify and describe customer service in an organisation

Internal and external customers

Internal customers

Internal customers may well be other employees. Some employees depend on others to supply them with essential services. In a school or college, for example, the reprographics manager provides a service to lecturing or teaching staff. Both are employees, but the staff are dependent upon the service given by the reprographics manager. If he or she takes a week to photocopy material required urgently, or goes on holiday without making alternative arrangements or informing the people who depend on that service, he or she is letting down internal customers by giving them a poor quality service.

 **Activities**

In groups, identify the people in your school or college who have internal customers, that is they supply a service to colleagues. Consider the resources available to them to provide that service and whether they are suitable.

External customers

Let us now relate this to external customers, whose needs may be more far-reaching.

There are two types of external customers that we will consider – individual customers and business customers.

1 **Customer service for individuals.** Customers may need further information about the product or service. They may wish to make a complaint. They may need advice as to which of a variety of products is the most suitable for their needs.
2 **Customer service for business organisations.** In industrial markets, the level of customer service is slightly different, because the level of personal contact between the organisations tends to be greater. For instance, a company supplying machinery must give a high level of rapid service. When machines break down, the workforce can find itself producing little or nothing very rapidly – yet the workforce must still be paid. The breakdown of a machine has potentially very serious financial consequences. Regular personal contact between the machinery supplier and the client – by visit or telephone –

is therefore one of the ways in which a good business relationship is maintained. The client must feel trust that the supplier will take appropriate action in moments of crisis.

 **Performance criterion**

3.3.3 Identify business communications which meet customer needs

> You never get a second chance to make a first impression.

There are many forms of business communications designed to meet the needs of external and internal customers and effective use of them is essential when making the all-important first impression.

Oral communications

Face to face and by telephone

These are particularly appropriate methods of communication for:

- sales representatives;
- sales assistants;
- customer service personnel.

Such verbal communication opportunities allow people to put questions and hear answers, have discussions, and listen to what the other person has to say.

How such opportunities are used depends on the reason for the meeting. If a sales representative is holding a sales meeting, the customer involved may well want to discuss his or her precise needs; successful sales people listen to those needs, asking closed or open questions (see pages 252–253) where appropriate. The sales person is then well placed to describe how the products or services on offer may meet the customer's needs.

The customer may just be 'fact finding' and not yet in a position to make a decision which product to buy, or even whether he or she wishes to buy. Sales assistants in shops frequently meet customers in these circumstances, especially those involved in selling more expensive merchandise such as curtains, carpets, shoes or cutlery, where the customer needs to make a detailed consideration of what each product has to offer, before deciding which to buy.

One benefit of face-to-face communication is that each party can observe the other – to identify genuine interest, perhaps confusion or even boredom!

From the customer service point of view, the telephone is an invaluable tool; customer contact may be easily and quickly established and problems solved without delay.

The success of promotional tools such as *Yellow Pages* and *The Thomson Directory* are testimony to the usefulness of the telephone in such circumstances.

Practising effective interpersonal communication skills and a positive telephone manner is time extremely well spent.

This is why it will be considered again in section 3.3.4, page 252.

Written communications

Written or typed communications in business are usually by means of:

- a letter;
- a memorandum.

Written communications like **letters** are permanent and they are one way. They may also be quoted at a later date; the opportunity to ask questions or discuss a matter is thus not only limited, but also protracted.

For this reason, it is frequently much more satisfactory to telephone a customer to identify and discuss precise requirements, whether it be an interest in purchasing a new product, a sales enquiry or a complaint.

A letter can then follow to explain a situation, list products, options and prices or give a written apology. This more formal communication then becomes a permanent record of a discussion.

However, a letter may satisfactorily answer a simple enquiry for further factual information.

A **memo** can be a less formal communication and is usually an internal company communication. As part of the salesperson/customer relationship, a memo is usually factual, concise and devoid of informal greetings as the example in Figure 97, page 319 shows.

Customer and product information.
Let us use as examples:

- statement of account;
- price list;
- guarantee;
- safety notices;
- brochure.

Statement of account
This is usually issued by the accounts department. The people working here are not felt to be always customer friendly, since their main interest is in ensuring that the customer pays for goods or services received.

Thus a statement of accounts tends to be blunt and to the point.

As a means of communication of new products, its use is limited, since it is presented to the customer at a time when he or she is being asked to pay, and therefore a further merchandise offer may not be received with open arms! There are exceptions and enclosures with a credit card statement of accounts, for example, have generated extra sales of all sorts of consumer products and services. An additional enclosure of this sort is known as a 'piggy back' mailing, since the account statement has to be sent, and therefore the extra postage to make the additional offer is minimal, if anything.

Price list
A price list is also often quite cheaply produced, printed in one or two colours, and is a separate document from a product brochure. This is to allow for price increases to take place without having to reprint an expensive colour brochure!

Price lists also tend to be blunt and to the point. The wooing of and picture painting for the customer takes place in the brochure. By the time the customer looks at the price list, a purchase is imminent!

Guarantee

This frequently has two main purposes; the first is to allow the customer to gain access to help in the event of the product or service not functioning properly within the first year or so following purchase.

The second purpose is for the supplier to gain further information about the type of person who made the purchase. For example, what other goods or services the customer purchases; age, sex, size of family, size of home and whether owned or rented, reason for purchase, where and when purchased.

This all gives the supplier invaluable information about the customer, as discussed earlier.

In rare instances, such information may be sold to a third party so that details of complementary products may be mailed to the customer by the third party's company. However, the law stipulates that the customer must be allowed to request that such details should not be forwarded in this way.

Safety notices

Safety notices must be clear, unambiguous, easily seen, read and understood. If not, they are not an effective warning and accidents could occur.

Brochure

A product brochure is designed to offer the customer with serious intentions to buy the information that enables him or her to differentiate between one product or service and those offered by competitors.

The brochure is a shop window for the products of a business, whether for the end consumer or for industrial goods or services.

For this reason, billions of pounds per year are spent by suppliers on designing and printing brochures to promote their wares.

The communication is one way: from supplier to consumer. Brochures may then prompt questions to a sales assistant in a store, or a telephone call direct to the business itself.

Brochures come in all shapes and sizes dependent on the product or service, the price and whether it is for industrial or consumer use.

More is spent per brochure by businesses promoting industrial goods, for which there are fewer customers, but each has the potential to spend much larger amounts of money than individual people buying goods for their own use.

 **Performance criterion**

3.3.4 Demonstrate business communications which meet customer needs

Face-to-face situations

Here are some ideas that I have found helpful in making effective business communications.

- **Make the other person feel pleased** that you are meeting, by striking up a common theme, such as the traffic, weather, parking.
- **Assume nothing** in your discussion. If in doubt, ask for clarification.
- **Speak clearly**, and at an appropriate speed.
- **Do not use complicated words unnecessarily.**
- **Do not interrupt.**
- **Think before you speak**, in order to speak logically.
- **Use a tone appropriate to the circumstances.**
- **Be polite.** The other person deserves the sort of respect you expect for yourself. From a customer relations viewpoint, it is much harder – if not impossible – to deliver customer satisfaction if you have upset him or her beforehand.
- **Practise asking open and closed questions.** Open questions encourage the other person to speak, closed questions beg yes or no short answers.
- **Practise active listening** – do not do all the talking! This means listening to the whole answer, not just the first part, as Figure 67 shows.

The respondent is asked a question to which he or she replies.

In segment one, the listener listens to the answer, as he or she should do. At segment 2, the listener starts to reflect over what was said in segment 1 and how it relates to what the person is trying to sell, or the other parts of the business dealing.

FIGURE 67 Analysis of a typical discussion between two people

This leads the listener on to another train of thought and at segment 3, the listener identifies the next question he or she would like to ask. By the time segment 4 is reached, the listener is looking for an opening to ask the next question.

The point of this diagram is that although the respondent has been giving relevant information throughout the answer (points X), only the first three (i.e. those in section one) were heard by the listener, because he or she was too busy moving towards the next question. Vital information may well have been lost. This is not an academic theory, this is what really happens in many business situations and it causes much misunderstanding.

Had the listener simply **listened** to the answer, much more information would have been gleaned.

Activity

Make a list of five situations in which you have been involved where you have not listened attentively for long enough to appreciate fully what you were being told.

One answer is to prepare yourself for these occasions, by writing down the questions you want to ask. With such a list, it is not necessary to think of the next question, you already have it written down.

When you are listening, give the other person your full attention. Sit straight opposite, look the person in the eye, do not cross your legs and do not fidget. Then, **relax and listen**.

As you gain experience in such situations, you will find that you can dispense with the list of questions as you are confident enough to cope with a situation that you have met many times before. Until that time arrives, some years hence, **use a list!** Furthermore, practise active listening!

Activities

Split into threes. One person acts as respondent, one as listener, one as observer. The respondent should talk, uninterrupted, for three minutes on a simple topic, perhaps, 'how I like to spend Christmas'; 'where I am going for my holidays'; 'my plans for when I win the National Lottery'; 'my childhood'.

The listener should simply listen, using the suggestions previously made.

The observer should check how closely the listener follows these points.

When the respondent has finished, the listener should re-tell what he or she has heard, back to the respondent. When he or she has finished, the respondent should confirm (or deny) its accuracy, and identify omissions.

Neither listener nor respondent should make notes.

At the conclusion, the observer should report on the listener's reactions – that is, changes in posture, how long he or she remained attentive and sitting directly opposite the speaker. Finally, the observer should check the accuracy with which the listener can remember what was said.

Do this three times so that each person has a chance to play each role.

The lecturer or teacher should monitor the timing.

At the conclusion, in a short plenary session, reflect how well a selection of the students recall their experiences.

This exercise may be repeated with the listener then allowed to ask some short questions; the observer should note how many open and closed questions are asked.

Speaking on the telephone

On the telephone the same practices broadly apply. The inability to see the other person means that the language must be straightforward to avoid misunderstandings. The chances of sales success are reduced on the telephone, but this is offset by the vast increase in the number of potential customers with whom contact may be made in a single day.

- Use straightforward language on the telephone.
- **Happiness is infectious, so sound happy** and even tempered. On telephone sales courses, the phrase 'smile when you dial' is sometimes used!
- **Open in a friendly way and say who you are.** 'Hallo, (pause) David Wilkins' welcomes an incoming caller, and identifies the speaker by both forename and surname. 'Hallo, Accounts' confirms that the caller has been connected with the right department. The other person cannot see you, so a one word, dour 'Jones' gives the impression that the call is unwelcome and an intrusion; if it is a customer, this should not be further from the case.
- **Always be polite:** courtesy costs nothing and can win you many friends.
- **Be brief.** Telephone calls cost money, so long discussions should be avoided. In any case, in business calls, people generally do not want to waste time with idle chat.

Some people have difficulty being courteous yet brief on the telephone; it is a skill worth acquiring. If you want to end a call without upsetting the other person, you can dream up something like 'the boss is signalling that he wants me', or 'I have a call waiting on the other line'. On a personal level, you can say 'somebody else wants to use the phone'. People understand this and are unlikely to be offended.

Of course, it is much the best to tell the truth and with practice, courteous, brief telephone calls become second nature.

Activity   This activity will involve you in role play.

Note to lecturers and teachers
Please see page 259 before introducing this activity to the students. It is strongly suggested that an observer should also be appointed, so that students work in groups of three.

With larger groups of students, they may work in pairs (i.e. two customers, two employees, two observers).

Useful evidence of competence may be gained by recording this activity on video. If used in small groups, this can also be a most powerful learning tool, as the students *see* how they appear to others when it is re-played.

When this activity has been completed discuss with the students concerned how the situation might have been handled differently had the scene taken place on the telephone, with the guest calling the receptionist from the room.

Then review in plenary session whether the people concerned focused on meeting customer needs, and the result.

Customer care role play
Employee's brief

You are the receptionist at a large hotel with conference facilities. It is your responsibility to receive payment from the guests as they leave.

There was a problem last night with the hotel's central heating system, but it has now been attended to.

However, you have noticed that this particular guest has been inquisitive to a degree almost amounting to fussiness, about all the hotel's facilities during the whole of the overnight stay.

The guest is about to ask you to prepare the invoice.

Written business communications

Business letters

Have another look at the letter on page 315. Pages 314–316 mention the ingredients of an effective business letter. Now let us put the letter into the context of effective customer service.

Activity

You recently had your car repaired at a garage unfamiliar to you, but which was recommended by a friend. The car was overheating.

You had driven five miles after collecting the car when the same symptoms re-appeared. You believe the garage has been negligent but when you subsequently discussed it with the foreman on the telephone, he was not interested in your plight.

Individually, write a letter to the service manager of the garage concerned.

Activity When everybody has finished the last activity, select certain individuals to read their letters aloud in order to compare and evaluate:

a tone;
b style;
c chosen vocabulary;
d effectiveness.

Swap letters with a neighbour and put yourself in the position of the service manager: write a reply to the customer.

When all have finished, select others in the group to read their replies and evaluate them for effectiveness using the above criteria. Finally, assess how effectively each meets the customer's needs.

Writing memos Memos are considered on pages 312 and 319. Let us now consider them in the context of internal customer service.

Activity You are the production manager for a chocolate company. One of the products for which you are responsible is a bar of honeycomb dipped in chocolate. It is currently machine wrapped, but finished off by a hand twist at either end.

The factory hates doing this operation. It is time consuming, and after repeated wrappings, the factory operatives' hands become blistered and repeated stress injury has been reported.

In addition, you can save 1p per bar on a cost of 9p if you could seal the product by machine. The bar would then be airtight. Under the current method there is always the risk that the twist may come undone, and air reaches the product and discolours it before it is sold. This has happened often in the past.

1 Individually, write a memo to the product manager responsible for marketing this product outlining your reasons for wanting to change to the automated system.
2 Select some memos and read them out to the whole group. Evaluate the effectiveness of each one as an example of internal customer service.

Performance criterion

3.3.5 Describe procedures in one business organisation for dealing with customer complaints

Activities

Split into groups of three or four. Arrange to visit a local manufacturer or service provider.

Write a report on the way in which customer complaints are handled:

a by telephone;
b by personal callers;
c by letter.

Identify how the supplier avoids a repetition of each particular complaint.

After your visit, evaluate how successful you believe this customer is in dealing with customer complaints.

Performance criterion

3.3.6 Identify relevant legislation to protect customers

Activity

Look again at pages 216 and 217 (Element 3.2) and pages 118 and 119 (Element 2.2). Make notes on them from the point of view of customer protection; consider *The Health and Safety at Work Act* from the point of view of employees as customers of employers.

Note to lecturers and teachers

Customer-care role play
Customer's brief
You have been staying overnight in a hotel and are about to settle your account.

The central heating system in your room did not work properly and you were very cold during the night.

The system was functioning normally to-day, so you cannot prove how cold your room was.

You want to tell the hotel about your experience with a view to receiving a discount on your bill.

Additional information to disclose if asked
You have been staying at the hotel because you think it may be suitable as a conference venue for 150 delegates, to be held later in the year. You will shortly decide where to hold the conference and where the delegates will stay.

 # Element 3.4 Present Proposals for Improvements to Customer Service

In the previous element we have looked at the theory of providing customer service and practised some techniques. This element uses both theory and practice formally to devise and present proposals.

Evidence indicators

- A record of a presentation proposing improvements to customer services in a business organisation. The presentation should show how improvements could help attract customers, secure customer satisfaction and customer loyalty, and enhance the organisation's image. The presentation should include examples of improvements to three of the following:

  a friendliness;
  b availability of goods or services;
  c speed of delivery;
  d policies for exchanges or refunds;
  e access to buildings (wheelchairs, buggies);
  f customer safety;
  g care for the environment.

- Notes to support the presentation describing customer services in one business organisation, stating how the organisation monitors its customers' satisfaction and outlining proposals for improvements to customer service.

 **Core skills**

This element gives students the opportunity to demonstrate these core skills:

Application of number
Element 2.1 Collect and record data

2.2 Tackle problems

2.3 Interpret and present data

Communication
Element 2.2 Produce written material

2.3 Use images

2.4 Read and respond to written materials

Performance criterion

3.4.1 Explain the importance of customer service in business organisations
Most people can think of examples of good customer service that they have received – at the hi-fi shop or the dry cleaner for example.

Similarly, nearly everybody has experiences of receiving poor service – perhaps at the council offices or in a clothes shop.

Activities

In groups, identify three occasions when you have received good customer service and three when you have received bad. In your groups, describe what happened on each occasion, and identify what made the experiences good and bad.

Customer service may be split into four categories:

1   gaining and retaining customers;
2   gaining customer satisfaction;
3   encouraging customer loyalty;
4   enhancing an organisation's image.

Gaining and retaining customers

In any business, it is very costly to win new customers.

It is said that when somebody receives extraordinarily good service from an organisation, that person will tell, on average, eight other people of the experience.

When somebody receives poor service from an organisation, that person will, on average, relate the experience to over three times as many: 25 people.

This is possibly the most powerful argument for ensuring that customers receive a high level of service when they come into contact with any organisation.

The best, and most profitable, business comes from existing customers coming back to place repeat business.

So, in addition to the above statistics, the case for retaining satisfied customers, as we saw on pages 205–206, is so strong, that it is impossible to underestimate its importance.

Gaining customer satisfaction

Japanese businesses do not have a history of product innovation – but they do have a history of giving customer satisfaction with reliable goods, and goods incorporating accessories that their customers want.

It has been said that the whole Japanese success of the past 20 years has been based on consistently delivering customer satisfaction.

Valued customers come back time and again and will frequently recommend the services to other people.

Customer loyalty

When a business has gained a new customer, and delivered satisfaction on a number of occasions, loyalty is engendered. Because the customer is confident of receiving satisfaction, repeat purchases are made, secure in the knowledge that he or she will receive value for money, a high level of customer service and a wide selection from which to make the final choice.

Enhancing an organisation's image

Ask anyone about the characteristics of Marks & Spencer, and the basis on which they have built their success. The chances are that at some point, somebody will mention the fact that goods may be returned and money refunded with few questions asked if the customer is not completely satisfied.

The effect of this is cumulative. The image of Marks & Spencer and its 'St. Michael' brand is one of quality, value for money and customer service.

Of course there is a cost involved in replacing or exchanging goods, training staff and giving customers the benefit of the doubt. But that cost is small compared to the positive image enhancement; and negligible by comparison with the negative cost of a poor reputation.

Many people remember a chance remark made in 1990 in an unguarded moment by the chairman of a well known jewellery retailer, when he criticised the products that his business sold. Sales plummeted, the share price fell, the business suffered untold damage. The shops were forced to change their name and their image; yet despite all this, even now, the business has not really recovered.

More recently, the Somerfield supermarket chain has considerably improved its level of customer service, and turnover and profits have risen accordingly.

Performance criterion

3.4.2 Identify how business organisations monitor customer satisfaction

Activities

Choose a local business with which you are in contact.

Devise a marketing research project to find out:

a how many customers that business has, compared to two of its competitors;

b the level of sales it achieves with a small selection of its products. (Note: students are recommended to choose fast-moving consumer goods like chocolate bars or newspapers so it will not be difficult to find purchasers);

c what customers like about the business;

d what customers dislike about the business.

When you have carried out your research, arrange to visit the business in your groups and identify how your research findings compare with those of the business itself.

Identify how the business monitors its customer satisfaction and the importance it places on its findings.

From your findings above, identify how the business can improve the level of service it delivers to its customers. Discuss this with the business concerned.

Performance criterion

3.4.3 Identify improvements to customer service

There are many causes of customer dissatisfaction. Here are some examples:

1 the product or service does not do what the business claims it can do;
2 the person who deals with the customer's complaint appears to be uninterested in helping to solve the problem;
3 cumbersome, and therefore frustrating, administration in the business.

Areas for improvement to customer services

The following pages discuss these important areas of customer service:

- reliability;
- friendliness;
- availability of goods or services;
- speed of delivery;
- published policy for exchanges or refunds;
- access to buildings for wheelchairs or baby buggies;
- care for the environment;
- customer safety.

Reliability

When somebody enters a shop, the customer needs to have some confidence that what they are buying is of a quality that they expect and that it will function as stated in the publicity material. If it does not, not only is that person likely to tell 25 other people, a lot of time and effort may be spent by the shop, the customer and the supplier to present the product in the condition that it should have been in the first place.

Let us consider this a little closer. If the product is faulty when the customer unpacks it at home, the customer has to pack it up again. It then needs to be returned to the shop from which it was bought. This may mean either a delay until the next visit or a special journey to the shop; this costs time and money.

Then somebody at the store must re-pack it and send it back to the supplier where it is unpacked and examined. The person who examines the faulty goods must be paid. When the fault has been identified, the product needs to be repaired, then re-packaged and returned to the shop. The shop then telephones the customer, who calls into the shop on the next journey and collects the goods.

What does the customer think of the supplier now?

How much better to have supplied a fault-free product in the first place!

Apart from the time and effort expended, the sheer cost of packing up, unpacking, repairing, re-packing and shipping could mean that nobody makes any profit from that particular product and the store may well have lost a customer, as well as all of his or her friends.

Reliability does not only concern the product. It also concerns the level of service that surrounds it.

Imagine that somebody wishes to buy something quite expensive, perhaps some new clothes. The person telephones the shop to check that it stocks the items and has the correct size. The customer makes a special journey to buy them – but by the time the customer arrives the shop has sold out of that size and shows no interest in attempting to order the garments specially.

Another example concerns cars. Many people have not the faintest idea what happens underneath the bonnet of a car, nor do they want to find out. They trust that the garage will service their car properly, and when they are faced with an invoice for £250, it is because the work involved was necessary and came to that amount. With cars in particular, it is also essential to know that the car will be ready without delay. Imagine if it took a fortnight to service your car, in the same way that some jewellers take two weeks to clean a watch!

Let us also consider the guarantee that a product or service has. A guarantee is a 'long stop' – that is the product ought to work reliably, but if it does not, the manufacturer will repair it within the first year free of charge. If the product breaks down and the manufacturer has gone out of business, the purchaser needs to know that it can be repaired by somebody else, otherwise the customer has a product which is useless.

In the case of holidays, if a tour operator becomes bankrupt while the customers are on holiday, it is vital that they can not only continue to enjoy their holiday, but that they can also get home without having to pay extra costs!

In recent years there are many cases of customers being left in the lurch, due to the unreliability of the supplier, manufacturer or retailer.

Much is due to the level of training, the company culture, the attitude of the people concerned, and the product design.

Friendliness

Friendliness within an organisation is also frequently down to the company culture and training, as well as to the attitude of the people concerned.

The success of companies like Sainsbury's and Marks & Spencer is proof that it is quite possible to be efficient, effective, friendly and business-like. It is also possible to work under pressure, to be interrupted, and *still* remain friendly. What is essential is to maintain a sense of proportion – and a sense of humour!

> Remember the John Egan quote: 'without satisfied customers there can be no future for any commercial organisation.' (see page 205). The customer must take priority; friendliness costs nothing and repays dividends.

Availability of goods or services

A company might produce the most desirable item in the world; if it is not available relatively easily, sales may be few.

Availability of goods and services is paramount.

On the other hand, it is a logistical and financial nightmare for national retailers to carry high stocks of a large range of products. The rate of stock-turn (turnover) is slowed, the retailer has to borrow large sums to pay for the stock, and the product range carried becomes out of date because more up-to-date items cannot be stocked until the old ones are sold.

Activity

Carry out a survey of personal stereos stocked by your local stockists. Identify the

a manufacturers,
b models stocked,
c price and
d product features

for three or four different retailers. How do they vary? Discuss the different perceptions that consumers have of the particular retailers.

Speed of delivery

About 140 years ago, W H Smith founded his newspaper business on the network of people he established around the country to receive and distribute the newspapers he shipped to them from London.

Just over 100 years later, Sir Joseph Lockwood used the same system to distribute EMI hit singles.

The characteristic of both these products is that customers want them immediately – without delay. People don't wish to pay money for yesterday's news or last month's pop hit. Time is money and vital to the success of the product and the business.

To a lesser extent, the same is true of many other products. Fashion clothes need to be supplied at the moment that they are fashionable – not a season later.

Availability of goods and services is about speed of delivery, as well as ease of access. For example, an immediate telephone call from the shop when an item on order becomes available makes for enhanced customer relations.

Published policy for exchanges or refunds

There are two aspects to exchanges and refunds – the legal side and the shop's policy. The legal aspect is covered mainly by the *Trades Description Act* and the *Sale of Goods Act*; both of these Acts are covered on page 216. If goods are supplied faulty, the customer has a legal right to return them and obtain a full **refund**; the customer need not accept alternative goods, voucher or credit note. However, the contract to buy is actually between the original purchaser and the shop, so it is that person who should return the faulty goods.

Many shops will exceed their legal obligations by exchanging goods should the customer change his mind, or where the recipient of an unwanted gift returns it. This is, course, is up to the discretion of the individual shop and is often promoted as a customer service.

In addition to the published policy, the local staff have some discretion to accept goods for exchange or refund beyond the company's published policy, again often in the interests of good customer service.

A more senior person is often approached by a junior member of staff and that person will consider the merits of the individual circumstances and people and decide accordingly.

Access to buildings for wheelchairs or baby buggies

As commercial awareness of the significance of customer service grows, so does an awareness of the special needs of certain groups of people.

For example, buildings which are on more than one level (such as railway stations with their bridges and platforms) nowadays incorporate ramps for wheelchairs and baby buggies. The aisles of many supermarkets are now similarly designed to accommodate both.

Public toilets incorporate facilities for parents to change their baby's nappy – in some cases, in both ladies' and gentlemen's' toilets.

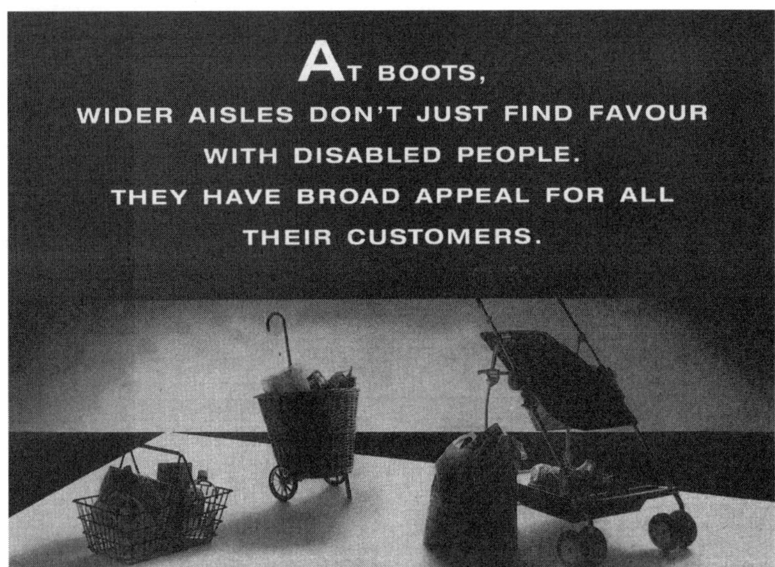

FIGURE 68 An advertisement designed to convey the vital importance of easy access to public buildings for the disabled

This new awareness of convenience for all users is demonstrated in most public buildings now being designed and built – colleges, schools, shops, offices and factories.

Care for the environment Concern for the environment was covered in greater detail in Element 1.2.

Awareness of the abuse of natural resources, especially wood in paper manufacture, dates from the growth of self-service stores and the consequent growth of the packaging industry.

The oil crisis of 1973 heightened public awareness of the cost of plastic packaging and now re-use of plastic packaging materials, like plastic bags, is encouraged by retailers and manufacturers alike.

Within stores re-using carrier bags not only helps to eliminate waste, it also reduces costs.

General re-use, or recycling, of packaging means that less is left around to disfigure country and town environments. Used food packaging, such as burgers and fish and chip wrappers are a different matter. In this case it is the customer who has a moral responsibility to dispose of them carefully not only to avoid germs spreading, but also because rubbish builds up very quickly when it is left lying around and does not degrade. In some cases build-up of rubbish can become a safety risk, which leads us smoothly into the next heading!

Customer safety This aspect of customer care depends on a number of factors.

1 The behaviour of customers themselves. Normal citizens behave responsibly; mentally disabled or disturbed people may need special attention to avoid the sort of dangers that most people would avoid of their own accord.
2 Health and safety, with special regard to the particular environment. Health and safety policy in a do-it-yourself store needs to take account of the fact that heavy goods are often moved by customers themselves so special lifting apparatus or transport is increasingly made available.
3 Procedure in the event of fire. Recent legislation following some awful incidents, most notably the fire at King's Cross underground station, as well as fires in old hotels built largely of wood, resulted in greater public awareness of fire hazards, and a dramatic review of fire regulations.

Shops, hotels and all public places now provide fire-fighting equipment such as fire blankets and extinguishers. Buildings which accommodate the public are obliged to practise fire drill. This is especially true of public buildings where special needs must be considered, such as people who are getting changed (leisure centres), customers who have not yet paid (supermarkets) and people in bed (e.g. hospitals and hotels).

Performance criterion

3.4.4 Present proposals for improvements to customer service in one organisation

Activities

Agree groups of three people.

Arrange to visit a local business of your choice. Make an appointment to talk to one of their employees about customer service. It does not matter whether customers are the general public, or employees of other businesses. Consideration should also be given to the concept of 'internal customers' as described on page 247.

Write a report on customer service within that organisation, using the following headings.

- Reliability
- Friendliness
- Availability of goods or services
- Speed of delivery
- Published policy for exchanges or refunds
- Access to buildings (wheelchairs, baby buggies)
- Care for the environment
- Customer safety

After your visit, discuss in your group how you believe these procedures and policies could be improved.

Arrange to return to the company and discuss your suggestions with the person you met. Listen to his or her comments.

Now finalise your report on how you believe these policies and procedures could be improved.

Unit 4 Financial and Administrative Support

The aim of this unit is the development of practical financial and administrative skills which help business organisations run smoothly and effectively. The unit builds on the skills in the Foundation Business GNVQ and supports progression to the Advanced Business GNVQ and other advanced courses in administration and finance. It introduces students to the fundamentals of money management which can lead to accounting at higher levels, and the production, storing and retrieval of data. The alphabetical and numerical ordering skills required for Element 4.3. are transferable skills particularly useful for electronic file management.

From: *Mandatory Units for Intermediate Business* GNVQ, May 1995

 # Element 4.1   Identify and Explain Financial Transactions and Documents

The importance of accounting and sensible management of finance to any form of business can hardly be understated.

There are many parties interested in the financial health of any business and this includes charities, churches and voluntary organisations. The phrase 'money makes the world go round' has its origins in keen observation!

Who are the parties interested? That depends upon the nature and type of business, which this element now examines in more detail.

Evidence indicators

- Three simple income and expenditure accounts which show how regular financial transactions are recorded. The three accounts show expenditure (all purchases) less than, equal to and more than income (all sales) and explain why such information is essential to a business.
- Examples of each type of financial document (purchase, sales, receipts) with explanations of the purpose of the documents, and a brief description of four payment methods.
- A list of security checks with an explanation of the importance of security to a business organisation.

Core skills

This element gives students the opportunity to demonstrate these core skills:

Application of number
Element   2.2 Tackle problems

Communication
Element   2.3 Use images

Information technology
Element   2.1 Prepare information

2.2 Process information

2.3 Present information

2.4 Evaluate the use of information technology

Performance criterion

4.1.1 Explain financial transactions which take place regularly in an organisation and explain why records of transactions are kept

Managing money

An essential part of life is the ability to manage money effectively and efficiently. On the one hand, money comes into somebody's ownership – **income**; on the other hand, money goes out of that person's ownership in return for purchases of goods and services – **expenditure.**

It is exactly the same in business and, just as in life, those who manage the financial side best, often end up with the most money.

Income

In business, regular income can be generated from many different sources:

1   **payments** from customers who have received goods or services;
2   **grants** from the government or elsewhere, if the business is eligible for them;
3   **loans** from the bank.

Expenditure

Expenditure also exists in different guises:

1   **wages** for the workforce;
2   **materials** necessary for the business: these can be components necessary for the manufacturing process and are sometimes referred to as **consumable** or **variable costs;**
3   **overheads**: these are costs related to the business and its premises – rent, rates and maintenance costs and also electricity and telephone charges. They are often known as **fixed costs,** since the business has to pay them irrespective of the amount of business they undertake.

Keeping records

An essential part of effective and efficient management of business finances is the need to track where all the money comes from, and where it goes to. In people's personal finances, there are normally relatively few sources of income and expenditure. In business, there are many more – most business have hundreds of customers, and several suppliers of different goods and services.

It is therefore vital for businesses to keep records of financial transactions. Here are some reasons for doing so.

1 So that the owners of the business can prove that certain transactions or payments took place at a certain time.
2 To monitor company performance for profitability, usually against forecast.
3 To provide accurate records for taxation purposes. The Inland Revenue (for corporation tax or, for small businesses, income tax) and Customs and Excise (for value added tax – VAT) have a right to inspect all business records and the owner has a legal obligation to keep accurate records and to make them available to tax inspectors at appropriate times.
4 In order to check that the business is paying its invoices, and that invoices owing are paid, at the correct times. There can be hundreds or thousands of incoming and outgoing payments at any one time and obviously all such transactions must be recorded – it would be impossible to rely on peoples' memories.
5 Limited companies must supply shareholders with a record of trading profits and losses at least once each year; further details are given below under 'Producing annual accounts'.
6 Partnerships and sole traders must report formally or informally to any investors in the business.

The importance of being able to trace all the stages of an order, its delivery and payment of the invoice, will be examined in greater detail later in this element on page 280.

General, purchase and sales ledgers

Businesses enter details of all purchases in a **purchase ledger**.

This used to be a book, but is now more commonly a computer file, which is usually kept alphabetically by **supplier name**. Each entry is made on the relevant page so that people within the business can easily see how much is owing to a supplier at any time.

In the **sales ledger,** businesses record sales to each customer, when they were invoiced and when payment was received. This is also kept alphabetically, but by **customer name,** so that any amounts owed by the customer are easily identified.

Any credit notes issued to the customer in respect of faulty or returned goods are also noted in the sales ledger.

In the **general ledger,** the total amount of purchases and sales is recorded, together with any returns, for which credit notes will have been issued.

The net figure, therefore shows the value of all purchases and sales made in a certain period, typically one month.

Producing annual accounts

At least for tax purposes, most businesses, no matter what their size, are obliged to present details of profits or losses recorded during the previous year's trading.

Both private and public limited companies must account regularly to their shareholders, normally once or twice per year, the turnover, profit and loss and the company's general trading situation.

For a public limited company, this is in the form of a formal, written annual report presented to shareholders at the annual general meeting and at mid-year, an interim statement of trading.

An annual report normally consists of four parts. The first is the chairman's statement, describing trading conditions for the year recorded, how the business has fared and the outlook for the future.

Then follows a statement of profit and loss for the previous trading year.

The report in Figure 69 shows how The Body Shop had a turnover (sales) of £219,700,000 in 1995. In 1994, the comparable figure was £195,400,000. 1995, therefore, recorded an increase in turnover of 12.4 per cent.

	Note	1995 £m	1994 £m
Turnover	2	**219.7**	195.4
Cost of sales		**89.6**	89.5
Gross profit		**130.1**	105.9
Net operating expenses	3	**95.6**	75.8
Operating profit	2, 5	**34.5**	30.1
Profit on disposal of subsidiary undertaking	22c	**–**	1.1
		34.5	31.2
Interest payable (net)	4	**1.0**	1.5
Profit on ordinary activities before tax		**33.5**	29.7
Tax on profit on ordinary activities	8	**11.7**	10.1
		21.8	19.6
Minority interests		**–**	0.2
Profit for financial year	9	**21.8**	19.4
Dividends paid and proposed	10	**4.5**	3.8
Retained profit	21	**17.3**	15.6
Earnings per ordinary share	11	**11.5p**	10.3p
Adjusted earnings per ordinary share	11	**11.5p**	10.1p

All amounts relate to continuing activities.

FIGURE 69 The Body Shop consolidated profit and loss account, July 1995

The trading year need not run from January to December. Many companies follow the tax year, which runs from April to March. Others record trading from July to June or October to September.

Gross profit is the turnover less cost of sales, that is the goods that were actually sold to raise the £219.7 million turnover.

Net operating expenses are selling and distribution costs, plus administrative expenses, which totalled £95,600,000.

In 1995, The Body Shop paid interest on bank loans of £1,000,000. Imagine how much money was borrowed to generate interest charges of £1 million!

Activity If interest rates are ten per cent, how much money would be borrowed to incur interest charges of £1 million?

The Body Shop had to pay tax of £11,700,000.

Of the £21,800,000 profit remaining, £17,300,000 was retained by The Body Shop for the future – to invest in new shops or a factory, for instance; perhaps even to buy another company.

As at February 1995

	Note	1995 £m	Group 1994 £m
Fixed assets			
Intangible assets	12	2.2	3.7
Tangible assets	13	73.6	67.9
Investments	14	0.5	–
		76.3	71.6
Current assets			
Stocks	15	38.6	34.6
Debtors	16	44.5	37.2
Cash at bank and in hand		29.0	24.9
		112.1	96.7
Creditors: amounts falling due within one year	17	51.2	35.6
Net current assets		60.9	61.1
Total assets less current liabilities		137.2	132.7
Creditors: amounts falling due after more than one year	18	23.7	32.4
Provisions for liabilities and charges			
Deferred tax	19	2.9	3.4
		110.6	96.9
Capital and reserves			
Called up share capital	20	9.5	9.4
Share premium account	21	37.0	35.7
Profit and loss account	21	64.1	51.8
		110.6	96.9

These financial statements were approved by the Board on 9 May 1995 and signed on its behalf by:
TG Roddick
Director

FIGURE 70 A balance sheet from The Body Shop Annual Report, July 1995

The difference (£4,500,000) is divided between shareholders, and each ordinary shareholder received 11.5p per share held.

Figure 70 shows the balance sheet. While the profit and loss account summarises trading over the whole year, the balance sheet is a snapshot of the business on the last day of the year in question, in this case 25 February 1995.

Fixed, tangible assets are buildings and equipment which the business owns.

Intangible assets include copyrights, patents and trade marks, together with the expertise involved in creating them.

Current assets are stocks which the company owns in their factories and stores throughout the world.

Debtors are included because these are people who owe the company money, but have not yet paid. On the assumption that they will pay in the new trading year, these amounts are included as assets, as valuable as cash in the bank or in the business itself.

Creditors are the people or organisations to whom the business owes money. The money owing to creditors should be subtracted from assets, as should the 'provision for charges' which is a stated amount of anticipated charges (bank, accountancy or auditors charges, for example.)

Deferred tax is tax not yet paid to either tax authority, but which will become payable in the future.

Following the profit and loss account and the balance sheet comes a description of the company's structure – how many companies there are, what they all do, and where they operate. The purpose of this is to give shareholders a more informed view of the company's trading, so that they have a better insight into how it functions.

For any business, producing regular sets of accounts for internal use enables effective control to be maintained.

If costs are rising higher than sales, then steps should be taken to reduce them; if sales are different to those budgeted, production may need to change emphasis to maintain adequate stocks of current items.

Monitoring business performance

Management accountants in a business monitor the costs incurred by the business against its forecast income and profits. This is called a **budget**, which is agreed by everybody involved in spending large sums of money on the company's behalf.

If profits turn out to be higher than forecast, there may be scope for additional spending; perhaps on advertising, in order to boost sales even more, perhaps on product development, which should reap future benefits.

When business is below forecast, it may be necessary to borrow more money to pay the costs, or the business may have to cut back on its expenditure.

Whatever the outcome, it is vital to monitor constantly – day-to-day – how the business is performing, with regular (usually monthly) reviews by senior managers and directors.

Ensuring security
Although businesses are no longer as vulnerable as they were when it was necessary for large amounts of cash to change hands, the extensive use of credit cards and cheques actually provides greater opportunities for dishonest transactions by customers – and employees who may have access to the company's finance.

Not all employers, employees and customers are honest and **auditors** regularly monitor businesses for honesty and integrity in their business dealings.

Security, honesty and integrity are also vital when reporting to the tax authorities.

Performance criterion · **4.1.2 Explain and give examples of purchases and purchase documents**

Purchases · Just as in a household, all sorts of purchases are made in a business. These can be **capital purchases**, 'one off' costs such as machinery, vehicles and new buildings. Whilst many of these items will one day need to be replaced, many capital purchases take place when a business is establishing itself.

The vast majority of **non-capital purchases** are made from a business's current account, costs that will be accounted for in full in the profit and loss account.

Such purchases may be for **materials** used in the business, such as components, packaging, and fuel for company vehicles. **Consumables** can include items like company notepaper, other stationery, printed brochures and promotional literature.

Other purchases may be for **services** which the business requires. These can range from car hire for executives to professional services from, for instance, outside accountants or the company's marketing and advertising agencies.

Wages are also a purchase in that the business is buying the labour of its employees and paying them for their time and skills.

In many businesses, there is a strict procedure for making purchases which must be adhered to ensure correct recording, and payment at the appropriate time.

So, whether the purchase is for materials or services from an outside supplier, an order is placed, initially verbally, then confirmed in writing.

Purchase documents

It may seem very simple to purchase goods or services from a supplier, but because both supplier and purchaser need to

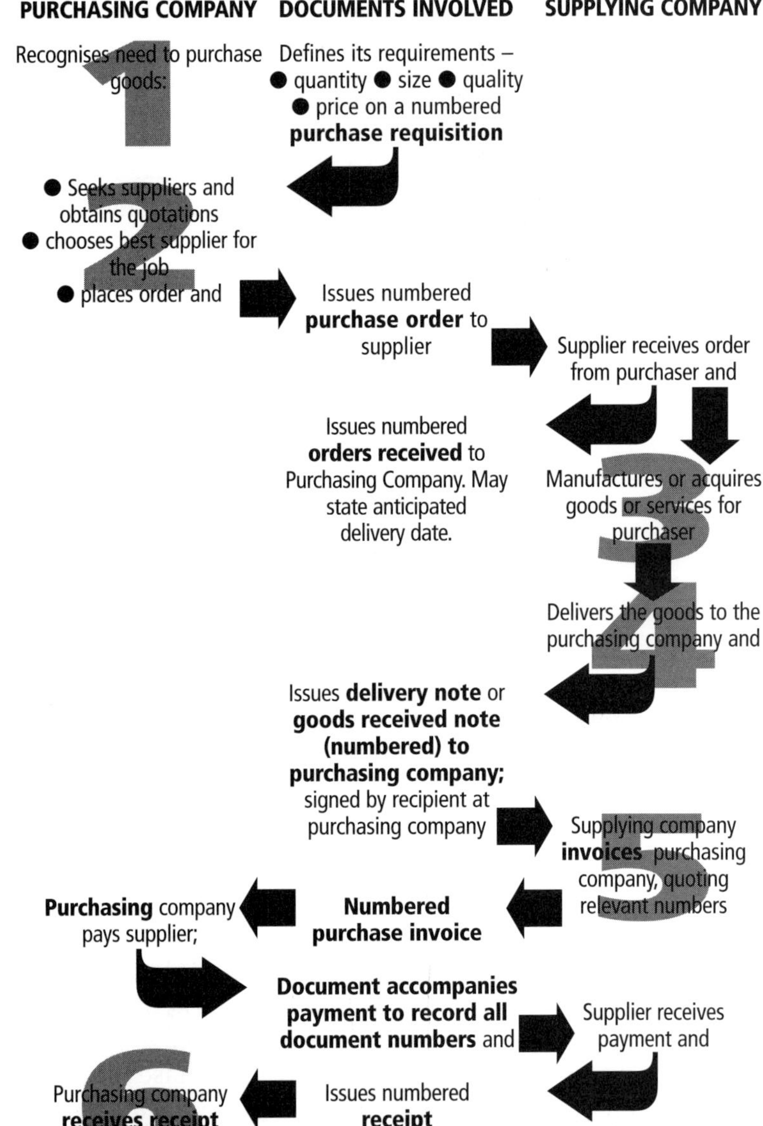

FIGURE 71 The paperwork involved in purchasing and supply

keep full records to account for their activities, a complex, but logical, flow of paperwork has to take place.

The chain of events, with accompanying documents is illustrated in Figure 71.

The order number follows the purchase throughout its life: placing the order, delivering the goods or service, invoicing and subsequent payment.

The paperwork involved seems complex, but in reality, many are simple forms, often produced on carbonless copy paper to

<table>
<tr><td colspan="2"></td><td colspan="2" align="right">GRM SYSTEMS plc
Tel: (01345) 678910
Fax: (01345) 678911</td></tr>
<tr><td colspan="4">PURCHASE ORDER RECORD</td></tr>
<tr><td>Order No:</td><td>22047</td><td>Date:</td><td>15/2/95</td></tr>
<tr><td>Supplier:</td><td>ABL</td><td>Delivery Required:</td><td>ASAP</td></tr>
<tr><td>Supplier Ref:</td><td>Peter Brown</td><td>Delivery Offered:</td><td></td></tr>
<tr><td>Supplier Tel:</td><td>Stroud 863298</td><td></td><td></td></tr>
<tr><td>Our Account No:</td><td></td><td>Date Received:</td><td></td></tr>
<tr><td>Project:</td><td>General/Stationery</td><td>Recipient:</td><td>Sue Philips</td></tr>
</table>

Quantity	Part Number	Description
50	A5 2D Ring PVC	Ring Binders
50	A5 PVC	Slipcases

CONFIRM BY FAX:	ORDER PLACED BY:	S. Philips
SUPPLIER FAX NO: 872150	APPROVED BY:	DG

23-Nov-94	(QAP 6, APPENDIX 7.1)	order.or

FIGURE 72 Sample of a typical purchase order

reduce the amount of administration necessary. Records are required at all stages by all the parties concerned:

1   the person actually placing the order;
2   the buyer (who issues the purchase requisition);
3   the delivery driver from the supplying company delivering the goods;
4   the operative in goods inwards, receiving the goods;
5   the person in accounts authorising payment to the supplying company.

Each person involved needs to be advised of what is happening. For example, the person in goods inwards needs to know whom to advise that the goods have arrived, and who should check that they are of the quality and quantity specified.

The examples in Figures 72–74 illustrate how sufficient detail is conveyed at each stage of the proceedings for this process to take place smoothly, accurately and efficiently.

FIGURE 73 Sample of a typical goods received note

Allison Works Trimedge

Sale, Glos GL0 2YZ

Tel 01345 678910   Fax 01345 678911

VAT Registered No 109 876 54

Advice No: 47391

Job No: M.175/95

Order No: Letter 16-2-95/
Order no. 22047

REP. 16

INVOICED TO:

GRM SYSTEMS PLC

1 Park Road,

Sale, Glos GL0 2YZ

DELIVER TO:

Quantity	Description	Price	£	p
50	Rb's s/s A5 x CD148 white rivets bound in			
	White PVC outside and Blue PVC inside over 32oz. boards with customers prints			
	encapsulated under front, spine and clear overlay on back cover sealed			
50	Slipcases to suit the above binders made in blue 819 PVC ovr 32oz. boards			
	Quality & quantity unchecked			

Accepted by **W Williams**

DATE **10/3/95**

Carriage to be charged

Goods sent by **Collected**

Invoice

WHITE – INVOICE. YELLOW – ACCOUNTS COPY. PINK – COPY INVOICE. GREEN – REP'S COPY.

FIGURE 74 Sample of
a typical purchase
invoice

▲ **Performance criterion**

4.1.3 Explain and give examples of sales transactions and sales documents

Obtaining and processing orders

Now let us consider this transaction from the sales side, from the supplier's point of view.

The supplier learns of the purchaser's interest in one of two ways.

1 If the purchaser is a regular customer the supplier's sales representative will call regularly to look after the customer's needs, and identify new opportunities for sales.

2 If the purchasing company is not a regular customer, the buyer may telephone or write to prospective suppliers to ask them to supply a quotation. If the order is potentially large, a sales representative may then make a personal visit to discuss the requirement in greater detail.

Whether the requirement is for goods or services, the amount of sales activity will probably be similar:

- **goods** sales may involve components, new machinery, printed materials, or stationery;
- **services** sales may involve looking after the photocopiers, servicing the company's vehicles, dictating machines or other machinery. Professional services can be from patent attorneys, accountants, or consultants.

Orders received

For some suppliers, the opportunity to obtain an order will come via a formal quotation, estimate or tender to supply goods or services for a certain price, The purchasing company may then seek to negotiate an additional discount, either for purchasing in quantity, or for prompt payment.

As we saw earlier, the purchasing company normally first indicates informally, verbally, to the supplier that an order will be placed.

The order is then confirmed in writing by the purchaser, so that both parties know where they stand. The confirming letter also states the price to be paid, including any special discount agreed between the two parties.

The supplying company can enter this on their 'orders received' file. This is a record which summarises all the orders that customers have placed. The file, when looked at over a period of months, or a year, will allow the supplying company to compare the total orders received to those received in the previous year or previous quarter.

The order may also count towards commission earned by the sales person. Accurate records of his or her transactions are therefore essential as this can represent a substantial part of that person's earnings.

One commercial service is worth special mention. Advertising agencies provide a specialist service and a request to develop a promotion from a business is likely to elicit a whirlwind of activity from agencies competing for this work. Agencies are normally requested to "pitch", which involves making a presentation to the company's senior management. This can include designs and suggestions for television commercials, press, magazine and poster advertising for the company. If an agency is successful, it may be appointed to handle such business for a specified period (normally one year at a time). For manufacturers such as Ford or Kellogg's, this can mean millions of pounds worth of business for the successful agency.

Delivery note

A delivery note will accompany the work being carried out, or the goods delivered to the purchasing company. The purpose of this is to confirm that the order has been fulfiled. The employee of the purchaser on the receiving end is not necessarily required to check goods for accuracy, merely to confirm that parcels have been delivered. The purchaser is informed how many days are available to check that the order has been delivered correctly. The recipient is asked to sign the delivery note; if the goods have not been checked, the employee may write 'Goods received but not checked' on the note.

Sales invoice

Following delivery, the supplier issues an invoice for the goods or service delivered.

This is normally sent to the person who placed the order (the person who initiated the purchase). That person is responsible for checking that the merchandise or work has been satisfactorily delivered before the originator approves the invoice for payment.

The invoice is then forwarded to the accounts department for payment.

Statement of account

The supplier may well enter this transaction onto the company's computer system, so that a regular statement of account is sent, usually monthly, to the main contact person in the purchasing company.

A statement of account is a summary of all the orders that the purchaser may have placed with the supplier and for which payment is still outstanding.

It is a diplomatic way of reminding valued customers that payment may be due or overdue, as the example in Figure 75 shows.

SHEFFIELD PROPERTY SERVICES

Management Dept.
10 Henry Street,
Sale
Gloucestershire GL0 6AB
Telephone: (01345) 161718
Fax: (01345) 161719

N Green Esq
Leyland
21 Seabrook Park
Sale
Gloucestershire
GL0 2XW

Our Ref.:   CJW/CDM

Your Ref.:

Re: 45 High Close, Sale, Glos

Invoice No.   LKF 21373A

Tax Point   27 March 1995

By Miss AB Philips – Contribution towards cost of checking Inventory of contents at end of tenancy			17	63
By Mr JD Lucas – First months rent due 18 March 1995 at £325pcm			325	00
Contribution towards cost of preparing and completing Tenancy Agreements			29	38
To Commission at $12\frac{1}{2}$% on £325	40	63		
To VAT at $17\frac{1}{2}$%	7	11		
<u>Fees</u>				
To Serving Notice under Section 20 of Housing Act 1988 and preparing and completing Tenancy Agreements for the furnished letting of the property to Mr JD Lucas on an Assured Shorthold Tenancy for 6 months from 18.3.95 at £325pcm	50	00		
To checking through Inventory of contents at the departure of Miss AB Philips	15	00		
VAT at $17\frac{1}{2}$%	11	38		

FIGURE 75 Sample of a typical statement of account

Performance criterion

4.1.4 Explain and give examples of payment methods and receipt documents

Payment

There are several ways in which people or businesses may arrange to make payments:

- cheque;
- cash;
- credit or charge card;
- debit card;
- credit;
- hire purchase;
- pay slip;
- petty cash voucher.

Cheque

This is a very secure way of making payment for both businesses and private transactions, since the transaction may be traced throughout the whole process. The party making the payment has, by completing the counterfoil, a record of when the cheque was written.

Receipt of the cheque by the supplier's bank triggers the bank to debit the purchaser's bank account.

The recipient's bank statement will identify when the cheque was paid into the account.

In addition, payment of a cheque may be stopped if the paying party has second thoughts, or if the recipient of the goods discovers an omission or sub-standard merchandise.

As Figure 76 shows, each cheque is numbered separately. The name of the payee (person to be paid) is written or printed on the cheque, as is the amount to be paid.

Cash

A business only uses cash to pay for items of very small value, usually paid out of petty cash, that is the small amount of ready cash that most businesses hold to reimburse employees for small purchases that they make on the company's behalf.

The same may apply to private purchases. A cash payment can only be proved when accompanied by a receipt and anybody carrying a large amount of cash is a natural target for pickpockets or other theft.

In addition, cash, especially banknotes, may be forged, which presents a further complication for the receiving party.

FIGURE 76 Sample of a typical completed cheque and cheque stub

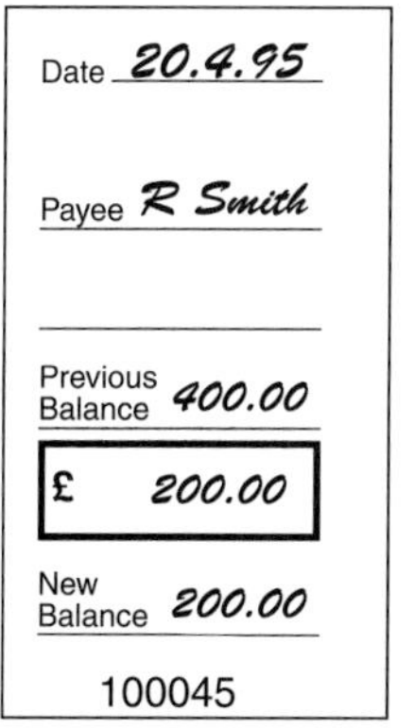

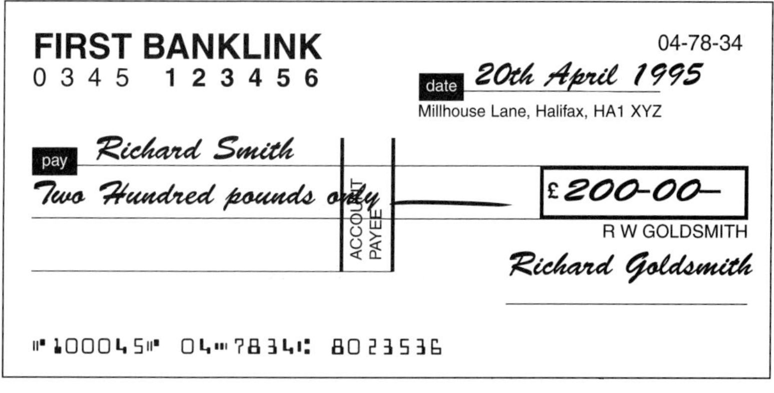

Credit or charge card

There are two kinds of credit card, one for private consumers and one for businesses. For both types of holders, there is a credit limit which applies to the total value of purchases in any one month. Businesses issue certain employees with a company credit card in order to pay for petrol and other authorised expenses, food and hotel accommodation while on company business.

Credit cards are so called because any purchase made using them does not need to be paid for until at least three weeks later, when a statement is sent to the holder by the credit card company.

Although credit cards are susceptible to fraud or theft, they offer a safer means than cash to pay for goods or services. In addition, insurance cover is available giving the holder entitlement to a refund in certain instances of breakage, or goods later proving to be substandard.

However, credit cards are a relatively expensive means of payment, even if the amount payable is settled in full as soon as the statement arrives.

There are three types of charges associated with credit card payments. The first is the fee which the holder must pay to the company which issued the card. This is about £10, payable annually. Charge cards, which operate in a similar way to credit cards, charge even more.

The second is the merchanting fee, which a business pays to the credit card company in order to clear the transaction and receive payment from the issuer of the credit or charge card. This can vary from one per cent to three per cent of the value of the transaction. In other words, if somebody pays £100 by credit or charge card for some goods, the seller actually only receives up to £99; the credit card company receives £1 for making the payment. This is one reason why the more widespread use of credit cards in the late 1980s was felt to be a significant cause of inflation, since some retailers, especially petrol stations, were forced to increase their prices to pay for their high credit card merchanting fees.

The final cost is the charge for the credit itself. When the whole amount owed on a credit card is not cleared within about three weeks from receipt of the statement, interest is charged on the outstanding amount.

This is usually at a far higher rate than usual – around 20 per cent, compared to 10 or 12 per cent on a standard bank loan.

Debit card

This is a more recent payment method than a credit card and owes its existence to the availability of technological innovation which allows a supplier to check the customer's ability to pay at the time of the purchase.

When the card is 'swiped' through the supplier's card machine, the card owner's details are checked for payment worthiness. If approved, the account is debited and the supplier's account credited forthwith.

In this way, the transaction is similar to that of a cheque, except that clearance is immediate.

There is normally no annual fee for holders of debit cards; they cannot be used as a source of credit, so no interest is payable. There is a small merchanting fee which the supplier must pay to use the debit card. Unlike a cheque (which may be stopped), or cash (which may be forged), once payment has been cleared, the supplier is virtually assured of receiving payment for the goods supplied.

Credit

Many businesses make purchases on credit and it is quite acceptable for companies which do a lot of business together to have 30, or, decreasingly these days, 60 or 90 days credit. In other words, if an invoice is sent on the first day of the month, payment is not required until the first day of the following month.

Clearly, for a business, this has implications for expenditure compared to income (the 'cash flow'), for the company may have to borrow the amount of the outstanding debt to make further purchases until payment is received. For this reason, businesses sometimes give a discount for quicker payment – within seven days or even by return. Such discount may be 2.5 per cent – enough to be worthwhile for both payer and payee. This discount is both an incentive for the payer and a way of reducing the payee's bank borrowing.

Thirty days is, however, a common length of time for credit to be agreed between well-acquainted businesses.

Hire purchase

This is a form of credit especially for higher-priced consumer goods such as electronics, cars and furniture. It is offered by the retailer to the customer, and operated by suppliers such as Lombard, Tricity Finance and Wagon Finance, many of whom are owned by the high street banks (Lombard, for example, is owned by Midland Bank).

The customer pays a deposit at the point of sale and then makes monthly payments to the finance house. It usually works out as a very expensive means of making purchases, since both the retailer and the finance house profit from such transactions.

In addition, the finance house is running some risk of default, since the loan is frequently unsecured.

Secured loans are when a householder owns property and gives the right of sale of that property to the lender in case of default of payment (such as when a building society lends money for house purchase.) In this case, the chances of the lender losing any money is small since repossession of the house will allow more than adequate recompense for the missed payments. Any balance is paid back to the defaulting customer.

In the event of the loan being unsecured, the finance house must repossess the goods then sell them to recoup losses. Under such conditions, the repossessed goods are frequently in unsaleable condition and money is lost by the finance house.

Receipts

The main purpose of a receipt is to provide proof of payment. Thus, receipts can exist in several forms, including cheque stubs, paying-in slips and bank statements.

The reason for giving a receipt is to provide written confirmation to the person paying that a sum of money has been received by the person or company for whom it was intended.

It may subsequently be useful for a variety of reasons, to prove that payment has actually taken place.

A receipt may be written on anything. All that is required is a written declaration by the recipient that the sum has been received, ideally dated and perhaps signed; the only necessity is that the receipt may be traced back to the payer of the money. Taxi drivers have been known to supply receipts written on the margin of a newspaper! Thus, a till receipt from a supermarket which states the amount paid and the name of the supermarket, provides evidence that this transaction has taken place. This is normally sufficient to allow trouble-free exchange of goods, or to receive a refund in the event of goods being unsatisfactory.

Ideally, the receipt should be duplicated so that both payer and payee have a copy, but this is not essential.

A cheque stub or counterfoil can act as a receipt – proof that on a particular day a cheque for the recorded amount, payable to recipient X, was written by the person concerned. Together with the bank statement, which shows when this sum of money was taken out of the bank account, this provides proof that the transaction has taken place.

Similarly, a stamped paying-in slip is proof of payment into a bank account and thus acts as a receipt.

By contrast, the acknowledgement given by a bank paying-in machine states that it is not a receipt, because the sum is received 'subject to confirmation'.

A train ticket acts as proof of payment for inspection and other purposes.

 **Performance criterion**

4.1.5 Explain the importance of security and security checks for receipts and payments

Financial security

Since business revolves around money, it is essential that its management is very tightly controlled.

For this reason, an organisation is quite vulnerable when money is changing hands and security checks therefore take place at each stage of the payment process. The reason for all the documentation mentioned under performance criterion 4.1.1, page 280 will now become apparent.

The three main stages in the process of order, delivery and payment for goods, from a financial point of view, are:

1 authorisation of orders;
2 invoices against orders and goods received notes;
3 authorised cheque signatories.

Authorisation of orders

In order to control spending within an organisation, only certain people, usually with some seniority, have a budget within their control.

These people are the only ones who can give authority for the organisation to spend sums of money on the organisation's behalf. In many cases, there will be a stated limit to the amount of money that that person is able to spend in any one purchase, and the type of goods that the person is able to buy for the business.

In order to prevent fraud specimen signatures may be held on file by the business so that, if necessary, authorisation signatures may be checked for authenticity.

It is vital that any supplier should recognise this authority before proceeding to supply the business. The consequences of proceeding without authorisation are that the business cannot receive – **nor pay for** – the goods!

This procedure is such common business practice that in only very rare instances does it present any embarrassment.

Invoices against orders and goods received notes

Before paying an invoice, the company should check that the goods have actually been received in good condition and in the right quality and quantity.

For this reason, the authorising signatory should reconcile the supplier's invoice with the purchaser's order and the goods received note that the warehouse or other receiving person signed when the goods were delivered.

If everything is in order, the invoice may then be approved for payment.

If not, the invoice needs to be queried with the supplier; perhaps by telephone, perhaps by fax or letter.

In rare instances of persistent errors, it may be advisable to change the supplier.

Authorised cheque signatories

An authorised cheque signatory is a person nominated to sign cheques on the company's behalf.

Such people are usually restricted to the owner, directors, or at least senior managers of the business. Certainly, not all budget holders, nor those allowed to authorise invoices, are allowed to sign cheques on behalf of the company.

The whole process should have been controlled for accuracy from start to finish, so at this stage in the payment process, signing the cheque is usually a mere formality. However, the responsibility for such action must rest with a senior person, who can ensure that the transaction makes overall sense – the supplier, the type and quantity of goods and the amount to be paid.

Since the signatory may well not have been involved beforehand in a particular transaction, the invoice and a copy of the goods received note normally accompany the unsigned cheque, so that the signatory may review details before committing the company to payment by signing the cheque.

Usually, the accounts department fills in the relevant details, since the signatory is a senior person and there is normally a large pile of cheques to sign; the signatory does not wish to spend time filling in such details, he or she merely wishes to approve them.

Authorised signatories of a business give specimen signatures to their accounts' department and to their bank, so that cheques may be verified for accuracy.

The whole process of order authorisation, invoice approval and regulated cheque signatories is designed to ensure maximum security of the company's finances.

Activities

1 Arrange to visit a local business, preferably a manufacturing company.
   a Explain **why** the business needs to record details of income and expenditure.

b Give examples of the **purchases** that the business makes. Explain, with samples of the relevant documents including receipts, how the business accurately records information relating to the purchases they make.

c Give examples of the **sales** that the business makes. This information may be available from catalogues or sales brochures.

d Explain, with samples of the relevant documents including receipts, how the business accurately records information relating to their sales.

2 Arrange to meet somebody in the finance or accounts department of a local business.

a Find out how many different methods the company uses to make payments. Give four examples, including claims for expenses if possible. Explain how the business uses each method.

b Find examples of the different types of receipt mentioned in the text and explain how the business uses the information each contains.

3 Discuss the security arrangements that the company has with regard to these procedures:
- purchase requisition;
- quality control of goods inwards;
- invoice approval;
- cheque signature.

4 Obtain three simple business income and expenditure accounts from parents, friends, or other source. These could be an extract from a day book, accounts payable, accounts due or other financial record. The annual accounts of The Body Shop on pages 276–277 could be one example.

Using different time periods as examples, show examples of expenditure for all purchases being:

a less than income (all sales);

b more than income (all sales);

c expenditure equalling income.

A balance sheet, accompanied by an explanation, would demonstrate this.

Explain why such information is essential to a business.

 # Element 4.2 — Complete Financial Documents and Explain Financial Recording

This element aims to extend the understanding gained in the last element by giving students the opportunity to complete some of the documents that were examined then. Students should gain an understanding of the financial information which supports budgeting, and the production of accounts in a business.

This element is almost entirely based on activities. The previous element may be useful for further reference.

Evidence indicators

- A clearly and correctly completed set of financial documents supporting a simple income and expenditure account over a stated period of time, showing total income and total expenditure.
- A list of computer software which a business could use to record and monitor financial information. The list should name the supplier, cost and features of the software.

Core skills

This element gives students the opportunity to demonstrate these core skills:

Application of number
Element 2.1 Collect and record data

2.3 Interpret and present data

Communication
Element 2.1 Take part in discussions

2.2 Produce written material

2.3 Use images

2.4 Read and respond to written materials

Information technology
Element   2.1 Prepare information

2.2 Process information

2.3 Present information

2.4 Evaluate the use of information technology

Activities   1   **A transaction between Jellymould UK Ltd and DIY Plc**

On 25 June, 1996,
   Jellymould UK Ltd, Unit 4, Woodcaster Industrial Estate,
   Michaelhampton, Gloucestershire GL15 1AB
place an order with DIY Plc for:

   4,000 2.5cm length rivets @ £16 per 1,000
   150 steel angle joints @ £1.25 each
   75 electric plugs fused 13 amp. @ 33 pence each.

The supplier's address is:
   DIY Plc, Springclean Lane, Lingfold, Surrey RH5 2YZ

and they deliver it to Jellymould on 5 July, 1996.

The goods are invoiced on invoice number 8769457J on 20 July 1996. Jellymould pay for it by cheque on 1 September, 1996.

You should note that in August, 1996, there is still an invoice outstanding from a delivery of June 1996, invoiced on 15 June, 1996, Invoice No. 1958473J for £754.96 plus £132.12p VAT, total £887.08p. Jellymould is a regular customer of DIY Plc and enjoys a 10 per cent discount on all purchases.

You are now going to fill in the relevant documentation for the transaction.

Purchase documents
- Purchase order placed (purchase order record) – Figures 72 and 80
- Goods received note – Figures 73 and 82
- Purchase invoice – Figures 74 and 81

Sales documents
- Orders received – Figures 77 and 83
- Sales invoice – Figures 78 and 84
- Delivery note – Figures 79 and 85
- Statement of account (for August 1996 in your exercise) – Figures 75 and 86.

Note: **For each of these tasks, number the document 1, 2, 3 and so on and explain why it is vital that this and all other information should be correct. Explain what might happen if it were inaccurate.**

Write out this documentation, using the completed illustrations in this and Element 4.1 for guidance, and the blank forms as a basis.

Memo	**ORDER ACKNOWLEDGEMENT**

TO: **GRM Systems plc**
FROM: ADRIAN BARKING LTD
DATE: **22.2.95**
SUBJECT: ORDER ACKNOWLEDGEMENT

ORDER #: **Letter 16/2/95/ Order no. 22047**

DATE RECEIVED: **17/2/95**

DESCRIPTION:

50 – Binders @ £1.99
50 – Sipcases @ £2.92

COST:

EML JOB #: **M175/95**

DESPATCH DATE:

W/E 10/3/95

....

ADRIAN BARKING LTD

FIGURE 77 Orders received

**FIGURE 78 Sales
invoice**

1, Bonham Park, Sale, Gloucestershire GL0 2XW
Tel: (01345) 873641 Fax (01345) 121315

South Western Bearings Plc
800 Park Avenue
Almondsbury
Bristol
BS12 4SE

For the attention of Malcolm White, Esq
Business Marketing

Invoice No; 235

Invoice Date; 23.11.92

I N V O I C E

To:

1. Supplying 'Business Connection' models on 18.11.92
ref. Quotation of 20.7.92

Balance (70%) of charge
(Total 400 sets x £6.11)   £1710.80

Origination – artwork (50%)   £240.00

author's corrections to artwork   £97.00

2. Supplying 200 sets GW 849 Pot Pourri
Dish Gift Pack ref. Quotation of 9.10.92   £1600.00

SUB TOTAL   £3647.00

VAT @ 17.5%   £636.36

TOTAL NOW PAYABLE   £4286.16

VAT Reg. No. 345 6789 10

EYE *for* **ID**

1, Bownham Park, Rodborough Common, Sa
Tel: (01345) 873641 Fax (01

South Western Printing Plc
Romney Avenue
Lockleaze
Bristol

For the attention of Mr Colin Wood

18 November 1992

D E L I V E R Y N O T E

Please receive herewith:

1. 198 individually gift-wrapped
Pot Pourri Dish Gift Packs

6 cartons of 31 Packs
1 carton of 12 Packs

Total 7 cartons

2. 398 boxed sets of 6 'Business Connection' coasters

7 cartons of 50 sets
1 carton of 48 sets

Total 8 cartons

Received..

Delivered..

VAT Reg. No. 345 6789 10

FIGURE 79 Delivery note

Jellymould UK Ltd

Unit 4, Woodcaster Industrial Estate,
Michaelhamton, Gloucestershire GL15 1AB
Tel: (01345) 016789 Fax: (01345) 016790

PURCHASE ORDER RECORD

Order No: ________________________   Date: ________________________

Supplier: ________________________   Delivery Required: ________________

Supplier Ref: ____________________   Delivery Offered: ________________

Supplier Tel: ____________________   ________________________

Our Account No: __________________   Date Received: __________________

Project: ________________________   Recipient: ______________________

Quantity	Part Number	Description

23-Nov-94   (QAP 6, APPENDIX 7.1)   order.or

FIGURE 80 Purchase order record.
See Figure 72 (page 281) for a completed example

PURCHASE
INVOICE

Springclean Lane,

Lingfold, Surrey RH5 2YZ

Tel 01883 558910   Fax 01883 558911

VAT Registered No 109 876 54

DIY PLC

Invoice No. :
Invoice Date/
Tax Point :
Account No. :

Invoice To:

Deliver To:

Our Order No.   Your Order Reference

Date Order Received   Date Despatched   Order Analysis Data

Part No.   Description   Quantity   List Price   Net Value

V/C   VAT Rate   Goods Amount   VAT Amount

Total Value

VAT

Total Due

TERMS OF PAYMENT STRICTLY NET
UNLESS STATED OTHERWISE
PAYMENT WITHIN 30 DAYS FROM DATE OF INVOICE

WHITE – INVOICE. YELLOW – ACCOUNTS COPY. PINK – COPY INVOICE. GREEN – REP'S COPY.

FIGURE 81   Purchase invoice note.
See Figure 74 (page 283) for a completed example

DIY PLC

Springclean Lane,

Lingfold, Surrey **RH5 2YZ**

Tel 01883 558910

Fax 01883 558911

VAT Registered No 109 876 54

Advice No: ______________

Job No: ______________

Order No: ______________

INVOICED TO:

DELIVER TO: REP. ______________

Quantity	Description	Price	£	p

Accepted by ______________   DATE ______________

Carriage to be charged	Goods sent by	Invoice

WHITE – INVOICE. YELLOW – ACCOUNTS COPY. PINK – COPY INVOICE. GREEN – REP'S COPY.

FIGURE 82 Goods received note. See Figure 73 (page 282) for a completed example

Memo   **ORDER ACKNOWLEDGEMENT**

TO:
FROM: JELLYMOULD UK LTD
DATE:
SUBJECT: ORDER ACKNOWLEDGEMENT

ORDER #:

DATE RECEIVED:

DESCRIPTION:

COST:

JOB #:

DESPATCH DATE:

....

JELLYMOULD UK LTD

FIGURE 83 Orders received note. See Figure 77 (page 297) for a completed example

Invoice

VAT Reg. No. 345 6789 10

FIGURE 84 Sales invoice.
See Figure 78 (page 298) for a completed example

Delivery Note

FIGURE 85 Delivery note.
See Figure 79 (page 298) for a completed example

DIY PLC

Springclean Lane,

Lingfold, Surrey RH5 2YZ

Tel 01883 558910

Fax 01883 558911

VAT Registered No 109 876 54

Statement

FIGURE 86 Statement of account. See Figure 75 (page 286) for a completed example

Complete the payment cheque and stub for the 1 September, 1995, as if you were a signatory for Jellymould UK Ltd.

- Cheque with cheque stub – Figures 76 and 91

Payments documents

Now switch roles and imagine that you are Charlie Brown, who works in the accounts department. Issue a receipt for the cheque you receive and complete a paying in slip for your bank.

- Receipt – Figures 87 and 93
- Paying in slip – Figures 88 and 92

FIGURE 87 Examples of receipts

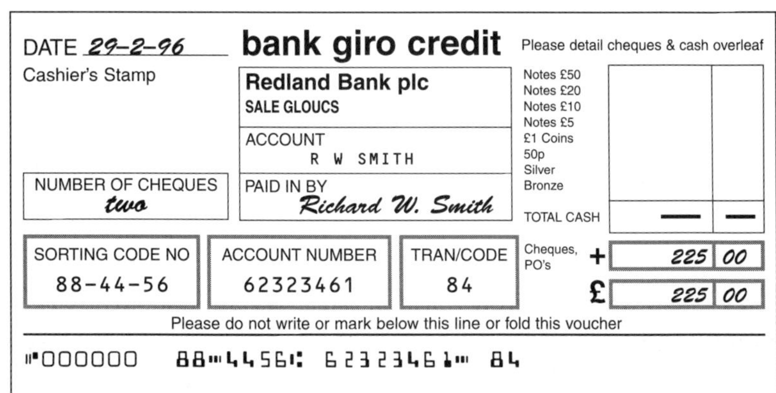

FIGURE 88 A completed paying in slip

Charlie Brown earns £9,600 p.a. in the accounts department. Work out his gross pay and mileage payment for June 1996, a month in which he travelled 47 miles for the company. The company reimburses employees at 56 pence per mile.

- Pay slip – Figure 89

	PAY ADVICE		
ADDITIONS		DEDUCTIONS	
GROSSPAY 995.00		SUPER(T) 59.70	
MILEAGE 22.00		TAX 169.91	
		NAT.IN.D 73.27	
**TOTAL* 1017.00		**TOTAL* 302.88	
		NET PAY 714.12	

Deductions are for Income Tax, National Insurance Contribution and for the company's Pension Scheme

FIGURE 89 A pay slip

While he was out on business, at his manager's request, Charlie Brown purchased a pen for £5.40. Complete the petty cash slip so that Charlie can reclaim his money from Jellymould UK Ltd.

- Petty cash voucher – Figures 90 and 94

Petty Cash Voucher

Date 26/10/95

Department Admin

For what required	£	p
Postage	12	80
	12	80

Signed A. White

Approved Brian Philips

FIGURE 90 A completed petty cash voucher

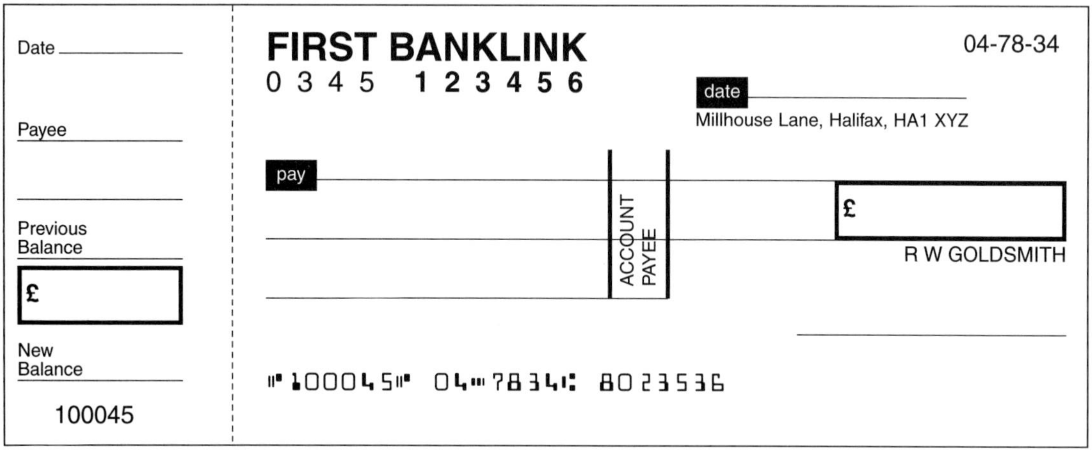

Date _______________

Payee _______________

____

Previous
Balance

£ _______________

New
Balance _______________

100045

FIRST BANKLINK

0 3 4 5   **1 2 3 4 5 6**

04-78-34

date _______________

Millhouse Lane, Halifax, HA1 XYZ

pay _______________

ACCOUNT PAYEE

£ _______________

R W GOLDSMITH

____

⑈100045⑈ 04⑈7834⑇ 8023536

**FIGURE 91 A cheque
to be copied and
filled in.
See Figure 76 (page
287) for a completed
example**

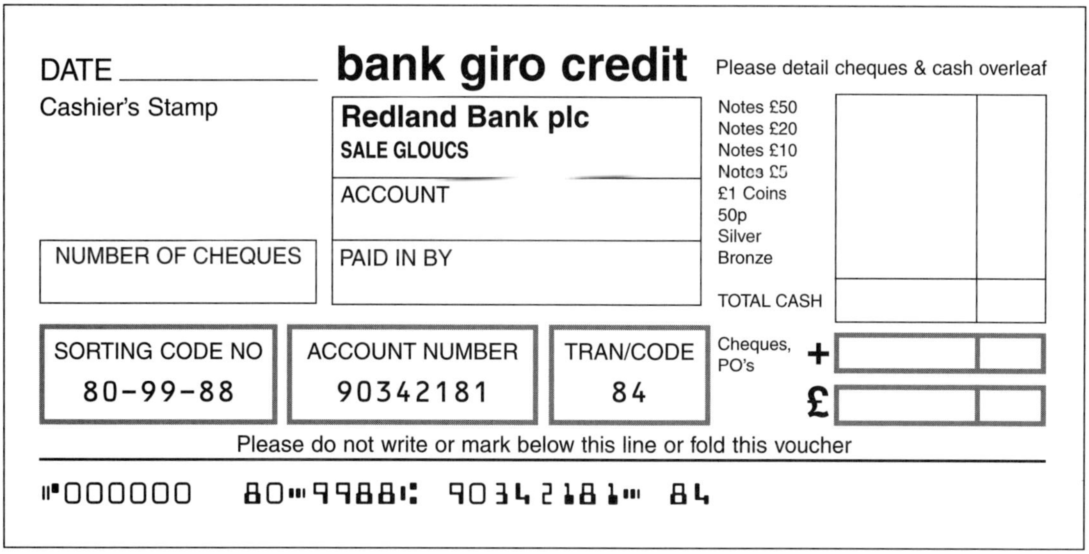

DATE _______________

Cashier's Stamp

NUMBER OF CHEQUES

bank giro credit

Redland Bank plc

SALE GLOUCS

ACCOUNT

PAID IN BY

Please detail cheques & cash overleaf

Notes £50
Notes £20
Notes £10
Notes £5
£1 Coins
50p
Silver
Bronze

TOTAL CASH

SORTING CODE NO	ACCOUNT NUMBER	TRAN/CODE
80-99-88	90342181	84

Cheques,
PO's   **+**

£

Please do not write or mark below this line or fold this voucher

⑈000000 80⑈9988⑇ 90342181⑈ 84

**FIGURE 92 A paying
in slip to be copied
and filled in**

No.: ....   Date: ....

Received with thanks

From ....

....

....

£

signed ....

FIGURE 93 A receipt to be completed

Petty Cash Voucher

Date ....

Department ....

For what required	£	p

Signed ....

Approved ....

FIGURE 94 A petty cash voucher to be copied and filled in

2   Find out from two local businesses, and your school or college, how their accounts departments use information technology to help them record and monitor financial information.

Evaluate the advantages and disadvantages that computerised systems have over manual ones.

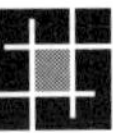

Element 4.3 Produce, Evaluate and Store Business Documents

About this element

Having focused on finance thus far in Unit Four, this element is all about the written word in business and how it is used as a means of conveying information.

The practical activities in this element highlight the role of business documents in organising work and emphasise the importance of safe storage and reliable retrieval. It is designed to help students to appreciate the conventions and formats used in business communications, and to assist them in developing filing skills which are necessary when using IT systems.

Evidence indicators

- A set of accurately and correctly produced business documents which includes a draft and final version for each document in the range, and notes evaluating the quality of appearance, style, format, spelling and grammar.
- Three examples of different methods of processing business documents, with a summary which compares them in terms of legibility, cost, time taken to produce, the ease with which they can be amended, and storage.
- A record of referencing, filing and retrieving at least 36 documents and six files.

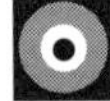

Core skills

This element gives students the opportunity to demonstrate these core skills:

Communication
Element 2.2 Produce written material

2.3 Use images

2.4 Read and respond to written materials

Information technology
Element 2.1 Prepare information

2.2 Process information

2.3 Present information

2.4 Evaluate the use of information technology

 **Performance criterion**

4.3.1 Explain the purpose of routine business documents

Technology has had an enormous impact on communication in business. The fax machine, mobile telephone, personal computer, main frame computer system, E-mail, telephone conferencing, and many other developments have revolutionised business life for most people.

These innovations offer more **support** to business; its basic purpose is unchanged. We have already seen the expression beginning 'business is people' on page 102. It ends 'knowledge is power'. People in business must communicate information. It may be done orally (by speaking), aurally (by listening), graphically (by seeing pictures), visually (by observation) and in other ways.

Communicating through business documents

Information may be conveyed through business documents for three main purposes:

- giving;
- receiving;
- recording.

Giving and receiving information

As a means of communication with customers, colleagues and other companies, business documents are simply a way of learning facts and opinions. They are there to be read; there is no opportunity for discussion or asking questions. Business documents are a **one-way communication**.

They should not normally be used, therefore, as the sole means of communicating a piece of information. Prior or subsequent discussion should take place around any document. If for no other reason, the person who wrote the document is thus certain that it has been seen and read!

In a bureaucratic or autocratic organisation, documents tend to be used as the sole means of communication when the writer is defending a particular course of action, wishes to hide something, or wishes to put pressure on colleagues if the piece of information is so important that it is their fault if they have not read it. This sort of attitude to communication does exist in business, especially in a bureaucracy or autocracy.

Recording information

Documents have a longer life than discussions, meetings, telephone conversations, or other instant communication media.

They can be stored: perhaps for later reference, perhaps simply to record an event that may be used to prove a fact on a subsequent date.

Different types of business documents

There are five types of business documents which need to be considered:

- letters;
- memos;
- invitations;
- notices;
- messages.

Letters

Business letters, in any language, are normally quite formal communications and have a unique etiquette. We shall consider business language later on in this chapter.

There are two kinds of business letter; the individual letter and the mailshot.

As a means of communication either is restricting for the reasons mentioned earlier – it is a one way communication and the reader is unable to ask questions.

Individual letters

The individual letter is a communication which often confirms in writing something that was discussed by telephone, in person or at a meeting.

However, it can also serve to advise somebody of certain information, perhaps prior to a meeting.

Mailshots

A business mailshot is usually used to inform potential customers about a product or service, in certain circumstances:

1 inviting them to meet on the business stand at a trade fair or exhibition;
2 inviting customers to a meeting or preview to be held at different venues around the country;
3 inviting the respondent to return a card to obtain further information.

In short, a business letter may be written by one person to one other person; by several people (who can all sign it) to one person or by one person to several people – in which case copies are made, signed and sent to the various recipients.

Sometimes, copies may also be sent to people who are mentioned in the letter, or who are affected by its contents. In this case, it is customary to state at the bottom of the letter who is to receive copies, using the abbreviation 'c.c.' (short for 'carbon copy', from the days of carbon paper and typewriters).

Memos

A memo (short for 'memorandum') is a written communication between people who work for the same company, or group of companies.

A hand-written note may use a spare scrap of paper which might be left on somebody's desk if that person is unavailable. A memo is unlike this: it is more formal.

Thus, a memo is an internal business letter, and may be used in exactly the same way as an external letter. A memo is similarly likely to receive more attention if it is discussed before or after it is sent. Otherwise, depending on its contents, written memos are easily ignored by their recipients.

Invitations

Invitations can vary from the individual invitation to a valued business partner to attend a test match, the opera at Covent Garden or a dinner to announce the launch of a new product, to a mass mailing inviting potential customers to try a new magazine free for a month.

In all cases the purpose of an invitation is to generate a positive response from the recipient; for this reason it should be worded in formal, polite but friendly language.

Often the third person is used as in Figure 95, for example.

Notices

The use of memos, meetings and notices are all a reflection of the type of business for which a person is working. Some businesses write memos by the ream, others hardly at all; some call regular meetings, others rarely.

Notices also fall into this category.

There are generally three kinds of notice:

1   to warn – for example, 'always wear eye protection when using welding equipment';
2   to advise – these are usually day-to-day happenings, such as a notice from the supervisor to say that she will be on holiday for two weeks from a certain date;
3   to announce – these are more important and tend by their nature to attract readers. Such notices can have far reaching implications, such as an announcement that the managing director has resigned.

FIGURE 95 A business invitation

Farnes Barnes Leisure Services plc

Charlie Farnes Barnes
requests the pleasure of
the company of

Hilda Greencushion

at the Finals of the
All England Tennis Championships
at Wimbledon
on 16th July at 10am.
Luncheon at 12.30, High Tea from 3.30

R.S.V.P.
Melinda Smithers
Farnes Barnes Leisure Services plc

Please bring this invitation with you

Messages

These may be on notice boards, computer screens, or on 'post-it' notes left on telephones. In all cases, they should be timed and dated, so that the person knows how old the message is, and legibly signed by the person who took the message, in case of any misunderstanding or questions.

 **Performance criterion**

4.3.2 Produce draft and final versions of business documents

Business language for correspondence

In most countries and languages there is an etiquette that is unique to business correspondence. Much of it is exists for very sound reasons, such as ease of understanding, but some does not.

For example, in what other form of letter would you write 'Yours sincerely' – and be sure that you should not have written 'Yours faithfully'? When would you write 'Yours faithfully'? Where else would you address as 'Dear' somebody you loathe?

Similar anomalies exist in French and German.

Formalities to observe in letters

There are some formalities which need to be observed. For example:

> **Dear Sir** or **Dear Madam** is followed by **Yours faithfully.**

> **Dear Mrs Smith, Dear Mr Brown, Dear Charlie,** or **Dear Miss, Rev. Dr or other named person,** is followed by **Yours sincerely.**

In general, the type of language used to a business acquaintance is more formal when written than when speaking directly to them.

Let us consider the letter in Figure 96.

Note, first of all, that it is on **company headed notepaper.**

1, Bownham Park, Sale, Gloucestershire GL0 2XW
Tel: (01345) 873641 Fax (01345) 121315

Geoff Green, Esq.
Marketing Director
ABC Girders Ltd.
704, Park Avenue
Aztec West
Almondsbury
Bristol BS12 1AB

24 March 1995

Dear Mr Green,

Ref: Model House

I write in response to your letter of 18 March 1995.

Thank you for sending me the brochure with a diagram of the idea for a model house.

On first inspection, there appears to be several different ways to realise this effectively which I would be very happy to progress with you.

I have pleasure in enclosing an initial quotation to devise and supply 5,000 units of such an item.

You will appreciate that the final price may be subject to some variation as the project develops, but I will be able to confirm prices once we start to develop the product.

As there is no requirement to score the board, there is a saving over the previous quotation, partly offset by small increases in print and board costs over the two years.

I will ring you early next week to progress.

Yours sincerely

Richard Smith

VAT Reg. No. 345 6789 10

FIGURE 96 A business letter
Then follows, on the **left hand side**, the **name**, **title** and **full postal business address** of the recipient.

After that, on the **right hand side** is the **date**.

Then the **salutation**, 'Dear Mr Green'.

So that Mr Green can quickly understand what the letter is about, the heading of the letter relates to the subject matter which follows.

'Ref.' stands for 'With reference to', in this case a promotional model of a house.

Note the **formal nature of the language,** 'I write in response to your letter ...', rather than 'I have got your letter of 18 March and this is my answer ...'.

The sentence 'Thank you for sending me' acts as a reminder to Mr Green of previous developments. In other words, Mr Green can pick up the letter and plunge straight back into the thought processes which he was exploring a week ago when Mr Smith and Mr Green last discussed the model house.

The benefit of this is that in business, many different things happen at once, and on occasions, it can be difficult to remember precisely what had been happening in a particular area under discussion.

The main difference between the written word and the spoken word is that people can usually see each other when they are speaking and, even on the telephone, phrasing and intonation can be heard.

In writing none of these aids exists, so , for example, a smile has to be written. Hence this letter states, 'I have pleasure in enclosing' rather than 'I am enclosing'. Both mean the same, but 'I have pleasure' infers that Mr Smith would really like to do business with Mr Green.

'I will ring you early next week to progress' is a formal statement in a form of business letter shorthand to clarify the next action. In this case, even if Mr Green does nothing, he will receive a telephone call from Mr Smith the following week.

This is not to say that language should be overcomplicated. It is vital to be precise and accurate and therefore use of appropriate words is essential. Over-complication is likely to mean that such written work is avoided, ignored or, at best, reluctantly considered.

Formalities to observe in reports

> The main purpose of writing anything in business is to make a statement which you hope will gain support.

For this and other reasons, there are some rules which apply particularly to reports and longer documents.

1 Facts should be presented dispassionately, analytically and objectively.
2 When figures are presented, their source should always be quoted.
3 An opinion should only be stated when requested. Then it may appear under a section entitled 'recommendations', or, with supporting arguments, the author may choose from a number of stated options.
From such a careful exposition, the stated opinion may well stimulate further discussion.
4 The passive tense is often used in reports and long documents. The reader will note that this book is written in an unemotional tone in order to allow the facts to emerge as objectively as possible. Phrases such as 'I recommend this', or 'you ought to do that', are avoided to allow the reader to grasp the facts and, after practising and learning from the activities, the reader may make his or her own decision.
5 Reports should go from the general to the specific: from the known to the unknown. Thus readers will be able to follow an argument. General statements may easily be understood, and specific statements emerging from them will follow logically. For instance:

'Woozle's pocket-money range of plastic toys has sold well, as the chart shows. It would be logical to develop this strength in our product range' is more likely to get heads nodding in agreement than 'we should launch a new cheap plastic toy range to sell in garage forecourts.' This last is more likely to receive puzzled looks and prompt the question 'why?'

Copyright When communicating by the written word it is important to respect the various laws of copyright that exist, notably the *Copyrights, Designs and Patents Act 1988.*

Copyright law restricts the right of people to copy or use

another person's work without permission. This applies to pictures, photographs, films, television programmes, press articles, books, hand-outs, song lyrics and music.

It also embraces trademarks, logos, illustrations, patents (such as new devices to do something, such as Mercedes' design for their door handle).

In general, copyright applies to printed words and music for a period up to 70 years after the writer's death. For pictures, recordings and films, the period is 70 years from origination.

Trade marks are renewable every seven years, but need to be registered first. The advice of a qualified patent or trade-mark lawyer is recommended for this.

Copyright is an area that warrants more consideration than there is space available here; all good reference libraries have further details if you would like to know more.

Performance criterion

4.3.3 Evaluate each business document produced

Activities

Figures 95–99 give samples of a letter, a memo, an invitation, a notice and a message.

Turn to the Core skill section on communication, on pages 341–349. There are several pointers and exercises to aid accurate written communication.

Write a written evaluation of each figure, taking into account:

a appearance – style and layout;
b language – spelling and grammar.

MEMO

To: Jane Williams

From: Peter Black

Date: 21 January 1996

Subject: Parents evening – Friday 26 January, 7.00 pm

I have been told by your Head of School that you teach full-time 16–19 students. As such, I wrote to you in December asking you to confirm your availability for Parents evening, on Friday 26 January. I haven't as yet received a reply. Please could you complete the slip at the bottom of the page and return it to me as soon as possible.

Please note that if you are not able to come, I need to know the name of the colleague you will be giving the information about your students to as well as the courses and subjects you teach. Please enter their name on the slip at the bottom of the page.

The minimum information needed about each student is:

1. Attendance in your class – with absences out of possible attendances
2. Test/mock exam results, unit/module performances, or other achievement
3. General progress and attitude
4. Likely achievement in your subject
5. Strengths and weaknesses

If you wish to make appointments, please do this through the students. (It may be useful to know that Graham Morris will be giving a talk to parents at 7.00 pm, 7.30 pm and 8.00 pm.)

Please reply as soon as possible so that I can complete arrangements for the evening.

To: Peter Black

From: <NAME>

Whether you are able to attend or not, please give the courses and subjects you teach full-time 16–19 students (for name signs etc.): ____

____

I am able to attend Parents evening at 7.00 pm on Friday 26 January   ❏

I am not able to attend Parents evening. I will give the information requested to

________________________________ (name of colleague)   ❏

FIGURE 97 A sample memo

FIGURE 98 A sample notice

STAFFROOM NOTICEBOARD

PLEASE NOTE!

The following message has been received from Geoff White:

Rank Xerox will be replacing the large 5065 photocopying machine in John Brown's department between 31 January and 2 February inclusive.

This copying facility will not be available during this time and apologies are expressed for any inconvenience this may cause.

Mary Williams

17 January 1996

FIGURE 99 A sample message

Dave,

Please, please have our assignments for tomorrow. Chris needs to send them off to be verified.
Thanks
Fred
ext 2621
1.15 pm

Monday 22.1.96

Performance criterion

4.3.4 Compare the methods of processing business documents

Methods of producing business documents

The methods used to produce business documents need to reconcile the need for speed with accuracy, professionalism, cost and above all, efficiency.

The options open to most people in business are handwriting, typewriting and wordprocessing including desk-top publishing.

The way in which a particular document is ultimately presented will depend upon the urgency, the person or people for whom it is intended, and the skills of the originator.

Handwriting

Of the list above **hand-written** documents are customary for:

- messages or notes left for somebody else;
- informal memos;
- informal notices.

In addition, these documents, too, may be hand-written:

- the front sheet of fax messages;
- character references;
- 'with compliments' slips.

When applying for a job using a word-processed c.v. (which it should be), it is a good idea to hand-write the covering letter, especially if the applicant has attractive handwriting. It shows another skill, as well as an ability to spell and present. This clearly works against the candidate, however, if the spelling or writing is of a low quality. In that case it is a good idea to use a wordprocessor with a spell-check!

Typewriting and wordprocessing

Typescript is nowadays very rare indeed and should only really be used in the event of power failure.

All documents should be produced using a wordprocessor and printer.

The use of printing or **desk-top publishing** is almost universal in business; while many letters and day-to-day business documents are produced on at least a good wordprocessing package from a personal computer, a desk-top publishing package would always be used for instruction books and often for reports.

It should be noted, however, that the quality of the content is the most important factor in the ability of a document to impress! However, presentation of information in business is extremely important. Documents intended for busy executives need to be easy on the eye and the key information immediately accessible.

Report writing is a skill on its own, but an attractive front sheet and well-laid-out contents will win people over to the writer's point of view far more easily than a packed document where the words are densely printed and poorly set out.

Photocopying

It is worth saying a little about photocopying, since countless documents are copied in business each day.

It looks best if everybody can have a laser printed original version of a document but the demands of cost, speed and size of circulation means that many documents are photocopied.

The machine needs to be used carefully so that the print on copies is straight, and the page neither under nor over-exposed. A little practice pays dividends since no two makes of photocopier respond alike to originals – some ignore pencil, others copy it as if it were black ink; some copy photographs extremely well, others, less so.

Practice makes perfect where these machines are concerned. One word of caution. Photocopies are cheap and it is easy to forget that forests are being consumed at prodigious rates to feed the paper-hungry Western world. If careful use of resources is an aim, it is worth considering whether each copy is really necessary.

Performance criterion

4.3.5 Reference, correctly file and retrieve business documents

Filing systems

Filing systems can be **manual** – filing cabinets full of files, or **electronic** – files stored in a personal or main-frame computer.

With the use of effective references, filing and retrieval becomes easy.

It is not necessary to have long reference numbers for either manual or electronic systems – they impress nobody and hinder accuracy. A reference may simply be the originator's initials.

Similarly, the simpler the filing system, the more effective it is. Provided it is logical it will be understood, even if the originator is unavailable.

In either case, speed of retrieval is the main consideration.

Activities

1   Consider the retrieval system for the work in your portfolio.

There are many different ways that it can be ordered:
- by subject;
- by completion date of each piece of work;
- by hand-back date, (i.e. when the work has been assessed and the evaluation has taken place);
- by lecturer or teacher.

Each method will have advantages and disadvantages. Consider them in groups for a few minutes, then refer back to the Introduction, pages 1–4 for the recommended system.

2   Write an evaluation, including advantages and disadvantages, of how successful you believe your own filing system has been. You should use IT to produce the evaluation.

What changes would you make to your portfolio filing system, if you were starting the course anew?

Performance criterion

4.3.6 Identify and evaluate ways to send and ways to store business documents

Sending and storing documents

The main factors that a business needs to consider when producing and sending documents are:

- urgency;
- convenience;
- cost;
- efficiency;
- security and confidentiality;
- availability of equipment;
- staff expertise;
- health and safety.

Urgency

If a document is urgent, the cost to a business to get it there on time becomes secondary.

The fastest way to send documents is by fax, and the cost is only the time taken to send the pages over a telephone line. It takes about 40 seconds to send one side of A4 script, anywhere in the world at any time of day or night, usually for under £2.

However, the client will end up with a document composed of the coarse dots of a fax, and with many fax machines (unless the fax is photocopied on receipt) the print will fade in time when exposed to the light.

For this reason, if time is not quite so tight and presentation is important (such as a brochure and tender for a potential client), use of a courier service will usually guarantee delivery anywhere on mainland UK within 24 hours.

The cost of this is about £10–20 per package.

For inter-company or inter-network communications, E-Mail is the fastest, most direct and cost-effective method.

Convenience

Fax is, of course, not only fast but also convenient. Most courier companies collect, so that, too is relatively convenient. Most Post Office and Red Star originated services require the package to be brought to the nearest depot – in this case, a main line railway station or a larger Post Office.

Standard first or second class post is both cost-effective and convenient, provided speed is less important. Most mail sent first class arrives the next day.

Cost

There are three aspects of cost: production, duplication and mailing.

Production costs

This is the cost associated with printing words and pictures, and binding documents.

Word-processed or desk-top published documents are cheap to produce, providing the wordprocessor or PC is available. If, however, the business is small, wordprocessing and copying services are available at secretarial bureaux located in most towns. Their rates vary, but about £4 to produce a page of word-processed print is average.

Duplication costs

The unit cost of printed documents, such as promotional literature, can work out very expensive, especially if the item requires colour pictures and only a small quantity is required.

The expense is high because it takes several hours to make the printing presses ready to print the job – even if the printing itself only takes a matter of minutes.

Printing in one colour (such as black, blue or red) is much simpler and, if the quantity required is small, this is often a sensible solution.

In this instance, black and white photocopies are about 10 pence each, whereas they cost about a penny on a leased photocopier, available in most businesses.

If colour illustrations form an essential part of the document, and only a small quantity is required, A3 and A4 size coloured photocopies give reasonable reproduction and cost about £1 each.

Mailing costs

There are three mailing services that warrant attention:

Special delivery This service is offered by the Post Office and guarantees delivery anywhere in the UK mainland within 24 hours. The charge depends on the weight of the package, but generally would be cheaper than the charges of a courier service.

Registered delivery This is particularly applicable when items of security or high value are being sent. It offers financial compensation in the event of the package becoming mislaid. Despatch and receipt are logged by the Post office and the package may be traced at all main points in the delivery process.

Red Star This is an overnight mailing service operated by British Rail and requires the package to be brought to the nearest railway station operating the service. It further requires the recipient to collect the package from the station of delivery. If this is acceptable to sender and receiver, Red Star is a quick, cost effective means of sending documents and other packages.

Efficiency

The days of secretaries typing letters, then re-typing them to correct errors, then re-typing them again because the manager has changed his mind, are thankfully long gone, with the advent of the automated electronic office.

Security and confidentiality
Frequently, a business wishes the contents of documents to remain confidential. Documents which contain details of profit and loss, bank borrowings, reports on takeover bids, and details of new products are examples.

E-Mail is somewhat vulnerable to outsider interference, known as industrial espionage, as are faxes.

Sending documents by registered mail, using the Royal Mail or a reliable courier service, is worth the extra cost in instances where security is paramount.

Availability of equipment
The acceleration in the pace of change, which has resulted in a staggering increase in the availability of high-quality equipment, has greatly reduced the cost of producing high-quality documents.

As stated above, fax machines, black and white (and, increasingly, colour) photocopiers and desk-top publishing facilities exist in most large organisations. The use of E-Mail is spreading rapidly.

Where such equipment is not available within the business, many local secretarial bureaux offer good facilities at reasonable charges.

Staff expertise
Clearly it is in the whole company's interest to have staff trained to use equipment, and that their skills are kept up-to-date by short training courses. Whilst such courses can seem expensive and the resulting absence of support staff inconvenient, such investment pays dividends when documents are produced efficiently, quickly and to a high standard. The business's image is enhanced as well.

Health and safety
Constant exposure to a VDU induces fatigue and eyestrain. It may even contribute to deterioration of eyesight.

When people work at a VDU for short spells, however, this is not the case, so regular breaks are essential in a well-lit, preferably daylit, area. This area should be well away from the vicinity of VDUs. Such provision is part of health and safety legislation and readily accepted by understanding employers.

Activities   Mention was made earlier of speed and efficiency with regard to producing business documents. Time and energy can be wasted paying a lot of attention to content and detail. However, in order to work efficiently and effectively, it is essential to practise, and to understand, how each document is put together.

1   Thinking about the room where you are now sitting, write a notice to inform people how to leave it in the event of fire or other emergency.

Consider that the notice must be understandable when people are under pressure to leave the room quickly. The notice must include where they should meet up again.

2   Write a letter to apply for the job vacancy advertised in Figure 100. It may be useful to re-read pages 314–316.

FIGURE 100 An advertisement for a job in sales

3   You are working late in the office one night and realise that the next day you are expecting a visitor from Gillan's, the company's stationery supply company. You do not have the telephone number for Gillan's but your colleague (Audrey Beames) does. Write a note asking her to postpone the meeting for you as soon as she arrives in the morning.

Note: Make use of the feedback that you receive, from your colleagues or your lecturer. Practise again until your presentation and use of language improves. This is a business skill that is well worth acquiring. For example, a busy personnel manager is unlikely to interview the writer of a poorly set out letter of application, even if the writer were in fact the most suitable applicant. The personnel manager would never know what had been missed – and neither would the candidate.

4   Student grants are continually being reviewed by government and education authorities. Despite this, more students are entering tertiary education than ever before, some preferring to stay closer to home to reduce costs and the need to borrow money from the banks.

Write a letter to your local newspaper on this subject. Support it with facts researched from the local education authority (such as the amount of grant available at the different levels of study, and the screening process necessary to obtain such funds), and articles in the press.

Note: With the above activities, at least one document must be hand-written, and at least one produced on a computer. Notes, draft and final text must be made available for each document produced for the purposes of assessment.

5   Identify the advantages and disadvantages of using IT for three of the documents that have been produced for these activities, in terms of:
    a   **origination** (including spelling, grammar and appearance);
    b   **production** (for (b) compare the time and effort involved in producing the work by hand and electronically, and the accuracy of the end result);
    c   **storage and retrieval.**

Core Skills

Section 1 Application of Number

Introduction

The ability to work with figures is a skill that can easily be acquired with practice. Here is an opportunity to do so!

This book offers opportunities to demonstrate competence with Application of number in the following elements:

Element		See mandatory unit elements:
1	Collect and record data	2.4; 3.1; 3.2; 3.4; 4.2
2	Tackle problems	1.3; 2.4; 3.1; 3.4; 4.1
3	Interpret and present data	1.3; 2.4; 3.1; 3.2; 3.4; 4.2

This section has been designed to help students understand the basic skills required, act as a reference guide and to give practice exercises to develop skills so that students are able to demonstrate an ability to use numbers in a business context.

Data really means numbers. The word 'data' is actually plural, so we should say 'Data really mean numbers'.

Adding, subtracting, multiplying and dividing

Activities

Try these calculations, without using a calculator.

1	$75 + 8 =$	2	$547 - 364 =$
3	$43 \times 86.7 =$	4	$96 \div 3 =$
5	$847 + 6854 =$	6	$8765 - 3456 =$
7	$84 \times 7 =$	8	$976.5 \div 37 =$
9	$75 + 86 =$	10	$756 - 965 =$
11	$43 \times 17 =$	12	$7664 : 83 =$

When you have completed them as best you can without using a calculator, check them using a calculator.

Squares and cubes

One advantage of a calculator is that it very quickly calculates squares and cubes.

> A **square** is when a number is multiplied by itself, for instance: $2 \times 2 = 4$, $5 \times 5 = 25$.

It is useful when working out how much carpet is needed to cover the floor of a particular room. Carpet is normally sold by the square metre; this means 1 metre long by 1 metre wide.

An example of its use in business concerns *The Health and Safety at Work Act 1974* which states that each employee should have 12 square metres of working space. Since area = length × width (or width × length) this would be an area perhaps 6 by 2 metres; 4 by 3 metres or 3.4641 metres square.

> The **cube** is a number multiplied by itself, then multiplied by itself again, for instance
> $$3 \times 3 \times 3 = 27 \qquad 5 \times 5 \times 5 = 125$$

This is useful to calculate how much volume is available. If a room is 2 metres high, then the volume of an employee's work space would be $4 \times 3 \times 2 = 24$ cubic metres.

Activities

Using your calculator, work out these squares and cubes in terms of square and cubic metres:

1 $4 \times 4 =$ 2 $26 \times 26 =$

3 $2 \times 2 \times 2 =$ 4 $17 \times 17 \times 17 =$

5 $139 \times 139 =$ 6 $26 \times 26 \times 26 =$

Data

Figures in all shapes and sizes are data. If they are unprocessed, simple numbers (for instance sales figures, total sales, monthly sales), with which no further calculation has taken place, they are known as **raw data**.

If, however, they have been added to other relevant figures, the resulting figures are known as **processed data**. For instance the monthly sales figures for January, February and so on until Septemberare added to the forecasts for October, November and December so that the projected sales figure for the whole of the year may be calculated.

Activity Look at the figures in the activity in Element 1.3, pages 73–82. Give three examples of raw data and three examples of processed data.

Conversions **Time**

The basis of time is normally considered to be Greenwich Mean Time (GMT), which is 0 degrees longitude. Time depends on whether a place is situated east or west of that line.

So, for example, New York is five hours behind Greenwich Mean Time; Los Angeles is seven.

Tokyo is nine hours in advance of Greenwich Mean Time, Sydney ten hours.

Activity If it is noon in Britain, what is the time in:
a Los Angeles
b Tokyo?

Is it advisable to telephone somebody in New York at the beginning or end of the working day? And should you telephone your colleague in Sydney when you arrive or leave the London office?

Temperature

To convert Fahrenheit to Centigrade (also known as Celsius):

Subtract 32 from the Fahrenheit temperature and divide by 1.8.

To convert Centigrade to Fahrenheit;

Multiply the Centigrade temperature by 1.8. then add 32.

Activity Convert these to Fahrenheit or Centigrade, first without using a calculator, then check your answers by using a calculator:

a 32 degrees Fahrenheit
b 35 degrees Centigrade
c 68 degrees Fahrenheit
d −4 degrees Fahrenheit
e −5 degrees Centigrade

Distance

1 inch = 2.54 centimetres

1 yard = 91.44 centimetres or 0.9144 metres

1 mile = 1.609 kilometres (5 miles = 8 kilometres)

1 centimetre = 0.394 inch

1 metre = 39.37 inches

1 kilometre = 0.621 miles

Activity Using a calculator, work out:

a how many kilometres there are in 3 miles; 63 miles and 258 miles?
b how many centimetres there are in 1 foot; 3 yards and 2 inches?
c how many miles there are in 36 kilometres; 596 kilometres and 4 kilometres?
d how many inches there are in 10 centimetres; 47 centimetres; 3 centimetres?

Volume and weight

1 litre = 1.76 pints

1 pint = 0.568 litre

1 gallon = 4.546 litres

1 kilogram = 2.205 lb

1 gram = 0.035 oz

> 1 imperial pound (lb) = 0.454 kilograms or 454 grams
>
> 1 ton = 1,016 kilograms

Activity Give answers to the following questions:

a How many pints is 0.2 litre?
b How many gallons are 10 litres?
c How many gallons are 45 litres?
d If petrol is £2.50 per gallon, how much must I pay for 36 litres?
e How many imperial pounds are three kilograms?
f How many tons are 10,000 kilograms?
g How many grams are four ounces?
h If cheese costs £1.25p per imperial pound, how much will 1 kilogram cost?
i How many ounces are 100 grams?
j How many ounces are there in a kilogram?

VAT

> To find out an amount that is net of VAT at 17.5 per cent, divide the amount by 1.175 and round up or down as necessary.
>
> To add VAT to an amount, multiply the net price by 1.175.

Thus £10 net of VAT is £8.51; the VAT is therefore £1.49p.

Estimating One of the greatest numerical skills that can be acquired in business is the ability to estimate. It has many applications, especially when converting distance, volume, weight and currency.

Distance

If you are travelling 300 kilometres, it is not always necessary to convert them to miles and yards! It is sufficient to know that 300 kilometres is approximately 200 miles. It is actually 186.41 miles, but since this makes a difference of less than 15 minutes to a three hour journey, it is more important to make a reasonable estimate quickly, than to make a precise calculation slowly.

Here are some useful estimates.

Distance and length
2 miles is about 3 kilometres
3 miles are about 5 kilometres
5 miles are 8 kilometres
8 miles are about 12 kilometres (why?)
Somebody who is 6 feet tall is about 1.8 metres high
1 inch is about 2.5. centimetres
10 centimetres are about 4 inches
1 metre is about 3 feet 3inches
1 foot is about 30 centimetres

Volume
1 litre is about 1.75 pints
1 pint is just over half a litre
4 litres are about 7 pints
4.5 litres are about a gallon
45 litres are about 10 gallons

Weight
500 grams are just over 1 imperial pound (lb)

Currency

In Germany
1 Deutschmark is about 45 pence
One pound sterling is about 2.2 Deutschmark
10 pence are about 22 Pfennig
100 Deutschmarks are about 45 pounds sterling

In France
1 franc is about 14 pence
One pound sterling is about 7.4 francs
10 pence are about 74 centimes
100 francs are about 13 pounds 50 pence

In the USA
1 dollar is about 66 pence
One pound sterling is about 1.5 dollars
10 pence are about 15 cents
100 dollars are about 66 pounds sterling

Activity

1 Convert these decimals to fractions:
   a 0.1   b 5.75
   c 6.375   d 0.67
   e 0.25

2 Convert these fractions to decimals:
   a ⅓   b ½₅
   c 3⅝   d 4⁴⁄₉
   e 2⅖

3 Convert question 2 above into percentages.

4 Calculate how much VAT is contained in bills for:
   a £25   b £5.76
   c £2.35   d £23.50
   e 50p

The following eight questions give you practice with estimating.

1 Approximately how many miles are:
   a 500 km?   b 25 km?
   c 4 km?

2 Approximately how many kilometres are:
   a 3 miles?   b 25 miles?
   c 250 miles?

3 Approximately how many centimetres are:
   a 10 inches?   b 6 inches?
   c 2 feet?

4 Approximately how many feet and/or inches are
   a 3 m?   b 1 km?
   c 25 cm?

5 Approximately how many litres are there in:
   a 4 gallons?   b 10 gallons?
   c 2 pints?

6 Approximately how many pints or gallons are there in:
   a 10 l?   b 96 l?
   c 2.5 l?

7 Approximately how many imperial pounds, ounces, or tons
are there in:

a 12 kg? **b** 120 kg?

c 3000 kg? **d** 2.5 kg?

e 30 g? **f** 10 g?

g 100 g?

8 Approximately how many kilograms or grams are there in:

a 3 lb? **b** 4 oz?

c 8 oz? **d** 2.5 tons?

e 10 lb?

The following two questions give practice in converting one
currency to another.

9 Convert into Deutschmarks, francs and dollars:

a £25 **b** 25p

c £367 **d** £5,000

e 80p

10 Convert into pounds sterling:

a DM25 **b** 68Pf

c DM359 **d** F13.50

e 76 centimes **f** F250

g $25.00 **h** 60 cents

i $250 **j** $3,750

Calculating costs for a business plan

The importance of forecasting and monitoring company
performance has been covered in earlier elements. Its value
when setting up a business is to identify when (or, in extreme
cases, if) the business will become profitable.

Very few businesses make profits immediately. A major
benefit of projecting costs and income is to establish when
the business will start to become profitable.

This is relevant not only to the owner but also to investors,
shareholders, banks lending money and the tax authorities.

It is vital to be as realistic as possible at all stages, for
businesses rarely work out as forecast! It is therefore essential
that everybody enters a new business with their eyes open to
the potential pitfalls.

Let us take the case of an imaginary newsagent, who in addition to the core stock of news and magazines, also sells confectionery, soft drinks and stationery. The three products are purchased from three wholesalers.

She is starting from scratch, planning to employ nobody else. She needs premises, with shopfittings, and to buy a car.

Let us consider this business in the first three years of trading, projecting best, worst and likely scenarios.

Fixed costs

A sensible start is to identify the **fixed costs** which the business has. These are the costs that she must pay, whatever **turnover** (i.e. sales value) the business may have.

For our example, the fixed costs are as shown below

	£ p.a.*
Rent	5,000
Electricity (including heating)	1,250
Telephone	750
Business rates	2,000
Car tax, insurance, petrol and servicing costs	2,250
Shop insurances	650
Maintenance costs, estimated	300
Advertising (**Yellow Pages**, local papers)	1,000
Total fixed costs per annum	**13,200**

*N.B. p.a. = per annum, meaning 'per year'

At the start, the newsagent would only need an estimated 30 per cent of this sum, since most of these large costs would be billed quarterly, that is every three months.

'One-off' costs

Then there are the start-up costs, the 'one-off' costs associated with starting the business. These might be as shown below.

	£
Agents and legal fees to acquire the premises	1,200
Purchase of used car	5,000
Shopfitting; shelves, till, security	3,500
Telephone line installation	125
Advertising new business to local people	750
Printed stationery	200
Total 'one off' costs	**10,775**

Variable costs

Finally, there are the variable costs to consider. These are the costs that vary according to the level of sales. In this case, it covers **the cost to purchase stock** from our three wholesalers.

In the worst scenario, the newsagent thinks she will sell:

	£ p.a.
Newspapers at 300 per day	£ 28,000
Confectionary and soft drinks	£ 50,000
Stationery	£ 25,000
Total cost of stock per year	**103,000**

Let us assume that at the start, the newsagent needs to spend £20,000 on stock.

The cost of starting up

In order to start up the business, the newsagent requires a lot of money – £10,775 to pay the 'one-off' costs, plus an estimated £3960 (30 per cent of the fixed costs), plus £20,000 to pay variable costs. She needs £34,735, plus her cost of living and some contingency. Let us say, she needs a total of £60,000.

Let us assume that she has saved £10,000. She therefore needs to borrow £50,000 from the bank. The bank will only allow her to borrow such a high amount for three years, and would demand a total repayment of £65,000 to include their interest.

If the mark-up on the goods she sells is an average 25 per cent, the stock she purchased would sell for £128,750.

Her profit margin is £128,750 less £103,000 = £25,750 p.a.

Note that £25,750 is 20% of £128,750 – the reason for stating this will become apparent later.

Total profit over three years would be £25,750 × 3 = £77,250

However, she needs to pay her 'one-off' costs of £10,775, reducing her profit margin to £66,475.

In addition, she needs to pay three years of fixed costs at £13,200 p.a; total £39,600.

Her actual profit becomes £66,475 less £39,600 = £26,875

Her bank loan is £65,000. So, in this instance, over three years the business would lose money: she only has £26,875 with which to pay off the £65,000 loan, leaving her with a loss (money owing) of £38,125.

Hardly an inspiring start for a business! If the turnover of £128,750 is felt to be realistic, the newsagent should *not* proceed.

Calculating break-even point
So, let us calculate the break-even point over three years.

	£
Fixed costs (£13,200 × 3)	39,600
'One-off' costs	10,775
Bank charges	65,000
Total overhead charges for three years	**115,375**

If the business trades at an average 20 per cent margin, the business must turn over £115,375 × 5 = £576,875 in order to break even.

This is an average turnover of £192,292 per year.

The key question that all interested parties must answer is: **'is this a realistic turnover?'** For at this point, the newsagent has earned nothing, so these figures should be regarded as a minimum for there are bound to be unforeseen expenses along the way.

However, in the fourth year of trading, the bank loan has been repaid, and the 'one-off' charges met, so the net profit would be 20 per cent of £192,292 (i.e. £38,458), less fixed costs of £13,200, leaving £25,258; a reasonable income which should increase as the business grows.

Section 2 Communication

<table>
<tr><td>

Introduction

</td><td>

There are four elements to the core skill in communication at Intermediate GNVQ level.

Communication is such a fundamental part not only of business life but also of everyday living, that these core skills may be demonstrated and recorded in many different ways.

Students have the opportunity to demonstrate competence in Communication skills in the following elements.

</td></tr>
</table>

	Element	See mandatory unit elements:
1	Take part in discussions	1.3; 2.1; 2.2; 2.3; 3.1; 4.2
2	Produce written material	1.1; 1.2; 2.1; 2.2; 2.3; 2.4; 3.1; 3.2; 3.3; 3.4; 4.2; 4.3;
3	Use images	1.2; 1.3; 2.1; 2.3; 2.4; 3.1; 3.4; 4.1; 4.2; 4.3
4	Read and respond to written materials	1.3; 2.4; 3.1; 3.2; 3.4; 4.2; 4.3

In addition, there are some activities within this section designed to reinforce skills.

Thus, the objectives of this section may be summarised:

1 to give additional practice in common weak areas of communication;
2 to act as a reference guide in other areas.

Taking part in discussions

It is one thing to discuss a topic with a colleague you know well.

It is quite a different undertaking to discuss a new topic with somebody you do not know well, or at all. Meeting new people in unfamiliar places can be an uncomfortable experience for many people. This may also apply to the other person in the meeting – a confident swagger may in fact conceal insecurity beneath the surface.

The most important consideration is to focus on **what is to be achieved** from the meeting.

Getting to know each other

Human beings, like any animal, show certain behavioural characteristics – in crowds, when alone and also when meeting people for the first time or faced with unfamiliar surroundings. It often takes some minutes for someone to become acclimatised to a new situation.

This is why it is often advisable to start with a general observation, such as 'lovely day', or 'there was a lot of traffic in town'. Neither has anything to do with the purpose of the meeting, but it allows both people to get to know each other on a superficial level: tone of voice, dress, appearance, manner and other things which distinguish each human being.

The first rule is to **relax!** People remember more and perform better when the dry throat and perspiration of nervousness is not allowed to hinder effective operation.

Consider **appearance**: a T-shirt, jeans, sneakers and an earring may look fine at college but will probably look out of place in an office, and may put off the other person in the meeting.

Think of **body language**. The signals that body and posture send out are usually far more explicit than spoken words. Watch out for the following instances of body language.

1 Facial expressions. A smiling face encourages and invites a friendly response, a dour expression could encourage an early termination of the meeting.
2 Eye contact. It is of course impolite to stare at somebody else, but it is courteous – and displays honesty and directness – to look the other person in the eye occasionally.
3 Gestures. A nodding head demonstrates agreement and encourages the other person to continue. It also shows attentiveness.
4 Attitude. Crossed legs and/or arms can mean the person has ceased to listen or formed an opinion that is not going to change. Scratching the back of the neck can signify that the other person is lying!

5 Personal space. In Western Europe, people generally like to have a reasonable amount of personal space between them and the next person. In a crowded train, notice how people have facial expressions that are fixed some distance away from the person next to them who under normal circumstances would be far too close for comfort! The message this gives is 'I know we are huddled closely together; there is nothing either of us can do about it, so I will pretend you are not there and look into the distance.' Try looking directly at the other person and see the response you receive!

Discussions take place for three reasons:

1 to give information,
2 to receive information,
3 to explore ideas

with the other people involved.

Reference should also be made to the exercises on active listening skills and asking questions in Element 3.3 on pages 253–256.

Written material The writing of reports, letters and other business communications was considered in Element 4.3.

It is worthwhile considering the range of reference material that exists to help resolve the uncertainties that confound us all from time to time!

Using a dictionary or spellcheck software
A dictionary is not only a useful tool to check the spelling of certain words, it also explains what the words mean.

Most wordprocessing software packages have a spellcheck that is well worth using, in order to avoid the elementary mistakes that can cause embarrassment.

Here are some words which are all too commonly mis-spelt in business communications:

accelerate (two 'c's, one 'l')
accurately (an 'e' before the 'ly')
acquire (a 'c' before the 'q')

across (only one 'c')
advertisement (an 'e' before 'ment')
applied (two 'p's and 'i-e-d')
appreciate (a 'c' in the middle)
association (a 'c' in the middle)
available ('a-i-l' in the middle)
basis (one 's' in the middle)
beginning (one 'g', two 'n's)
casualty (note the 'u' in the middle)
competitive (one 't', then 'i' – twice!)
conscientious (the series 's-c-i-e-n-t-i' fools many people)
definite ('f-i-n-i' in the middle)
description ('p' then 't')
develop (has no 'e' at the end)
different (two 'f's, then 'e' followed by 'r')
disciplinary (note the 'c', and the 'a' towards the end)
discussion (two 's')
environment ('n' followed by 'm')
excel ('c' and one 'l')
excellent (two 'l's then 'e')
excitement (watch for the 'c', then the 'e' follows the 't')
excited (watch for the 'c')
filing (two 'l's makes 'filling'!)
financial (note the 'c' followed by 'i')
fulfil (one 'l' at the end)
fulfilling (two 'l's in the middle)
honourable (one 'n', then 'our' then 'able')
imaginable (no 'e' in the middle)
imaginative ('a' follows the 'n' - not an 'e'!)
important (has an 'a' three letters from the end)
improvement (has an 'e' in the middle!)
improving (has no 'e' in the middle!)
intelligence (two 'l's followed by 'i')
interested ('e' follows 't' both times)
leisure ('e' then 'i')
(driving) **licence** ('c' at the end – **noun**)
Licensed to kill ('s' at the end – **verb**)
manageable (has an 'e' in the middle)
Managing Director (has **no 'e'** in the middle)
necessary ('c' followed by two 's' then 'a')
necessarily (as above, and one 'l' at the end)
negotiating (the fifth letter is a 't')
noticeable (note the 'e' after the 'c')
opportunity ('o' follows the 'p's, with 't-u-n' in the middle)
persuade ('e' after the 'p')
Principal of the College (meaning 'chief')

a person of **principle** (somebody with a conscience)
professional (one 'f', two 's')
pursue (unlike 'persuade', this one has a 'u' after the 'p')
questionnaire (two 'n's in the middle and an 'e' at the end)
recommend (two 'm's)
response (an 's' before the 'p')
responsibilities (four i's, one 'l')
responsibility (three 'i's, one 'l')
satisfactory (an 'o' after the 't')
school ('ch' followed by double 'o')
slowly (no 'e' before the final 'y')
stationary ('remaining in one place' - 'a' at the end)
stationery (writing materials - 'e' at the end)
strategic ('t-e-g')
subsidised (two 'i's and an 's' at the end)
success (two 'c' then two 's')
successful (as above, then only one 'l' at the end)
technological ('ch' then 'no', then 'logic', with 'a' before the final 'l')
technology ('ogy' at the end)
technician (has a 'c' towards the end)
technical ('al' at the end)
their idea (i.e. of them)
over **there** (answers the question 'where?')
useful ('e' in the middle, one 'l' at the end)
waste (has no 'i' in the middle)

And remember, letters which start 'Dear Sir' or 'Madam' end 'Yours **faithfully**'; letters which start 'Dear Miss Brown' end 'Yours **sincerely**', and note that it has two 'e's!

 **Activities**

1 To, too, or two?
   a … err is human, … forgive divine.
   b … times … is four.
   c You are … impatient to succeed.

2 Past or passed?
   a I … my driving test yesterday.
   b She … me the ball.

3 Waste or waist?
   a Up to my … in muck and bullets.
   b Some television programmes are a … of time.

4 Affect or effect?
   a Nothing you can do will … the way I feel.
   b Thunder is a very dramatic …

5 Whose or who's?
   a … shoes are these?
   b … wearing my shoes?

6 There or their?
   a Look at the windmill over …
   b … coats are on … pegs.

7 Its or it's?
   a … over there.
   b Have you seen … winter plumage?

8 Correct these sentences:
   a She done it all by herself.
   b We was delighted with the result.
   c I wish you could of seen it.

Data presentation

A picture table, graph or chart can sometimes present facts more powerfully than words!

Pictures, tables and so on can also be used to break up a piece of writing so that it looks attractive and easy to read. It is important to display data so that it both looks logical and reads clearly. There are many different ways to display data.

Statistical tables

It is not necessary to be good at maths to understand tables. It *is* necessary to consider the headings carefully. These often extend on both **axes** (the **vertical axis** goes **up and down**, the **horizontal axis** goes **across** the page).

Tables are frequently an expressive way to demonstrate the relationship between two or more measurable factors.

On the next page is an example from a survey of men's participation in housework. The two **variables** here are where the men live and the number of hours per day that they spend doing housework.

The table shows the number of hours worked per day by the men in each of three counties, by percentage.

County	Hours per day				Total
	More than 2	1–2	Below 1	None	
Cornwall	5%	10%	17%	68%	100%
Sussex	3%	11%	25%	61%	100%
Yorkshire	6%	7%	20%	67%	100%

Men's participation in housework by county

Graphs

A graph, like a statistical table, shows the relationship between two variables. On a graph, the variables are shown by the vertical (up and down) and horizontal (across) axes which should be labelled.

In the example in Figure 101 the two variables are the different years and people over 65 as a percentage of the total population.

The graph shows how the percentage changes from 1911 to 2001.

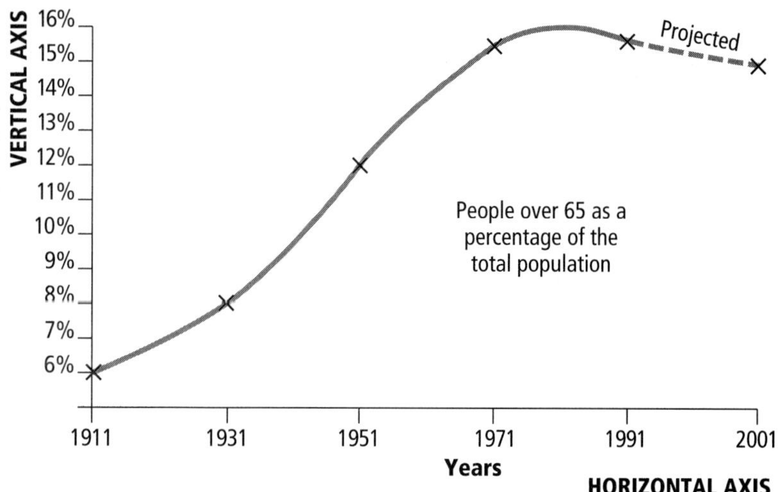

FIGURE 101 The percentage of people over 65 in the population, 1911–2001

The figures for 2001 were not known when the graph was drawn so the figure is a projection, taken from existing statistics.

The purpose of the graph is to provide an immediate visual impression of population trends. In order to look for a trend consideration needs to be given whether the line is higher or lower at the end than at the beginning, and what does it do in between?

It can clearly be seen from the graph that the percentage of people over 65 increased dramatically from 1911 to 1981.

Note that it is not always necessary to start at 0. In this example, the vertical axis starts at about 3 per cent, and the first noted percentage is 6 per cent.

Pie charts

Pie charts are one of the simplest ways of displaying data or information. For example, the pie chart in Figure 102 shows age groups as proportions of the total population.

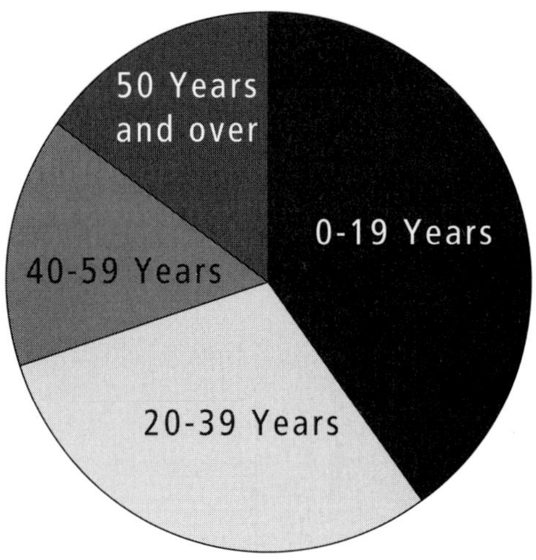

FIGURE 102 Age groups as proportions of the total population

It can be readily seen that the largest group is the 0 to 19 year olds. Pie charts are thus very useful for a quick impression of how something is shared out, but not very accurate for showing small differences.

Bar charts

Like graphs, these give an immediate visual display of information. They are similarly based on two axes.

The bar chart in Figure 103 is another way of showing information about the elderly in the population.

It shows a consistent pattern: notice that there are substantially more women over 60 than there are men over 65. The trend of an increasing proportion of elderly in the population is once again shown, though the projection that was made prior to 1981 is that this will fall eventually.

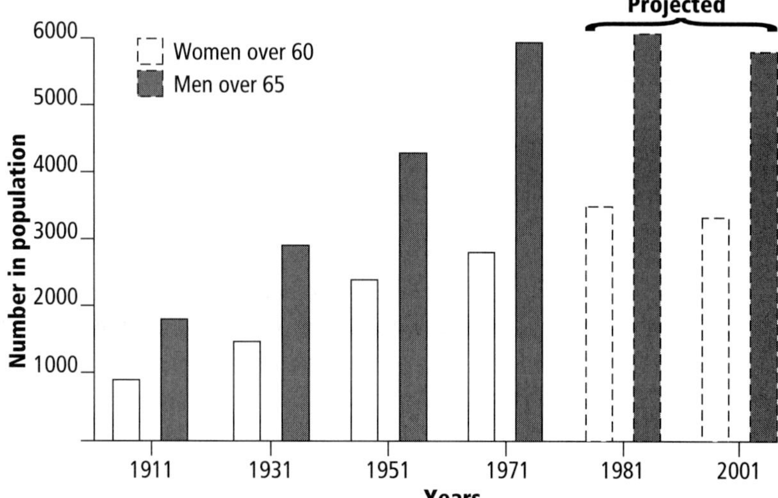

FIGURE 103 The numbers of elderly people in the population, 1911–2001

Histograms

These allow for more detail than is possible with pie or bar charts.

In a histogram the bars are drawn so that they merge into one another. The histogram in Figure 104 shows the percentage of population in each age group.

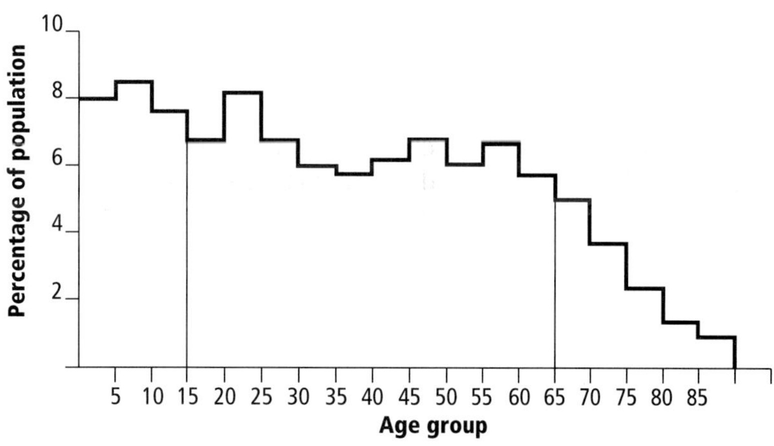

FIGURE 104 The percentage of population in each age group

Section 3   Information Technology

Introduction

There are many opportunities within the activities of this book to demonstrate competence in the four areas of the core skill of Information Technology:

Element	See mandatory unit elements:
1 Prepare information	2.1; 2.2; 2.3; 2.4; 3.1; 3.2; 3.3; 4.1; 4.2; 4.3
2 Process information	2.1; 2.2; 2.3; 2.4; 3.1; 3.3; 4.1; 4.2; 4.3
3 Present information	2.1; 2.2; 2.3; 2.4; 3.1; 4.1; 4.2; 4.3
4 Evaluate the use of IT	2.1; 2.2; 2.3; 2.4; 3.1; 4.1; 4.2; 4.3

Since most students arrive on the Intermediate GNVQ programme with increasing awareness of the immense opportunities that information technology presents, as well as wide knowledge and skills, the purpose of this section is merely to re-state the boundaries within which IT operates.

Those students who have yet to develop IT skills are strongly recommended either to sit at a machine and start – it is certainly easier than many people expect to acquire quite a high degree of proficiency by learning alone – alternatively the advice available on an IT course is recommended. This book is not large enough to describe all the different possibilities which exist within the different hardware systems and software programmes.

It is however, worthwhile to consider the framework within which IT operates.

Different types of information

The information used in IT is called data. It falls into three categories:

Text

This includes letters and words in any language, using any alphabet. Most computer programmes adjust the keyboard by accessing the appropriate part of the software to give the user access to a foreign alphabet. This can range from French or German, where the addition of a small number of accents is counterbalanced by a small reduction in the number of letters, to Russian which has its own alphabet!

Numbers
IT uses these in many creative and illuminating ways. Their simplest use is in everyday work for they are incorporated into the standard keyboard and can easily be used in passages of text.

More complex uses involve automatic calculations which are incorporated into spreadsheets or dedicated programmes, of which more later on pages 355 and 356.

Graphics
Computers of all types these days have the capability to receive a number of different graphics packages. At their simplest, such packages can be used to produce graphs, pie and bar charts; at their most complex, company logos, technical drawings and other artwork can be produced to professional standards.

The appearance on paper of such graphics depends very much on the quality of the printer which is connected to the computer; a colour laser printer gives the highest quality.

CAD (computer aided design) is a means of designing new products using a computer programme. It further allows for the product to be turned round, inverted and reversed electronically, enabling the designer to identify elementary shortcomings in the product thus saving the expense of designing a prototype unnecessarily.

Hardware Figure 105 refers to the different components that make up a computer. They fall into four categories:

Input devices
These are the means used to put data into the computer in a form which the computer understands. Data input is based on electrical pulses.

The most usual data-input devices are the computer keyboard and the mouse; the mouse is used first to highlight information displayed on the screen and then input it.

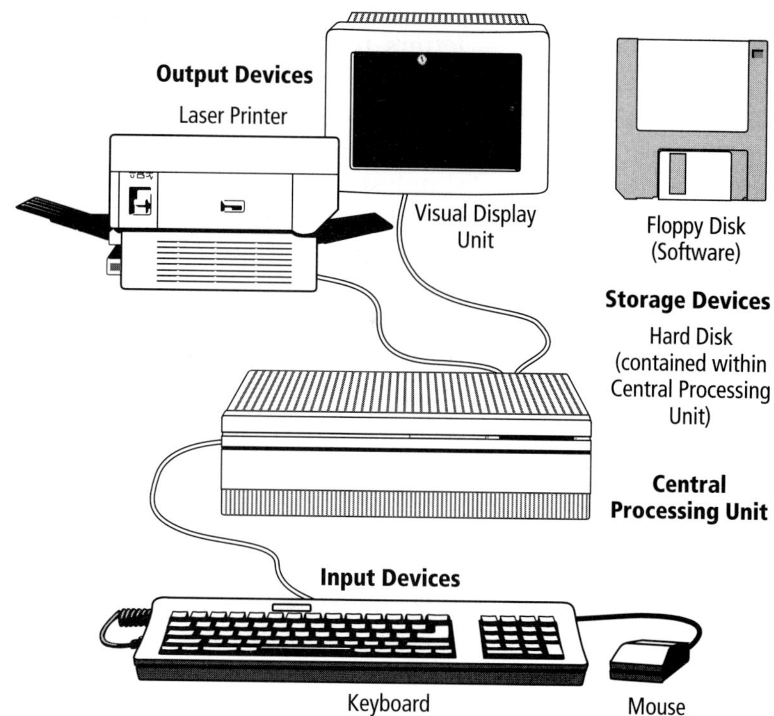

FIGURE 105

Other possible input devices are fax machines, and other forms of electronic data conversion.

Central processing unit

This is the part of the computer which actually does the work! It contains the micro-processors and other electronic paraphernalia which accept and process data. Data are not accepted and processed in a form which is recognisable by anything other than another central processing unit.

Output devices

Once the computer has accepted the information or processed it as requested by the user, the output devices are the means by which it displays the results it has recorded.

In most computers this is done via the visual display unit (VDU) screen – which looks like a television screen but uses a different display system – or via the printer.

The simplest printers are dot matrix ones. This means that each letter, number or symbol is formed by a number of dots grouped together to form the symbol. These are now rather old and tend to give quite low quality print.

The more modern version of these are bubble jet printers, which work on the same principle as dot matrix printers, that is each character is formed from a series of dots. However, the bubble jet printer uses much smaller dots, with far higher-quality printing.

Bubble jet printers are available in monochrome (black and white) or full colour.

The highest-quality printing is achieved by laser printers, which print monochrome or colour to professional standards. Their price falls by the month and a laser printer of average quality may now be purchased for quite a reasonable price.

Storage devices

These are the places where raw or processed data are stored, usually **hard disks**, usually incorporated into the central processing unit of the computer. Alternatively, **floppy disks** store data and may be inserted into the central processing unit as required.

Back-up disks are usually floppy disks which contain a copy of all the data on the hard disk in case this becomes inaccessible or is inadvertently erased!

Types of computer

There are two major types of computer.

1 **Main-frame computers** are housed at the head office of a large corporation; network terminals access them from branch networks.
   For example, when a transaction is made through a large building society, it is recorded by the person in the branch office, using a keyboard. That keyboard has direct access to the main-frame computer which may be located hundreds of miles away – even abroad.
2 **Stand-alone computers,** on the other hand are computers which work with no other support. They are sometimes known as **personal computers,** or PCs for short. Some PCs are portable, incorporating input device, central processing unit, storage and output device into one small unit. These are known as **laptops,** for obvious reasons.

Memory

Computers generally have two types of memory, known as **ROM** and **RAM.**

ROM is short for **read only memory.** ROM cannot be changed or deleted. The operating system of computers is usually stored in ROM, so that each time the computer is switched on, the ROM operates at a basic level, loading software programmes such as DOS or Windows which are stored in RAM.

RAM stands for **random access memory.** This memory can be read and changed by the user, but data are lost when the computer is switched off. For this reason it is essential to save any wanted work using a hard disk, preferably supported by a back up-floppy disk.

Software

There are two types of computer software: **systems programs** and **applications programs.** Both are loaded into the computer to tell it what to do.

Systems programs

The systems program tells the computer how to function. The most common is **DOS** (short for disk operating system).

Many people also use **windows.** This allows the operator to work on several different tasks at the same time. It is also easy to learn, using a series of **icons** or simple logos which lead the user into different parts of the program.

Applications programs

These are loaded on top of the systems programs and point the computer in a particular direction.

Applications programs are frequently sold as a package. This is usually a series of disks, an instruction manual and possibly a demonstration disk.

In other cases, applications programs are specifically designed by a computer software house for a particular company, such as the program used by Abbey National plc to run its main-frame computer which records all the transactions made by its customers through branch offices.

Typical applications programs
Word-processing packages

These enable the computer to produce letters, memos and other written documents. Sometimes a **template** is used to conform to a pre-existing format for letters, memos or reports.

Otherwise the computer assumes that the words are to be printed onto a sheet of A4 paper inserted short side first (portrait) into the printer.

Spreadsheets

A spreadsheet is like an enormous sheet of paper with lots of vertical and horizontal columns.

One of the advantages of having this placed on computer is that with a spreadsheet package, the computer will add, subtract, multiply, divide or perform other calculations to all the columns in the spreadsheet.

This not only cuts out a lot of work but, provided the information is correctly input, there is no room for error.

Spreadsheets are particularly useful for accounting and other financial workings.

They are also used to project income and expenditure. For example, the computer can be asked 'what would happen to our profit if our costs from supplier x increased by 3 per cent?'

Desktop publishing (DTP)

Such packages are used to create business documents. They usually include a wide choice of **fonts** (typefaces) which have unusual names such as Courier or Helvetica.

They allow the user to create an attractively printed document which, when also thoughtfully laid out creates an air of professionalism.

Database packages

A database package stores information in a convenient way so that people can use it in a number of different ways.

For example, a company may keep details of its customers on a database. Such information may be accessed by:

1 postcode;
2 alphabetically;
3 size of company;
4 value of sales in the preceding year;
5 businesses with unpaid invoices;

It may be seen that each of these different routes to access is of value to different parts of the company.

Accounting packages

These are frequently based on the spreadsheet (see above), but are dedicated to a particular format, such as book-keeping, with income on one side, expenses on the other.

Another file may calculate income and expenditure for VAT, or end of year accounts.

Dedicated packages

These are programs specifically designed to do a particular job, For example, a company may commission a dedicated package to calculate the payroll for all employees, then print out a payslip with an accompanying cheque or bank credit transfer instruction which is then implemented for each employee.

Graphics packages

These are used by studios for artwork, posters and other design work. Simplified versions with fewer options are also available at lower cost to other people. Many schools and colleges have such packages for use by tutors and students.

Questions Unit 1

Business Organisations and Employment

Element 1.1 Explain the purposes and types of business organisation

For questions 1, 2, and 3 read the beginning of the sentence in each question, then select which of A, B, C, or D is the correct ending.

1   An example of a business in the tertiary sector is:
    A   coal mining
    B   steel making
    C   car manufacture
    D   hotel

2   An example of a business in the private sector is:
    A   a nationalised industry
    B   a local government organisation
    C   a public limited company
    D   a state-owned business

3   The owners of a private limited company are:
    A   the banks
    B   the shareholders
    C   the directors
    D   the families of the directors

For the next two questions, read the two statements carefully. Circle **one** *of the letters that follow it to indicate which combination you believe is correct.*

4   Decide whether each of these statements is true (T) or false (F)
    (i)   All partnerships enjoy limited liability.
    (ii) All businesses run by the state try to make as much profit as possible regardless of the level of service they provide.

    Which option best describes the two statements?
    A   **(i)** T   **(ii)** T
    B   **(i)** T   **(ii)** F

    C (i) F   (ii) T
    D (i) F   (ii) F

5 Decide whether each of the following is true (T) or false (F).
   (i) The Post Office is an example of a monopoly.
   (ii) When the government wishes to privatise a business, it offers its shares for sale on the stock exchange.

   Which option best describes the two statements?
   A (i) T   (ii) T
   B (i) T   (ii) F
   C (i) F   (ii) T
   D (i) F   (ii) F

*For the next two questions, choose the **two** endings for each statement which you believe are correct and circle the appropriate letters.*

6 Because BP extracts crude oil from the earth or sea, then refines it, it operates in these two sectors:
   (i) primary
   (ii) secondary
   (iii) tertiary
   (iv) public
   A (i) and (ii)
   B (i) and (iii)
   C (ii) and (iii)
   D (iii) and (iv)

7 Examples of renewable resources are:
   (i) iron ore
   (ii) natural gas
   (iii) forests
   (iv) fish
   A (i) and (ii)
   B (i) and (iii)
   C (ii) and (iii)
   D (iii) and (iv)

For the next three questions, choose from the four options A, B, C and D the appropriate answers to each question; you may use each answer more than once.

These are the most common types of business in the private sector:
   A sole trader
   B partnership

    C   limited company
    D   franchise

Which type of business would most suit:

8 somebody who has just been made redundant, but who has little experience of working alone?
    A   **B**   **C**   **D**

9 five accountants?
    A   **B**   **C**   **D**

10 a family newsagent?
    A   **B**   **C**   **D**

Element 1.2 Examine business location, environment, markets and products

For questions 11, 12 and 13, read the beginning of the sentence in each question, then select which of A, B, C, or D is the correct ending.

11 A major consideration for a shoe manufacturer when choosing where to site the business is:
    A   the availability of skilled labour
    B   distance from the nearest town
    C   the climate
    D   distance from London

12 One of the main reasons that supermarket chains finance computers for schools is:
    A   for the benefit of their health
    B   they are seen to be helping the local community
    C   because children spend a lot of money in their stores
    D   it helps to reduce their tax liability

13 A business which manufactures goods solely for the domestic market:
    A   makes most of its sales abroad
    B   imports finished products from abroad
    C   sells all of its products in the country where it makes them
    D   makes some of its sales abroad

For the next two questions, read the two statements carefully. Circle **one** *of the letters that follow to indicate which combination you believe is correct.*

14 Decide whether each of the following is true (T) or false (F).
   (i) The government is a major purchaser of some products.
   (ii) Consumer durables are low-priced goods which are frequently bought by customers.

   Which option best describes the two statements?
A	**(i)** T	**(ii)** T
B	**(i)** T	**(ii)** F
C	**(i)** F	**(ii)** T
D	**(i)** F	**(ii)** F

15 Decide whether each of the following is true (T) or false (F).
   (i) Most charities are funded by donations from the government.
   (ii) A market led business is constantly trying to find out precisely what its customers want.

   Which option best describes the two statements?
A	**(i)** T	**(ii)** T
B	**(i)** T	**(ii)** F
C	**(i)** F	**(ii)** T
D	**(i)** F	**(ii)** F

For the next two questions, choose the **two** *endings for each sentence which you believe are correct and circle the appropriate letters.*

16 Mass produced products are
   (i) made in large quantities to keep the price low
   (ii) intended to maximise customer choice of colours, shapes and sizes
   (iii) often dependent on advertising to generate high consumer demand
   (iv) designed to give the customer an air of exclusivity
   A (i) and (ii)
   B (i) and (iii)
   C (ii) and (iii)
   D (iii) and (iv)

17 Two functions of product development in a business are:
   (i) to ensure that sufficient funds are available to develop the business

(ii) to develop new products that meet customers' needs and expectations

(iii) to up-date existing products that no longer satisfy market needs

(iv) to manufacture products as cost effectively as possible

A (i) and (ii)

B (i) and (iii)

C (ii) and (iii)

D (iii) and (iv)

For the next three questions, choose from the four options A, B, C and D the appropriate answer to each question; you may use each answer more than once.

These are four considerations for choosing to re-locate a business:

A availability of natural resources

B availability of specialist creative services

C access to customers

D transport services

Choose which consideration is most likely to concern:

18 an advertising agency?

    A   B   C   D

19 a paper mill?

    A   B   C   D

20 a distribution business?

    A   B   C   D

Element 1.3 Present results of investigation into employment

For questions 21, 22, and 23 read the beginning of a sentence given in each question, then select which of A, B, C or D is the correct ending.

21 An entrepreneur is essential for a business to:

A keep one step ahead of its competitors by identifying new opportunities in the market

B establish an effective administrative department

C ensure that all customer accounts are up-to-date

D maintain staff discipline

22 One advantage that part-time employees have over their full-time counterparts is that:

A such employees have fewer legal rights than full time employees

B the pay is less

C a parent may be at home when the children come home from school

D when business is slow they tend to be the first people to be made redundant.

23 Regular breaks for employees are important because:

A it gives them an opportunity to gossip about the rest of the staff

B people lose concentration and effectiveness when they work for long periods

C it enables them to go out and do some shopping

D they can telephone home to see that everything is all right

For the next two questions, read the two statements carefully. Circle **one** *of the letters that follow it to indicate which combination you believe is correct.*

24 Decide whether each of the following is true (T) or false (F).

(i) Employees have no legal obligation to act responsibly.

(ii) A multi-skilled workforce is inadvisable because it has to be paid more wages.

Which option best describes the two statements?

A (i) T (ii) T
B (i) T (ii) F
C (i) F (ii) T
D (i) F (ii) F

25 Decide whether each of the following is true (T) or false (F).

(i) One of the advantages of self-employment is that the person is free to develop the business according to his or her skills.

(ii) The chances of a new business failing in its first three years are higher than an established one.

How are these two statements best described?

A (i) T (ii) T
B (i) T (ii) F
C (i) F (ii) T
D (i) F (ii) F

*For the next two questions, choose the **two** endings for each sentence which you believe are correct and circle the appropriate letters.*

26 Skill shortages are caused by:
- **(i)** employees laid off by one firm being re-employed elsewhere to do something else
- **(ii)** a sudden surge in demand
- **(iii)** lack of training
- **(iv)** an influx of workers from Continental Europe
- **A** (i) and (ii)
- **B** (i) and (iii)
- **C** (ii) and (iii)
- **D** (iii) and (iv)

27 Two of the causes of the growth in numbers employed in service industries are:
- **(i)** less people employed in the retail sector
- **(ii)** increased activity in drilling for oil and gas
- **(iii)** the decline in traditional manufacturing businesses
- **(iv)** the growth in foreign travel and tourism in the UK
- **A** (i) and (ii)
- **B** (i) and (iii)
- **C** (ii) and (iii)
- **D** (iii) and (iv)

For questions 28, 29 and 30 choose from the four options A, B, C and D the appropriate answer for each question; you may use each answer more than once.

These are four different types of employment
- **A** self employment
- **B** temporary employment
- **C** unskilled employment
- **D** full-time employment

Which of these is likely to be the most suitable for

28 an independently minded enthusiastic entrepreneur?

    A   B   C   D

29 an ice cream seller?

    A   B   C   D

30 a labourer?

    A   B   C   D

Questions Unit 2

People in Business Organisations

Element 2.1 Examine and compare structures and working arrangements in organisations

For questions 1 and 2, read the beginning of the sentence in each question, then select which of A, B, C or D is the correct ending.

1. In a hierarchical structure, there is a tendency to:
   A   have very few staff
   B   adopt an autocratic management style
   C   use job titles and authority limits
   D   ignore tiers of management

2. A flat management structure is particularly effective for:
   A   informal decision making
   B   effective delegation by senior management
   C   employees to work on their own initiative without interference from senior staff
   D   teamwork at all levels within the organisation

*For the next two questions, read the two statements carefully. Circle **one** of the letters that follow it to indicate which combination you believe is correct.*

3. Decide whether each of these statements is true (T) or false (F).
   (i)   In a small shop, the decision whether or not to hold a sale would be made by the owner.
   (ii) In a democratic organisation, employees are encouraged to take part in the decision-making process.

   How are these statements best described?
   A   (i) T   (ii) T
   B   (i) T   (ii) F
   C   (i) F   (ii) T
   D   (i) F   (ii) F

4. The following two statements have been made:
   (i)   Chasing up customers who have not paid their bills is

the responsibility of the finance department.
(ii) The production department is responsible for
developing new products.

How are these statements best described?

A	**(i)** T	**(ii)** T
B	**(i)** T	**(ii)** F
C	**(i)** F	**(ii)** T
D	**(i)** F	**(ii)** F

For the next two questions, choose the **two** *endings for each sentence
which you believe are correct and circle the appropriate letters.*

5 Two of the functions for which marketing is responsible
are:
(i)   warehousing
(ii) promotion
(iii recruitment
(iv) packaging
A (i) and (ii)
B (i) and (iii)
C (ii) and (iv)
D (iii) and (iv)

6 Two benefits of teamwork to a company are that:
(i)   people work more effectively
(ii) people can socialise more outside office hours
(iii) problems are easier to solve
(iv) work ceases when a team member is ill
A (i) and (ii)
B (i) and (iii)
C (ii) and (iv)
D (iii) and (iv)

*For the next two questions, choose from the four options A, B, C and D
the appropriate answer for each question; you may use each answer
more than once.*

Here are descriptions of the main responsibilities of four
senior executives:
A   recruitment policy, salary scales, employee
confidentiality and training
B   press releases and consumer competitions
C   overseas' sales
D   investing the company profits

Which of these describes the work of

7 the promotions' manager?

   A   B   C   D

8 the personnel director?

   A   B   C   D

Element 2.2
Investigate employee and employer responsibilities and rights

For questions 9 and 10, read the beginning of the sentence in each question, then select which of A, B, C or D is the correct ending.

9 *The Health and Safety at Work Act 1974* states that employers must:

   A   pay employees a minimum wage
   B   provide a safe working environment and adequate welfare facilities
   C   ensure each employee contributes to a pension scheme
   D   keep personal data confidential

10 ACAS stands for:

   A   Association of Chartered and Articled Solicitors
   B   Advice, Counselling and Auxiliary Services
   C   Advisory, Conciliation and Arbitration Service
   D   Against Corruption in the Armed Services

For the next two questions, read the two statements carefully. Circle **one** *of the letters that follow it to indicate which combination you believe is correct.*

11 Decide whether each of the following is true (T) or false (F).

   (i) ACAS acts in cases of dispute between an employer and an employee, even if the employee is represented by a trade union.
   (ii) If an employee is accused of theft, he or she is not entitled to seek legal representation.

Which option best describes the two statements?

   A   **(i)** T   **(ii)** T
   B   **(i)** T   **(ii)** F
   C   **(i)** F   **(ii)** T
   D   **(i)** F   **(ii)** F

12 Decide whether each of the following is true (T) or false (F).
- **(i)** Since women retire earlier than men, the law allows an employer to pay women slightly less than men to do the same job.
- **(ii)** An employee has a legal obligation to behave responsibly towards colleagues.

Which option best describes the two statements?

A	**(i)** T	**(ii)** T
B	**(i)** T	**(ii)** F
C	**(i)** F	**(ii)** T
D	**(i)** F	**(ii)** F

*For the next two questions, choose the **two** endings for each sentence which you believe are correct and circle the appropriate letters.*

13 In most cases an employer is entitled to know:
- **(i)** everything about an employee's previous criminal record
- **(ii)** everything about an employee's previous criminal record except for minor offences and 'spent' convictions
- **(iii** what the potential employee chooses to reveal about the past
- **(iv)** the employee's previous employment record with dates that the person started and left the business

- **A** (i) and (ii)
- **B** (i) and (iii)
- **C** (ii) and (iv)
- **D** (iii) and (iv)

14 Employees have the right to:
- **(i)** stop work if they feel ill
- **(ii)** go home if they feel ill
- **(iii)** a minimum of two weeks' paid holiday in each full year worked
- **(iv)** be absent from work in the event of the death of a close relative

- **A** (i) and (ii)
- **B** (i) and (iii)
- **C** (ii) and (iv)
- **D** (iii) and (iv)

For the next two questions, choose from the four options A, B, C and D appropriate answer for each question; you may use each answer more than once.

Within the personnel function of a business, activities take place at different levels, according to the work involved and the seniority of the executive. Consider these situations:

A   A member of staff has been allowed to take an extra week's holiday unpaid.

B   Decisions must be taken about improving facilities and employment opportunities for less able-bodied people.

C   A programme is to be developed to improve teamwork and co-operation between staff at all levels and in all departments.

D   Training must be arranged for selected people in first aid.

Which situations is this person most likely to handle?

15 The training manager?
    A   B   C   D

16 The personnel director?
    A   B   C   D

Element 2.3 Present results of investigation into job roles

For questions 17 and 18, read the beginning of the sentence in each question, then select which of A, B, C or D is correct.

17 The PR manager would be employed in:
    A   Finance
    B   Personnel
    C   Marketing
    D   Production

18 The task of buying components for the manufacturing process is most likely to take place in:
    A   Finance
    B   Personnel
    C   Marketing
    D   Production

*For the next two questions, read the two statements carefully. Circle
one of the letters that follow it to indicate which combination you
believe is correct.*

19 Decide whether each of the following is true (T) or false (F).
  (i) In a large organisation, if your computer breaks down,
  you should try to fix it yourself.
  (ii) One of the benefits of working in a small organisation
  is the breadth of experience to be learned in many
  different areas.

  Which option best describes the two statements?
  A (i) T   (ii) T
  B (i) T   (ii) F
  C (i) F   (ii) T
  D (i) F   (ii) F

20 Decide whether each of the following is true (T) or false (F).
  (i) The finance director is most likely to decide where to
  locate a new factory.
  (ii) One of the tasks of the managing director is to set the
  profit targets for the organisation.

  Which option best describes the two statements?
  A (i) T   (ii) T
  B (i) T   (ii) F
  C (i) F   (ii) T
  D (i) F   (ii) F

*For the next two questions, choose the **two** endings for each sentence
which you believe are correct and circle the appropriate letters.*

21 Democratic decision making:
  A involves transferring a lot of trust by senior managers
  to people in more junior positions
  B encourages commitment to the organisation by
  employees at all levels
  C means that the managing director must be involved in
  the day-to-day operating of the business
  D promotes rumours and ill feeling among employees

22 The two main differences between a director and a
  manager are:
  A unlike a manager, a director sits on the board and is
  an integral part of the strategic decision making
  process of the business

    B   unlike a director, a manager runs the day-to-day activities in a particular function of the business

    C   unlike a manager, a director is there to give orders to subordinates

    D   unlike a director, a manager makes long term decisions for the business

For the next two questions, choose from the four options A, B, C and D the appropriate answers for each question; you may use each answer more than once.

Various tasks have to be undertaken by staff in distribution, for instance:

    A   Establishing company policy with regard to purchasing trucks or using outside carriers.

    B   Negotiating carriage rates with carriers.

    C   Directing incoming vehicles where to discharge their load.

    D   Loading up vehicles with the company's goods.

Which task is most likely to be carried out by:

23 the distribution manager?
    A   B   C   D

24 the warehouse foreman?
    A   B   C   D

Element 2.4 Prepare for employment or self-employment

For questions 25 and 26, read the beginning of the sentence in each question, then select which of A, B, C or D is correct.

25 A hotel receptionist works in the:
    A   secondary sector
    B   public sector
    C   private sector
    D   primary sector

26 One of the advantages of working for a large company like Ford or Nestlé is the opportunity to gain experience in a:
    A   family run business
    B   multinational company
    C   private limited company
    D   nationalised industry

For the next two questions, read the two statements carefully. Circle
one *of the letters that follow it to indicate which combination you*
believe is correct.

27 Decide whether each of the following is true (T) or false (F).
  (i) The Training and Enterprise Council exists to develop
        commercial skills of the workforce on a regional basis.
  (ii) The Training and Enterprise Council is run entirely
        from central government with no involvement of
        industry.

  Which option best describes the two statements?
  A **(i)** T   **(ii)** T
  B **(i)** T   **(ii)** F
  C **(i)** F   **(ii)** T
  D **(i)** F   **(ii)** F

28 Decide whether each of the following is true (T) or false (F).
  (i) A franchise is a business concept which is transferable
        to another area
  (ii) A disadvantage of a franchise is that the franchiser
        often takes a percentage of turnover each year of
        operation

  Which option best describes the two statements?
  A **(i)** T   **(ii)** T
  B **(i)** T   **(ii)** F
  C **(i)** F   **(ii)** T
  D **(i)** F   **(ii)** F

For the next two questions, choose the **two** *endings for each sentence*
which you believe are correct and circle the appropriate letters.

29 In order to start a new business, it is essential for the
  owner to:
  A employ people to help with all menial tasks
  B have large, expensive looking premises to create an
     impression of success and wealth
  C know precisely why customers will want to change
     from their existing suppliers and buy instead from the
     new business
  D keep a very strong control over costs

30 Charitable organisations:
  A rely on voluntary workers to carry out many essential
     tasks

B are heavily subsidised by the government
C form part of private sector business
D pay heavy taxes to the government

For the next two questions, choose from the four options A, B, C and D the appropriate answer each question; you may use each answer more than once.

A Somebody is setting up a printing company with large, expensive machinery funded by bank borrowing.
B A group of trained estate agents are starting a business to let industrial property.
C A private limited company is seeking funds for large scale expansion.
D An executive is setting up as a consultant.

31 A private limited company would be advisable for:
   A   B   C   D

32 A public limited company would be advisable for:
   A   B   C   D

Questions Unit 3

Consumers and customers

For questions 1 and 2, read the beginning of the sentence in each question, then select which of A, B, C or D is the correct ending.

1 A petrol refiner has just developed a fuel for cars which is more environmentally friendly than unleaded petrol, without affecting the performance of the car. This is likely to succeed mainly because:
   A consumers are concerned about the effect of fuel emissions on the environment
   B it might be cheaper than petrol is currently
   C it will mean consumers having to make adjustments to their car engines
   D petrol producers will still be able to make large profits

2 The main reason why sales of cheap 'own label' products increase when customers incomes are falling is:
   A they taste better than the branded equivalents
   B people cat more at such times
   C supermarkets promote such merchandise more
   D customers want to buy the same amount of food for less money

*For the next two questions, read the two statements carefully. Circle **one** of the letters that follow it to indicate which combination you believe is correct.*

3 Decide whether each of the following is true (T) or false (F).
   (i) A **need** is something that people cannot survive without.
   (ii) A **want** is something that people would like to have.

   How are these statements best described?
   A (i) T   (ii) T
   B (i) T   (ii) F
   C (i) F   (ii) T
   D (i) F   (ii) F

4 Decide whether each of the following is true (T) or false (F).
   (i) Information about the amount of pocket money that children are given is useful to an ice cream manufacturer.
   (ii) Information about the differences in peoples' eating habits on the Isle of Wight would be of interest to a confectionery business operating in the mass market.

   Which option best describes the two statements?
   A (i) T   (ii) T
   B (i) T   (ii) F
   C (i) F   (ii) T
   D (i) F   (ii) F

For the next two questions, choose the **two** *endings for each sentence which you believe are correct and circle the appropriate letters.*

5 Two examples of consumers of goods and services, from a marketing viewpoint, are:
   (i) domestic pets
   (ii) businesses
   (iii) the government
   (iv) babies

   Which option best describes the two statements?
   A (i) and (ii)
   B (i) and (iii)
   C (ii) and (iii)
   D (iii) and (iv)

6 Increasingly, products such as cars , trainers and confectionery are marketed on a global basis to a world-wide audience. This is because:
   (i) it is just as expensive to develop a product for one country as it is for the whole world
   (ii) improved communications have encouraged similarity of consumer preferences throughout the world

   Which option best describes the two statements (T – true, F – false)?
   A (i) T   (ii) T
   B (i) T   (ii) F
   C (i) F   (ii) T
   D (i) F   (ii) F

For the next two questions, choose from the four options A, B, C and D the appropriate answers for each question; you may use each answer more than once.

Four different characteristics of customers in this country are:

A   age
B   whether they are working or retired
C   gender
D   number of children in a household

Which would be the major characteristic of interest to suppliers of these products and services?

7   A travel agent specialising in off-peak holidays for older people?
A   B   C   D

8   An insurance company which specialises in recently qualified drivers?
A   B   C   D

Element 3.2 Plan, design and produce promotional material

For questions 9 and 10, read beginning of the sentence in each question, then select which of A, B, C or D is the correct ending.

9   A company is deciding whether or not to sponsor the British Olympic swimming team. The key factor in this decision is:
A   whether the team is likely to win
B   the amount of consumer demand for the company's products that this would generate
C   whether the marketing manager is a keen swimmer
D   the likely cost-effectiveness of this promotional outlet compared to others

10 A group of students wishes to publicise a fund-raising event they are planning for a local charity. They have a couple of weeks and no budget to spend. They would be best advised to:
A   advertise in the local press
B   talk to the local press to obtain editorial coverage
C   have some leaflets produced by a local printer
D   hope that people will come to see them and give money anyway

*For the next two questions, read the two statements carefully. Circle **one** of the letters that follow it to indicate which combination you believe is correct.*

11 Decide whether each of the following is true (T) or false (F).
   (i) Posters are an extremely effective medium to promote all the benefits of a new product because there is room for plenty of copy.
   (ii) Public relations are an extremely effective method of promotion because the producer of the press release has complete control over what the newspapers print.

Which option best describes the two statements?
A **(i)** T   **(ii)** T
B **(i)** T   **(ii)** F
C **(i)** F   **(ii)** T
D **(i)** F   **(ii)** F

12 Decide whether each of the following is true (T) or false (F).
   (i) Government legislation forbids the promotion of contraceptives on television.
   (ii) Government legislation forbids the promotion of smoking on television.

Which option best describes the two statements?
A **(i)** T   **(ii)** T
B **(i)** T   **(ii)** F
C **(i)** F   **(ii)** T
D **(i)** F   **(ii)** F

*For the next two questions, choose the **two** endings for each sentence which you believe are correct and circle the appropriate letters.*

13 The two most important factors in the rise and effectiveness of direct marketing as a promotional medium are:
   (i) people think they might have won a fortune in a prize draw
   (ii) recent improvements in printing and production methods have increased the creative possibilities for this medium
   (iii) the increase in consumer choice in viewing channels and their use of video means that television commercials are less effective
   (iv) consumers enjoy opening unsolicited mail and are consequently more likely to go out and buy the product

A (i) and (ii)
B (i) and (iii)
C (ii) and (iii)
D (iii) and (iv)

14 The two main advantages of advertising at peak time on television are:
(i)   television airtime is very cheap
(ii) you can easily show it to your friends
(iii) it has colour, sound and movement
(iv) it is simultaneously accessible to a large audience
A (i) and (ii)
B (i) and (iii)
C (ii) and (iii)
D (iii) and (iv)

For the next two questions, choose from the four options A, B, C and D the appropriate answer for each question; you may use each answer more than once.

Here are four different types of promotion:
A direct mail
B competitions
C sponsorship
D advertising on local commercial radio

Which medium would be most effective for:

15 a local store seeking to promote a sale?
A   B   C   D

16 a charity seeking to contact people in person at home to appeal for donations?
A   B   C   D

Element 3.3
Providing customer service

For questions 17 and 18, read the beginning of the sentence in each question, then select which of A, B, C or D is the correct ending.

17 An absent-minded old lady is lost in the department store where you work; her middle-aged daughter has asked for your help. Your best course of action is:
A   both of you to search for the old lady
B   write down the details immediately in an incident book

    C   ask the daughter to wait while you contact the manager and the security staff

    D   immediately announce over the Tannoy system a detailed description of the old lady

18 In the same store an extremely irate customer confronts you with a receipt showing that his faulty personal stereo was sent for repair a month ago and has still not been sent back by the workshop. You are very busy unpacking for display some merchandise which has just arrived. The best action to take is:

    A   politely explain that you are very busy and could he possibly come back later

    B   explain quietly and patiently that it is nothing to do with you and ask if he would explain the situation to one of your colleagues

    C   stop what you are doing, telephone the workshop to find out what has happened and when the equipment will be repaired; then offer the customer the option of collecting the goods in person or sending it to him through the post

    D   offer him a replacement personal stereo from the display

For the next two questions, read the two statements carefully. Circle **one** *of the letters that follow it to indicate which combination you believe is correct.*

19 Decide whether each of the following is true (T) or false (F).

    (i)   The main purpose of *The Sale of Goods Act 1979* is to prevent customers from being tricked into buying goods which are not fit for sale.

    (ii) Under *The Sale of Goods Act 1979* merchandise must be fit for the purpose for which it is intended.

Which option best describes the two statements?

A	(i) T	(ii) T
B	(i) T	(ii) F
C	(i) F	(ii) T
D	(i) F	(ii) F

20 Decide whether each of the following is true (T) or false (F).

    (i)   Somebody who folds their arms when listening to a customer may be indicating that they have shut themselves off from the customer's problem.

    (ii) It is not a good idea to contact a supervisor if you are

unable to help a customer as this looks as if you do not
know what you are doing.

Which option best describes the two statements?

A	(i) T	(ii) T
B	(i) T	(ii) F
C	(i) F	(ii) T
D	(i) F	(ii) F

For the next two questions, choose the **two** *endings for each sentence
which you believe are correct and circle the appropriate letters.*

21 You have discovered that a gentleman has left his wallet
behind in the store. The first **two** things that you should do
are:
(i)   telephone or write to the person
(ii) look inside it for a contact telephone number or
      address
(iii) announce it over the Tannoy system
(iv) look to see how much money there is inside
A   (i) and (ii)
B   (i) and (iii)
C   (ii) and (iii)
D   (iii) and (iv)

22 The two most important points about communicating
with customers are:
(i)   that you can talk to them by name
(ii) that you listen to what they have to say before saying
      anything
(iii) that you are honest with them about the extent to
      which you can help them
(iv) that you know what you are talking about
A   (i) and (ii)
B   (i) and (iii)
C   (ii) and (iii)
D   (iii) and (iv)

*For the next two questions, choose from the four options A, B, C and D
the appropriate answer for each question; you may use each answer
more than once.*

A manufacturer chooses to offer these services to its
customers:
A   an overnight delivery service for an extra charge
B   regular visits from the sales team

C a computerised ordering system
D a telephone sales service

Which of these services is intended for:

23 a long term relationship between supplier and customer?
A   B   C   D

24 supplying customers who need supplies quickly?
A   B   C   D

Element 3.4 Present proposals for improvements to customer service

For questions 25 and 26, read the beginning of the sentence in each question, then select which of A,B,C, or D is the correct ending.

25 A loyal customer will usually return if:
A   he or she is supplied with goods that are not quite right because he or she likes the staff and does not want to make a scene
B   courteous and efficient service is evident on every visit
C   the sales staff always stop for a chat and gossip
D   he or she is politely asked to wait until all the sales assistants have returned from lunch

26 Telephone sales are most effective to business customers when:
A   cold calling to sell advertising space
B   the customer knows personally and trusts the people in the caller's business
C   it is disguised as a marketing research exercise
D   the caller creates a friendly atmosphere by discussing the weather and the latest developments in the previous evening's soaps

For the next two questions, choose the **two** *endings for each sentence which you believe are correct and circle the appropriate letters.*

27 It is a legal requirement for businesses to consider the health and safety of two of these categories:
(i)   customers
(ii) visitors to the premises
(iii) shareholders
(iv) consultants
A   (i) and (ii)
B   (i) and (iii)

C   **(ii)** and **(iii)**
D   **(iii)** and **(iv)**

28 You buy a pair of shoes which fall apart ten days
afterwards. The shop refuses to help.
Two sources of assistance are:
(i)   The Trading Standards Office
(ii) The Citizens Advice Bureau
(iii) The local Police Station
(iv) The County Court
A   **(i)** and **(ii)**
B   **(i)** and **(iii)**
C   **(ii)** and **(iii)**
D   **(iii)** and **(iv)**

*For the next two questions, read the two statements carefully. Circle
one of the letters that follow it to indicate which combination you
believe is correct.*

29 Decide whether each of the following is true (T) or false (F).
(i)   It is easier and cheaper to find new customers for a
business than to sell more goods to existing ones.
(ii) Dissatisfied customers tend not to tell anybody when
they have received poor service.

Which option best describes the two statements?
A   **(i)** T   **(ii)** T
B   **(i)** T   **(ii)** F
C   **(i)** F   **(ii)** T
D   **(i)** F   **(ii)** F

30 Decide whether each of the following is true (T) or false (F).
(i)   After-sales service is a vital part of the sales process,
particularly for consumer durables.
(ii) It is possible to deal effectively with customers even if
a long delay is involved, as long as this is explained at
the outset.

Which option best describes the two statements?
A   **(i)** T   **(ii)** T
B   **(i)** T   **(ii)** F
C   **(i)** F   **(ii)** T
D   **(i)** F   **(ii)** F

For the next two questions, choose from the four options A, B, C and D the appropriate answers for each question; you may use each answer more than once.

On a customer-care training course you learn to:
A   take the customer gently by the arm and quietly ask if he or she needs any help
B   give the customer your undivided attention and do not interrupt
C   give a polite greeting and let the customer browse at leisure
D   look at the person then speak distinctly and clearly

This action would be the most appropriate

31 if the customer were annoyed and had a complaint to make
A   B   C   D

32 if the customer were blind
A   B   C   D

Questions Unit 4

Financial and Administrative Support

For questions 1, 2 and 3, read the beginning of the sentence in each question, then select which of A, B, C or D is the correct ending.

1 When a business bills a customer for goods that it has supplied, it sends a:
   A goods received note
   B statement of account
   C sales invoice
   D sales credit note

2 An auditor is somebody who:
   A controls the contents of a newspaper
   B manages a company's computer systems
   C keeps a company's security systems in order
   D checks that financial records and transactions have been correctly carried out

3 Telephone and electricity bills, business rates and building maintenance costs are all examples of:
   A overhead costs
   B income
   C materials costs
   D variable costs

For the next two questions, read the two statements carefully. Circle **one** *of the letters that follow it to indicate which combination you believe is correct.*

4 Decide whether each of the following is true (T) or false (F).
   (i) Security for a business is as much concerned with the procedures and behaviour of its employees as it is with its customers.
   (ii) The orders received record is a guarantee of income in coming months and years.

How are these statements best described?

A (i) T (ii) T
B (i) T (ii) F
C (i) F (ii) T
D (i) F (ii) F

5 Decide whether each of the following is true (T) or false (F).
   (i) One of the ways of making a regular payment through a bank is by letter of credit.
   (ii) Banking automated clearing services (BACS) is used by businesses which have many banking mandates to operate at any one time.

How are these statements best described?

A (i) T (ii) T
B (i) T (ii) F
C (i) F (ii) T
D (i) F (ii) F

*For the next two questions, choose the **two** endings for each sentence which you believe are correct and circle the appropriate letters.*

6 Two of the main advantages of an efficient security system to a business are:
   (i) it reduces the costs to the business
   (ii) it increases sales
   (iii) it generates confidence and trust among employees and customers
   (iv) it creates employment for security companies
   A (i) and (ii)
   B (i) and (iii)
   C (ii) and (iii)
   D (iii) and (iv)

7 Two examples of documents which acknowledge receipt of payment are:
   (i) a goods received note
   (ii) a credit note
   (iii) a bank statement
   (iv) a cheque stub
   A (i) and (ii)
   B (i) and (iii)
   C (ii) and (iii)
   D (iii) and (iv)

For the next three questions, choose from the four options A, B, C and D the answers for each question; you may use each answer more than once.

Here are four documents that are essential to effective administration of a business:
- A purchase invoice
- B pay slip
- C cheque
- D delivery note

This document would be of particular importance to:

8 a wages' clerk

   A   B   C   D

9 a buyer

   A   B   C   D

10 a warehouse foreman

   A   B   C   D

Element 4.2
Complete financial documents and explain financial recording

For questions 11, 12 and 13, read the beginning of the sentence in each question, then select which of A, B, C or D is the correct ending.

11 COD stands for:
- A complete order delivered
- B credit on demand
- C cash on delivery
- D copper on duty

12 On an invoice, VAT is normally added:
- A at the beginning
- B after each item
- C before the final total
- D after the goods section and before labour costs

13 A business is likely to enjoy credit terms from a supplier when
- A it has had trouble paying bills on time in the past
- B a relationship of confidence and trust has been established
- C the bank has refused to honour one of their cheques
- D The supplier has a high credit rating with its bank

*For the next two questions, read the two statements carefully. Circle **one** of the letters that follow it to indicate which combination you believe is correct.*

14 Decide whether each of the following is true (T) or false (F).
- **(i)** Trade discount is a percentage reduction in price that is enjoyed by a wholesaler or tradesman in return for bulk or regular purchase.
- **(ii)** The term 2.5 per cent 30 days means that discount is given for prompt payment.

How are these statements best described?

A	**(i)** T	**(ii)** T
B	**(i)** T	**(ii)** F
C	**(i)** F	**(ii)** T
D	**(i)** F	**(ii)** F

15 Decide whether each of the following is true (T) or false (F).
- **(i)** A debit note is sent to a company to adjust their account when they have been overcharged on an invoice.
- **(ii)** A remittance advice is intended for the accounts department so that they know for which goods payment is being made.

How are these statements best described?

A	**(i)** T	**(ii)** T
B	**(i)** T	**(ii)** F
C	**(i)** F	**(ii)** T
D	**(i)** F	**(ii)** F

*For the next two questions, choose the **two** endings for each sentence which you believe are correct and circle the appropriate letters.*

16 Two examples of typical credit periods enjoyed by customers with an established relationship with their suppliers are:
- **(i)** 7 days
- **(ii)** 30 days
- **(iii)** 60 days
- **(iv)** 120 days

A	(i) and (ii)
B	(i) and (iii)
C	(ii) and (iii)
D	(iii) and (iv)

17 Two common ways that businesses pay their invoices are:
  (i) by credit transfer
  (ii) by cheque
  (iii) by postal order
  (iv) by cash
  A (i) and (ii)
  B (i) and (iii)
  C (ii) and (iii)
  D (iii) and (iv)

For the next three questions, choose from the four options A, B, C and D the appropriate answer for each question; you may use each answer more than once.

These are examples of the establishments a business may contact if it wishes to take up a reference before allowing credit for a new customer:
  A the customer's bankers
  B another supplier to that customer
  C a credit control agency
  D the county court

The main reason that you are contacting the establishment is:

18 to find out if it has a history of unpaid debt
  A **B** **C** **D**

19 to check whether the new customer is over committed in its financial dealings
  A **B** **C** **D**

20 to see if it usually pays its bills on time
  A **B** **C** **D**

Element 4.3 Produce, evaluate and store business documents

For questions 21, 22 and 23, read the beginning of the sentence in each question, then select which of A, B, C or D is the correct ending.

21 In order to check whether a business is achieving its sales targets and maintaining costs within the boundaries it set itself, it will monitor its performance against:
  A sales forecast
  B budget
  C trial balance
  D cash flow forecast

22 The main disadvantage of using a fax machine to send
details of a brand new product innovation to the
managing director when she is on an sales visit to the USA
is:
A   the time difference between the UK and the USA
B   the time it takes to send a fax
C   the lack of confidentiality
D   the expense involved

23 The main piece of legislation which limits the type of
information that a company may divulge to third parties
about its employees is:
A   *The Health and Safety at Work Act*
B   *The Trades Description Act*
C   *The Data Protection Act*
D   *The Companies' Act, date*

*For the next two questions, read the two statements carefully. Circle
one of the letters that follow it to indicate which combination you
believe is correct.*

24 Decide whether each of the following is true (T) or false (F).
   (i)   A well-written, grammatically correct document is
         greatly enhanced if it is printed using desktop
         publishing.
   (ii) Even if it is printed using desktop publishing, a
         business document is unlikely to be taken seriously if
         the spelling and grammar are incorrect.

   How are these statements best described?
   A (i) T   (ii) T
   B (i) T   (ii) F
   C (i) F   (ii) T
   D (i) F   (ii) F

25 Decide whether each of the following is true (T) or false (F).
   (i)   If files are stored on the hard disk of a PC, there is no
         need to store them on a floppy disk as well.
   (ii) A letter which starts 'Dear Sir' should end 'Yours
         sincerely'.

   How are these statements best described?
   A   (i) T   (ii) T
   B   (i) T   (ii) F
   C   (i) F   (ii) T
   D   (i) F   (ii) F

*For the next two questions, choose the **two** endings for each sentence
which you believe are correct and circle the appropriate letters.*

26 Two of the most logical ways to store customer files of
major customers is:
(i)   by descending order of the value of business placed
(ii) alphabetically
(iii) chronologically, starting with the most recent order
(iv) geographically, working from east to west
A   (i) and (ii)   C (ii) and (iii)
B   (i) and (iii)   D (iii) and (iv)

27 The two most important factors to bear in mind when
writing a report are:
(i)   that it should be as detailed as possible
(ii) the needs of the people for whom it is intended
(iii) that the information should be as concise and
accessible as possible
(iv) the need to demonstrate that the writer is fully
conversant with the subject
A   (i) and (ii)   C (ii) and (iii)
B   (i) and (iii)   D (iii) and (iv)

*For the next three questions, choose from the four options A, B, C and D
the appropriate answer for each question; you may use each answer
more than once.*

There are many different forms of written business
communications:
A   fax
B   report
C   letter
D   memo

This would be the most expedient way of communicating:

28 detailed information about competitive products that are
currently available
A   B   C   D

29 urgent confirmation of an important internal matter
A   B   C   D

30 urgent confirmation of a large order
A   B   C   D

Answers

Element 1.1

| 1 | D | 2 | C | 3 | B | 4 | D | 5 | A |
| 6 | A | 7 | D | 8 | D | 9 | B | 10 | A |

Element 1.2

| 11 | A | 12 | B | 13 | C | 14 | B | 15 | C |
| 16 | B | 17 | C | 18 | B | 19 | A | 20 | D |

Element 1.3

| 21 | A | 22 | C | 23 | B | 24 | D | 25 | A |
| 26 | A | 27 | D | 28 | A | 29 | B | 30 | C |

Element 2.1

| 1 | C | 2 | A | 3 | A | 4 | B | 5 | C |
| 6 | B | 7 | B | 8 | A | | | | |

Element 2.2

| 9 | B | 10 | C | 11 | B | 12 | C | 13 | C |
| 14 | B | 15 | D | 16 | B | | | | |

Element 2.3

| 17 | C | 18 | D | 19 | C | 20 | C | 21 | A+B |
| 22 | A+B | 23 | B | 24 | C | | | | |

Element 2.4

| 25 | C | 26 | B | 27 | B | 28 | A | 29 | C+D |
| 30 | A+C | 31 | A | 32 | C | | | | |

Element 3.1

| 1 | A | 2 | D | 3 | A | 4 | B | 5 | C |
| 6 | A | 7 | B | 8 | A | | | | |

Element 3.2

| 9 | D | 10 | B | 11 | D | 12 | C | 13 | C |
| 14 | D | 15 | D | 16 | A | | | | |

Element 3.3

| 17 | C | 18 | C | 19 | A | 20 | B | 21 | C |
| 22 | C | 23 | B | 24 | A | | | | |

Element 3.4

| 25 | B | 26 | B | 27 | A | 28 | A | 29 | D |
| 30 | A | 31 | B | 32 | A | | | | |

Element 4.1

| 1 | C | 2 | D | 3 | A | 4 | B | 5 | C |
| 6 | B | 7 | D | 8 | B | 9 | A | 10 | D |

Element 4.2

| 11 | C | 12 | C | 13 | B | 14 | A | 15 | C |
| 16 | A | 17 | A | 18 | C | 19 | A | 20 | B |

Element 4.3

| 21 | B | 22 | C | 23 | C | 24 | A | 25 | D |
| 26 | B | 27 | C | 28 | B | 29 | D | 30 | A |

Index

ACAS (Advisory, Conciliation and Arbitration Services) 115
accounts 101, 150, 275, 276, 293, 356
ACORN profiles 244–245
advertisements 210, 225, 327
advertising media 210–214, 218–225
Advertising Standards Authority (ASA) 208, 217
affinity groups 243
after-sales service 67, 206, 241
application of number 177, 330–340
assets 277
auditors 279
autocratic decision making 132

balance sheet 277
Belbin, Meredith 134, 169
body language 342
borrowing facilities 151
BRAD (British Rate and Data) 229
break-even point 340
Budget 101, 102, 278
business
    communication 176, 241, 248–252, 257
        written 310-323, 341–349
    founding or starting up 89, 178–180
    growth 108
    large 21
    letter 314–316
    location 42, 47, 50, 51
    medium 21
    objectives 20
    organisations 17, 59, 261
    ownership 25
    performance 278
    plan 144, 337
    small 21
    strategy 144
    structures 88–94
businesses
    seasonal 71

CAB (Citizens' Advice Bureau) 167
capital goods 188
careers offices 163
cash flow 289
centralised systems 105
CFC propellants 55, 195
chain of command 93
chambers of commerce 165
charities 20, 21, 22
cheque 287, 291, 293, 305, 307
Civil Service 11, 24, 35, 160
co-operative joint ventures 33
co-operatives 25, 32
commission 122
company structure *see* business structures
compassionate leave 120
competition 21, 44, 52–53, 109, 175
competitions 100, 215, 218, 227–228
computer
    services 101
    systems 151, 351–356
computer-aided design (CAD) 102
computer-aided manufacture (CAM) 103
conservation 54–55
consumer
    goods, different types of 187–188
    protection 208, 216
consumers 109, 187–191
    kinds of (individuals, businesses, governments) 187–189, 206
contract of employment 116
contracts 151
copyrights 151, 317
corporate
    hospitality 227
    image 150, 262–263
cost of living 203
costs 273, 338–339
credit control 154
creditors 278
criminal activity 125

CTN (confectioner, tobacconist and
    newsagent) 162
customer
    complaints 258
    loyalty and retention 233, 261, 262
    safety 269
    satisfaction 262
    service 99, 155, 247, 261, 264
customers 152, 174, 191, 205, 206, 234,
    240–247, 250
Customs & Excise 274

de-centralised systems 105
debtors 277
decision making 91, 114, 142, 145, 169
deed of partnership 27
delivery note 285, 297, 299, 304
demand 189, 194, 202
democracy 22
democratic decision making 91, 131, 132
demographic structure 195
desktop publishing 321, 355
despatch note 280
directors 93, 130, 131
Disabled Persons (Employment) Act 1958 127
disciplinary procedure 121
dismissal 121
disposable income 194
distribution 97, 98, 154, 155, 226, 244
DTI (Department of Trade and Industry) 166
durable goods 60
duty of care 117

E-mail 71, 176
economy 13, 187, 188
ED (Employment Department) 167
employee
    benefits 121
    consultation 113
employment 69–77, 158, 160, 162, 182
    Acts 128
    agencies 164
    contracts (working contracts) 106
    self-employment 70, 72, 158, 160, 162,
        174, 178, 181, 182
entrepreneurs 26, 44
environment 54–55, 195, 269
equal opportunities 115, 118
Equal Pay Act 1970 127
European Court of Justice 114, 116
European Union grants 50

expenditure 273
extractive industries 14

Factories Act 1961 126
family business 161
fax (facsimile) 46, 106, 176
Federation of Small Businesses 164
filing systems 322
financial transactions 273
flexi-hours 105
forecasting 278
franchise 25, 30, 31, 162

goods received note 282, 296, 301
government 22, 23, 35, 60, 166, 190 (*see also*
    consumers, kinds of)
    grants 273
Government Enterprise Scheme 161
guarantee 251, 265

health and safety at work 118, 123, 150, 195,
    323, 326
Health and Safety at Work Act 1974 119, 122,
    127, 155
health and safety inspectors 123
hierarchical company structure 92, 104
holiday and sickness pay 71
holidays 85
human resourcing 148

incentives 49
income 273
Income Tax 119
industrial
    accidents 55
    tribunals 114, 115
information technology 177, 350–356
Inland Revenue 119, 274
interdependence of departments 96
interest 288
invoices 274, 285, 292, 297, 298, 302

job
    centres 163
    roles 148
    security 71, 160

labour 13, 22, 47, 279
    cost 47
    quantity 48
land 13, 22, 47, 49

lapsed users 234
leadership skills 150
ledgers 274–275
levels of seniority 130
liability for debts 29
limited companies 25, 28, 29, 33, 274, 275
loans 120, 273, 290
local government 24, 35
location of business 42

management
    senior, middle and junior 91, 130, 132
    skills 150
    styles 90–93
manufacturing process 97
market
    led businesses 65
    share 19, 58, 59
marketing 65, 99, 102, 153, 209
    analysis and research 153
    communications 66, 100
    mix 100
    plans and planning 100, 220–223
    research 64, 65, 242–246
markets 17, 56, 242–246
    types of 56, 57, 58, 59, 61
maternity leave 71
matrix company structure 94
media 100, 164
mission statement 143, 144
multinational companies 25, 32

National Insurance contributions 119
nationalised industries 24, 35, 160
natural resources 11, 13, 47, 48
needs 11, 12, 61, 62, 189, 204, 240, 241, 244,
    246

Offices, Shops and Railway Premises Act 1963 126
order confirmation 280
orders received 280, 284, 297, 301
organisation chart 90, 95
organisational structures *see* business
    structures

partnership 25, 27, 162, 274
Partnership Act 1890 27
patents 151, 318
paternity leave 71, 120
PAYE (Pay As You Earn) 119

payment methods 286–290
pension schemes 71
personnel department 96
petty cash 306, 308
planning permission 49
point-of-sale material 209
price 63, 154, 209
    list 250
primary sector 11, 14, 15
private sector 11, 20, 25, 160
problem solving 142, 146, 150, 170–171
producer co-operatives 32
product
    costs 103
    design and development 64, 100, 153,
        241
    positioning 231, 235
    rejuvenation 154
production 97, 150
products (goods and services) 60, 149, 187,
    209
profit 20, 36, 150, 276, 278, 339
profit-sharing schemes 122
promotion and promotional campaign 100,
    153, 154, 209–229, 236
promotional plan 218
promotions – legislation 216
public relations 100
public sector 11, 20, 22, 23, 24, 36, 160
purchase
    invoice 280, 283, 296, 300
    order 280, 281, 296, 299
purchasing 97, 98, 279–280

quality circles 113
quaternary sector 14

race relations 115
Race Relations Act 1970 127
RAM (random access memory) 354
receipt 280, 290, 291, 305, 308
record keeping 274
recruitment and selection 96, 103
regional development areas 50
Rehabilitation of Offenders Act 1974 128
remuneration 122
report writing 317, 321
retail co-operatives 32
Retail Price index (RPI) 203
ROM (read only memory) 354

salary 122
Sale of Goods Act 216, 267
sales 233
    department 98, 226
    literature 66
    promotions *see* promotion and
    promotional campaign
secondary sector 11, 14, 15,
secretarial function 151
sectors of industry 11–17
security 156, 279, 291, 323, 326
selling *see* sales department
separate legal personality 33
services – essential and non-essential 20, 24,
    188
setting and achieving targets 142, 147
sex discrimination 115
shares and shareholders 28, 30, 34
skilled workers 72
skills 13, 47, 168, 178
social grading 243
sole trader 25, 26, 274
sponsorship 214, 218, 227
staff
    administration 97
    associations 123
    discounts 121
    welfare 97
statement of account 285, 286, 297, 304
Stock Exchange 29
strikes 112
Sunday trading 195
supervision skills 150
supervisors 133
suppliers 174

Tannenbaum and Schmidt management style
    continuum 132
target setting and achieving 172–174
taxes 22, 23
team work 133, 134
technical department 98, 102
TECs (Training & Enterprise Councils) 166
telephone 248, 254
tertiary sector 12, 14, 16
trade marks 151, 318
Trade Union Acts 128
Trades Description Act 216, 267
trades unions 114
Trading Standards Office 217
training 84, 96, 112, 134, 262
transport 98, 150

unfair dismissal 115
unique selling proposition (USP) 230–231
unskilled workers 103

VAT (Value Added Tax) 274, 334
VDU screens 85, 326, 352
voluntary organisations 21, 22, 160
VSO (Voluntary Service Overseas) 167

wages 122, 273, 279
wants 11, 12, 62, 189, 204, 241
warehousing 97, 154
warnings – verbal and written 121
working
    alone and with others 174, 176
    conditions (*also* working hours,
    arrangements and environment) 52,
    83–85, 84, 104, 107, 122